Corporate Social Responsibility in Europe

Corporate Social Responsibility in Europe

Rhetoric and Realities

Edited by

Regine Barth

and

Franziska Wolff

Environmental Law and Governance Division, Öko-Institut, Germany

Edward Elgar

Cheltenham, UK • Northampton, MA, USA

Published by
Edward Elgar Publishing Limited
The Lypiatts
15 Lansdown Road
Cheltenham
Glos GL50 2JA
UK

Edward Elgar Publishing, Inc.
William Pratt House
9 Dewey Court
Northampton
Massachusetts 01060
USA

A catalogue record for this book
is available from the British Library

Library of Congress Control Number: 2009900689

PEFC
PEFC/16-33-111
CATG-PEFC-052
www.pefc.org

ISBN 978 1 84720 764 7

Printed and bound in Great Britain by MPG Books Group, UK

Contents

PART I   ANALYTICAL FRAMEWORK

PART II   MAPPING CSR: SURVEY DATA ON SELECTED
          ISSUES IN FOUR SECTORS

Figures

Tables

Contributors

Regine Barth is head of the Öko-Institut's Environmental Law and Governance Division and was the Coordinator of the RARE project. She has specialized in environmental and administrative law, both at German, EU and international level. Over the years she has carried out extensive interdisciplinary research on policy instruments including Corporate Social Responsibility (CSR). She regularly engages in participatory policy processes.

Maria Bohn is a Research Associate at the Stockholm Environment Institute, with its Policy and Institutions Research Programme.

Hajnalka Csáfor works as an Assistant Professor at the Department of Corporate Economics of Eszterhazy Karoly College in Eger, Hungary. She also works as a PhD student at the Budapest University of Technology and Economics (BUTE). Her main research interest is in CSR with a focus on developments in Europe and Hungary and also on regional aspects.

Mária Csete is a part-time Research Fellow at the Department of Environmental Economics, Budapest University of Technology and Economics (BUTE) and a full-time Research Fellow at the Adaptation to Climate Change Research Group of the Hungarian Academy of Sciences at the Budapest Corvinus University. Her research interests include regional and rural development, sustainable settlements, the socio-economic effects related to the mitigation of and the adaptation to climate change.

Miklós Füle is an Associate Professor at Budapest University of Technology and Economics (BUTE). His main research topics are environmental economics, specific small regional sustainable development scenarios and environmental aspects of bankruptcy proceedings.

Christian Hochfeld is Deputy Director of the Öko-Institut and Head of its Berlin office. He works with the Infrastructure and Enterprises Division. His main fields of research and consultancy are corporate sustainability strategies and CSR, sustainable product development and life cycle assessments.

Elin Lerum Boasson is a PhD student and a Research Fellow at the Fridtjof Nansen Institute. Her research interests are European and EU energy and climate politics, with specific attention to how the European developments affect Norwegian energy producers.

Noémi Csigéné Nagypál is a Research Fellow at the Department of Environmental Economics, Budapest University of Technology and Economics (BUTE). She graduated at BUTE as an engineering manager and has specialized in environmental management. Her research fields are monetary environmental valuation and CSR.

Daniele Nicolai is a Senior Researcher of the CSR and Sustainable Management Programme at the Fondazione Eni Enrico Mattei (FEEM). His research interests are in corporate governance, sustainability issues and CSR reporting. His main focus is on the energy and banking sectors.

Tamás Pálvölgyi is an Associate Professor at the Department of Environmental Management, Budapest University of Technology and Economics (BUTE). His research fields include climate change impact and adaptation in socio-economic systems. He has also experiences in researches related to environmental policy integration and sustainable development policies, as well as in the coordination of strategic environmental assessments.

Katharina Schmitt is a Research Fellow with the Environmental Law and Governance Division of the Öko-Institut. Her main area of research is CSR from a company, consumer and politics perspective, particularly in the area of food and retailing. She works on issues ranging from environmental protection to fair trade and social inclusion.

Irmgard Schultz holds a PhD in political science. She is a Senior Researcher and a co-founder of the Institute of Social-Ecological Research (ISOE) in Frankfurt/Main. She heads the research department 'Everyday Life Ecology and Consumption'. Her work focuses on approaches to conceptualizing the gender dimension in inter- and transdisciplinary sustainability research; everyday life ecology and sustainable development; and gender and environment.

Jon Birger Skjærseth is a senior researcher at the Fridtjof Nansen Institute. His research interests lie in the field of international, EU, national and corporate environmental policy, with main emphasis on climate change and marine pollution.

János Szlávik is a Professor and Head of the Department of Environmental Economics, Budapest University of Technology and Economics. His research interests are sustainable development and evaluation methods of environmental capital.

Federica Viganò holds a PhD in Philosophy and is a Senior Researcher in the CSR and Sustainable Management Programme at Fondazione Eni Enrico Mattei (FEEM). Her main interest is in CSR as a vehicle of wider social justice, wealth redistribution and democracy (systemic logic).

Jørgen Wettestad is a Senior Research Fellow and Programme Director at the Fridtjof Nansen Institute. His research interests are European and EU energy and environmental politics, with specific attention to the EU emissions trading system.

Peter Wilkinson is an independent consultant in corporate responsibility, specializing in countering corruption in the private sector. He is a Senior Advisor to Transparency International, the global coalition against corruption.

Franziska Wolff is a Research Fellow and project leader with the Environmental Law and Governance Division of the Öko-Institut. Her research interests are governance issues pertaining to sustainable businesses, a sustainable economy and natural resources, ranging from agriculture to fisheries and biodiversity.

Foreword

Like societies elsewhere, European societies face serious social and environmental challenges, ranging from an ageing population and social exclusion to industrial restructuring and climate change mitigation. In order to address such complex challenges, all sectors of society need to contribute, including business, consumers, policy makers, academia and the media. Business' contribution to sustainability in this context is Corporate Social Responsibility (CSR), which is understood by the European Commission as a 'concept whereby companies integrate social and environmental concerns in their business operations and in their interaction with their stakeholders on a voluntary basis'. CSR can therefore promote sustainability while enhancing Europe's innovative potential and competitiveness.

In the European Union the debate on the role of CSR started in the late 1990s. It intensified as of 2001 with the publication of a Green Paper and the 2002 launch of the EU Multi-Stakeholder Forum on CSR chaired by the Commission. The European CSR strategy was further developed through two Commission Communications from 2002 and 2006 and through the backing of a new European CSR Alliance as an umbrella for responsibly minded enterprises.

As the Commission and European Parliament have stressed, it is now time to move the debate to the material and measurable outcomes and impact of voluntary business contributions – the acid test for CSR. While CSR cannot replace social and environmental regulation, this book shows how it contributes to a number of public policy objectives, including investment in skills development, efficient use of natural resources, human rights and poverty reduction. However, the precondition for this is that CSR should deliver on its social and environmental promises. More knowledge of CSR's actual impact on sustainability, its potential and its limits as a governance instrument is hence crucial to developing effective policy mixes for sustainable development.

The research project on which this book is based was funded by the Commission under the EU's Sixth Framework Programme. The project deserved the Commission's support because of its critical, impact-oriented research focus and its dedication to the question of whether and how CSR can contribute to the fulfilment of EU policy goals.

I hope that the lessons learned will be welcomed by a wide audience among CSR practitioners, policy makers, civil society and academia.

Vladimír Špidla
European Commissioner for Employment,
Social Affairs and Equal Opportunities
Brüssels, April 2008

Acknowledgements

We would like to thank the European Commission, DG Research, for their financial support for this book and the research project on which the book is based. The project 'Rhetoric and Realities: Analysing Corporate Social Responsibility in Europe' (RARE) was funded from 2004 to 2007 within the EU's Sixth Framework Programme (contract number No. CIT2-CT-2004-506 043). Our special thanks go to Dominik Sobczak for administering the project so smoothly. Dominique Bé, Robert Strauss and Geneviève Besse from the Commission's DG Employment, Social Affairs and Equal Opportunities, as well as José Jorge Diaz Del Castillo from DG Environment also supported us at various points during the project.

Sincere thanks are also given to all members of the RARE project team. Apart from the authors of this book, this includes a number of other researchers from the seven involved organisations – the Öko-Institut (Germany) as project coordinator, the Budapest University of Technology and Economics (Hungary), Fondazione Eni Enrico Mattei (Italy), Fridtjof Nansen Institute (Norway), the Institute for Social-Ecological Research (Germany), Peter Wilkinson Associates (United Kingdom) and the Stockholm Environment Institute (Sweden). They all contributed to our discussions, to individual project deliverables and to the development of our common understanding of this research endeavour: Bettina Brohmann, Jordi Cadilla, Vanessa Cook, Michael Chi Chen, Miriam Dross, Ludovico Ferraguto, Carolin Günsche, Lars H. Gulbrandsen, Rike Krämer, Tanja Kreetz, Arild Moe, Ria Müller, Sabina Nicolella, Linn Persson and Olivia Voils. The book authors, of course, merit our special thanks for their contributions; they all did tremendous work and had to endure many tiresome requests from our side.

We highly appreciate that 49 companies participated in our CSR surveys and case studies, thus enabling us to gain empirical data for our research. Especially, we would like to thank those company representatives who kindly agreed to be personally interviewed and who provided valuable and sometimes critical company information. This includes chief executives, purchasing managers, marketing and quality assurance staff, risk managers, human relations managers, advisors and many more informants from Caja Madrid, Dexia Group, Gottfried Friedrichs KG, Hydro, MOL Plc, Monte dei Paschi di Siena, Shell Plc, Shell Hungary, Unilever and Young's

Bluecrest. We would of course like to extend our thanks to the interviewees from civil society organisations such as Friends of the Earth, Greenpeace, Transparency International and the World Wildlife Fund for Nature; from private sector associations such as Confederación Española de Cajas de Ahorros, Associazione Bancaria Italiana and the European Savings Banks Group; as well as from public institutions including Instituto de la Mujer and Instituto Universitario de Investigación José Ortega y Gasset.

In the context of an expert workshop, a number of CSR researchers and practitioners gave us very fruitful feedback on our conceptual building blocks and thus helped us in shaping our research approach. Apart from the above mentioned EU Commission officials, they include Davide Dal Maso, Stanislas Dupré, Kate Grosser, Stephen Hine, Jonas Moberg, Jeremy Moon, Antonio Rueda, Paul Scott, Bernd Siebenhüner, Jette Steen Knudsen and Roberto Zangrandi. We would also like to thank those that contributed as speakers, discussants or moderators to the RARE project's final conference: Bernhard Bauske, Geneviève Besse, Giorgio Capurri, Tony Clark, Paul de Clerck, Elizabeth Guttenstein, Richard Howitt, Jane Leavens, Mike Mitchell, Arild Moe, Jan Noterdaeme, Guido Palazzo, Orsolya Pallaghy, Jette Steen Knudsen, Marion Swoboda, Ralph Thurm and David Vogel.

Finally, it remains to thank most warmly those that not only secured the organisational success of the conference but also did a great job in editing this book and preparing its print: Nathalie Hahn and Heike Unruh from the Öko-Institut. Without them, this publication would not have been possible. Likewise, we are highly indebted to Ben Booth from Edward Elgar Publishing Ltd for his trust in the manuscript and his patience with us.

Regine Barth and Franziska Wolff
Darmstadt / Berlin, April 2008

PART I

Analytical framework

1 Corporate Social Responsibility and sustainability impact: opening up the arena

Regine Barth and Franziska Wolff

1.1 INTRODUCTION

In the past years, the concept of Corporate Social Responsibility (CSR) has gained much attention, both academic and political. While the idea that companies contribute to societal welfare beyond their legal obligations has a longer tradition in the Anglo-Saxon countries and especially in the US, it is less practiced in continental Europe. There, many social and environmental responsibilities of corporations are defined legally which are voluntary elsewhere. In the context of the sustainability debate, the CSR concept has become more prevalent globally: the enormous challenge of 'satisf[ying] the needs of the present generation without compromising the chance for future generations to satisfy theirs' (Brundtland Commission 1987) cannot be dealt with by governments alone. It requires all possible contributions by all societal players.

Against this backdrop, the acid test of CSR is the degree to which companies' voluntary social and environmental efforts are in fact effective in contributing to sustainable development. This is the subject of the book at hand: What sustainability impact is achieved through CSR? Is it rhetoric or reality? Do companies that acknowledge social and environmental responsibility sufficiently change their operations and daily practices? And do these changes in corporate practice lead to substantive social and environmental benefits outside the company? To what extent do voluntary business activities hence contribute to the achievement of sustainability goals set by policy makers? These are the questions that we have discussed for a number of European business sectors and for selected sustainability issues. The focus is on CSR impacts created within Europe and aiming at EU policy goals. We shall draw from the results of a European research project, which was carried out by seven research institutions from 2004 to 2007 with funding from the European Union's Sixth Framework Programme.[1]

In this chapter we shall set forth our understanding of CSR as the overarching framework that spans the whole book. We follow the understanding that CSR is essentially a voluntary business contribution to sustainable development and is based on the integration of social and environmental concerns into business operations. However, in addition to a business tool, we understand CSR also as a societal and political (that is to say, public policy) mode of sustainability governance. We shall conceptualize how CSR processes within companies lead to effects both within companies and outside companies, namely on society and the environment. We shall also show why such sustainability impact in our view is the acid test of CSR. In Section 3 of this introduction, we shall then explain the structure of the book and the main findings presented in its chapters. The individual contributions are self-standing but interrelated and all of a piece, due to the common framework of the mentioned research project. The chapters following this introduction describe our frameworks for assessing and for explaining the sustainability impact of CSR. Chapters 5 to 9 present and synthesize four empirical surveys that map CSR perceptions and activities in European CSR leadership companies. We take a critical look at the oil industry, the banking sector, the fish processing sector and at small and medium-size enterprises (SMEs) in the automotive sector. Thematically, the focus is on a selected number of CSR issue areas: the mitigation of climate change and chemical risk, resource management in marine fisheries, promotion of gender equality and countering of bribery. Chapters 10 to 14 include in-depth case studies of ten companies in which we assess and explain sustainability effects of CSR in one of each of the issue areas. Chapters 15 to 17 finally deal with CSR and public policy – what is the contribution of CSR to achieving EU sustainability goals? How do CSR practices and EU integration in new EU Member States interrelate? And finally, what are the policy implications of the book's findings?

1.2   OUR UNDERSTANDING OF CORPORATE SOCIAL RESPONSIBILITY

Despite – or probably because of – the abundant literature on CSR and related concepts, there is not one agreed on definition or concept of CSR. This has to do with a number of factors. Firstly, the very practice of CSR is multifaceted and substantial differences exist between approaches to CSR management. Non-financial reporting, supply chain management, sustainable R&D, cultural sponsorship and stakeholder management, labour rights, pollution reduction and local sports events – the range of CSR instruments, activities and issues is vast. Secondly, there are parallel and overlapping concepts that co-exist with the notion of CSR. Early examples include 'Social Responsibility' (Bowen 1953), 'Corporate Social Responsiveness' (Ackermann and Bauer 1976; Frederick 1978) and 'Corporate Social Performance' (Carroll 1979; Sethi 1975; Swanson 1995; Wood 1991). The 1970s and 1980s also saw the coining of the 'stakeholder' paradigm (Freeman and Reed 1983) and the emergence of 'business ethics' (Behrman 1988; Solomon and Hanson 1983). The concepts of 'environmental management' (Steger 1990; Welford 1998), 'corporate sustainability' (Roome 1998; Atkinson 2000; Sharma and Starik 2002) and the 'triple bottom line' (Elkington 1997) witness the 1990s influence of the environmental and sustainability debate. More recent conceptual contenders are 'corporate accountability' (Gray 1992; Zadek et al. 1997), 'corporate citizenship' (Marsden and Andriof 1998; Warhurst 2000) and 'corporate responsibility' (Wulfson 2001; Zadek 2004). While each of these concepts deals with business-society relations, their focus and emphasis varies and definitions are hard to delimit. Finally, the third reason why there is no single agreed on understanding of CSR is the cultural-institutional differences in national business systems. These imply that what companies do as CSR in some countries corresponds to the fulfilment of legal requirements in others (Matten and Moon 2005).

Still, some 'mainstream' definition of CSR has emerged in Europe. It is summarized by the European Commission (2001, p. 6) as 'a concept whereby companies integrate social and environmental concerns in their business operations and in their interaction with their stakeholders on a voluntary basis. Being socially responsible means not only fulfilling legal expectations, but also going beyond compliance . . .'. Throughout this book we shall apply this definition. In the following sections we discuss its core dimensions: 'beyond compliance' voluntariness and sustainability integration. To begin with, however, we place the definition within a wider conceptualization of corporate action as socially and ecologically embedded. Against this backdrop, CSR is presented as a mode of sustainability governance both for corporate, societal and public policy actors.

1.2.1 Corporate Action in a Societal and Ecological Context

The starting point of our reflections is that companies act in complex social and natural environments. They trigger and take part in processes of economic and social exchange. Thereby, they draw on people (as workforce and consumers), on society as a collective (as carriers of social norms and providers of public goods) and make use of the natural environment (as scarce resource base, energy source and waste sink) (Costanza 1991;

Hoffman 2001; Midttun 2005). In return, companies create economic and social assets, contribute to the provision of public goods, provide work and livelihoods for people, and offer opportunities for people's social inclusion and self-realization. Companies not only compete for resources and customers, but also for political power, societal recognition and institutional legitimacy (Aldrich 1979; DiMaggio and Powell 1983). From a macro perspective, corporate practices can be seen as being formed by, and embedded within, particular economic, social, cultural and institutional structures and belief systems. At the same time, they constitute order and change the nature of these encompassing structures. This interplay between agency and structure is generally described as a process of 'structuration' (Giddens 1984).

Companies are part of a world that faces massive challenges, a number of which relate to 'sustainable development'. Sustainable development in the famous Brundtland Report in 1987 is defined as 'Meeting the needs of the present generation without compromising the ability of future generations to meet their needs.' The concept resulted from an attempt to integrate environmental protection into strategies of economic development. In its most common form, sustainability means the balancing of economic, ecological and social development. Established as a guiding principle for societal development at the UN Earth Summit in Rio de Janeiro in 1992, it was taken up in business concepts in the mid-1990s. The role and responsibilities of the private sector concerning sustainable development are threefold: firstly, companies contribute to sustainability problems and hence are casually co-responsible for them. For example, they (over-) use natural capital, producing waste and emissions that strain nature's carrying capacity, and interfere with ecosystem interactions. Socially, they impact on the health and lives of their workforce, possibly exploit child labour and abuse power. Due to globalization, these impacts occur increasingly internationally and often indirectly, that is, through suppliers. Secondly, companies are perceived to possess the means to contribute to the solution of sustainability problems. They have the means to reduce their own negative impacts; they create economic and social assets, provide work and livelihoods and opportunities for people's social inclusion. Finally, society attaches duties to their role of companies in the economy and society. Following Hart's (1968) work on the responsibility of individuals, this may be termed 'role responsibility'.

1.2.2 CSR as a Business, Societal and Political Mode of Sustainability Governance

Within the described setting, we understand CSR to be a mode of sustainability governance that actually integrates three dimensions: a business,

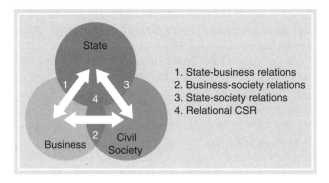

Source: Based on Albareda et al. (2007, p. 395).

Figure 1.1   Relational model of CSR

a societal and a political (in the sense of public policy) dimension. This integrated view links up with the 'relational model' of CSR which stresses the triangular relations between companies, civil society and public administration (Albareda et al. 2007; Figure 1.1).

The relational model draws attention to the diversity and reciprocity of actor relations in CSR processes. Note that, unlike in earlier models of social relations, the state is not the hub around which all social relations revolve. Where all three actor spheres overlap, truly 'relational' CSR is practiced. Overlaps also indicate areas of 'co-responsibility' or 'complex responsibility' between different actors that are not fully responsible for a problem – and that cannot fully solve it on their own (Lozano 2000). The latter reflection is the starting point of our thinking: we underscore that in CSR the capacities of (sustainability) governance are actually distributed among business and non-business actors. We define 'sustainability governance' as institutional arrangements or mechanisms to promote sustainability. 'Governance capacity' means the formal and factual capability of actors to define and implement measures that contribute to such arrangements and mechanisms (cf. Knill and Lehmkuhl 2002).

We stated above that CSR is a mode of sustainability governance with a business, societal and political dimension. The business dimension refers to the corporate rules and practices by which companies strive to become more socially and environmentally friendly. CSR is a means for businesses to respond to sustainability challenges and to cope with the uncertainties that result from these. Companies assess whether such challenges might turn into a risk or represent an opportunity for them (for more detail, see Section 1.2.5.1). They can define and implement measures to adjust their processes or products. Outside their immediate sphere of influence, for example in supply chain management, companies' governance capacity is more indirect. It relies on obligatory clauses in supplier contracts, incentives and moral suasion. CSR instruments provide the business sector with 'templates' for the required changes of rules and practices. At the same time, the use of well established CSR instruments signals that a company engages in recognized and legitimate business practices rather than in 'heretical' missteps (Fineman 2001; Hoffman 2001; DiMaggio and Powell 1983).

CSR, however, is more than a business affair. Because consumers, civil society organizations and even social movements contribute to shaping and pushing CSR, it is also a societal mode of sustainability governance. It provides a channel through which stakeholders can assert to companies their norms and expectations regarding sustainable development. While traditionally, these demands have been directed towards the state, economic globalization prompted societal pressure groups to increasingly target companies. The governance capacity of societal actors in CSR lies in granting or refusing buying power, legitimacy and knowledge. This depends on the actors' concrete, either antagonistic or cooperative initiatives: boycotts, legal action, participation in stakeholder dialogues, development or even implementation of CSR instruments.

Finally, governments stimulate and to some extent even regulate CSR (see Chapter 15 as well as Aaronson and Reeves 2002; Buckland et al. 2006; European Commission 2004b and 2006b; Fox et al. 2002). In such cases, CSR becomes a means of political governance. Governments may stimulate CSR, for example, through the provision of legal and institutional frameworks for voluntary instruments (for instance, the EU's Environmental Management and Auditing Scheme, EMAS), through capacity building, the greening of public procurement, financial incentives or CSR related networking. Governments have also started to regulate formerly voluntary activities, such as non-financial company reporting. Such forms of indirect regulation increasingly complement direct sustainability regulation by which governments, endowed with a legitimate monopoly of force, have traditionally determined the social and environmental responsibilities of companies (so-called 'implicit' CSR, Matten and Moon 2005).

We shall now exemplify how the described modes of sustainability governance intertwine in the use of CSR instruments (Table 1.1).[2] By 'CSR instruments' we mean governance tools that systematically cause or facilitate the incorporation of sustainability concerns into a company's operations. They may be applicable across many companies (standardized instruments) and in this case are often established by third parties, such as UNEP, multi-stakeholder bodies or sector associations. Alternatively, they may be tailor-made to meet the demands of an individual firm

Table 1.1 CSR instruments and distributed governance capacities

CSR area	CSR instrument	Examples	Governance capacity
Management	Codes of conduct	Ethical Trading Initiative base code, Global Compact, ILO Tripartite Declaration, OECD Guidelines on Multinational Enterprises and so on	• Company • Stakeholders: sponsor of instrument
	Management system	EMAS, ISO 14000, ISO 26000, OHSAS 18000, SA 8000 and so on	• Company • Stakeholders: sponsor of instrument
	Accounting and reporting	Global Reporting Initiative (GRI), Greenhouse Gas Protocol Initiative, AA 1000, ISEA 3000 and so on	• Company • Stakeholders: sponsor of instrument
	Stakeholder cooperation	Clean Clothes Campaign, European Multi-Stakeholder Forum, stakeholder engagement in CSR reporting and so on	• Company • Stakeholders: civil society organizations, governments
	Corporate citizenship activities	Donating, sponsoring, foundations, CRM, volunteering and so on	• Company • Stakeholders: civil society organizations
	Non-standardized instruments	Company's tailor-made tools, for example Unilever's Traffic Light System for assessing the sustainability of fisheries	• Company • Stakeholders: no generalization possible
Consumption	Social and ecological labelling	Energy Star, EU organic label, European eco-label ('Flower'), Fairtrade Mark, FSC, MSC and so on	• Company • Stakeholders: sponsor of instrument (labelling organizations), consumers
Investment	SRI funds and indexes	Institutional SRI, consumer SRI; FTSE4Good, Dow Jones Sustainability Index and so on	• Company • Stakeholders: shareholders, fund managers, screening organizations, index providers • Company

Source: Authors.

9

(non-standardized instruments).[3] To show how the capacities of sustainability governance are distributed among different actors in CSR, we shall differentiate between instruments of responsible management, responsible consumption and responsible investment (European Commission 2004a).

Instruments of responsible management help companies to put their CSR approaches into concrete terms. They include codes of conduct, management systems, accounting practices, stakeholder engagement and cooperation, Corporate Citizenship activities and non-standardized instruments.

Codes of conduct are formal statements of principles that define standards for specific company behaviour, and in some cases for the behaviour of subsidiaries, contractors and suppliers. The governance capacity is distributed between companies that implement the codes and those actors that design them (their 'sponsors'). Sponsors may be the companies themselves or their associations, like the chemical industry's Responsible Care Global Charter on Product Responsibility. Typically, however, non-business stakeholders are included in or even spearhead an instrument's design. The ILO Tripartite Declaration, for example, was developed by governments, employers and workers represented in the International Labour Organisation. In some cases, such as the UN Global Compact review mechanism and learning forum, the sponsors of a code require specific follow-up mechanisms. They may also tighten the codes' standards over the years.

Management systems are tools that provide procedures and specifications for integration into a company's everyday practices. The obligations inherent in management systems either relate to corporate processes or to performance. Management systems can be deployed across the whole organization, as in the case of ISO 14 000, or may be exclusively site-based, such as the Social Accountability 8000 standard. Governance capacities are split up between companies and their stakeholders in the same way as described for codes of conduct.

Social and environmental accounting is the voluntary process of assessing and communicating organizational activities and impact on sustainability. Accounting includes both 'auditing' (the measurement and checking of data) and 'reporting' (the communication of data). Guidelines on the content and methods of accounting have been developed, most notably by the Global Reporting Initiative (GRI). As regards governance capacities, external stakeholders can play a more comprehensive role than in the case of codes or management systems: they are not only potential instrument sponsors, but are sometimes directly involved in the accounting processes to verify data or provide assurance on the reports' materiality.

Another instrument of responsible management is stakeholder engagement and cooperation. It includes various – bilateral or multilateral, formal or informal, issue-specific or more comprehensive – types of interaction between companies and their societal stakeholders. These may be driven by companies and industry associations (such as the Common Code for the Coffee Community Association), by civil society (such as the Clean Clothes Campaign) or by governments (such as the former European Multi-Stakeholder Forum). Influence of the stakeholders over the definition and implementation of sustainability measures varies strongly between more consultative and more cooperative forms of interaction. Where the say of stakeholders ('voice') is low, their influence is limited to the threat of stopping the cooperation ('exit').

Corporate Citizenship activities finally encompass a variety of specific community measures, such as donations, sponsorship, the establishment of foundations, cause-related marketing (CRM) or employee volunteering. As regards governance capacities, the social or ecological projects in Corporate Citizenship initiatives are typically designed and implemented jointly with or exclusively by civil society stakeholders.

Apart from the above standardized instruments, a host of non-standardized CSR instruments exist. These are company-specific, tailor-made tools by which businesses strive to increase their social responsibility. In terms of issues and governance mechanism, the instruments can vary widely, ranging from a firm's principles for ethical trading to action plans on its carbon footprint. Some of them derive from standardized instruments, simplifying these or adapting them to specific contexts. Regularly, companies use standardized and non-standardized instruments in parallel. Being designed to account for a company's individual demands, non-standardized instruments may actually play a greater role than standardized ones in changing corporate practices. However, since each differs from the other, no generalization can be made on how governance capacities are shared between companies and other actors.

Let us now turn to instruments of responsible consumption. These include above all social and ecological labelling. Labels are market-based CSR instruments that aim to influence purchasing decisions of customers, retailers, traders and end consumers in favour of more sustainable products. The award of a certificate that may be used for the marketing of a product is linked to a company's compliance with sustainability criteria. These relate to a product's characteristics (such as energy efficiency), its production (for example, respecting labour standards) or trading (fair producer prices). With instruments of sustainable consumption, governance capacities are distributed among labelling organizations[4] that define the label criteria; companies that implement the criteria; and buyers that prefer the labelled product to a less sustainable one, hence causing a sustainability impact.

Finally, the prime instrument in the area of responsible investment is socially responsible investment (SRI). It links the access to capital of publicly listed companies not only to the financial targets of investors but also to their social, environmental and ethical considerations. SRI works through two channels: shareholder activism or 'screening'. In the first approach shareholders directly influence a company's orientation towards socially responsible behaviour. This happens through dialogue, pressure on management and voting in shareholder meetings. In the second approach investors influence companies' preferences indirectly by selecting the assets for their portfolios on social and environmental grounds. Social or ethical screening can be done either by including companies that are rated to have a good sustainability performance or by excluding companies that produce specific adverse products, such as alcohol or weapons. Governance capacities here lie with (institutional and retail) investors. They are being informed by research, screening and rating agencies which supply SRI data; index providers such as FTSE4Good or the Dow Jones Sustainability Index which set criteria and create transparency on SRI markets; and finally companies which react to shareholder activism and may take into account in their policies SRI screening criteria.

1.2.3 Specifying the 'Voluntary' and 'Beyond Compliance' Nature of CSR

As mentioned above, the mainstream definition of CSR is based on the premise that CSR is voluntary and 'beyond compliance'. While 'voluntary' describes the motivation of corporate behaviour, 'beyond compliance' specifies the relative level of implementation. The latter refers to whether only the legal standards or additional measures are implemented. There is a lack of clarity with regard to this mainstream definition, however. For example, according to this designation, is CSR possible in such areas as countering bribery? Bribery is defined as a crime by basically all legal systems and may not be tolerated in companies and their counterparts. Why then should we describe corporate measures to prevent bribery as CSR, as something voluntary? And is legislation pertaining to CSR, such as transparency obligations, a contradiction in terms? In order to answer these questions, we shall scrutinize the elements of the above definition and refine them.

In our view, 'compliance' can relate to both goals and measures. Goals may be quantitative or qualitative, mandatory or voluntary; they set targets or define the illegality of actions. Measures are activities by which goal attainment may be increased (performance measures) or ensured (implementation measures). Going 'beyond compliance' in relation to a goal means to overachieve a given target or to set a target for the company where policy makers have not formulated one. Going 'beyond compliance' in relation to measures, on the other hand, means that a company carries out activities and adopts rules or practices which are not prescribed by regulation. Still these may serve to systematically approach or implement a legally prescribed goal.

The reduction of environmentally harmful emissions shall exemplify the above. We assume there is a legally defined threshold for emitting a substance. In addition, several implementation measures are prescribed regarding verification and reporting of the emissions. In a case like this, a company can go beyond compliance, both with regard to the goal and further measures. Concerning the goal, a CSR commitment could mean that the company decides to reduce its emissions by a further 5 per cent. Concerning measures, the firm might decide to verify and report more frequently and extensively than required, or to report publicly and with independent verification even if this is not stipulated.

Although there will be instances where the line between the two ways of going 'beyond compliance' are blurred, this distinction is helpful. This is the case when legal goals do not leave room for a company to go beyond compliance, as in countering bribery. Due to the total ban for bribery, it is impossible for companies to overachieve this goal. It is nevertheless possible to carry out measures which companies are not legally obliged to follow. Even a company that has a record of bribery – and thus is below compliance regarding the overall goal – can adopt the voluntary Business Principles Countering Bribery and subsequently implement organizational changes to prevent the occurrence of bribery. In such cases, CSR means undertaking voluntary measures to help the company to become compliant with obligatory goals.

Another special case regarding the relation between voluntariness and 'beyond compliance' is the (so far rather sparse) law governing CSR itself. A case in point is the EU's EMAS legislation. Companies desiring to use the EMAS logo have to submit to legally defined procedures and obligations. Implementing EMAS nevertheless is CSR, as an EMAS certification itself is voluntary.

1.2.4 Specifying the Integration of Sustainability Concerns into Business Operations: 'Built-in' and 'Bolt-on'

The integration of social and environmental concerns in business operations and in the interaction of businesses with their stakeholders is part of the definition of CSR that has become widely accepted within Europe (European Commission 2001, p. 6). We suggest distinguishing different

Source: Authors.

Figure 1.2   'Built-in' and 'bolt-on' CSR

degrees of integrating social and environmental concerns into management. When less integrated, CSR encompasses societal commitment that lies outside – and hence is 'bolt-on' to – a firm's immediate business activities. This type of CSR is often referred to as corporate citizenship (CC).[5] When more integrated, CSR is about building social and environmental concerns into a company's operations, the process and product decisions directly relating to its business activities (Figure 1.2).

In 'bolt-on' CSR companies engage in individual initiatives and extra-activities beyond their core business operations. Although such Corporate Citizenship activities are often regular and routine measures that may even be strategically linked to the core business,[6] they do not intervene with the company's business operations. Activities include donations, sponsorship, company charitable trusts or foundations, employee volunteering and cause-related marketing.[7] These reflect the companies' commitment in the local, national or international communities in which they operate. By definition, external parties profit directly or indirectly from such measures.

We can distinguish four ways of 'building in' CSR (Belz and Pobisch 2004). Stakeholders may in principle be integrated into all four options. The first way is to make corporate processes more sustainable. CSR here may encompass sustainable resource management in raw material extraction; the greening of sourcing decisions, of production and distribution processes; fair trade practices; efforts to increase female representation in top management as well as compliance to ILO's labour standards. This is where standardized instruments of responsible management are used most often. The second way to build in CSR is by improving the ecological and social properties of the products or services themselves. A firm's production and business operations hence become immediate objects of its responsibility. CSR then also extends to research and development, the product portfolio, the setting up of distribution channels and market development. Thirdly, 'built-in' CSR may include the sphere of sustainable consumption. Apart from providing consumer information, companies can promote the consumption of sustainable products, among others, by means of pricing and marketing. Finally, in the broadest sense, CSR extends to the shaping of social-ecological framework conditions that govern production and consumption. In this case, companies use their influence in legislative processes, industry norm-setting and public discourses[8] to promote rather than obstruct ambitious sustainability standards.

As Figure 1.2 indicates, CSR can be more or less 'bolt-on' or 'built-in', and many intermediate forms exist between the poles. In principle, standardized CSR instruments can be used in all cases. However, the deeper social and environmental responsibilities are integrated into business activities, the more instruments will need to be supplemented by changes in corporate processes, products and stakeholder relations. Finally, both forms of CSR have the potential to produce sustainability impact, though in the first case this impact is likely to lie outside a company's business activities.

1.2.5   Specifying CSR Processes and Effects

In the following sections we turn our attention to the concrete processes through which companies integrate social and environmental concerns into their operations and stakeholder relations, and to the resulting effects. These effects we shall call CSR 'output', 'outcome' and 'impact'. We provide a systematic model which describes CSR process steps and CSR effects as two sides of the same coin.

1.2.5.1   CSR process steps
Within companies we assume that the CSR processes preceding the creation of sustainability impact can roughly be categorized into three phases: commitment, strategy formulation and implementation (cf. Wheelen and Hunger 2004, pp. 9–16). Before the commitment phase, and thus the actual CSR process, companies scan their environment. In this step the firm recognizes the existence of sustainability challenges like climate change, poverty reduction and equal opportunities. These sustainability challenges for companies translate into a range of more specific 'issues', such as transport emissions, micro lending or equal pay for men and women. Issues represent areas of current or expected future stakeholder interest, for which responsible corporate behaviour is or might be requested. Sustainability issues can take the form of (intentional or unintentional) direct consequences of company actions, such as greenhouse gas emissions, workers' accidents, overfishing and so on. Or they may be broader societal problems which exist quite independently of company action (Schmitt 2004). The latter include, for example, poverty, starvation or AIDS. Having screened the sustainability issues, businesses assess – in the light of internal and external factors – whether they represent a risk or opportunity for them.

Risks include, for instance, damages to reputation, forfeit of licence to operate or the missing of business opportunities, while opportunities involve increased resource productivity and employee motivation, a positive corporate and brand identity as well as premium prices for products produced in a socially or ecologically friendly way (Salzmann et al. 2005; Willard 2002).[9] Companies then review CSR as an adequate response to this risk or opportunity.

In the commitment phase the company acknowledges responsibility by deciding to address one or more sustainability challenges. It sets overarching objectives which are to be integrated into its vision and values. In the phase of strategy formulation the commitment is put into more concrete terms: medium to long-range plans are developed which specify targets and policies for the effective management of sustainability issues. This can include formulation of an overarching CSR or sustainability strategy, and of single-issue strategies (for example, on climate change) respectively. Furthermore, CSR concerns can be integrated into other strategies, such as business, functional, growth, competitive, sourcing and R&D strategies. In the process of strategy formulation managers may also decide to adopt specific CSR instruments. From the adaptation of existing and development of new strategies, the company moves on to the stage of implementation. During this phase the strategies and policies are put into action by way of programmes, resources and procedures. This includes the concrete implementation of CSR instruments, among others, through carrying out specific activities (for example, change to a less CO_2 intense production method). Implementation in a more encompassing sense also covers the establishment of wider organizational structures through which responsibilities are assigned, and verification and control are ensured. Note that it is difficult to draw clear dividing lines between the different phases, and that a strictly chronological and linear accession of the process steps is not necessary.

1.2.5.2 CSR effects
The above process steps can create different types of effects within and outside companies. In this section we distinguish these CSR effects into 'output', 'outcome' and 'impact'. We have transferred these concepts from public policy analysis to CSR research. Public policy scholars (Dunn 1994; Oberthür and Gehring 2006; Prittwitz 2003; Underdal 2004) originally developed the terms to describe the effects of governmental policies, but we found the typology fertile for analysing the effects of corporate policies as well.

CSR outputs are changes both in corporate commitment and strategies with regard to a company's social and environmental performance. They may include, for example, the development of an environmental or diversity policy with targets and timeframes as well as a decision to adopt the Global Compact or other CSR instruments. CSR outcomes are changes in companies' concrete practices resulting from the implementation of CSR outputs. For instance, a company operationalizes and implements a management system to counter bribery, greens its supply chain or 'gender-mainstreams' its vocational training. Both output and outcome are crucial preconditions for achieving impact and thus for the success of CSR. CSR impact finally describes the substantive consequences in the social or environmental realm (outside the company) caused by the changes in corporate practices. It encompasses direct and indirect sustainability benefits, such as pollution reduction and the diffusion of solutions for pollution reduction. The typology of CSR outcome, output and impact will be described in more detail in Chapter 2.

As can be seen from Figure 1.3, we link CSR process steps and CSR effects as follows: CSR commitment causes changes in corporate strategy, and thus 'output'. Implementation of the altered strategy yields changes in corporate practice, and thus 'outcome'. Outcome leads to substantive effects in the social and environmental realm, in other words, to 'impact'.

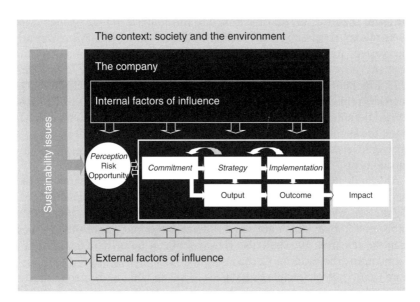

Source: Authors.

Figure 1.3   A framework for analysing the creation of sustainability impact through CSR

Figure 1.3 illustrates the described context of environmental influences and in-company CSR processes that ideally lead to a beneficial impact on society and the environment. Sustainability challenges are part of companies' natural environment, but also their social context within which the societal and environmental problems become interpreted and turned into societal demands on the private sector. How sustainability issues are perceived and further 'processed' within the company depends on a range of factors internal and external to companies that will be elaborated in Chapter 3. These factors influence, among others, how CSR commitment becomes specified and implemented, thus yielding output and outcome. Sustainability impact accrues outside the company, in its societal and natural environment.

1.2.6   Rhetoric and Reality: Sustainability Impact as Acid Test of CSR

The title of this book refers to the 'rhetoric and realities' of CSR. Rhetoric (from the Greek ῥήτωρ, rhêtôr, orator or teacher) classically describes the art or technique of persuasion through the use of language. In its everyday use the term often suggests a somewhat skeptical opposition to 'reality' in the sense of 'action' or 'facts'. In organizational and management theory the term 'rhetoric' has become linked to the analysis of management fashions or fads (Abrahamson 1991; Collins 2001; Kieser 1997). More recently, the concept of CSR and components of it, such as environmental management, have been subjected to critical reviews along these lines (Crane 1995; Fineman 2001; Guthey et al. 2006; Roberts 2003; Windell 2005). Our interest in this book is less with the construction or diffusion of CSR as a potential 'fad', but with the sustainability impact created through it. In this sense, the slightly simplistic formulation of 'rhetoric and realities' refers to varying levels of substance and effects of social responsibility within and outside firms.

Although they are highly illustrative, we shall, however, not employ the categories of 'rhetoric' and 'reality' for our analysis proper. Rather, in the analysis we shall stick to the terms 'output', 'outcome' and 'impact' as elaborated above, which are more differentiated and established in social scientific research. We shall also refrain from an immediate translation of output into 'rhetoric' and outcome into 'reality'. In our view, output is more than 'rhetoric', while outcome is less than what we understand to be bottom-line 'reality'. As regards the first point, CSR output, among others, includes sustainability changes in corporate strategies and adoption of instruments. This goes beyond mere corporate rhetoric, defined by Rhee and Lee as 'a company's environmental [or social] intention declared externally or internally in formal arguments, including written and published symbolic statements, declarations and slogans about environmental [or social] management' (Rhee and Lee 2003, p. 177, own brackets). As regards the second argument, we feel that CSR outcome, while certainly going beyond 'rhetoric', cannot be equated with 'reality' either. This is because socially and environmentally motivated changes in corporate practices do not necessarily (albeit in many cases they do) affect society and the environment – our ultimate benchmark of 'reality'.

Why is it important to understand the impact that CSR has on society and the environment? Knowledge of the impact of CSR on society and the environment is potentially relevant for various stakeholders. For academia, insights into the sustainability impact of CSR can partly fill an existing research gap: up to now, scant research has been carried out addressing this topic. Whilst research into CSR has mainly focused on CSR management within companies and the impact of such commitment on corporate organization, strategies and financial performance (for an overview see Chapter 3), policy studies have concentrated on public rather than corporate policies to date. We attempt to bridge the resulting gap by enquiring into how the private sector can contribute to sustainable development, and in particular to achieving politically set sustainability goals. For businesses, learning more about the effectiveness of their voluntary activities in terms of sustainability is decisive. With additional insights into how to really make a difference businesses can also counter criticism on CSR being a mere 'greenwash'. From the point of view of public policy makers, knowing more about the sustainability potential and limits of CSR helps them to differentiate between a policy fashion and a potentially effective means of governance. In this spirit, the European Parliament announced in a 2007 resolution 'that the EU debate on CSR has approached the point where emphasis should be shifted from "processes" to "outcomes", leading to a measurable and transparent contribution from business in combating social exclusion and environmental degradation in Europe and around the world.'[10] These insights can help to create the most effective policy mixes for sustainable development. For societal stakeholders, such as civil society organizations, it is important to learn about possible positive or negative effects of CSR in relation to their concerns and to appreciate how the creation of sustainability impact through CSR can potentially be promoted.

1.3   THE STRUCTURE OF THE BOOK

The book is divided into four parts. Part I, which contains Chapters 1 to 3, elaborates the methodological framework of the book. While in this chapter we have developed our understanding of CSR, Skjærseth and

Wettestad in Chapter 2 tackle the methodological challenges of assessing the sustainability impact of CSR. They discuss the criteria for differentiating compliance from beyond-compliance activities in order to establish a baseline for the impact of CSR. Based on this, Skjærseth and Wettestad outline two approaches for assessing CSR impact, a 'relative improvement' and a 'goal attainment' strategy. The authors highlight the need to disentangle by process tracing the causal links between the different levels of CSR effects, namely CSR 'output' (changes in strategy), 'outcome' (changes in practices) and 'impact' (sustainability gains). Finally, they place their approach – which is the basis of empirical work presented in subsequent chapters – in relation with existing research.

In Chapter 3 Viganò et al. develop a framework for explaining the sustainability impact of CSR. In a first step, they break down the question about sustainability effects into more specific operational research questions. Drawing on both institutional and management literature, they then work out a set of factors that influence the achievement of CSR effects, and above all of CSR impact. These factors are: design of the CSR instruments employed, corporate strategy and organization, corporate culture, the business environment, civil society and the political-institutional setting. Linking the factors to the operational research questions, a number of propositions are formulated that will be empirically discussed in Part III of the book.

Part II presents a first set of empirical studies by which we map CSR in different European industries, with a focus on selected social and environmental issues. These include the mitigation of climate change and of chemical risk, sustainable resource management, the promotion of gender equality and countering bribery. We consider these issues as highly relevant for sustainable development in its social, environmental and economic dimensions. In terms of sectors, the oil industry, the fish processing sector and the banking business were chosen since they also have a high impact on and potential for sustainability. Also they link up with the targeted issues: 'fuelling' our fossil economy, the oil industry has a share of responsibility for climate change and chemical risks (ecological sustainability). With fishery resources globally declining, fish processors are at the intersection of ecological and economic sustainability in the field of resource management. The banking sector has implications both for economic and social sustainability: as financial institutions they must exert responsibility and due diligence for countering bribery and they have a pivotal role in anti-money laundering; and as a sector with a high rate of female employment it has a high potential to promote gender equality. Finally, the three sectors lend themselves to a cross-cutting analysis of the targeted issues. For example, gender equality can be analysed in the banking as well as the fish

Table 1.2   CSR issues and sectors studied

Sustainability dimension	'Focus' issue	Sector
Ecological sustainability	Mitigation of climate change and chemical risks	Oil sector
Economic sustainability	Sustainable management of (fisheries) resources	Fish processing sector
	Countering bribery	Banking sector
Social sustainability	Promoting gender equality	

Source: Authors.

processing sector, bribery in oil companies and banks, and environmental issues in the fish processing and oil industries.

Apart from the sectors' sustainability implications, we sought to analyse industries from different macro sectors: the primary (oil and gas), secondary (fish processing) and tertiary sector (banking). This creates variance with regard to the products and production processes that have CSR relevance. Finally, we were interested to include both industries with a long-standing CSR experience, such as the oil and banking sectors, and a 'CSR newcomer' like the fish processing industry.

The oil, fish processing and banking sectors are the subject of empirical research throughout the whole book. The focus within these sectors is on larger, partly multinational companies operating in various EU countries. To get an additional and contrasting perspective, Chapter 8 analyses SMEs. The SMEs are of either Hungarian or Austrian origin. This makes possible an additional comparison: that between companies headquartered in new and old EU Member States. We selected the automotive supply chain as it is a relevant industry in both countries, has substantial sustainability impact and SMEs of this sector are active in CSR, including our targeted issues.

In Chapter 4 Schmitt sets out the common foundations of Chapters 5 to 8. These chapters contain structurally similar surveys carried out among 49 companies in the four sectors. Companies were selected that are active in CSR and, in particular, in the targeted issue areas. The surveys cover their CSR commitment, strategies and implementation, thus revealing CSR 'output' and 'outcome'. They also inform about measurement practices and to some – very indicative – extent about the sustainability impact that companies think they achieve through CSR.

Boasson et al. demonstrate in Chapter 5 that the oil industry is rather advanced in terms of CSR. Though based on a striking conceptual diversity, the nine European companies surveyed address all four targeted issue areas in strategic terms, in implementing activities – including through a high number of standardized instruments – and in performance measurement. The authors, however, raise the critical question of how such a broad portfolio is handled in practice: will its width not reduce the depth of its impact?

For the fish processing sector, Schmitt and Wolff in Chapter 6 draw a less advanced picture. The eight sampled companies' commitments focus on the issue closest to their core business: the sustainability of fisheries, which is not only critical to the ecosystem but also to the industry's supply base. This is the only issue more or less consistently translated into corporate strategies and activities. Purely environmental concerns, such as the industry's carbon footprint, or social issues have not yet been seriously tackled. While performance measurement is unsatisfactory, individual firms perform notably with regard to sustainable sourcing.

The survey of 17 European banks carried out by Viganò and Nicolai in Chapter 7 confirms that the sector has reached some sophistication with regard to CSR. To a substantial extent, banks strategically integrate their responsibilities and transpose them into targets, relating to own operations as well as those of suppliers and other partners. A major challenge for implementing CSR in banks is to address not only their direct but also indirect responsibilities, for example in lending policies. With regard to these, the banks' efforts of measuring performance as well as the actual self-assessed performance are limited.

In Chapter 8 Pálvölgyi et al. highlight that the 20 SMEs surveyed in the Austrian and Hungarian automotive supply chain also have institutionalized social and, in particular, environmental responsibilities. However, compared with the larger companies targeted in the preceding chapters, they use a less formal and strategically planned approach to CSR, and adhere less frequently to standardized instruments. Concrete activities tackle 'traditional' environmental issues – climate change not yet being a priority – and gender equality. Differences between Austrian and Hungarian respondents were less distinct than expected.

Schmitt synthesizes the four surveys and compares evidence across the different sectors and company sizes in Chapter 9. She highlights varying degrees of CSR diffusion in the sectors and different implementation patterns. In terms of similarities, it is striking that businesses of all sectors and sizes conceptually emphasize compliance rather than going beyond compliance as most relevant for their social responsibility. Another similarity is that even among the selected CSR leaders, many do not systematically assess their CSR impact.

Part III contains company case studies. Their objective is to assess in some more depth the sustainability impact selected enterprises have achieved – or have failed to achieve – through CSR, and to causally explain this impact. From the oil, banking and fish processing sectors, two to three firms surveyed in Part II were chosen. While the criteria for the selection of the companies differ – partly aiming at most similar, partly at most different cases (Przeworski and Teune 1970) – the authors seek to identify factors for success and failure in achieving CSR impact. All case studies are based on the framework for explaining CSR effects laid down in Chapter 3 and address propositions developed there.

In Chapter 10 Boasson and Wettestad find out that adoption of selected CSR instruments in Shell and Hydro does not always lead to an adaptation of the companies' climate-related practices to the instruments' requirements. The level of sustainability effects rendered by CSR instruments differ in the two companies. Even where executives are committed and corporate cultures favour CSR implementation, limited strategic control and a lack of organizational integration hamper impact. The crux of climate-related responsibility for the oil business is that high environmental impact requires restructuring the very basis of business.

Wolff and Schmitt in Chapter 11 study three high-performing fish processors: Unilever PLC, Young's Bluecrest Ltd and Friedrichs KG. Factors that contribute to promoting 'on the water' impact through their supply chains include management alignment, organizational integration and tight supplier relations. Also all companies have particular traditions or identities which link up with the sustainable fisheries issue. Finally, environmental organizations and partly retailers facilitate effective CSR implementation too. However, limited availability of sustainable fish, weaknesses in public fisheries management and lacking familiarity with the MSC label constrain the creation of impact.

In Chapter 12, Schultz analyses the effects of gender-related CSR in Caja Madrid and Dexia. While implementation models differ in the two banks, both banks substantially foster gender equality. Importantly, both implementation models 'fit' with the companies' stakeholder demands and gender equality is integrated into corporate culture. Strategically, the gender topic requires a long-term perspective and an emphasis among the various other diversity issues (for example disabled). In organizational terms, cross-sector functions for gender equality and ongoing internal communication prove to be crucial. Finally, in both cases national gender equality award systems foster gender impact.

Wilkinson discusses policies of two leading European banks – Caja Madrid and Monte dei Paschi di Siena – to counter bribery and money laundering in Chapter 13. Whilst the banks recognize a special responsibility to anti-money laundering, they have no specific commitments to counter bribery. Nevertheless, they carry out voluntary activities in both these issue areas, including communications, training and implementation of (self-tailored) instruments. Key contributors to achieving CSR effects are the banks' traditions of community commitment and stakeholder governance, the influence of banking associations as well as procedures and targets provided by anti-money-laundering laws.

In a synthesis of the case studies in Chapter 14 Wolff argues that the case studies identify sustainability impact in some issue areas and sectors, but less so in others. In general, there are few examples for high impact; more often findings suggest low to medium impact. Across the studies, there are no systematic patterns linking output, outcome and impact. When explaining CSR effects, strategic integration and hierarchical control play a crucial role both for instrument choice and adherence (CSR output) and for changes in corporate practices (CSR outcome) and resulting impact. Other factors, including the demands or pressures from civil society, were also relevant to some extent.

Finally, Part IV tackles the interrelations between CSR and public policy from various perspectives. Wolff et al. in Chapter 15 conceptually discuss the roles of public policy for CSR, and of CSR for public policy. While public policy stimulates and even procedurally regulates corporate responsibility, CSR can – if it is real rather than rhetorical – increase the sustainability effect aimed for by public social and environmental policies. This holds true not only where companies go 'beyond compliance', but also where command and control or incentive-based public governance exists. Based on empirical evidence, the authors finally examine to what extent CSR activities address EU sustainability goals in the fields of climate, fisheries, gender equality and anti-bribery policy.

In Chapter 16 Pálvölgyi et al. examine how EU integration affects and interacts with the practice of CSR in the new EU Member States. Focusing on Hungary, they demonstrate how EU integration slowly transforms the socio-economic framework conditions of formerly socialist countries into which present-day CSR activities are embedded. Through the example of a national oil company and the Hungarian subsidiary of an international oil corporation, the authors compare concrete CSR practices in a Europeanizing market. They also discuss whether these practices in turn have repercussions on EU integration.

Chapter 17 wraps up the discussion on the rhetoric and realities of CSR. Wolff et al. sum up the book's core findings on the sustainability impact of CSR. They point out where CSR impact is more likely to be found and where there are systematic limits of CSR in creating sustainability impact. Finally, they present implications from the book results for public policy and research.

NOTES

1. The project 'Rhetoric and Realities: Analysing Corporate Social Responsibility in Europe' (RARE); for more information, see the Acknowledgements.
2. A more extensive version of the below reflections can be found in Wolff and Barth (2005).
3. In Chapter 3.3 we shall elaborate the role of standardized and non-standardized instruments in our overall research design.
4. These may be civil society organizations, governmental bodies, multi-stakeholder committees or specialized businesses.
5. Note that not all authors make the distinction between CC and CSR. Andriof and McIntosh (2001, p. 14), for example use the terms synonymously. We follow Mutz et al. (2001) in that we conceptualize Corporate Citizenship as part of CSR.
6. A strategic link between a company's business and corporate citizenship activities exists, for example, when a firm with sites in Africa donates to AIDS projects, or a global food company supports projects fighting child mortality.
7. While some authors regard cooperation with citizens and other external stakeholders as a Corporate Citizenship instrument (Habisch 2003; Maaß and Clemens 2002), we classify stakeholder engagement as a CSR instrument. It may be more or less 'bolt-on' or 'built-in' to a company's business operations.
8. An example of such discursive influence is to counter the widespread interpretation that 'ecological' equals 'expensive' (Belz and Bilharz 2005, p. 251).
9. Note that perceiving CSR as a potentially profitable approach to sustainability issues for businesses does not limit CSR to 'win win' situations: in some instances behaving responsibly goes hand in hand with forgoing certain benefits. An example is the increase in labour costs when a company decides not to use (cheap) child labour.
10. European Parliament resolution of 13 March 2007 on corporate social responsibility: a new partnership (2006/2133(INI)).

2 A framework for assessing the sustainability impact of CSR

Jon Birger Skjærseth and Jørgen Wettestad

2.1 INTRODUCTION

If Corporate Social Responsibility (CSR) wants to be recognized as a substantive and not only rhetorical exercise, there is a need to show that it indeed achieves what its proponents claim: that companies, by voluntarily adopting and integrating social and environmental concerns into their business operations, add to social and environmental improvement and hence to sustainability. But what activities 'count' as CSR in the first place? How can we determine the sustainability impact of CSR? And how do we establish causal relationships to make sure that the improved environmental performance of a company, which it may claim to result from its beyond compliance efforts, is indeed caused by the corporation taking on specific environmental responsibility – and not merely, for instance, by closing an uneconomic site?

The purpose of this chapter is to tackle these questions. We shall present key analytical challenges related to CSR impact assessment and hence introduce the approach which is guiding the empirical studies presented in this book. We are not the first to suggest a framework for CSR impact assessment (see, for example, Annandale et al. 2004; Figge and Hahn 2004; Kolk and Mauser 2002). Our approach is in many ways in line with dominant trends within management literature, such as working with a model distinguishing stages in the process and including both internal processes and external influencing factors (as further elaborated in Chapter 3).

The specific contribution of this approach lies, firstly, in a systematic approach to assess the actual sustainability impact of CSR. There is a quite limited research available on the actual effect and impact of voluntary sustainability approaches such as CSR – although such initiatives have over time been quite well described (Annandale et al. 2004). This has to do with the fact that measuring the impact of specific 'drivers' of company performance is a methodologically difficult exercise. Still, we believe that it also has to do with a shortage of analytical frameworks that focus directly on actual impact. It is this dimension that forms the very core of our interest and hence this book. Therefore, we combine management literature with literature rooted in political science and particularly in the evaluation of the effectiveness of national and international policies and institutions (for example, Miles et al. 2002; Oberthür and Gehring 2006; Underdal 2004). Secondly, our approach strives to benchmark the corporate sustainability achievements against public policy goals. This perspective is rather uncommon, as students of management literature tend to be more interested in the business implications than in the public policy effects of corporate action, while policy analysts often focus on the impact of public rather than private decisions. Thirdly, as regards the methodological realization of the impact assessment, the combination of surveys (in different industrial sectors) and a number of in-depth case studies used is not common in the field of CSR assessment.

The next section explores what constitutes CSR and different criteria for evaluating the impact of CSR. The third section discusses the key concepts of CSR 'output', 'outcome' and 'impact' as different effects of CSR processes and discusses how to draw causal inferences from CSR commitments to actual impacts. Conclusions from the exercise are presented in Section 4.

2.2   CRITERIA FOR EVALUATING THE IMPACT OF CSR

In the first part of this section we discuss what actually constitutes the object to be assessed or evaluated. The second part explores different criteria for evaluating the impact of CSR.

What is then the object of our assessment – that is, what is CSR and how can we identify a starting point for assessing the sustainability impact of CSR? The assessment of the impact of CSR presupposes the existence of something that qualifies as CSR in the first place. As described in Chapter 1, we understand companies to employ CSR in order to react to sustainability challenges in the company's social and natural environment. These challenges (or 'issues') are perceived by the business either as risks or as opportunities. The first process step of CSR then is when a company commits itself by acknowledging its responsibility for an issue and develops a strategy to tackle the issue, among others by determining goals, policies and adopting CSR instruments.[1] The result of this first step is summarized as the company's CSR output. This output may or may not lead to other activities through a process of implementation, such as switching to new technologies or establishing programmes to enhance gender equality or counter bribery (outcome). Such activities may have consequences for the social or environmental problem in question, for example, reducing greenhouse gas emissions or bribery (impact). We shall return to the various stages and effects in Section 3. The object to be evaluated is hence the consequences of the initial perception of sustainability challenges: the resulting CSR commitment and strategy, including the adoption of CSR instruments, plus their subsequent effects.

CSR instruments should be understood in a wide sense. They may be standardized and hence used by many companies in the same sector or even across different sectors, or purely company-specific. Some instruments pertain to specific sustainability issues, such as child labour, security and human rights in the extractive sector, or gas flaring by oil companies; others cover a whole range of issues from human and labour rights to environmental protection. Among the instruments of socially responsible management, we can distinguish codes of conduct, management systems, accounting and reporting, stakeholder engagement and, beyond the companies' immediate business sphere, corporate citizenship activities, such as donating, sponsoring or volunteering. Instruments of socially responsible consumption cover labels relating to social (for example fair trade) or environmental product or production qualities, with companies adhering to the label standards. Instruments of socially responsible investment (SRI) include SRI funds as well as sustainability indexes for stock-market listed firms and are not employed by companies themselves but by investors.

CSR is further conceived of as a voluntary and beyond-compliance strategy of companies (European Commission 2006b, p. 2). The distinction between mandatory and voluntary corporate action is difficult, but important for establishing a baseline for CSR impact. When CSR is defined as a beyond-compliance strategy, we need to know what constitutes compliance with mandatory obligations before we start to assess the impact of CSR. Compliance will then serve as the 'business as usual' baseline. This implies, strictly interpreted, that we should try to isolate the 'amount' of corporate activities that exist beyond compliance. This is particularly challenging in cases which are heavily regulated, such as chemicals. In such densely regulated cases there will be substantial involuntary action geared towards improving companies' sustainability performance. Companies can adopt codes of conduct (partly) as a response to mandatory obligations or turn to labelling as a response to anticipated regulation at a later stage. For our assessment purpose, however, motives for adopting CSR – such as the degree to which CSR is a response to anticipated regulation – are less relevant.[2]

What are the criteria for evaluating the impact of CSR? We have learned from the study of policy and regime effectiveness (for example, Underdal 2002) that there are essentially two strategies available: a 'relative improvement' and a 'goal attainment' strategy. Firstly, we can measure CSR impact as a relative improvement caused by the CSR instruments and activities. This 'relative improvement' strategy is suitable to answer whether CSR matters. Our baseline will then be (the construction of) a hypothetical situation without any 'voluntary' CSR activities: would the companies behave differently in the absence of a CSR commitment and strategy? This counterfactual question is extremely difficult to answer conclusively, but one indication of such behaviour is the extent to which companies have adopted beyond-compliance CSR strategies and actually behaved beyond compliance. Our empirical baseline from which we would measure changes would then be 'compliance'. The following empirical steps can be indicated for an ideal-type 'relative improvement' strategy of CSR impact assessment:

- Which mandatory obligations exist in the relevant policy field? As an example, let us assume there is legislation requiring 20 per cent of women in leading corporate positions.
- How would the company behave in a compliance situation? Obviously, the company would employ 20 per cent of women in leading positions.
- To what extent has the company adopted CSR commitment, strategy and instruments beyond compliance? It may have adopted goals and measures to secure 50 per cent of women in leading corporate positions.
- Has the company behaved beyond compliance? For example, has the number of women in leading positions exceeded 20 per cent?
- To what extent can the difference between compliance and actual behaviour be explained by CSR commitment and strategy? Have the changes indeed been caused by CSR or do they result from other motives and developments?
- Outside the company, what is the effect on society and/or the environment of the company's CSR-induced beyond-compliance behaviour?

A second strategy is to relate CSR impact to the attainment of a predefined goal. This 'goal attainment' strategy is appropriate if we want to know whether CSR instruments are sufficient to solve the problem at hand. What could be accomplished can be measured by relating what is accomplished to the given objectives. Objectives could be located at different levels, from company to nation state and EU level. While we recognize that companies with their CSR activities do not necessarily aim to fulfil goals set by governments, our interest in the business contribution to social and environmental governance suggests that we base the assessment on public (EU) objectives within the relevant issue areas or policy fields. One major challenge with this strategy is that obviously a number of public policy goals do not directly address companies. For example, the EU's Sixth Environmental Action Programme[3] requires among others 'promoting greater integration of environmental considerations in the Common Fisheries Policy', a goal that needs to be met by European governments rather than by companies. Also, the EU's commitment under the Kyoto Protocol to reduce greenhouse gas emissions by 8 per cent in the period 2008–12 addresses states.

However, this policy goal, though not immediately directed at companies, is transferable to companies. That is, companies can voluntarily contribute to it if they choose to do so, beyond potential legal requirements at national level. Benchmarking companies' CSR impact against public policy goals requires a detailed analysis of such goals which takes account of the extent to which companies can contribute to their achievement. A further methodological challenge of the 'goal attainment' strategy of impact assessment is that policy goals tend to vary in terms of their level of ambition over time and between different policy fields, thus making a comparison difficult. Since objectives also vary significantly in preciseness, it is hard to measure them. Relevant empirical steps of an ideal-type 'goal attainment' strategy include:

- What have the companies accomplished? Tackling this question requires an analysis of company data on their performance, for example with regard to gender equality.
- Which public (for example EU) policy goals have been adopted, and to what extent do they relate to or are transferable to companies? In our example this would require an analysis of policies tackling the work-life balance of employees, the gender pay gap, anti-discrimination and so on.
- To what extent have the companies contributed to attaining the identified policy goals? An assessment of the distance between what has been achieved and what can be achieved according to gender equality goals is necessary.
- Is goal attainment causally related to CSR efforts?
- Outside the companies, what is the effect on society and/or the environment of the company's CSR-induced beyond-compliance behaviour?

Notice, firstly, that the definition of CSR as 'voluntary and beyond compliance' requires an assessment of existing mandatory goals and measures with regard to both strategies. Secondly, the 'relative improvement' and 'goal attainment' strategies of CSR impact assessment ideally complement each other. This is because in some cases there may be high goal attainment, but low absolute CSR impact. For example, a given oil company may have succeeded in reducing emissions of greenhouse gases due to lower oil and gas production and technological changes that are not causally related to CSR instruments. In other cases there may be low goal attainment, but high impact from CSR instruments. Another oil company may have succeeded in reducing emissions significantly due to implementation of CSR instruments, but it may nevertheless fall short of a given target.

2.3   DISENTANGLING COMPLEX CAUSAL RELATIONSHIPS: DISTINGUISHING CSR 'OUTPUT', 'OUTCOME' AND 'IMPACT'

CSR can create different types of effects within and outside companies. In order to get a better grip on the challenge of understanding and disentangling complex causal relationships, as indicated above, we have suggested breaking down the impact assessment into three main types of effects. Building upon central concepts used in other impact assessment work (for example, Dunn 1994; Oberthür and Gehring 2006; Underdal 2004), we therefore draw from and work with the distinction between the 'outputs', 'outcomes' and 'impact' of corporate decision-making processes.

In a very rough outline this may be translated into 'what corporations say' (output), 'what corporations do' (outcome) and 'what corporations achieve' (impact). These three types of effects are based on each other. That is, outcome presupposes output and impact presupposes output and outcome. Let us have a closer look at these seminal concepts in turn.

2.3.1   Output: CSR Commitment, Strategy and Instruments

Decision-making processes may in a first step result in norms prescribing, proscribing or permitting behaviour (or collectively agreed knowledge) as their immediate output (Oberthür and Gehring 2006, p. 34). In this sense and with reference to the typology of CSR process steps as identified in Chapter 1 (commitment, strategy, implementation), we define CSR outputs as commitment and strategies with regard to integrating social and environmental concerns into business operations and stakeholder relations. Commitment and strategies may include, for example, the development of an environmental or diversity policy with targets and timetables as well as the decision within a company to adopt the Global Compact or other 'standardized' CSR instruments. The actual adoption of such instruments will then be the effect and qualify as 'output'. Commitment, strategy and the adoption of instruments are pre-implementation and denote 'what companies say' rather than what they do.

Consider the following example. When trying to identify what counts as CSR outputs in the case of a specific company, such as the Norwegian oil corporation Hydro (see Chapter 10) or the Spanish bank Caja Madrid (see Chapters 12 and 13), we would first of all check whether the company has an overall vision, mission or objectives with regard to their responsibility to society and the environment, expressed if possible in a written statement. We would then try to find out what strategic importance the company attaches to a social or environmental issue. Further relevant aspects are: does the company translate its social and environmental responsibilities into roadmaps, either by developing self-standing policies or strategies, or by integrating them into existing policies or strategies, such as its sourcing, human resources, corporate, growth and R&D strategies, as applicable? Has the company formulated targets with regard to its beyond-compliance social and environmental performance? Finally, we would check what voluntary instruments the company has adopted for systematically managing social and environmental issues.

As noted, although this book deals with the issue 'rhetoric vs realities' of CSR, we do not equate 'output' with 'rhetoric'. CSR instruments resulting from commitment and strategy are preconditions for outcome and impact which should not be written off and discouraged by labelling them to be simply rhetorical. The information necessary to identify a company's CSR output is in many cases publicly available. This does, however, not hold for aspects such as the firm's assessment of what strategic relevance a CSR issue has for them. In the studies we carried out this information was gained through company questionnaires.

2.3.2 Outcome: Changes in Corporate Practices

In order to become effective, a company's output must generate some form of behavioural change (outcome). We hence define CSR outcome as changes in companies' concrete practices. Changes in practices mean bottom-line changes, such as withdrawing investment from irresponsible activities and redirecting investment to responsible ones; adjusting innovation processes and greening the company's product portfolio; sourcing more sustainable inputs; implementing environmental management systems; installing eco-efficient technologies; better recognizing disadvantaged groups in recruitment; implementing a whistle-blowing mechanism that is capable of countering bribery and so on. In our understanding, outcome is by definition the result of an output, that is, of a CSR commitment, strategy or instrument.

In some cases it is somewhat fuzzy to distinguish between CSR outputs and outcomes. For example, when companies on the basis of a sustainability commitment adopt a CSR instrument, is this not already an act of implementation and hence an outcome? And what about social accounting – to what extent does it change corporate practices and thus qualify as an outcome? In general, we accept that there is some leeway in the classification process. For our purposes, we have defined instrument adoption to be an output, since an instrument first needs to be translated into action to become effective. However, we understand actual reporting to be a change in the company's social (transparency-related) practices and hence as an outcome.

Generally, we can expect that some time – sometimes a long time – passes between the adoption of a strategy or instrument and its implementation through concrete activities and changes in practice. Hence, an output may be translated into an outcome with a certain time lag. Given the rather new and recent character of many CSR instruments, this time lag represents an analytical problem. The reason why outputs have seemingly not resulted in outcomes, that is, in behavioural changes, may simply be that it takes time to alter institutions and too little time has passed.

Outcomes may be of different quality. The implementation of CSR reporting, for example, with regard to the achievement of sustainability impact, could probably be regarded as a rather 'weak' outcome compared, for example, with investments in energy efficient production technology or in more environmentally friendly products and services.

When it comes to empirically identifying CSR outcomes, not much information is publicly available on the social and environmental activities that companies carry out, on their changes in organizational structures and resource allocation, in investment, product development, sourcing and production practices. In the CSR assessments that are presented in this book we therefore above all made use of questionnaire data. But in addition, interview information was important, as it is hard to get a good grip on causal connections within the CSR processes of companies only on the basis of written reports and statements.

2.3.3   Impact: Implications for Society and the Environment

Behavioural outcomes may or may not result in an impact on society or the environment. CSR impact denotes the substantive consequences in the social or environmental realm outside the company. CSR impact can also be described as sustainability benefit. Impact in a narrow sense covers consequences for the problem itself, such as a reduction of CO_2 emissions, of bribery or discriminating pay practices. In a wider sense, impact of CSR can be understood as consequences for the societal – that is, company-external – capacity to solve the respective problem. Impact then includes the 'diffusion' of innovative solutions.[4]

An example of such wider impact is that technological or social innovations resulting from a company's CSR commitment are adopted by other firms or are taken up in public policies. The latter was the case, for example, with the introduction of an internal emissions trading programme in the oil corporation BP which served as an inspiration for the public EU Emissions Trading System, EU ETS (Skjærseth and Wettestad 2008).

There are some analytical challenges related to assessing impact across different issue areas. For environmental issues it is relatively easy to think about CSR impact, as these genuinely emerge outside the company. This holds, for example, with a reduction in polluting emissions, with resource preservation through material efficiency and so on. In many cases, impact will directly 'mirror' outcomes. For example, if a company replaces an old technology by a new, more energy efficient one (outcome), this will automatically lead to a reduction of greenhouse gas emissions (impact) in the outside world.

With regard to social issues such as the ones tackled in this book – gender equality and countering bribery – impact is often more intangible. Partly, the desired social impact equals the outcome at company level. For example, an increase in female representation at board level would be an outcome (internal to the company), but at the same time it enhances the societal quota of women in top positions and contributes to changing societal gender relation, hence creates impact. With regard to fighting bribery, implementing relevant policy leading to a greater understanding of the problem among employees is an outcome, while wider changes in society's opinions constitute an impact. Within a CSR impact assessment, it is in most cases not possible to 'prove' such societal impact, but their likelihood and plausibility should be discussed. The most relevant benchmarks for us to assess impact against are the EU's sustainability goals.

2.3.4   The Challenge of Causality

Both the 'relative improvement' and 'goal attainment' strategy of assessing the sustainability impact of CSR as described above involve the challenge of establishing causal relationships between the various effects of CSR. The empirical approach to assessing the sustainability impact of CSR which we suggest and make use of in Parts II and III of this book is based on a combination of extensive and intensive research strategies.

The extensive approach consists of a questionnaire-based company survey as a first step, the intensive approach of interview-based case studies as a second step. The extensive strategy is suitable for establishing general patterns between dependent and independent variables, that is, the correlation between CSR instruments or activities and the final impact by comparing similarities and differences between companies or change over time. Surveys are a tool to map general patterns in the extensive analysis. They are also a tool for selecting the most interesting case studies for further intensive scrutiny.

The extensive strategy is, however, less suitable for establishing causal inferences. In-depth case studies can be used for this purpose, as they are suitable for process tracing, identification of mechanisms linking cause and effect and the control for rival explanations (Elster 1989; George and McKeown 1985; King et al. 1994, p. 227). With regard to CSR impact assessment, we need to causally relate CSR output to outcome (as a result of output implementation) and then to social and environmental impact wherever feasible. This implies that we should show how the commitment, strategies and instruments have been implemented and actually caused the observed change in behaviour. This is far from trivial. Within the oil industry, for example, it may be difficult to assess the 'cause and effect' relationship between voluntary climate instruments and corporate emissions of greenhouse gases: if a company divests of coal for competitive reasons and then points to the coal divestment as a climate activity, we are confronted with a classic 'chicken and egg' problem.

We have then tried to combine process tracing with control for possible rival explanations. We should always ask whether the links between output, outcome and impact might have been caused by factors other than the CSR efforts made. For environmental issues, relevant rival explanations and control factors include the use of new technology unrelated to corporate CSR strategy or the availability of alternative waste disposal options. For societal issues, changes might occur owing to underlying demographic trends rather than to CSR. For example, growth in the use of banking by minorities might be owing to a greater confidence and assimilation rather than CSR actions of banks in making available specialized services and products. The increase in employment of females might be owing to rising standards of educational performance of girls relative to boys rather than to improved diversity practices. Each of the different dimensions outlined above and the different policy fields raise their own problems of measurement that will be discussed in each case study.

2.4 CONCLUSIONS

Do companies, through voluntary CSR commitment and strategy, add to social and environmental improvement? As a starting point for approaching this question, we identified a general need for analytical frameworks focusing directly on how to assess and evaluate the actual impact of CSR, particularly in relation to public policy goals as most studies in this field have been directed towards description of CSR activities. Based on the insight from a combination of CSR management literature and political science approaches to evaluate effectiveness, we first asked what activities 'count' as CSR. We should first note that any assessment of the impact of CSR presupposes the existence of something that qualifies as CSR in the first place. This 'something' which should be voluntary and beyond compliance includes all company efforts to integrate social and environmental concerns into their business operations and stakeholder relations. We distinguish between three types of CSR effects. The basic effect is CSR output, which ranges from the very first commitment (acknowledgement of responsibility) to the development of strategies (plans to determine goals and policy) that may, or may not, include the adoption of CSR instruments. Such instruments constitute the practical tools that systematically facilitate the incorporation of sustainability concerns into a company's operations. Depending on the implementation of such CSR output, changes in corporate practice and behaviour may result within the company itself (outcome). Finally, such changes may lead to substantive consequences in the social and environmental realm outside the company (impact).

How can we then determine the sustainability impact of CSR? There are essentially two criteria available for assessing the impact of CSR. Firstly, we can measure CSR impact as a relative improvement caused by the relevant CSR instruments and activities. Secondly, we can relate CSR impact to the attainment of a predefined social goal that is transferable to companies. In any case, we need to establish causal relationships between the observed performance and the CSR instruments and activities adopted. We combine an extensive and intensive research strategy. The extensive strategy is used for mapping general patterns and for selecting the most interesting cases for in-depth analysis. The intensive strategy is used for establishing causal inferences through process tracing, identification of mechanisms and control for rival explanations.

NOTES

1. As companies integrate social and environmental concerns into their operations in a variety of very different ways, CSR instruments should be understood as a variety of practical tools that systematically facilitate the incorporation of sustainability concerns into a company's operations.
2. What are the motives for CSR and whether it is a response to anticipated regulation will, however, gain some relevance in the discussion of success factors since the impact of voluntary CSR instruments can turn out to be spurious and simply reflect adjustment to anticipated regulation. Note that corporations represent a social interest group with a significant potential to influence governmental policies (for example, Fuchs 2004; Risse-Kappen 1995).
3. Decision No. 1600/2002/EC of the European Parliament and of the Council of 22 July 2002 laying down the Sixth Community Environment Action Programme. *Official Journal of the European Communities*, 10.09.2002, L 242/1.
4. Policy diffusion is an established concept within comparative politics focusing on a horizontal (across states) spread of policy instruments through learning based on effective communication, which can be applied to companies as well.

3 A framework for explaining the sustainability impact of CSR

Federica Viganò, Franziska Wolff and Daniele Nicolai

3.1 INTRODUCTION

The previous chapter discussed how to assess the sustainability impact of Corporate Social Responsibility (CSR). Here, we want to turn to explaining such impact. What are the causes for high sustainability impact through CSR or, in other words, what are CSR success factors? And what factors prevent the achievement of substantial social and environmental benefits?

Before developing a framework for explaining the sustainability effects of CSR, we place our approach in relation with the current CSR discourse (Section 2). In Section 3 we break down the basic question: 'What factors promote the achievement of sustainability impact through CSR?' into more specific, better researchable sub-questions. We apply the three categories of CSR effects as elaborated in Chapter 2, that is, CSR 'output', 'outcome' and 'impact'. Drawing both on institutional and management literature, Section 4 then sets out the factors by which we shall explain the achievement of CSR impacts. These factors partly occur within companies and partly exist in the companies' environment. They include corporate strategy, organization and culture, on the one hand, and the business environment, civil society and the political-institutional setting, on the other hand. The design of specific CSR instruments is regarded as a further factor that may explain the sustainability impact of CSR. In Section 5 we set out a number of propositions that relate these explanatory factors to the research questions about CSR impact. Section 6 sums up the main insights and draws some conclusions.

The framework developed on the following pages will be used as a basis for the case studies presented in Chapters 10 to 13.

3.2   THE CSR DISCOURSE AND THE IMPACT QUESTION

The construct of CSR has substantially evolved over time. A turning point was the seminal work of H. R. Bowen (1953) on the *Social Responsibility of the Businessman*. In the past decades the scholarly debate has grown exponentially and has fanned out into a number of different perspectives, approaches and also different disciplines: agency theory (Friedman 1970), stakeholder theory (Freeman and Reed 1983; Donaldson 1999; Donaldson and Preston 1995; Philips 1997), social contract theories (Donaldson and Dunfee 1999; Gray et al. 1996), corporate ethics (Crane and Matten 2004; Roberts 2003), corporate social performance (Carroll 1979; Preston 1978; Wood 1991), institutional theory (Jones 1995); leadership theory (Waldman et al. 2006); strategic management theory (Baron 2001; Burke and Logsdon 1996; Husted and Salazar 2006; McWilliams et al. 2006; Murray and Montanari 1986; Reinhard 1998; Smith 2003; Werther and Chandler 2005) and its offsprings, the market-based view of the firm (Porter and Kramer 2006) and the resource-based view (Barney 1991; Hart 1995; McWilliams et al. 2002; McWilliams and Siegel 2001; Russo and Fouts 1997). Today, corporate social responsibility appears as a landscape of theories, approaches, terminologies and disciplines – ranging from management studies, marketing and economics, social sciences and legal studies, to ethics, psychology and environmental sciences. This diversity leaves the concept open to progressive development and conceptual as well as to practical-managerial statements.

When considering the findings and frontiers of CSR research so far, also with regard to the impact of CSR, a sort of 'ideological divide' still seems to characterize the field: the literature is carved up between those that advocate the prevalence of an economic orientation of CSR and those that advocate a normative or ethical model (Joyner and Payne 2002; Smith 2003). The first model largely follows the reasoning initially developed by Milton Friedman (1970) that corporate responsibility goes no further than maximizing shareholder value. The second model follows the perspective of CSR as based on ethical-normative choices (Carroll 1991). In systematic terms, the sustainability-driven CSR debate – which this book forms part of – largely follows the ethical model, focusing on the normative call for inter- and intragenerational justice. In-between these two models the debate still struggles on what the primary interest of a corporation should be, whether profitability or a less self-centred, more societal perspective. Regarding the direction of future research, the question is whether studies should keep running along separate tracks or whether a more comprehensive theory should be sought (Matten et al. 2003; Swanson 1999). A shared research programme could be more explicative also with regard to the sustainability impact of CSR.

Presently, the division between the two models is reflected in the different foci of analysis of the two schools. Within the economic paradigm a number of studies tackle the question of impact. However, they focus on the financial impact of CSR and the link between CSR and financial performance (Dowell et al. 2000; Griffin and Mahon 1997; Joyner and Payne 2002; McWilliams and Siegel 2000; Orlitzky et al. 2003; Porter and Kramer 2006; Salzmann et al. 2005; Waddock and Graves 1997; Wagner and Schaltegger 2003; Willard 2002). With proponents of the economic models developing their evaluation of CSR effects on the basis of economic and financial cost benefit analysis (McWilliams and Siegel 2001), impact is defined in terms of short- or long-run stock prices or accounting profitability, such as return on equity, return on investment or operating profit (Paul and Siegel 2006). According to Windsor (2001), economic paradigms dominate both the research and practice of CSR. This is one of the reasons why research findings are still unsatisfactory with regard to the sustainability impact of CSR, which is a largely non-financial impact as defined according to the ethical model. It includes, for example, contributions to the larger social good, a more equal distribution of wealth in society, diffusion of sustainable practices by firms or an intergenerational attention in the use of resources.

Literature dealing with the sustainability dimension of CSR, however, tends to neglects research into the (social and environmental) impact of CSR. It often focuses on motives for CSR (for example, Dummett 2006; Hemingway and Maclagan 2004; Bansal and Roth 2000; Prakash 2001) or on procedural and management aspects of CSR (AccountAbility 2003; Doppelt 2003; Hass 1996; Jonker and de Witte 2006; Kolk and Mauser 2002; Loew et al. 2004; Schaltegger et al. 2002 and many others). This may be due, among other things, to the fact that a lot of this literature strives to develop management recommendations. An additional methodological cause is that the firm rather than the sector tends to be used as the unit of observation. Finally, while company-level financial data is relatively easily accessible, measuring the impact of CSR on society and the environment is harder since the relevant data is complex and accrues outside companies. Recognizing these difficulties, we shall nevertheless attempt in the following to combine the impact perspective of the economic paradigm with the sustainability orientation of the ethical model.

3.3   OPERATING RESEARCH QUESTIONS ABOUT SUSTAINABILITY IMPACT

Our central question is: *What factors promote the achievement of sustainability impact through CSR?* We suggest breaking down this overall research question into several narrower and more specific operational research questions. In this way, our overall research interest can be more easily approached and examined. An important intermediate step is our distinction between different, progressively emerging types of CSR effects, namely CSR output, outcome and impact. As elaborated more extensively in Chapter 2, we understand CSR output as changes in corporate commitment and strategies with regard to a company's social and environmental performance; this includes the adoption of specific CSR instruments. CSR outcome includes the changes in the company's practices that result from the implementation of CSR output. CSR impact finally encompasses the substantive consequences in the social or environmental realm – that is, outside the company, but caused by internal changes in the company's social and environmental practices.

Note that CSR instruments – although they constitute only one dimension of CSR output – play a specific role in the operational research questions and in our subsequent research design. This is because instruments help to systematically incorporate sustainability concerns into companies' operations. In particular, standardized instruments, such as the GRI Guidelines, Global Compact, ISO 14000 or the Business Principles for Countering Bribery, will be of interest. As against company-specific instruments and wider CSR policies, these standardized CSR instruments provide a better basis for comparison: because they are generic, companies that adopt the instruments subscribe to the same goals and procedures.[1] These goals and procedures are typically described in public documents, such as codes of conduct or ISO standards. The systematic and standardized nature of instruments allows us to gain comparative insights in two respects. On the one hand, when companies use different CSR instruments to tackle the same sustainability issue, differences in the companies' sustainability impact allow conclusions on how conducive the instruments as such are to creating impact (effective instrument design). On the other hand, when companies employ the same instrument, variance in the companies' sustainability impact indicate that the instruments were implemented either more or less successfully (effective instrument implementation). Despite the relevance of standardized instruments, we also acknowledge in our research design that companies implement a number of non-standardized CSR instruments and activities.

Drawing on the distinction between CSR output, outcome and impact, we shall now specify and substantiate four operational research questions.

1. *Why are some CSR instruments more conducive to impact than others?*
   In relation to our typology of CSR effects, this operating question links CSR output, which includes the adoption of instruments as one main

element, with sustainability impact. The underlying assumption of the
question is that there are characteristics inherent in the design of CSR
instruments that promote the achievement of sustainability impact.
However, the influence of these design characteristics is empirically difficult to disentangle from other influences, above all from the effects of
the – more or less effective – instrument implementation. In our empirical in-depth analyses (Chapters 10 to 13) this difficulty is compounded
by the limited number of company cases and the fact that the use of
the same instrument across the companies was not the prime criterion
for selecting the companies. As a consequence, we shall not investigate
this question empirically but through an analytical a priori examination. We graphically represent this in Figure 3.1 by merely dotting the
line between output (instrument design) and impact. The figure more
generally portrays the relation between operating research questions
and the CSR effects.

2. *What factors determine a company's instrument choice?*
    This question again tackles CSR output. For the reasons set out above,
    we focus our respective research to a large extent on CSR instruments.
    There are two aspects to consider in this regard: adoption of (any)
    and choice of (specific) CSR instruments. The first aspect – why does
    a company adopt a CSR instrument? – is largely congruent with the
    question of why companies engage in CSR at all. Although we recog-
    nize that the motives for CSR may indirectly affect its success, we feel
    that with a view to sustainability impact, the second aspect may be
    more relevant: why does a company select a specific instrument, that
    is, instrument A as opposed to instrument B? The background to this
    is our assumption that some CSR instruments are more conducive to
    impact than others (see above). The choice of CSR instruments may
    thus lay the foundation for subsequent sustainability impact. In this
    chapter as well as in the case studies of Chapters 10 to 13 our emphasis
    is hence on the latter aspect, though we do cover the first one as well.

3. *What factors drive an effective implementation of CSR instruments
    within companies?*
    This question addresses factors that promote the achievement of CSR
    outcomes resulting from CSR output – that is, changes in company
    practices resulting from the effective implementation of CSR instru-
    ments. In order to achieve CSR 'outcome', CSR outputs (which may
    be more or less explicit or formal) need to result in changes of corpo-
    rate behaviour, for example, through introducing concrete beneficial
    activities or refraining from harmful ones. Hence, beyond the adop-
    tion of a potentially effective instrument, its company-specific imple-
    mentation is decisive. Whether a code of conduct is translated into a

fully-fledged management system, whether a social performance or pollution reduction target is operationalized through procedures and activities, whether a gender equality strategy is backed up with organizational capacities – each choice will influence their effectiveness. Apart from efforts within companies, the level of outcome may also be influenced by external restrictions. For example, sustainable sourcing strategies depend on the supply of sustainable inputs, and gender-sensitive staffing policies on the availability of qualified women.

4. *Why do certain instruments create more impact by some companies than by others, even though as effectively implemented?*

   The fourth constellation we identify relates to sustainability impact. The underlying assumption is that even if a potentially effective instrument were chosen and implemented well, it might be possible that the actual impact differs among different companies. In the terms of the typology of CSR effects, the question is whether impact can differ among companies even though the levels of output and outcome are comparable. Reasons for these differences could be the sector environment, country-specific conditions or other contextual factors, such as the lack of consumer acceptance. In our empirical research, however, we found little evidence for this constellation. As a consequence, we decided to concentrate our research on the first three questions.

When it comes to sustainability impact, note that we also assume a direct relation between the achievement of outcome and the production of impact. This is because we posit that once companies have changed their innovation and sourcing practices, their production processes or human relations activities as a result of their CSR commitment, these changes will in many cases automatically 'translate' into societal and environmental impact (see the triangular arrow from outcome to impact in Figure 3.1).

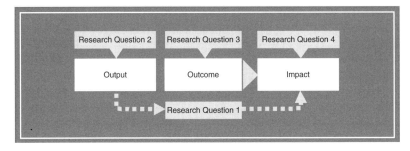

Source: Authors.

Figure 3.1   Operating research questions and their relation to CSR effects

For example, a high ratio of female recruitment into manager positions will contribute to a societal reality in which leadership positions are more equally distributed between men and women. Similarly, the production of more fuel efficient cars in the automotive industry will reduce traffic-induced CO_2 emissions.[2] Hence our underlying assumption with regard to CSR impact is: a verifiable and positive change in a company's social and environmental behaviour will lead to a positive impact on sustainability – and hence, indirectly, contribute to the achievement of politically defined goals on sustainable development. During our empirical analysis, this assumption will be triangulated with existing secondary data on the sustainability impact of CSR instruments applied within the companies. Only where we find valid information confirming our assumption as to the instrument's positive sustainability impact will we maintain the heuristic equation of outcome and impact.

By specifying the above operating research questions, we focus our attention on specific aspects of the output-outcome-impact chain that we feel are critical for the creation of sustainability impact. In proposing answers to the above questions, we shall now suggest a number of factors internal and external to companies that may explain the achievement of sustainability impact through CSR. We draw both on an actor-related perspective supported by management literature and on an institutional perspective based on new institutionalism and organizational analysis.

3.4   EXPLANATORY FACTORS FOR THE ACHIEVEMENT OF CSR EFFECTS

In the following we shall develop a framework for explaining CSR effects – output, outcome and the subsequent sustainability impact. Our purpose is not to build a normative model outlining what directions companies should take in order to become more sustainable, but first and foremost to construct an analytical 'lens' through which to observe (and simplify) reality.

Our starting point is that there exist factors both within and external to companies which influence CSR processes and contribute to the achievement of CSR effects. Based on (neo-) institutionalist scholarship, on the one hand, and on approaches to environmental and sustainability management in firms, on the other, we identify five sets of explanatory factors or independent variables which we consider particularly relevant. These are: corporate strategy and organization, corporate culture, the business environment, civil society as well as the political-institutional setting (Table 3.1). In addition to these, we assume that the design of

Table 3.1   Factors explaining CSR effects

Factors internal to companies	Factors external to companies
→ Corporate strategy and organization	→ Business environment
→ Corporate culture	→ Civil society
	→ Political-institutional setting
→ Design of CSR instrument	

Source: Authors.

CSR instruments – which may originate from within or from outside the company – can explain some of the effects that CSR efforts create.

The set of explanatory factors has been drawn from management and institutionalist approaches which both provide explanatory perspectives on organizational change. The strength of the management approach is its grasp of strategic processes and conflict; the strength of institutionalist thinking lies in its attention to longer-term processes of change and the recognition of embedding socio-cultural contexts. However, there are some ontological differences between the approaches. Management theory tends to focus on agency and – often implicitly – posits that actors behave in a rational, utility-maximizing and strategic way. Compared with this, institutional theories assume that the behaviour of agents is habit-driven, rooted in shared interpretations of reality and strongly influenced by social structures, culture and institutions. The question hence arises whether the two approaches can indeed coalesce? Generally, combinations of theoretical approaches may prove to be more holistic and hence better explain complex reality. At the same time, they risk mixing conflicting ontologies if it is not made clear that their foundational assumptions are sufficiently similar (Geels 2007; Lewis and Grimes 1999).

Looking briefly at how our two approaches deal with the key ontological dimensions of structure, agency and change,[3] we feel, however, that they are commensurable. Firstly, both approaches recognize the role of structure, even though management literature focuses on organizational and industry structures while institutionalist thinking highlights social structures, such as norms and cognitive frames. Secondly, agency also exists in both approaches. Management literature emphasizes it more strongly and argues that structures restrict or stimulate but do not determine a specific behaviour. In institutionalist accounts, though actors rely more on routines, they actively interpret and enact pre-existing rules and structures; and in the medium term the resulting variation of practices can transform structures if reproduced more widely ('structuration', Giddens 1984). This partly answers the third question about (organizational) change – which in our framework is a precondition for achieving CSR impact. Both approaches allow for change, while institutionalism, in addition, accounts for inertia or stasis. The basic difference lies in the time horizon. Focusing on more material structures, management literature tends to treat change as a potentially quick matter of strategic interaction following changes in preferences or restrictions. Dealing with more durable and taken-for-granted social and cognitive structures, institutionalists conceptualize change slower. In this sense, the approaches complement each other: in shorter time periods, where the context for social interaction is stable, the rationalistic approach of management literature is promising. In the longer term, where social structures, rules and cognitive frames transform and hence the very basis for utility calculation and strategic interaction changes, institutionalism can better account for change. Given the foundational similarities and complementarities of the two chosen approaches, a combination of them seems justified – and makes it possible to exploit the approaches' respective strengths and complement their weaknesses.[4]

Our framework reflects structures, agency and change. Change is what we ultimately want to explain: change in corporate commitment, instrument use and strategy (output), in corporate practices (outcome) and, consequently, in the state of society and the environment (impact). We explain this change by factors that strongly reflect agency, such as corporate strategy and the interventions of civil society, and by factors that are more 'structural' and institutional in nature, such as corporate organization, the informal rules of corporate culture or industry structure.

We shall now define the explanatory factors for CSR impact. We have deduced these from the two approaches and will locate them in the academic discourse. The mechanisms by which the factors are assumed to affect CSR output, outcome and impact will be specified in the subsequent Section 5.

3.4.1 Instrument Design

CSR instruments are standardized or company-specific tools that systematically facilitate the incorporation of sustainability concerns into a company's operations. Organizational literature understands instruments as 'institutions' in the sense that they are a more or less coordinated set of rules and procedures that govern the interactions and behaviours of actors (Powell and Di Maggio 1991). Like other (policy) instruments, they also structure actors' perception and 'sense-making' of corporate processes by inducing a particular problematization of the issue (Lascoumes and Le Gales 2007).

We can distinguish different types of instruments that may either relate to the socially responsible management of companies – above all codes of conduct, management systems, accounting and reporting, and forms of stakeholder involvement – to socially responsible investment or to socially responsible consumption (European Commission 2004a). Both the management sciences – with regard to CSR instruments, see among others AccountAbility 2003; Schaltegger et al. 2002; Smith and Feldman 2003 – and the public administration literature (Adger et al. 2003; Bemelmans-Videc 1998; Jordan et al. 2003; Majone 1976; Richards 2000; Salamon 2002) address variance of instrument design and its implications on effectiveness or, more specifically, on sustainability. Such variance in instrument design may relate to an instrument's material obligations, for example, its specificity and stringency, as well as to the governance mechanisms required or recommended by the instrument to enforce it, such as monitoring mechanisms, internal or external verification, forms of accountability or sanctions.

3.4.2 Corporate Strategy and Organization

Significant strands of strategic and environmental management literature view the actions of corporations as determined by corporate strategies and organizational structures. Strategies are roadmaps of organizations towards attainment of their long-, medium- and short-term goals and objectives. By organizational structure we mean the formal set-up of a company's value chain components in terms of work flow, communication channels and hierarchy (Wheelen and Hunger 2004, p. 87). Both corporate strategies and structures provide formal rules and are largely determined by corporate executives (Egri and Pinfield 1996; Levy 1997).

Sustainability management can be described as the increasing integration of social and environmental objectives into business policy and strategy, on the one hand, and into managerial systems and organizational structures, on the other (Figge et al. 2002; Kolk and Mauser 2002; Zadek 2001). The model of strategic management implies that within companies CSR processes are subject to a – more or less – 'planned and programmed adjustment of the structures, systems and activities of a business in response to the perceived and anticipated changes in the business environment, taking into account the organization's capacity to change' (Roome 1992, p. 16). The process of strategic control covers as a first step the scanning for external opportunities and threats. The screening of external conditions is complemented by an organizational analysis of the internal strengths and weaknesses in reacting to these. This is followed by the formulation of a strategy, the implementation of programmes, the measurement of performance and, finally, a review loop (Hitt et al. 2003).

The relation between corporate strategy and organizational structure is

subject to a long-standing debate. While some hold that changes in corporate strategy lead to changes in organizational structure ('structure follows
strategy', Chandler 1962), others argue that at the same time structure
influences strategy (Mintzberg 1979). Both positions have been received in
the CSR literature: on the one hand, implementing CSR strategies is held
to require adaptations in hierarchical command, oversight and reporting
lines as well as vertical integration of different units and functions (Doppelt
2003, p. 80). On the other hand, the organizational structure of a company,
for instance its openness to organizational innovation and the way it
manages knowledge, can influence its reaction to claims upon its social
responsibility (Neef 2003).

3.4.3   Corporate Culture[5]

Corporate culture denotes the informal, normative rules and routines
within companies. The concept is linked to the assumption that members
of organizations act in accordance with what is perceived as culturally
appropriate (Christensen and Røvik 1999; March and Olsen 1989). This
perspective regards corporations not only as organizations which ensure
that technical tasks are set out but more broadly as institutions infused
with values and symbols (Selznik 1957). The degree of institutionalization
will vary from organization to organization. Scott (1995, p. 33) describes
institutions as consisting of 'cognitive, normative and regulative structures and activities that provide stability and meaning to social behaviour.
Institutions are transported by various carriers – cultures, structures, and
routines – and they operate at multiple levels of jurisdiction.'

The role of culture as regards corporate behaviour was first put forward
by organizational theory in the 1950s (for example, Selznik 1957). This
approach rests on the assumptions of bounded rationality (Simon 1947;
Cyert and March 1963). Moreover, it sets forth that people are rule-following
actors: rather than taking decisions on the basis of a 'logic of consequence'
according to which they calculate their maximum utility, they follow a 'logic
of appropriateness'. This means that actors need to determine what kind of
situation they are in, which role they have in this situation and which are the
appropriate rules to follow in this situation (March and Olsen 1989, p. 23).
Within organizations members of the organization need to 'make sense',
that is, create a shared understanding of the organization's purpose, performance and the challenges it faces and how to resolve these (Weick 1995).
In accordance with this approach, the cultural school of management sees
strategy formation and implementation as a process of social interaction
based on shared beliefs (Brooks 2005; Mintzberg et al. 1998).

Whereas members in organizations which are weakly institutionalized tend to follow formal rules, members of highly institutionalized organizations will tend to follow informal, culturally defined rules (Christensen and Røvik 1999).[6] A company's culture will be marked by events in the early years of its life: the circumstances under which a company was established will crucially affect its internal socialization processes and future development (Pierson 2004; Selznik 1957; Thelen 2000). However, corporate culture may also be malleable to incremental change, which again may be path dependent. This implies that former events will create 'positive feedback' and thus generate development trajectories difficult to reverse and branching patterns of institutional development (Pierson 2004, p. 21). Thus, the culture of an organization will constrain its response to new events, such as a performance crisis or diverse exogenous shocks (Thelen 2000; Christensen et al. 2004, p. 54).

3.4.4 Business Environment

We are interested in two dimensions of a company's business environment. The first dimension covers the prevailing business opportunities and restrictions the company is faced with within the sector. This includes, among others, the preferences of investors, suppliers, customers and consumers. The second, complementary, dimension encompasses the understanding and legitimacy of CSR among competitors and peer companies within and beyond the sector, for example, in business associations. The business environment can become relevant at domestic, EU or international level.

The first dimension of 'business environment' – the role of business opportunities and restrictions for corporate social responsibility – is discussed extensively by management literature (Hansen and Schrader 2005; Porter and Kramer 2006; Salzmann et al. 2005). The wider context is provided by the market-based view of strategic management (Porter 1990), according to which an industry's structure crucially shapes the strategic environment of a firm. Five forces play a special role: the bargaining power of customers and that of suppliers; the threat of new entrants; the threat of substitute products; and the resulting level of competition. Taking account of these five forces, companies develop competition strategies, such as cost leadership, product differentiation or market focus strategies. With regard to (environmental) sustainability, Steger (1993) argues that a firm's strategic positioning in the market is related, on the one hand, to its exposure to sustainability risks and, on the other hand, to the market opportunities arising from the promotion of sustainability.

The second dimension we shall look at under the heading of 'business environment' – the understanding and legitimacy of a concept such as CSR among peer companies and competitors – is tackled by institutionalists in organizational analysis (Hoffman 2001; Powell and DiMaggio 1991; Sahlin-Andersson and Engwall 2002). They argue that companies' organizational processes are not only influenced by the market context, but by sense-making and legitimacy concepts within the business environment or larger socio-economic context. Business environments as core segments of organizational fields[7] are characterized by shared beliefs and assumptions about competition practices, legitimate behaviour and best practice standards, including for CSR. The sharing of such beliefs and assumptions by many actors in the field occurs among others through processes of socialization in business schools and professional associations or through the imitation of leaders (DiMaggio and Powell 1983). They guide the behaviour of managers and other actors, though not in a deterministic or completely stable way.

3.4.5 Civil Society

The role of civil society expectations, pressure or support for corporate (CSR) processes is recognized both by management-oriented approaches, such as stakeholder theory (Freeman and Reed 1983), or the resource dependence view of strategic management (Pfeffer and Salancik 1978) and by institutional approaches (Arts 2002; DiMaggio and Powell 1983). Civil society stakeholders encompass social movements and non-governmental organizations ranging from trade unions to 'green', social, charity, consumer organizations and issue-focused networks, such as the Clean Clothes Campaign. Unlike business stakeholders, they do not have contractual relations with companies,[8] and unlike governments, they are not linked with them through authoritative relations of regulation and enforcement. Pursuing particular societal objectives, such as environmental protection or human rights, civil society is an articulator and carrier of norms and values (Midttun 2005).

The underlying view is that a company exists in open systems. This means that the perceptions and activities of the business organization are inescapably influenced by its environment (Hoffman 2001; Fineman and Clarke 1996). Constituents in its environment influence the company's interpretation of its external environment. These constituents may also hold resources which a business organization perceives as crucial to the realization of its internal objectives. In the case of civil society these resources include knowledge and legitimacy. Knowledge that may be interesting to companies and that members of civil society organizations dispose of as experts or practitioners can relate to facts (for example, on the causes or consequences of sustainability problems) and to action (for instance, on the responses to a sustainability problem). Legitimacy is 'a generalized perception or assumption that the actions of an entity are desirable, proper, or appropriate within some socially constructed system of norms, values, beliefs, and definitions' (Suchman 1995, p. 574). Civil society groups can avail themselves of these 'resources' vis-à-vis companies in a supportive or an antagonistic, pressurizing way (McIntosh et al. 2003; Murphy and Bendell 2002). According to resource dependence scholars, organizations will try to diminish their dependence on external resources as they are held among others by civil society. They may apply different strategic responses to achieve this, ranging from acquiescence to the expectations of civil society and compromise with their demands, to avoidance, defiance and manipulation (Oliver 1991; see also Pater and van Lierop 2006).

3.4.6 Political-institutional Setting

Companies operate within a political-institutional setting. In a narrow sense and with a focus on our research interest, this includes social and environmental policies as well as governmental expectations on CSR. In a wider sense, it encompasses the institutional arrangements governing the social systems of production and consumption, for example, the system of industrial relations or the rules of competition. In the cases we shall look into the political-institutional setting can be relevant at domestic, EU or international level.

Simplified, the state can be seen as the locus for legitimate political aggregation of collective interest and, through setting and enforcing rules, as a provider of public goods. Institutionalist literature in the political sciences analyzes how traditionally hierarchical relations between the state and the business sector have become more cooperative (Kooiman 1993; Rosenau 1992) and how the role of the state has changed from enacting command and control regulation to more procedural and communicative functions (Jordan et al. 2003; Mayntz 1998). In this vein we interpret the trend among European governments to stimulate CSR through a range of incentive measures and procedural regulations, and through networking, capacity building and awareness raising. Voluntary corporate action is also affected by the more complex institutional arrangements underlying the social systems of production and consumption (Hollingsworth et al. 2002; Mol and Spaargaren 2006; Post and Mahon 1980). These include the degree to which the market economy is liberal or coordinated; the role that philanthropic work has traditionally played within the social welfare system; parameters of the financial markets; gender relations on the labour market; corruption cultures; the extent to which industrial relations between employers and trade unions are conflict- or consensus-oriented; or the scope to which the national innovation system is geared towards 'green' innovation. In addition, the political-institutional environment influences the problem perception as well as the self-perception of firms. Companies, finally, are held to adhere to rules set by the state in exchange for access to public goods and in reaction to societal expectations (Midttun 2005). They also provide material resources for the state to (re-) distribute. At the same time, they try to influence the political-institutional setting in which they operate, through lobbying, resistance and more subtle discursive strategies.

3.5   PROPOSITIONS

How do corporate strategy, civil society, the business environment and the other explanatory factors described above affect the sustainability impact of CSR? In this section we develop a number of propositions that link these independent variables to our dependent variables – CSR output, outcome and the subsequent impact, as tackled in the operating research questions. The propositions will be discussed empirically in Chapters 10 to 14, though not all conjectures need to be taken up in each chapter.

In a brief summary, these are our propositions:

- *Why are some CSR instruments more conducive to impact than others?*
  Our a priori assumption is that an instrument's design – its inherent level of specificity and obligation – contributes to the level of sustainability impact which the instrument may create.
- *What factors determine a company's instrument choice?*
  We propose that – apart from the sheer availability of pre-existing instruments – the instrument's strategic and organizational fit as well as its legitimacy in the business environment and governmental promotion policies are crucial determinants of instrument choice.
- *What factors drive an effective implementation of CSR instruments within companies?*
  Factors we shall discuss include the strategic and organizational integration of CSR, the fit within a long-standing identity of corporate social responsibility (corporate culture), the existence of business or organizational benefits for the company, civil society pressure and the threat of regulation ('shadow of hierarchy').

We shall discuss these questions separately and shall set our propositions in italic. The propositions also set out the causal mechanisms by which we assume that the respective factor will affect CSR output, outcome or impact.

3.5.1   A Priori Assumptions on Instrument Design[9] and CSR Impact

Our assumption is that the instrument's very design affects the extent to which a CSR instrument is likely to create sustainability impact. *Specifically, we argue that instruments that feature high levels of specificity and obligation will be more conducive to sustainability impact than instruments without these features.*[10] An instrument is more specific than another instrument when it requires specific and substantive activities rather than procedural improvements. The instrument is also more specific when it has quantifiable rather than qualitative targets and when its targets are more ambitious than comparable targets set by other instruments. The basic assumption underlying these posits is that the instrument requires more substantive action, and that there is less room for interpretation and deviation in fulfilling this purpose. An instrument has a higher level of obligation if it is independently verified,[11] requires a public commitment and is linked to some form of enforcement or sanction. In these cases achievement of targets can be assumed to be more critically reviewed, tracked by management and be more binding. As a consequence, underperformance will create risk, for instance, by reducing the credibility of a company's CSR commitment or exclusion from a business opportunity. Thus, enterprises have a stronger incentive to strive for better results.

Considering the vast diversity of instruments and instrument types, both standardized and tailored company-specific ones, we are conscious that not all of these facets of specificity and obligation are applicable to all instruments. There may also be additional factors that might be relevant for an instrument to create sustainability impact, such as continuous improvement requirements. However, we feel that the above elements capture the most important design criteria and even if not all of them apply in all cases, they may serve as benchmarks.

3.5.2   CSR Output and Instrument Choice

What factors determine a company's instrument choice? Instrument choice means in this context both selection among competing pre-existing standards and development of own, custom-made instruments. It is of course especially interesting why (or why not) a company chose an instrument that may be regarded as highly conducive to sustainability impact according to the above criteria. We suggest that apart from the sheer availability of pre-existing instruments, an instrument's strategic and organizational fit as well as its legitimacy in the business environment and governmental promotion policies crucially influence instrument choice.

Based on the above assumptions on the relevance of strategy and organizational structure, *we assume that companies decide to adopt an instrument because they expect it to promote their strategic goals. When choosing between alternative instruments, they will select one instrument over another because it has a better fit with their strategic goals or their organizational structure.* A given CSR instrument – and more precisely its issue focus and its implementation characteristics – may be perceived by corporate decision makers to either fit or conflict with the company's overriding strategies (for example, its business, corporate or growth strategies) or with its functional strategies (sourcing, marketing, human resources and the like). A fit occurs, for example, when an instrument is linked with a label that can be communicated in synergy with a sustainability-oriented marketing strategy. If it is a company's business strategy to become cost leader for a certain product, a sustainability label – that essentially signals a special quality and thus a premium price – would however conflict with the strategy to offer cheap products. In the latter case strategic fit of the CSR instrument (label) would not be given. Similarly to the concept of strategic fit, instruments will be preferred which are perceived to fit in with the existing organizational setting and systems. Sticking with the above example, introduction of an eco-label is facilitated if a quality management system is already in place. Having said that, an instrument is less likely to be chosen if its implementation requires extensive restructuring. The effect of a new instrument on organizational resources – the tangible and intangible inputs into a company's production process (capital, equipment, skills and so on) – is also an element to consider.

With regard to companies' organizational culture, *we assume that the more informal rules of corporate culture play no significant role in instrument choice.* While the general commitment to CSR may or may not fit with a firm's corporate culture, this culture will be too diffuse to 'call for' a specific instrument.

When it comes to the role of the business environment, we regard the portfolio of existing CSR instruments as an obvious restriction on instrument choice. If there is only one instrument available to tackle a specific CSR issue, and the company is committed to tackling this issue, it will have little leeway but to 'choose' this one instrument. As an alternative, the company may forge its own tool or may work with others to develop a sector tool. Depending on how complex the issue to tackle is, the costs of such efforts may be perceived as prohibitively high within many companies. However, *if there are alternative instruments to select from, we hypothesize that the one instrument will be chosen which the company is most familiar with and which has the highest legitimacy within the business environment.* The more well-known and 'legitimate' an instrument is – that is, the more it is supported and accepted by powerful, high-status actors – the more likely a company is to jump on the bandwagon and endorse the instrument itself (Fligstein 1991; Hoffmann 2001). This works through a mechanism called 'mimetic isomorphism' in organizational analysis (DiMaggio and Powell 1983): within an industry imitation of an organizational form (such as a CSR instrument) is a typical response when a company is uncertain about what is the efficient and effective reaction to a specific challenge. A highly legitimate instrument takes on a taken-for-granted quality, which in turn reduces uncertainty. Rather than 'rationally' assessing how well an instrument fits with its strategic and organizational setting, the company 'follows the leader' and copies the practices employed by legitimate or more successful organizations, or recommended by business associations. This proposition hence contrasts with the above hypothesis on strategic and organizational fit, although there may be cases where both strategic calculations and mimetic isomorphism point into the same direction, or where an organization rationalizes one by the other.

We assume that civil society demand does not play a significant role with regard to instrument choice. We expect societal stakeholder demand to be more broadly related to the uptake of social and environmental activities as such, but not geared towards selecting a specific instrument.

With regard to the political-institutional setting as explanatory factor for CSR instrument choice, we propose that *companies may decide in favour of a specific CSR instrument because the instrument is supported within the political-institutional setting.* Public policies can create expectations and market opportunities around an instrument, for instance, by financially promoting its use, by recognizing its substance in public procurement strategies and by reducing administrative requirements for its users (Hass 1996). The latter is, for example, the case with the German EMAS privilege ordinance which exempts certified facilities from certain approval processes and audits. In a wider sense, companies may prefer one CSR instrument to another because its logic is more strongly reflected in the political culture and policy style of their home country – a style which they are familiar with and for which they have developed expertise. In this sense, companies with headquarters in consensus democracies (Lijphart 1984) may be expected to be more prone to stakeholder involving instruments and learning networks, such as the Global Compact, than to competitive, benchmarking-oriented CSR instruments.

3.5.3   CSR Outcome and Instrument Implementation

What factors drive (or prevent) an effective implementation of CSR instruments within companies? Effective implementation, we argue, leads to the achievement of CSR outcomes, that is, to changes in corporate practices.

We shall discuss the role of strategic and organizational integration of CSR, the fit within a long-standing identity of corporate social responsibility (corporate culture), the existence of business or organizational benefits for the company, civil society pressure and the threat of regulation ('shadow of hierarchy').

Tackling the role of strategy and organization for CSR processes, *we propose that CSR output is likely to render greatest effects if corporate leaders link it to the core strategies of the company and integrate it organizationally*. The strategic integration of CSR should ideally range from overarching strategies to functional strategies (Burke and Logsdon 1996; Jonker and de Witte 2006). At the level of the business strategy,[12] CSR may be employed as a differentiation strategy, that is, the firm's competitive advantage is sought through the creation of a non-materialistic quality or added-value of a product, brand or firm. CSR can also be mainstreamed into a company's corporate strategy,[13] especially its portfolio decisions, by replacing non-sustainable products with more sustainable ones. The concrete CSR issue will determine which of the company's functional strategies CSR needs to be integrated in and how these strategies need to be vertically coordinated. Strategic integration will foster the achievement of CSR outcomes by proactively preventing conflicts between the achievement of CSR-related goals and of other business objectives.

By organizational integration of CSR we mean the creation of responsibilities for CSR issues at different hierarchical and functional levels, the setting up of communication channels between relevant units, the involvement of mid-level management, staff training and provision of sufficient resources, as well as the establishment of monitoring, continuous improvement processes and performance measurement (Smith 2003; Winn and Angell 2000). Organizational integration will promote the achievement of CSR outcomes by embedding behavioural change into processes and routines. It also provides the means for strategic or hierarchical control (Roome 1992), that is, for the communication of CSR goals set by corporate leaders at executive level (Prakash 2001) through the organization by means of clear lines of oversight and command, and the transfer of performance information back to the top. In addition, organizational integration enables vertical communication between the units, with their respective logics, involved in CSR implementation. Finally, organizational integration will foster process ownership of mid-level management and staff at functional and operational levels that actually carry out the behavioural changes related to CSR implementation (Berry 2004; Bruijn et al. 2004; Collier and Esteban 2007).

In addition to formal rules, corporate culture, as the informal norms and routines that evolve with a company's history and coin its present action, can be assumed to affect behavioural change as necessitated by the implementation of CSR. *We propose that corporate culture fosters change in an organization's social and environmental practices in particular if CSR is rooted in a long-standing and well-developed identity of the organization as being socially responsible.* This is because intrinsic pressures are created to produce verifiable sustainability impact. Through the medium of a strong and consolidated corporate culture, employees come to regard their work as linked to the company's success (Willmott 2000). To the extent that corporate culture is based on the belief in the organization's social responsibility, 'success' will include achievement of social and environmental improvements. CSR that is predominantly rhetorical (window dressing) will be at odds with the motivation of agents in an organization with such an identity (Collier and Esteban 2007).

The business environment may influence a company's CSR implementation efforts as well. Here, we focus on the business opportunities. *We suggest that CSR instruments are implemented all the more successfully, the more the respective changes in social and environmental practices are experienced as a business benefit for the company.* Business benefits related to CSR may include tangible and intangible benefits, such as access to capital through Socially Responsible Investment funds and lower risk premiums, increased resource efficiency, the attracting of recruits and staff motivation, good supplier and more generally business relations, enhanced reputation and brand image as well as sales prospects for 'responsible' products and services (Porter and Kramer 2006; Salzmann et al. 2005; Willard 2002). The experienced business benefits will work as inherent incentives for the effective implementation of CSR policies, rendering the respective behavioural changes quasi self-enforcing.

With regard to civil society, *our hypothesis is that the demand of civil society stakeholders promotes effective implementation of CSR instruments and high levels of CSR outcome.* This is because of the pressure civil society organizations may exert on companies when their CSR strategies fail to deliver, or because of the support they may lend to CSR implementation. Pressure strategies – informing the public, naming and shaming, organizing boycotts, bringing legal action against companies, advocating or facilitating regulatory changes – can withdraw legitimacy from companies and affect their market opportunities (Gereffi et al. 2001; Karliner 1997). Companies will therefore strive to improve their performance and sustainability impact. When cooperating with companies, civil society organizations will support them with knowledge and expertise crucial for effective implementation. The deeper they are involved in concrete decision making, the more they can use cooperative strategies to build up pressure from inside the cooperation, for example, by threatening to end the cooperation when the firm's CSR outputs do not lead to outcomes and impact.

Finally, *we assume that expectations and norms within the political-institutional setting as regards the effective implementation of CSR instruments also foster the achievement of CSR outcomes within companies.* Such (governmental) expectations can relate to the success of voluntary industry initiatives and may be linked to the threat of regulation if the voluntary solution fails to produce genuine social or environmental impact ('shadow of hierarchy', Dummett 2006; Scharpf 1997). Companies, in order to prevent a formal regulation that will deprive them of leeway and of competitive advantages, may decide to more effectively implement their CSR instruments, and respectively change their practices more radically in line with their CSR commitment. Political norms that may foster CSR outcomes include concrete standards on how to effectively implement voluntary activities, for example, in the context of publicly provided CSR instruments such as EMAS or gender award systems, or sustainability norms in public procurement. Political expectations and norms can both signal to corporate actors what behaviour is socially appropriate and provide incentives to comply with these.

3.6   CONCLUSIONS

In this chapter we presented a framework for explaining the sustainability effects of CSR. We distinguished different types of CSR effects, ranging from changes in commitment and strategy (CSR output) to adaptations of corporate practices (CSR outcome) and the resulting social and environmental consequences outside companies (CSR impact). Operating research questions were developed that address each of these effects (our dependent variables). Subsequently, we laid out a set of factors (independent variables) influencing the CSR effects. These operate from within or from outside companies and include corporate strategy and organization, corporate culture, the design of CSR instruments used as well as the business environment, civil society and the political-institutional setting. The factors were drawn from two sets of literature – (green) management literature and (neo-) institutional theories. By seeking to identify factors successfully leading to change rather than tracking or theorizing the underlying processes, our framework is a variance model as opposed to a process model of organizational change (Poole et al. 2000, p. 36). This results, among others, from the practical interest in developing recommendations for companies and policy makers on CSR success factors which we pursue beyond our academic curiosity. Finally, this chapter set out a number of propositions that link our explanatory factors (independent variables) to different CSR effects (dependent variables) and put forward the respective causal mechanisms.

We would like to acknowledge that our focus on the above explanatory factors is of course not a must. Some factors, such as the pressure from financial investors or leadership processes, could have been covered very prominently, while other factors to some critics may seem dispensable in this context. Our choice is a consequence of both our theoretical background and of a research interest in factors we found most promising with regard to the creation of sustainability impact. However, applying the framework in practice does not mean that factors missing from our set need to be disregarded when they surface in the empirical field work. And factors not elaborated here may turn out not to be vital for certain issues, sectors or companies. This, however, needs to be determined empirically on a case-to-case basis.

We feel that our approach can add to the academic CSR discourse in several ways. Firstly, it explicitly tackles the sustainability impact of CSR, while presently the main body of literature covers business and financial impacts of CSR. Secondly, whereas at present studies dealing with the sustainability side of CSR often focus on motivational, procedural and management aspects, we address impact and the substantive results of CSR. Thirdly, while some literature does tackle individual factors that may explain the achievement of sustainability impact through CSR, we try to integrate various such explanatory factors to also account for their interaction. Our approach is not a 'model' in the strict sense but rather a looser framework from which we deduct propositions. Because of this loose format, we are able to integrate the two promising approaches mentioned above. Both provide interesting perspectives and we leave it to the empirical discussion of our propositions to determine how fruitful these literatures are for explaining the sustainability impact of CSR.

This empirical discussion of the propositions is the subject of the case studies in Chapters 10 to 13. Our framework will form the basis, though not a Procrustean bed for these. Discussing the conjectures with empirical material from nine firms in three different sectors dealing with four CSR issues will give us the opportunity to analyze company, sector and issue specific variance. However, it should be kept in mind that the case studies are essentially qualitative in nature. As each of them includes two to three companies, we meet the 'small-n' problem typical of much social scientific research: the imbalance between the number of variables and the number of cases. As a consequence, the extent to which results can be generalized is limited. This should, however, not discourage our endeavour since qualitative research will deepen our understanding of the processes by which companies improve their sustainability performance through CSR and of the respective causal relations.

NOTES

1. Note, however, that standardized instruments are often not very specific when it comes to the activities through which they are to be implemented.
2. The latter example at the same time points us to the limits of equalling CSR outcome with sustainability impact: consumers may overcompensate the efficiency effects achieved by the automobile industry simply by driving more – thus cancelling out any positive sustainability effect. This, however, is outside the immediate sphere of companies' influence and should hence not be 'set off' when discussing the impact of their CSR activities.
3. 'Structure' and 'agency' (or 'action') are basic categories in the social science and social philosophy debate on the nature of social behaviour. While structuralist theories assume that behaviour is ultimately a product of larger social structures, of institutions, socialization and interaction, agency-based approaches regard individuals to act without such constraints and exclusively of their own creative volition; many approaches find some middle ground. Social 'change' can be regarded as the result in time of agency (within structures).
4. On the part of management literature, these weaknesses include its inability to account for the formation of preferences and hence the construction of actor strategies; and on the part of institutionalism, there is a disregard for interest conflicts and power struggles.
5. We would like to thank Elin Boasson for her substantial contribution to this section.
6. In line with Krasner (1988), organizations in which the members follow informal cultural rules rather than formal ones may be labelled strongly vertically institutionalized. Institutionalization also has a horizontal dimension. Strong horizontal institutionalization implies that all of the company's sub-organizations share the same cultural traits. In order for a corporation to be strongly institutionalized, both the vertical and horizontal dimensions must be strong (Christensen et al. 2004, p. 53, Krasner 1988).
7. The concept of organizational field is wider than the industry concept. Field refers to 'those organizations that, in the aggregate, constitute a recognized area of institutional life: key suppliers, resources and product consumers, regulatory agencies, and other organizations that produce similar services or products' (DiMaggio and Powell 1983, p. 148).
8. We count business associations, though 'non-governmental' in status, among the business stakeholders as this better accounts for their interests and logics of action.
9. We would like to thank Maria Bohn for her substantial contribution to this section.
10. In a dynamic perspective we might expect an older, more mature instrument to create more sustainability impact than a new instrument. This is because the instrument's institutional development over time – through pressures from the instrument's sponsors or stakeholders – is likely to increase the levels of specificity and obligation.
11. Tying to a scoring system is equivalent to independent verification in the case of an Excellence Model.
12. By business strategy we mean a company's roadmap on improving its competitive position.
13. A corporate strategy is the company's strategy on its overall direction in terms of growth and the management of its various business and product lines.

PART II

Mapping CSR: survey data on selected issues in four sectors

4 Introduction to the surveys

Katharina Schmitt

The following chapters contain the core results of structurally similar surveys carried out on Corporate Social Responsibility (CSR) in four European sectors in 2005 and 2006: the oil industry, fish processors, the banking sector and the automotive supply chain.[1] While the surveys in the first three industries focused on large companies, the latter sample included small and medium-sized enterprises (SMEs) only.

The surveys form one core part of this book's empirical analysis of CSR in selected companies and of its potential contribution to sustainability. The selection of companies mirrors this research interest in CSR performance and impact by focusing on CSR 'leaders' and in particular on companies active in the targeted issue areas. These include the mitigation of climate change, the promotion of gender equality and the countering of bribery in all four sectors analyzed. Additionally, the issue of minimizing chemicals risks was added for all but the banking sector, and concerns about sustainable fisheries were integrated as a key issue among fish processors.

With sample sizes ranging from 8 to 17 companies, the questionnaire-based surveys are not representative. Rather, they can provide qualitative insights into the framing, implementation and – to some initial extent – effects of CSR in different sectors, different issue areas and across different company sizes. Excepting minor variations necessary because of issue specific and sectoral differences, the survey questionnaires all follow the same structure: they cover the CSR commitment, strategies, implementation and performance of the companies selected, following a schematized implementation path (Figure 4.1).

In the section on corporate commitment, we asked companies to describe

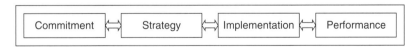

Source: Authors.

Figure 4.1   Survey structure

their understanding of responsibility to society and the environment. The section on corporate strategy dealt with the companies' strategic assessment of different CSR issues and how these were addressed via corporate strategies, policies and targets. The questions on implementation tackled how CSR strategies were operationalized through the use of instruments, through concrete implementation activities in certain CSR issues, organizational structures and resources provided to promote CSR. In order to shed some light on the potential difference between rhetoric and reality in CSR, we finally enquired about the CSR performance recordable and documented by companies. By following this model of CSR stages, the surveys reveal the companies' interpretation of their responsibility. In addition, they map CSR 'output', 'outcome' and to some degree the self-perception of their CSR 'impact'.

The summaries presented in the following chapters provide some striking findings from these surveys. Thus, they do not necessarily present the entire range of answers given by companies but rather a selection of these.

NOTE

1. For background information on the selection of these sectors, please refer to Chapter 1.3.

5 CSR in the European oil sector: a mapping of company perceptions

Elin Lerum Boasson, Jørgen Wettestad and Maria Bohn

5.1 INTRODUCTION

Compared with other businesses, the oil industry has been especially active in both developing and applying Corporate Social Responsibility (CSR) instruments. But do they all approach CSR similarly? And what issues are their CSR activities directed towards? This chapter aims to track down the prevailing CSR perceptions in the oil sector.

What is the 'oil sector' in this context? In Europe this sector is highly dominated by a relatively small number of multinational oil companies. We found it appropriate to include major companies as well as ensuring geographical representation encompassing different parts of Europe and major actors with a basis abroad. Most of the companies are involved in upstream as well as downstream activities. Moreover, we checked relevant federations' member lists[1] and added the criterion of being central companies/ operators on the British, Dutch and Norwegian shelves. On this basis, we singled out a set of 15 relevant companies: Amerada Hess, BP, Conoco, ENI, ExxonMobil, Gaz de France, Hydro, NAM, Orlen, Repsol, RWE-DEA, Shell, Statoil, Talisman and Total. After considerable effort, we managed to get a response from nine of these companies; mostly the European ones (Table 5.1). This is not surprising, as there appears to be some CSR 'questionnaire fatigue' among companies these days, not least in the big oil companies. As many of the dominating companies on the European scene chose to participate in the survey, the respondents do however represent a large part of the sector's activities in Europe.

This report is structured in the following manner: in Section 2 we address the issue of 'corporate commitment', that is, the terms the companies use to describe their social responsibility, the extent to which they agree with the EU's insistence on CSR referring to activities beyond mandatory

Table 5.1   Survey respondents

	Turnover Million €	Employees	Country
Amerada Hess	–	–	USA
BP	241 233	102 900	UK
Hydro	19 131	36 936	Norway
Orlen	90.39	19 997	Poland
Repsol	41 689	–	Spain
Shell	213 490	112 000	The Netherlands
Statoil	37 693	24 000	Norway
Talisman	3 775	1 870	Canada
Total	122 700	111 410	France

Source: Authors.

legislation, and their 'visions' and statements on issues targeted in this book (that is, climate change, chemicals, gender equality and the countering of bribery). Section 3 moves on to the issue of 'corporate strategy', including the companies' perceptions and ranking of the most important social and environmental issue areas and their 'translation' of responsibilities into policies/strategies. Section 4 discusses CSR instruments utilized by the companies, 'implementing activities', and relevant organizational structures established and resources set aside. Section 5 describes the companies' efforts towards measuring the impact of their CSR efforts. The last section sums up the main findings.

5.2   CORPORATE COMMITMENT: CONCEPTUAL DIVERSITY AND EMPHASIS ON ACHIEVING COMPLIANCE

5.2.1   Terms Used to Describe the Responsibility of Companies to Society and the Environment

In our main analytical model and way of thinking about CSR, we look upon corporate 'commitment' as the first step in our impact assessment and its causal chain leading up to an assessment of overall performance and CSR impact. In order to assess what companies tell us about their commitment to this issue, we need to know more about their understanding of the CSR concept. If their terms vary, this may indicate that they do not have a common notion about the nature of CSR and thus extra caution would be required in our subsequent interpretation of their responses. This is why, as the very first step, we asked for the main terms used by companies to describe their responsibility for society and the environment.

The striking overall response was diversity – and hence possibly also confusion! 'Corporate responsibility' and 'corporate social responsibility' were the most popular terms in our sample and were mentioned by four. Two of the terms we asked them about – 'business ethics' and 'corporate citizenship' – were mentioned by two. The other terms were mentioned only once. The companies stated seven new terms in addition to the seven we suggested. It is interesting to note that two important actors did not use any of the terms we presented, including the CSR term, to describe their responsibility to society. One preferred the term 'sustainability', which is of course something of a general buzzword in this context. Another used the term 'viability'.

The upshot of this is that there is significant basic conceptual diversity among the oil companies, and even among companies having the same national origin. This is in line with findings in other academic works on CSR. Moreover, this conceptual confusion is surely a complicating factor both in research efforts and in the broader dialogue between companies, policy makers and the research community. We cannot rule out that the companies may use diverging concepts on purpose because they find it convenient that there is no common notion about how their responsibility is to be understood. Diverging concepts and understandings make it more difficult to compare their performance and hard to hold them responsible for their actions.

Given the ongoing turf battle about what CSR means, and what seems to be an emerging prevalence of the EU Commission's definition of CSR as primarily pertaining to efforts going beyond formal legal compliance, we asked the companies about their understanding of this issue. Do they see CSR, for instance, primarily as a tool in the process of achieving compliance with mandatory commitments – or do they adhere to the EU's insistence on CSR as a concept referring to activities that go beyond mandatory legislation?

All oil companies in our sample found compliance with mandatory social and environmental legislation 'very relevant' (Figure 5.1). Moreover, for three of the companies this was in fact the only statement they assessed as very relevant. Four out of nine companies found that a contribution to meeting non-mandatory governmental recommendations was a very relevant part of this discussion. Three companies considered CSR very relevant as a contribution to political processes that lead to mandatory processes. Interestingly, all companies except one stated that going beyond mandatory legislation was relevant in their understanding of their responsibility. Only one of the companies indicated that activities

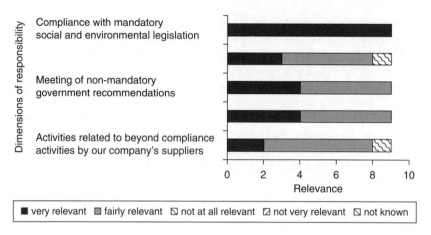

Source: Authors.

Figure 5.1   Dimensions of responsibility

related to 'beyond-compliance activities by our company's suppliers' were very relevant.

What is the upshot of this? First, it is clear that the oil companies included in our sample seemingly do not agree with the EU Commission's insistence on focusing this concept on voluntary activities beyond compliance. For them, CSR is a much broader concept. CSR instruments seem to be very relevant in their efforts to achieve compliance. This does not mean that the voluntary, beyond-compliance part of CSR was not acknowledged. In fact, it received substantial support. Overall, however, and probably not surprisingly, the companies embraced the 'achieving compliance' part of the CSR issue a little more wholeheartedly than the more daring 'going beyond compliance' part.

5.2.2   CSR 'Visions' and Statements on Selected Issues

Moving closer to the core of the commitment issue and based on the notion that companies as a very first and basic step must acknowledge that they have some sort of responsibility for how their activities affect the social and environmental surroundings, we asked the companies if they had a written overall CSR vision statement and not least if they had such a statement on the issues particularly targeted in the context of this book, that is, mitigating climate change, minimizing the risk from chemicals, promoting gender equality and countering bribery.

All of the companies have a written corporate statement of an overall vision, a mission or objectives. For three of the companies, this was a quite recent development. Others claimed that such an overall vision was introduced in the 1990s (one as early as in 1992, three others in 1997/1998).

With regard to the targeted sub-issues, all companies stated that countering bribery and promoting gender equality (with one exception) were covered by the statement. Seven of nine companies had statements that covered mitigating climate change and minimizing risks from chemicals. All of the companies indicated that they had statements on other issues than those targeted by us. From this we can possibly conclude that the companies perceived the somewhat more 'generic' and cross-cutting issues of countering bribery (which is also actually forbidden!) and promoting gender equality to be a little closer to the core of their interpretation of the CSR issue than the environmental and resource management issues.

5.3 CORPORATE STRATEGY: GOOD NEWS, BUT KEEP THE CHAMPAGNE ON ICE

5.3.1 The Most Important Social and Environmental Issue Areas

In our way of thinking about CSR, we look upon the formulation of corporate strategy as the second step in our impact assessment and the causal chain leading up to an assessment of overall performance and CSR impact. What social and environmental issues were perceived as most important for our selected companies in the formulation of their strategies?

Our ranking request was received a bit lukewarmly by the companies. One company mentioned three issues but refused to rank them and one refused to give any answer at all. Those that ranked did this in different manners. Hence, it is not very meaningful to present the response to this question in the form of a figure. Of the seven companies that made some sort of ranking, five of them point to climate change as the most important issue area. All but one of the eight companies that answered mentioned climate change as an important issue. One company ranked human rights as the most important issue. Other important issue areas mentioned include integrity, anti-corruption, ocean protection, local development, stakeholder consultations, preventing accidents, reduction of environmental footprint, reduction of pollutant releases and protection of sensitive areas.

From this we can conclude that climate change has clearly established itself as an important issue area for European oil companies. The ranking of other issue areas probably reflects differences in operations and

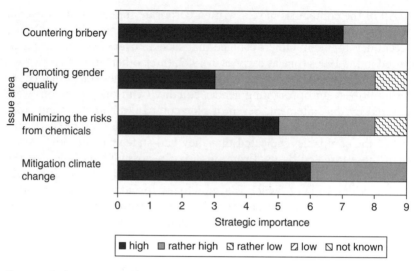

Source: Authors.

Figure 5.2   Strategic importance of selected CSR issue areas

institutional history among the companies. For instance, given the quite recent controversy within one of the companies over bribery issues, it is not surprising that this company gave this issue a quite high ranking. The reluctance of some companies to rank issues may once again have something to do with the somewhat different character of our targeted issues in the questionnaire (although these were not explicitly mentioned in this particular question), and also with issues more generally related to CSR. For instance, fighting climate change and fighting corruption are two very different types of social activities and challenges, and hence it may not necessarily seem very meaningful to compare and rank them in terms of importance.

A certain reluctance to rank differing issues is reflected in the responses to our request for a ranking of the strategic importance of our targeted issue areas for the companies (Figure 5.2).

Countering bribery scored best, with seven companies stating this issue as being of high importance, whereas climate change was chosen by six companies. It should be noted, however, that the companies overall simply indicated that all issues have high or rather high strategic importance for them. Taken at face value, this is good news for those striving to make companies more environmentally and socially responsible. However, it is important to keep in mind that our sample of companies which responded to the questionnaire did only include one American company. We know that the latter companies overall have a more critical perspective, for instance, on the issue of climate change. The companies were asked specifically about the strategic importance of the above concerning new member states. The results show that they did not perceive the issues differently in this respect.

It is noteworthy that climate issues are given the highest priority with regard to importance in general and high value when stressing strategic importance whereas the former section showed that climate issues were not defined as being at the heart of CSR. These findings imply that being perceived as a CSR issue does not necessarily imply high saliency.

5.3.2 Translating Responsibilities into Corporate Strategies and Policies

We also asked the companies how they more specifically translated social and environmental responsibilities into their policies and/or strategies. This included the development of specific policies targeting our focused issue areas, the integration of these focused issue areas into existing corporate strategies as well as the setting and coverage of relevant targets.

Nearly all companies stated that they have developed specific policies for climate change, chemicals, gender equality and bribery. In addition, most companies have also integrated many of the issues into their existing corporate strategies. In general terms, this should probably be counted as good news. At least in the companies included in our sample, important formal elements to accommodate various environmental and social concerns seem to be in place. However, a policy to mitigate climate change may range from producing an information leaflet asking employees to turn off the lights in their offices in the afternoon to establishing an internal emissions trading system. In other words, the champagne should be kept on ice for a while yet.

On the more specific issue of targets, seven of our eight companies have set such targets regarding the issue of climate change. Targets on chemicals likewise exist in seven companies, while only four respondents have gender equality and anti-bribery targets.

All companies stated that targets apply to the company's own operations, whereas three companies in addition reported that targets apply to products and services by suppliers and service providers. Three of the companies stated that they have set such targets for all of our targeted issues, whereas one has developed such targets for climate and chemicals, but not for gender equality and countering bribery, while another has developed a target for climate change only. The latter two cases may have something to do with target setting in the field of bribery being perceived as less meaningful and common than, for instance, the field of climate change.

5.4   INSTRUMENTS AND IMPLEMENTATION: CONFUSING VARIETY

In our analytical model we look upon CSR instruments utilized and the implementation of 'CSR activities' as key elements of the outcome part of our impact assessment and the causal chain leading up to an assessment of overall performance and CSR impact. Hence, we asked the companies about the CSR instruments they use. We also asked about the specific activities they carry out in the selected issue areas which could be meaningfully categorized as CSR activities. A final element in this section enquired about the particular CSR organizational structures and resources established and/or set aside by the companies.

5.4.1   CSR Instruments: A Wide Selection Utilized

Turning first to the issue of CSR instruments, we presented the companies with a list divided into six main sections: 'codes of conduct'; 'management systems'; 'forms of stakeholder engagement and co-operation'; 'non-financial accounting and reporting'; 'conformance with requirements of social and ecological product labels or awards' and 'others'. Overall, the companies utilized a considerable number of instruments. The top scoring company applied 24 instruments; two others applied 22 and 20, respectively; three others applied between 15 and 20 instruments; while three applied between ten and 15 instruments. It should be noted, however, that this overview also includes 'company-specific instruments'.

As to 'codes of conduct', a first central finding is that all companies adhere to the Global Compact. Second, four other such instruments are of considerable relevance, that is, the OECD Guidelines for Multinational Enterprises, the Business Principles for Countering Bribery, the Energy and Biodiversity Initiative and Responsible Care. A third finding is that 'company-specific codes' are also of considerable relevance. Finally, most of the companies utilize additional codes of conduct not initially identified by us (Figure 5.3).

Turning to 'management systems', all but one apply ISO 14 000, four apply EMAS and three apply OHSAS 18 000. Moreover, five of the companies state that they have company-specific management systems.

With regard to 'forms of stakeholder engagement and co-operation', all companies collect information about/from stakeholders and set out consultation of stakeholders. All but two engage in multi-stakeholder initiatives in the issue area of climate change; all but three engage in multi-stakeholder initiatives in the field of bribery; five companies engage in multi-stakeholder initiatives in the issue area of chemicals and three

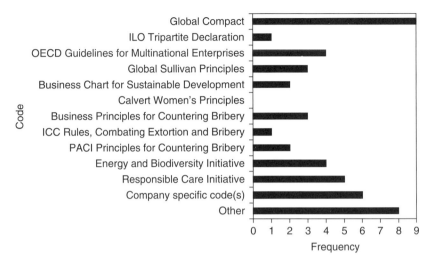

Source: Authors.

Figure 5.3 Adherence to codes of conduct

companies engage in such initiatives on gender equality. Moreover, four companies include stakeholders in decision making.

Moving on to 'non-financial accounting and reporting', all of the companies have their own reports and all, except two, do their reporting on the basis of the Global Reporting Initiative (GRI). With regard to other instruments, the two most commonly adhered to are the Petroleum Industry Guidelines for Reporting Greenhouse Gas Emissions and the International Standard on Assurance Engagements ISAE 3000. The Petroleum Guidelines are adhered to by five companies; the same goes for the International Standard on Assurance Engagements ISAE 3000.

We also asked the companies if they required business partners to comply with any of these instruments, or if such partners placed such requirements on the companies.

Almost all companies generally stated that contractors and suppliers are required to comply with company-specific standards (except for two which did not answer this question). The companies mention various additional instruments in this respect, with two specifically referring to ISO 14 000. Most of the companies also quite generally stated that their business partners are required to comply with company-specific standards. Three companies specifically referred to ISO 14 000 in this connection.

Regarding the extent to which the companies carry out community activities of issue-specific relevance, this seems to be generally limited, and there are marked differences between the companies. All, except one, contribute within the issue of climate change. One supports volunteering of staff, and it does so within all issue areas; another supports volunteering of staff within climate, chemicals and gender issues; others again only within chemicals or climate change issues. It seems to be common for oil companies to contribute added value, donate to or sponsor social or environmentally committed organizations within all of the fields asked about, although chemicals and bribery received lower ranking than the other issue areas. None of the oil companies align product sales to social and environmental causes.

In addition to the standardized instruments, we asked the companies to indicate which issue-specific, voluntary, beyond-compliance activities they were engaged in. The reply options were restricted to certain activities of relevance to EU policy goals in the policy fields of climate change, chemicals, gender and bribery. The companies were also asked to indicate whether the activity was at least partly required by law.

In the field of climate change the activities were divided into activities aimed at reducing greenhouse gas emissions, activities aimed at developing new renewable energy sources, and activities related to carbon removal and storage. All companies are active in all three categories of the climate change mitigation issue, but there is variation between them regarding the number of different activities they pursue within these categories. Two companies stand out as being involved in the development of a greater number of renewables than the others. One differs from the others as it does not have activities relating to any of the mentioned new renewables. When it comes to activities related to carbon removal and storage, all companies except one fund research on carbon removal and storage. It is interesting to note that all three companies have plans for full-scale carbon removal and storage projects before 2010.

When it comes to chemicals, gender and bribery, the activities asked for are hard to compare as the answers lack a general pattern. All companies (apart from two smaller ones) are active in all three categories of activities. There is, however, some variation between the companies in the number of different activities they pursue within each category, the complexity of the issues asked for makes it hard to assess the responses.

5.4.2   Assignment of Responsibility Within the Company

Based on the assumption that the level of organizational responsibility for CSR affects outcomes and impact, the companies were asked to describe how they had allocated responsibility within their organization for the different policy fields.

Interestingly, for seven of the eight companies that answered the question, there was no variation across the policy fields in the assignment of responsibilities, at least as far as the standardized options were concerned (board level responsibility, senior management level responsibility, functional responsibility, compliance control and auditing responsibility). The most common feature for all issues is that they are managed by seniors other than executive directors.

Overall, more companies place responsibility at the two highest levels (that is, board level and senior management level responsibility) than at the other, lower levels. However, one company had board level or senior management responsibility for all issue areas except chemicals. The companies were also asked to state if there were bodies that considered the issues regularly, and here we found some differences between the policy fields.

The oil sector is a high-risk sector when it comes to bribery, due to operations in regions with high levels of corruption. Oil corporations often pay large sums of money to governments that are accused of corruption. As noted previously, all but one company stated that countering bribery was covered by their CSR statement. A corollary question to the previous one was about expenditures related to CSR instruments and activities, and how these had changed over the past three years. One-third of the companies answered that they do not have data on such expenditures; another third gave no answer; while the remaining third indicated both significant expenditures and also increases ahead.

5.5   PERFORMANCE: UNCERTAINTY AND LACK OF MEASUREMENT

The final part of our survey addressed the key aspect of 'performance'. Here, we sought insight into the companies' measurement practices and performance with regard to the instruments and activities discussed above, including specific mechanisms used to implement the instruments. Still, the answers reflect company perceptions and are not assessed in accordance to external information. The questions in this section have low answer rates and the respondents have added comments which indicate that they found it complicated to address these issues. Thus, we only refer to some of the questions and the results must be interpreted with care.

5.5.1   Performance Measurement

For each policy field, the companies were asked if they measured their performance. The response was almost unison; performance was measured in nearly all areas. In order to get a rough picture of how they perceived improvement in performance, we asked the companies to judge whether their performance, as measured by some specific key performance indicator (KPI), had been 'rather low', 'medium' or 'rather high', since they started using the indicator. This turned out to be a difficult question for the companies to address. A few companies rated their development in accordance to KPIs but too few to get a reliable impression of how this is perceived.

The most interesting result from this question is not the assessments themselves but the difficulties the companies have in stating KPIs and their development over time. The comments made by the companies indicate that the coordinating challenge regarding performance measurement at the corporate level is in itself tremendous. Other factors may also have affected the companies' reluctance, such as fear of disclosing information on performance for competitive reasons.

In order to find out which instruments contributed most to supporting good performance, the companies were asked to name one instrument that related most to their performance in the four issue areas in focus. Only five of the companies answered this question. They pointed to company-specific instruments in most of the issue areas, but regarding chemicals two companies stated that they also had applied ISO 14 000. One of the smaller companies stated solely 'responsible care'. On bribery, three companies answered 'company-specific instruments' and one 'PACI'. Around half of the respondents gave input to this question. Nonetheless they indicate that the companies perceived the internally developed instruments as more important than externally introduced instruments in order to improve their own CSR performance. Externally introduced instruments may be an inspiration for changes in performance, but are not perceived as crucial tools.

5.5.2   Governmental Support Needed

Lastly, we posed a question concerning what kind of support the companies want policy makers to lend in order to improve the companies' performance – answers vary quite a lot. Except for wanting policy makers to contribute to raising awareness among companies, investors and consumers, there is no clear pattern to be found in the statements (Figure 5.4). As the EU is very eager to introduce CSR in business thinking through education, it is interesting that only one company requested this kind of assistance from policy makers.

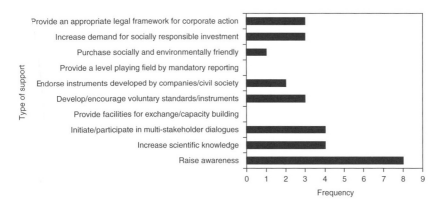

Source: Authors.

Figure 5.4   *Public policy support for CSR*

5.6   CONCLUDING COMMENTS: WHAT DO THESE RESULTS TELL US ABOUT CSR AND EUROPEAN OIL COMPANIES?

Before we sum up the main findings and wind up with some concluding reflections, let us briefly note that we experienced some 'questionnaire fatigue', but managed to overcome at least some of it. We ended up with a response rate above half of the original sample, getting more or less complete responses from nine companies. A not very surprising lesson is of course that carrying out quite extensive surveys is an ambitious and time-consuming exercise. Thus we recommend other researchers to plan carefully and expect delays! A very specific lesson is: seek to avoid the end of the year, when company executives are busy fulfilling internal reporting duties and so on.

Let us then turn to a summary of the main findings concerning how the oil companies perceive CSR. As the first step, we attempted to get an understanding of the companies' 'commitment' to CSR. With regard to terms used to describe companies' responsibility to the society and environment, the most striking feature was probably the significant conceptual diversity, although the terms 'corporate responsibility' and 'corporate social responsibility' were the most popular terms. Given that the research project on which this book is based links up with the EU Commission's emphasis on CSR primarily pertaining to efforts going beyond formal legal compliance, we asked the companies about their understanding of this issue. The main finding here was that the companies included in our sample do not agree with the EU Commission, as they place prime emphasis on CSR being a tool to achieve compliance with mandatory social and environmental legislation. On the issue of overall corporate CSR 'visions' and statements, all companies had such written statements. Almost all included countering bribery and promoting gender equality and a majority also included mitigating climate change and minimizing the risks from chemicals.

Moving on to 'corporate (CSR) strategy', we enquired about the companies' ranking of social and environmental issues in their formulation of strategies. Although the companies were reluctant to carry out such a ranking, it is at least clear that climate change has established itself as the most important issue for European oil companies. Countering bribery also has fairly high strategic importance. When translating responsibilities into corporate policies/strategies, almost all companies have developed specific policies targeting our four focused issue areas. Target setting is also common, although a bit more so in the case of climate change than, for example, bribery.

The next main issues addressed were CSR instruments, activities and organization. Regarding instruments adhered to, the impression at first glance is certainly impressive, with six companies adhering to 15 or more (with one company's 24 instruments topping the list). The most popular instruments are not surprisingly the Global Compact, OECD Guidelines, Responsible Care, ISO 14 000 and the Global Reporting Initiative. This formal diversity is also matched by some specific activities and practices, although the causal relationship between the two is unclear. The companies were in fact engaged in a considerable number of activities within all our four targeted issue areas. They also signal priority to CSR issues by assigning internal responsibility for such issues to high-level functions (that is, board level and senior management level responsibility). A critical question, however, is: what does the adherence, for instance to Global Compact, mean for the behaviour of companies? Does it mean that they do things noticeably differently? Moreover, although adhering to 15–20 CSR instruments in theory sounds impressive, how is such a broad portfolio handled in practice? Is there a harmonious, synergistic relationship – or are there conflicting requirements? In the same vein, is there a case of 'spreading out the resources thinly', instead of concentrating them to do a good job? Furthermore, what do the companies mean by 'company-specific codes'; are they instruments in the same league as the general instruments – or just a new label for 'business-as-usual'?

With regard to implementation and activities, it should be noted that all companies, except one, are active in all three categories of climate change mitigation (that is, reducing emissions, developing renewables and developing carbon capture options). This indicates that the European oil companies operating in Europe follow up their rhetorical support to the Kyoto Protocol with at least some realities.

Finally, what did the companies tell us about relevant performance? There is clearly some measuring going on. However, responding to the 'key performance indicators' formulated by us turned out to be difficult. One complication in this picture was a reluctance to disclose performance information for competitive reasons. This also limited the companies' willingness to inform us about possible instances where they had refrained from investments due to social/environmental concerns. As to the contribution of CSR instruments to performance, the most important ones were clearly the 'company-specific' instruments and to a much lesser degree the more 'standard' instruments.

NOTE

1. That is the European Petroleum Industry Association (EUROPIA) and the International Association of Oil and Gas Producers (OGP).

6 CSR in the European fish processing industry: not just fishing for compliments

Katharina Schmitt and Franziska Wolff

6.1 INTRODUCTION

How sustainably do European fish processors behave? What instruments do they use, what activities do they carry out to voluntarily go beyond their legal obligations? And to what extent do these activities help companies to improve their sustainability performance and create an impact on society and the environment?

This chapter addresses these questions and summarizes the results of a survey carried out in 2005 among eight European fish processors committed to Corporate Social Responsibility (CSR). We approached 41 companies (that is, achieved a response rate of 19.5 per cent) with CSR activities in place and with a reputation for CSR, in particular with regard to sustainable fisheries concerns and the other CSR issue areas chosen: climate change mitigation, chemicals, gender equality and countering bribery. The questionnaires sent to the companies followed the structure as sketched out in Chapter 4.

Our eight respondents are Domstein ASA, FF Skagen, Frosta AG, Gottfried Friedrichs KG, Icelandic plc, Rhabek Fisk A/S, Unilever plc/N.V. and Young's Bluecrest; they come from Denmark, Iceland, Germany, Norway and the UK. The companies partly operate in different markets, both with regard to geographical coverage within Europe and with regard to products (frozen fish, smoked fish and so on). With its sample and focus, the survey does not strive to give a representative picture of the whole European processing sector, but to give insights into the practices of selected CSR forerunners.

So far, the European fisheries and fish processing sector has not been scrutinized for its corporate responsibility practices in a more encompassing fashion, although in this sector, like in others, CSR has gained prominence in the past years. There are some general organizational analyses of individual companies and some studies, partly self-reported, on their CSR initiatives (for example Fieldhouse 1978; Jones and Miskell 2005; Unilever 2002, 2005a; Wilson 1968). There is also a growing body of literature on relevant CSR instruments, especially the Marine Stewardship Council (MSC) certification (for example, Constance and Bonanno 2000; Cummins 2004; Fowler and Simon 2000; Gardiner and Viswanathan 2004; Gulbrandsen 2005; Hoel 2004; Steinberg 1999; Wildhavens 2004). While the company case studies mostly focus on CSR in individual companies without conveying a broader picture across the sector and rarely tackle performance and impact, the instrument literature does not go into the company-level processes tied to using the CSR instruments. This chapter strives to tackle this gap.

6.2 CORPORATE COMMITMENT: SPANNING THE ISSUES AND DEFENDING THE COMPLIANCE APPROACH TO CSR

6.2.1 No Breakthrough for the EU Reference Concept

Assuming that organizations differently interpret such abstract concepts as CSR and derive different strategies from the respective interpretations, we were at first interested in how companies make sense of this concept. Our expectation was that companies would refer to a term that is anchored in their environment, be it the environment of industry peers or that of stakeholders.

'Corporate Social Responsibility' (CSR) as the concept promoted by the European Commission (2002, 2006b), along with 'Corporate Sustainability' are currently used very rarely by the companies polled. Only two of them refer to these concepts. With regard to CSR this might indicate that the Commission's CSR Strategy has not yet reached the fish processing sector, or that some form of understanding on the issue was developed before this strategy was introduced. Indeed, more (that is, four) companies refer to the older concept of 'Business Ethics'. However, the same number of companies employ the term 'Corporate Responsibility' (CR), which is rather recent, thus possibly indicating that newcomers selected a concept different from the EU's official reference term. Interestingly enough, both these preferred concepts do not necessarily imply an environmental dimension of well-doing. As shall be seen later, this is slightly contradictory to the fact that the concrete CSR activities of fish processors focus on the environment and on sustainable fisheries.

6.2.2 Emphasis on Achieving Compliance Instead of Moving Beyond Compliance?

When asked in some more detail how they interpret their own social or environmental responsibility, the companies unanimously stress that compliance with mandatory social and environmental regulation is very relevant (Figure 6.1)

The meeting of non-mandatory government recommendations is considered as 'fairly relevant' by all but one respondent. Some companies furthermore include contributions to political processes as a part of their responsibility understanding. 'Activities that go beyond mandatory legislation' seem to be the most contentious part of the companies' social and environmental responsibility: respondents attached different levels of importance to this element, ranging from very relevant to not at all relevant. This is striking, as CSR is commonly framed as a 'beyond compliance strategy'. In accordance with this, the EU explicitly defines CSR as activities going beyond mandatory obligations (European Commission 2002, 2006b). Again, a mismatch between the public policy expectation and the corporate interpretation becomes apparent, as the fish processors seem to pursue CSR as a compliance rather than as a beyond-compliance strategy.

It is more congruent with our expectations that supply chain activities are seen as very or fairly relevant in six out of seven answers given: especially with regard to the CSR issue of 'sustainable fisheries', the companies' CSR practices ultimately depend on the behaviour of their suppliers, that is, the fishing industry.

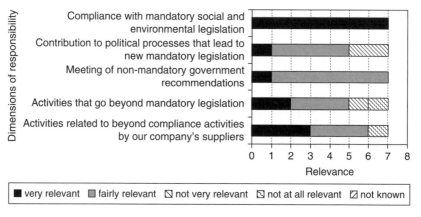

Source: Authors.

Figure 6.1   Dimensions of responsibility

6.2.3 Commitment Focuses on Core Business

We were curious about how companies substantiated their commitment towards society and/or the environment. Five of the eight companies polled declare that they have introduced an explicit written statement, thus making their engagement public. The issue area of 'sustainable fisheries' is most extensively covered in the companies' written statements. This is not surprising and confirms the common assumption that companies relate their commitment tightly to their core business and to issues that constitute a business case – such as the preservation of fish stocks, which is not only an environmental issue but a question of economic survival of fish processors. It was quite unexpected, therefore, that this crucial issue is only covered in the statements of five of the surveyed fish processing companies.

While 'mitigation of climate change', 'minimizing risks from chemicals' and 'promotion of gender equality' are further issues covered in the written statements of three of the companies, 'countering of bribery' comes out last (one respondent). This may either be due to the fact that bribery is no major problem in the fish processing industry, or that it is at least not perceived as such by the companies and their stakeholders.

6.3 CORPORATE STRATEGY: CORE BUSINESS IS CALLING!

Do companies consistently transform their commitment into strategies? In order to understand the step from commitment to strategy we were interested to see which social and environmental issues are identified as relevant by the companies, and how they manage these issues and integrate them into their policies and strategies.

6.3.1 Strategic Focus on Core Business, but Some Inconsistencies

Consistent with the impression that companies focus their commitment on issues linked to their core business, it emerges that they also set their strategic emphasis on these. When enquiring about the strategic importance that the companies attach to certain issues, 'sustainable fisheries' – again as expected – by far scores highest ('high importance' attached by seven of eight respondents). It is followed by the issue 'minimizing the risk from chemicals', which covers, for example, avoidance of toxic substances for vessels' paints and nets ('high' or 'rather high importance' by five companies). Promoting gender equality is still seen to be highly or rather important by four respondents, unlike countering of bribery (two respondents) and the mitigation of climate change (one processor). Interestingly, the most heterogeneous picture emerges on countering bribery where assessments vary widely.

It is rather surprising how little importance companies attach to climate change: one might assume that there is a real sustainability challenge here for the fish processors – namely to limit CO_2 emissions in the cold chain – which is closely related to their core business. Also, climate change is high on the agenda of potential pressure groups, such as civil society, governments and investors, thus forcing it onto the agenda of companies as well. This could be explained by analysing how a strategically important issue is addressed in written CSR statements: climate change here is still relatively well covered. We might assume that companies use their written statements to pay lip service to stakeholders' expectations, while not (or at least not yet) fully recognizing the strategic importance of climate change mitigation.

6.3.2 Selective Integration of CSR Issues into Strategies

When translating their social and environmental responsibilities into corporate policies and/or strategies, companies may either opt to develop specific self-standing policies or they may integrate their concern for the issues into pre-existing policies and strategies. All of the European fish processing companies surveyed state they have self-standing policies on sustainable fisheries. Specific policies on climate change, the risks from chemicals and gender equality concerns exist in two to three companies, whereas the fight against bribery is not institutionalized into their own policy by any of the respondents.

Companies furthermore integrate their responsibility into pre-existing, cross-cutting policies and strategies. However, this integration seems to be selective: while sustainable fisheries concerns are integrated by most companies (seven out of eight), only a minority of the fish processors polled integrate climate change issues, chemicals concerns and the countering of bribery into cross-cutting strategies. The pre-existing policies and strategies into which social and environmental responsibilities are integrated include above all the sourcing and marketing strategies as well as product development and product placement.

6.3.3 Target Setting Not Clearly Aligned to Strategic Importance

A further crucial step in the CSR process of a company is the translation of strategies and policies into specific targets. The survey reveals that only five of the eight companies have defined targets. To our surprise, however, targets exist for all issue areas except 'countering bribery'. In all cases the targets apply to the companies' own operations as well as to suppliers and service providers, respectively, to the impacts of their products and services.

We checked more systematically whether the setting of targets is linked to a company's assessment that a specific issue is strategically important. For most of the issue areas to which companies assign a high or rather high strategic importance at least 50 per cent of companies have set themselves targets with regard to this specific issue area. As could have been expected, the sustainable fisheries issue is, in absolute terms, the one most frequently translated into concrete targets within the companies that attributed high relevance.

6.4   CSR IMPLEMENTATION: A 'ONE-ISSUE SHOW'?

Understanding the concrete implementation of a company's voluntary social and ecological commitment as precondition for sustainability impact, we asked companies what CSR instruments and activities they adhered to and how they implemented and anchored them in organizational terms.

6.4.1   No Preference for Specific Instrument Types, but Clear Thematic Focus

The survey reveals that the respondent fish processing companies do not seem to have specific preferences with regard to the types of instruments. Codes of conduct, management systems and labels are equally used. As regards content, the focus is on instruments that relate to sustainable fisheries, to food safety and the environment.

In the category of codes of conduct six respondents refer to the FAO Code of Conduct on Responsible Fisheries (FAO 1995) as a point of reference for their own principles; two have company-specific environmental principles. The management system most frequently employed (by six respondents) is the Hazard Analysis and Critical Control Point (HACCP), which relates to food safety, and own company-specific management systems (three companies) in the form of quality manuals and 'boat to plate' traceability systems. Stakeholder engagement is an instrument used by about half of the respondent companies. One of the most important instruments is the MSC label, a certification programme on sustainable fisheries. The label is frequently applied to some products out of a larger product range offered by fish processors.

In a tentative way the number and form of CSR instruments used by a single company can be linked to the ownership structure of that company and more specifically to its stock market listing. The stock market listed companies in our sample have a greater affinity to use CSR instruments. However, the statistical basis is small and company size might be an intervening variable: bigger companies have more resources and are potentially more exposed to the public limelight which pressures them to implement CSR instruments.

6.4.2   Voluntary Activities in Selected Issue Areas

Besides the use of standardized CSR instruments, as they were discussed above, CSR manifests itself in very concrete beyond-compliance activities and in changes of companies' daily practices. The survey enquires specifically about such activities in the five selected issue areas.

6.4.2.1   Sustainable fisheries activities: maintaining fisheries resources rather than tackling ecosystem impacts

In the issue area of sustainable fisheries voluntary activities frequently relate to specific fish stocks. A company may source fish from a stock managed according to legal requirements or it may source fish from other stocks that are managed more sustainably than legally required.

In order to get a more comprehensive picture of the extent of voluntary activities with a view to different fish stocks, companies were asked to specify their activities both with regard to: (a) the fish stock that earns the company the greatest turnover, and (b) a fish stock that the company catches or sources from explicitly sustainable fisheries (worldwide). The information relating to (b) will give us insights into what responsibility measures are taken in an 'ideal' case, while data on (a) will indicate what measures the company takes with regard to the economically most relevant stocks (Table 6.1).

Table 6.1 reveals that only for one company the fish from explicitly sustainable fisheries is also the economically most relevant one. To the extent the information was stated, the estimated share of fish sold from sustainable fisheries in relation to company's total fish sales is relatively high (average: 38 per cent).

For systematic reasons, we differentiate in the following between activities that contribute to sustaining marine fisheries resources (target and non-target species; Figure 6.2) and activities that minimize the impact of fishing on the wider marine ecosystem (Figure 6.3).

Among the top-scoring five activities to sustain marine fisheries resources, companies source fish from certified stocks (for example, by

Table 6.1 Fish stocks sourced from and percentage of sales

Company	1	2	3	4	5	6	7	8
(a) Fish with greatest turnover								
Species	Alaskan pollock	Atlantic cod	Alaskan wild salmon	Atlantic cod	Industrial fish in general	Cod	Plaice	–
Species' share of total sales	5%	20%	30%	–	–	–	15%	–
(b) Fish sourced from sustainable fisheries								
Species	Salmon	Alaskan pollock	Alaskan wild salmon	Haddock	Herring	-	Alaskan pollock	Pacific hoki and Alaskan pollock
Species' share of total sales	0.5%	12%	30%	–	–	–	10%	–

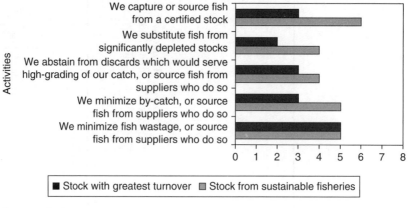

Source: Authors.

Figure 6.2 Voluntary activities to sustain marine fisheries resources (the five top scores)

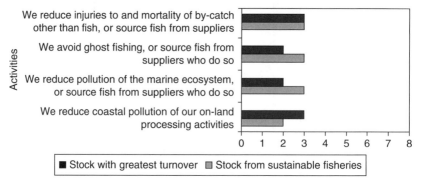

Source: Authors.

Figure 6.3 Voluntary activities to minimize impact on the marine ecosystem (top scores)

the MSC or KRAV) or from stocks that are being managed in a sustainable manner according to other requirements. These include, for example, criteria defined in the FAO Code of Conduct, own fishery assessment schemes and so on. Apart from the minimization of fish wastage, most of the measures vary between economically important and explicitly sustainable stocks. This might be attributed to the fact that the respective activities are obligatory under certain certification schemes (for instance, the MSC), but are not so widespread with regard to stocks not managed sustainably. In addition to the above described top-scoring activities, certain measures that we asked for are conducted rarely or not at all by the companies under study. For example, only two respondents implement supplier standards concerning technical measures of responsible fishing practice, and invest in or support stock monitoring and assessment. Likewise, just one of the companies states that it sources from suppliers that reduce fishing effort in specific cases. Even though the latter is a very effective measure to sustain marine fisheries resources, it is not widespread as it affects companies' competitiveness if the measure is not carried out collectively. None of the companies polled promotes closed areas (no-fishing zones) or closed seasons, or invests in research on sustainable fisheries methods.

As regards minimizing the impact of fishing on the marine ecosystem, it is evident that the level of CSR activities is significantly lower than compared to target and non-target fish. The most common activities carried out with regard to the marine ecosystem aim at reducing injuries to and mortality of by-catch other than fish, at avoiding ghost fishing, at reducing coastal pollution through on-land processing as well as pollution of the marine ecosystem (for instance, through oil spills, on-board processing or waste water). However, even with regard to the fish from explicitly sustainably managed stocks, these activities are carried out by a maximum of 40 per cent of our sample companies. This finding underlines that CSR activities representing a win-win situation (business case) are preferred to other activities. It also confirms the impression that companies view sustainable fisheries as a resource issue ('sustaining one's business tomorrow') rather than an environmental issue ('avoiding ecosystem impacts').

6.4.2.2 Chemicals activities: focus on risk management
Minimizing risks from chemicals is the issue in which the fish processing companies surveyed are engaged second most frequently. Their voluntary activities in this area cover above all chemical risk management rather than substituting to less hazardous or non-chemical alternatives. Risk management includes the proper servicing of equipment containing refrigerants, which six of the companies are engaged in, as well as the establishment of systems or activities for workers' safety. Only one company reduces its use of toxic substances for vessel paints and nets and two companies substitute away from the use of CFCs and HCFCs as refrigerants.

6.4.2.3 Climate change activities: little urgency
The mitigation of climate change does not seem to be an urgent issue area among the fishery companies surveyed. Only two respondents work to

reduce greenhouse gas emissions through diverse measures in their processing and transport operations and through energy efficiency improvements. Two companies are switching to renewable energy sources.

6.4.2.4   Gender equality activities: emphasis on the work-life balance

Among the social issue areas enquired about, voluntary activities of those polled clearly focus on the promotion of gender equality. The companies' emphasis in their activities is on the work-life balance of employees, rather than on equal opportunity and equal pay. For example, four respondents state to have established flexible working time arrangements. Also, specific action to promote parental leave of fathers is taken in two of the cases. With regard to the promotion of equal opportunities and equal pay, only two of the companies are more active. They work to close the gender pay gap and to ensure gender equality of full-time workers and part-time workers as well as contract employees.

6.4.2.5   Anti-bribery activities: no relevance?

Activities to counter bribery are sparse among the fish processing companies surveyed. This corresponds to the low profile that companies give to the issue within their commitment and strategies. Only two companies restrict or control facilitation payments, and restrict or control the giving and receiving of gifts. A management system comprising guidelines for employees and business partners, training, whistle-blowing mechanisms, internal control systems and possibly sanctions, reviews and public reporting of performance is implemented in none of the companies. One company explicitly stressed that bribery was not relevant to its operations.

6.4.3   Organization: Some Incongruity Between Issue Importance and Assignment of Responsibilities

Concerning the organizational set-up and the assignment of responsibility for CSR, our simplistic assumption is that the more institutionalized and the better endowed CSR activities are, the more likely it is that sustainability impact will be generated. We also expect that the level of institutionalization and endowment is related to how strategically important companies consider an issue area.

The latter expectation is met by the result that the processing companies have assigned organizational responsibilities above all with relation to the issue of sustainable fisheries. In seven companies an executive or non-executive director takes care of the issue, and in three of the respondent companies a senior manager is responsible as well. Functional responsibilities for sustainable fisheries (for instance, in the form of heads of fish purchasing, human resource directors, technical directors) and compliance control or auditing are established in two to three of the companies.

The issue that is institutionalized second best is gender equality: although the issue is less anchored at board level, the organizational responsibilities at all other managerial levels are equally developed. This comes as a surprise since in strategic terms, gender equality does not rank highly with most of the surveyed companies. The fact that gender issues are a more 'traditional' part of human resource policies might account for this. Organizational responsibilities for chemicals issues, although they feature relatively high in strategic terms, are not well developed. The fact that there are hardly any organizational responsibilities for climate change issues or countering bribery (apart from in one company) again conforms to our expectations.

6.5 PERFORMANCE AND IMPACT: A MATTER OF FAITH DUE TO A LACK IN MEASUREMENT PRACTICE

'Rhetoric or reality?' is the core research question of this book. We therefore also asked how and how successfully companies perform with regard to the action they take to meet their social and environmental responsibilities. Do the instruments and activities discussed above lead to bottom-line impacts, does CSR make a difference?

6.5.1 Deficits in Performance Measurement

Learning about impact and performance presupposes that companies measure certain CSR variables that indicate the achievement of positive effects. The survey reveals, however, that most companies of our sample do not measure their CSR performance. Considering the pressure on companies to prove that CSR is no 'greenwash', this finding is rather striking.

When asked why they do not measure performance, companies state that other organizations carry out the measurement; that there is no demand for such measurement; that resources are lacking; or that they have not defined concrete objectives to be measured anyway. Nevertheless, this is a problematic condition: on the one hand, without measurement there is no basis for assessing success or failure of CSR policies, and hence for developing remedies. On the other hand, not taking stock of actual performance and impact stemming from CSR promotes the public impression that CSR is a mere PR instrument.

Companies that do measure performance use so-called 'Key Performance Indicators' (KPIs). The indicator most often stated is the proportion of MSC certified fish purchased in relation to the company's overall fish portfolio. The building of indicators seems to be preferably linked to the MSC label, the implementation of which is easily proven, while the implementation of supplier standards appears not to be systematically measured.

6.5.1.1   Reluctant, but positive assessment of performance improvements

In our questionnaire we asked companies to assess their demonstrable improvement of performance in the selected issue areas according to a rough scale ('rather low', 'medium', 'rather high'. The assessment should be carried out on the basis of the companies' own KPIs and with regard to the time period since the KPI was introduced.

The first insight from this exercise is that the fish processors surveyed are reluctant to evaluate their own progress: only three of the respondents replied at all. The second insight is that in most cases demonstrable improvement is assessed to be at least medium. With regard to activities aimed to sustain marine fisheries resources (target and non-target stocks), the respondents estimated improvement to be medium or rather high. Impact is assessed to be higher with regard to sustainable fisheries than with regard to other issue areas. Within the issue area of sustainable fishing, progress is more pronounced with regard to sustaining resources than to reducing ecosystem impact. Both results tally with the earlier findings on the instruments adopted and activities carried out.

With a view to the other issues surveyed, mixed results were obtained. Only one company gave particulars with regard to the mitigation of climate change, which was assessed as 'medium' to 'rather low'. The company that assessed its gender-related performance considered demonstrable improvement with regard to equal opportunities to be medium. Two companies specified the share of female members in the board of management and indicated that their senior management comprised 5 per cent and 20 per cent women. These numbers suggest that equal opportunities at executive level are still a challenge. No data was given with regard to the companies' performance in countering bribery.

Although in the case of sustainable fisheries the specified performance improvement is encouraging, the overall lack of answers from the majority of companies is rather sobering. It means either that the question was not adequate; or that the companies – due to not measuring performance – cannot actually assess their improvement. If the latter is the case, some serious problems arise: companies cannot judge their own progress and take remedying measures. Neither can they communicate their (demonstrable) progress to their stakeholders and the public – and thus profit from improved reputation, and possibly an increased brand identity, competitiveness and attractiveness for employees.

6.5.1.2 MSC considered the instrument most conducive to improve performance

Which CSR instruments help companies best to improve their social and environmental performance? In order to be able to generalize on best practice, we asked companies to specify which of the CSR instruments they think contributed most to an improvement of their performance.

The fish processing companies in our samples very clearly chose the MSC certification to be the instrument most conducive to their CSR performance. Especially, companies referred to the effectiveness of externally communicating their adherence to the MSC as a major lever for creating impact. The regular monitoring of compliance with the MSC criteria, the engagement with diverse stakeholders as well as the independent verification were also judged to be important mechanisms of the MSC that lead to performance improvements.

6.5.1.3 Policy support: a preference for soft options

How can policy makers support fish processing companies to further improve their CSR performance? Confronted with a list of possible options, our respondents opted above all for 'soft' policies: they wish public policy to raise awareness, preferably among consumers, other companies and investors. Business schools, however, were not seen as relevant addressees of awareness raising measures.

State agents are furthermore asked to initiate and participate in multi-stakeholder dialogues, to develop or encourage voluntary standards in issue areas where there are none, and to endorse company or civil society instruments. Public policy that possesses more 'clout' – such as capacity building or consideration of CSR in public purchasing – was asked for by only one company. The clear preference is hence for soft options. The low popularity of 'responsible' public purchasing policies (for example, procurement of MSC certified fish for public cantinas, hospitals and schools) is somewhat puzzling, as the companies could be expected to benefit directly and in monetary terms from such measures.

6.6 CONCLUSIONS

Our most important findings include that companies use terms and concepts in their CSR strategy different from the one applied by the EU Commission to describe their voluntary sustainability activities, viewing these above all as a means to ensure compliance with mandatory legislation rather than to go beyond compliance. Companies assign strategic importance merely to those issues that relate to the companies' core business – that is, sustainable fisheries and to a minor extent chemicals – rather than to issues relating to their wider sphere of influence, be it with regard to climate change, gender equality or bribery. The focus on core business is mirrored when analysing CSR implementation (instrument use, activities, organizational set-up), though the relation between the implementation efforts and the strategic importance assigned to the issues is not always consistent. When it comes to sustainability impact, it emerges that the respondents are reluctant to assess their CSR performance. To the extent that they evaluate their performance improvement as caused by CSR, this evaluation is cautiously confident, at least with regard to sustainable fisheries issues. Performance improvement in other issue areas is either not assessed or less satisfactory, indicating that no sufficient amounts of CSR activities are carried out, or that the activities undertaken are not effective. The reluctance of many of the respondents to specify performance improvements is, among others, caused by the fact that few companies systematically measure their own performance at all. This is problematic as measurement is the basis for systematic review and improvement processes. While the survey cannot provide independent verification of performance data, it gives insights into the companies' self-assessment of their CSR performance – which may be understood as an upper limit, allowing for some overrating in self-assessments – and indicates which activities, instruments and structures have contributed to achieving the respective performance. The case study of Chapter 11 will help to deepen insights into sustainability impact and its drivers.

7 CSR in the European banking sector: evidence from a survey

Federica Viganò and Daniele Nicolai[1]

7.1 INTRODUCTION

According to literature, the banking sector has considered and reacted to the issue of sustainability relatively slowly, despite its high exposure to related risks caused by its intermediary role in the economy. The relevant literature from 1990 to 2000 shows that banks began to address sustainability by considering environmental issues first and social issues second (Bouma et al. 2001; Jeucken 2001, 2002). The prominent initial interest for environmental issues was a consequence of the direct risks banks could be held liable for, such as polluting activities. Only in the later years the indirect risks, such as reputation and the responsibility of banks related to lending activities, were duly considered by the sector, mainly because the concept of risk management, traditionally focused on financial risks, extended to environmental and social risks related to the investments made. Lending money to clients with dubious sustainability performances constitutes a reputational risk, which can lead to negative repercussions throughout the markets.[2]

Direct and indirect sustainability impact, measures to enhance societal benefits while limiting negative externalities, and motivations and policies of the banking sector have been explored by the survey presented hereafter. It was conducted among 17 European banks committed to Corporate Social Responsibility (CSR), in countries where the sector is rather developed.[3] It provides reliable information on how the sector is interpreting the challenging issues of sustainability and how it is dealing with the societal impact of CSR. The sample includes mainly large groups; the selection criteria preferred banks with an explicit CSR profile and a good CSR performance. Out of the 36 banks[4] approached at the end of 2005, 17 (47 per cent) responded to the questionnaire.

Within the issue areas targeted in this book (climate change, gender equality and bribery), the survey on banks addresses the analysis of CSR impact through the investigation of both direct and indirect aspects, where some of the most significant externalities lie. For instance, mitigating climate change can be addressed thoroughly if indirect aspects are chiefly considered, with banking being a relatively clean sector (low direct impact on the environment compared with other business sectors, such as oil and gas, fisheries, transportation and so on). Conversely, banks have a high potential to influence the behaviour of their clients, even the most polluting ones: access to credit is one of the major drivers for companies' strategies and actions.

7.2   SURVEY RESULTS

The results of the CSR banking survey are presented in accordance with the schematised path of corporate decision making outlined by the methodology described in Chapter 4. The analysis starts with a corporate commitment to responsibility, and then ventures into strategy building, implementation and performance measurement.

7.2.1   Corporate Commitment: Beyond or Through Compliance?

The questionnaire's focus on corporate commitment has given some interesting insights and confirms the explicit CSR profile of the chosen banks. Indeed, 16 out of 17 banks have a written corporate statement of overall vision, mission or objectives that clarifies their responsibilities towards society and the environment. The issues investigated (climate change, gender equality and bribery) are included in nine corporate statements and it is fairly relevant that 14 statements cover other CSR issues which are not covered by the three topics.

Banks are familiar with CSR-related terminology and chiefly relate their social and environmental responsibilities to the corporate sphere by choosing terms where the corporate duty is clearly implied ('CSR' and 'corporate responsibility'). The concept of 'corporate sustainability' follows while other terms, such as 'business ethics', 'corporate accountability' and 'triple bottom' line are less used.

When it comes to understanding how CSR is actually perceived by our sample with regard to the EU definition of CSR as beyond compliance policies or practices within the organizations, banks were asked to rank the importance of dimensions determining their responsibility to society and the environment. It is interesting to note that the EU Commission's definition seems to be challenged by the survey's result. The large majority of the banks (14) consider 'compliance with mandatory social and environmental legislation' much more important than 'activities that go

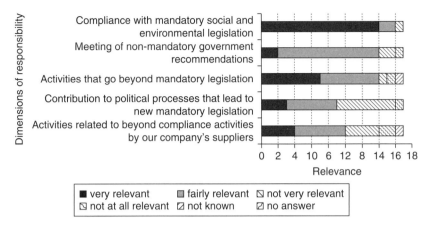

Source: Authors.

Figure 7.1 Dimensions of responsibility

beyond mandatory legislation' (ticked as 'very relevant' by seven banks only). It is inferable, therefore, that practitioners do not understand CSR just as beyond compliance; rather they see compliance as a relevant part of responsible behaviour.

As Figure 7.1 shows, when aggregating the two frequency boxes 'very relevant/fairly relevant' in order to stress the positive results, no significant difference emerges between the relevance given by companies to the compliance and the non-compliance dimensions (16 banks versus 14). Since it is a multiple choice question, it is likely that the same banks signed the two opposed dimensions without perceiving a clear contradiction. We interpret the result as follows: presumably CSR and its related activities are perceived as a path leading both to compliance and beyond; companies perceive more a 'continuum' rather than a sharp division between the two dimensions. Moreover, the continuum hypothesis seems to be confirmed by the fact that banks attribute a similar relevance to the 'meeting of non-mandatory recommendations' (the so-called soft law).

7.2.2 Corporate Strategy: Extending Responsibility From Direct To Indirect Aspects

The importance of the indirect aspects of CSR is more evident when analysing the integration of environmental and social CSR issues into banks' strategies and policies, concerning specifically the indirect risks deriving from lending activities, financing transactions and equity investments.

7.2.2.1   What is strategic?

Asked to provide an indication about what issue areas are strategically most relevant, half of the sample specifies areas which include an indirect responsibility via customers. This is relevant for the level of awareness concerning the responsibility they have in activities, such as lending operations, management of assets, Socially Responsible Investment (SRI) funds, financial products and consulting. The other issue areas identified as relevant are related to employees, as well as to social and environmental issues concerned with direct aspects.

Moreover, 3 banks out of 17 list the issue of financial inclusion as relevant: this aspect is gaining momentum as social exclusion is a diffuse phenomenon involving above all micro-small enterprises, households and social categories, such as immigrants, women, young and old people.

When moving to the ranking of the three issue areas investigated, the empirical evidence shows that climate change, gender equality and bribery score similarly and are considered strategically relevant by more than three-quarters of the banks.

7.2.2.2   Translating responsibilities into corporate policies and strategies

Moving from commitment into planning and acting, 15 banks state that they are developing specific policies covering all the three issue areas. Most banks are concerned with developing policies to promote gender equality first, then to counter bribery and finally to mitigate climate change. Most banks (12) also integrate their new policies into existing strategies, showing that CSR is not perceived as a 'bolt-on' activity, but rather as a 'built-in' activity.

An interesting qualitative result has been observed in the mitigating climate change issue area. Some banks specify to integrate the latter issue into 'risk and asset management'. This confirms that the relevance attributed by banks to indirect environmental responsibility (via customers) is translated into banking strategies (lending and investments, asset management).

7.2.2.3   Where are CSR-related organizational responsibilities assigned?

The assignment of social and environmental responsibilities within the organization can be a useful way to test the strategic relevance of the three issue areas declared by the large majority of the banks. Banks deal with the three issue areas at different levels, according to effectiveness and risk considerations. Indeed, countering bribery is mainly managed at the top level (board) and frequently by a compliance auditing unit. Instead, gender equality is managed at the level of senior managers, while climate change is primarily managed by functional bodies. The responsibility seems to lie where the control can actually take place: the more technical the control gets, the lower in the corporate hierarchy does the responsibility lie.

We can observe that the assignment of responsibility is subject to variation: as the perception of risk changes, due to evolving legislation or new market opportunities, the assignment of responsibilities can shift accordingly. This will probably be the case for climate change: if the survey shows that nowadays it is managed at a functional level, it is likely that, with the application of the EU Emission Trading Scheme and Carbon Credit Trades under the Kyoto Protocol Scheme, the issue of climate change will grow in importance, and responsibility will be assigned at higher levels within the corporate hierarchy.

7.2.3 Implementation: Manifold CSR Instruments, Few Sustainable Products

7.2.3.1 CSR instruments

Codes of conduct are the most relevant type of instrument used in the banking sector (89 entries). It is followed by non-financial accounting and reporting (62), forms of stakeholder engagement and co-operation (61) and management systems (34). Table 7.1 illustrates the top scoring instruments within the different categories.

Concerning codes of conduct, 15 banks out of 17 have developed company-specific codes to systematically manage social and environmental issues and to reinforce corporate identity. A sizeable share of the sample, however, refers to international guidelines promoted by the United Nations (UN Global Compact and UNEP Statement by Financial Institutions on the Environment and Sustainable Development), which are probably seen as an authoritative source as well as a good window for the enhancement of corporate reputation. It is important to stress that eight banks, almost half of the sample, adopt the Equator Principles, which address the indirect environmental responsibilities of banks in project financing. Furthermore, eight banks adopt the Financial Action Task Force (FATF) on Money Laundering and five banks use the Wolfsberg Principles: these instruments are related to money laundering which is aligned to the countering bribery issue area.

Sustainability reporting is a very popular instrument in the banking sector: all banks have developed their own reports, 15 banks follow the Global Reporting Initiative (GRI) reporting framework and 12 use the GRI supplements for the financial sector.

Stakeholder engagement activities and forms of stakeholder co-operation

Table 7.1   CSR instruments most frequently used by respondents

	Absolute frequencies	Relative frequencies
Codes of conduct		
Company-specific codes	15	88%
Global Compact	13	76%
UNEP statement	12	71%
Equator Principles	8	47%
FATF on money laundering	8	47%
All companies	17	
Total frequencies	89	
Non-financial accounting and reporting		
Own report	17	100%
Global Reporting Initiative (GRI)	15	88%
GRI financial services sector supplements	12	71%
Other	7	41%
ISAE 3000	5	29%
All companies	17	
Total frequencies	62	
Forms of stakeholder engagement and co-operation		
Collecting information about/from stakeholders	16	94%
Consultation with stakeholders and dialogue	15	88%
Participation in multi-stakeholder initiatives	15	88%
Inclusion of stakeholders in decision making	11	65%
All companies	17	
Total frequencies	61	
Management systems		
ISO 14 000	12	71%
Company-specific management systems	8	47%
EMAS	5	29%
EFQM excellence model	3	18%
SA 8000	2	12%
All companies	17	
Total frequencies	34	

Source: Authors.

should be encouraged in the banking sector: according to our sample the great majority of banks collect information on and from stakeholders, consult stakeholders and take part in multi-stakeholder initiatives. These are interesting findings that, however, need to be further investigated. There are many different interpretations of what stakeholder engagement is, ranging from one-way information to participatory decision making. So, even if 11 companies state that they actually do include stakeholders into decision-making processes, it is still unclear to what extent and on what topics this happens. Are the issues on which stakeholders are engaged material to the banking sector? Indeed, the range of issues on which stakeholder engagement takes place leads to some interesting considerations: 12 banks engage in multi-stakeholder initiatives on climate change while the initiatives taken up in the other issue areas are much less (six companies in countering bribery and three in gender equality). While it is very difficult to find direct stakeholders of banks affected by their climate change policy, and therefore to engage them concretely, participatory decision making and project co-operation with directly affected stakeholders would be possible in other issue areas, especially in the gender equality issue area. However, it could be assumed that banks participate in climate change initiatives to increase their reputation ('rhetoric'), but also that they are envisaging the strategic importance of financial products related to climate change mitigation ('reality').

The most frequently employed management system is ISO 14 000 (while EMAS – the environmental management system promoted by the EU – is adopted to a lesser extent), and company-specific management systems follow. Our sample shows that banks adopt less management systems than other instruments, such as codes or stakeholder engagement: this might be due to the fact that banks do not have directly polluting activities, nor are they big energy consumers. Therefore, the impact of an environmental management system is less effective than in other businesses.

The average number of CSR instruments adopted by each bank is 17, which is a high result even though this does not yet prove the scope and the depth of their CSR activities.

The repercussions of CSR instruments have been investigated by considering constraints and requirements on the wider value chain. On the one hand, most banks (14) require compliance from their contractors and suppliers with different instruments (ISO 14 000, EMAS and UN Global Compact) or with their underlying standards (ethical codes for suppliers, ethical charters, environmental and sourcing policies, requirements against the employment of child labour). In fact banks, like other large companies, are clients able to impose CSR conditions on their suppliers through their purchasing policies. On the other hand, more than half of the banks are required to be compliant by their customers (borrowers and recipients of investment funds) with the following instruments: one-third of the sample specify the Equator Principles in project financing, while four banks credit directives, company guidelines, code of business ethics and CSR policies.

7.2.3.2   Voluntary activities in the three issue areas

Activities in the different issue areas have been explored concerning both direct and indirect aspects of banks' responsibilities.

For what concerns the direct aspects of mitigating climate change, the large majority of banks is carrying out usual activities, such as reducing energy use in their premises, substituting business travel with video phone conferences, and introducing new technology to reduce direct GHG emissions from sources owned or controlled by the banks themselves. However, the most innovative activities carried out by banks in this field can be found when dealing with indirect aspects. The most common activities that banks carry out voluntarily are: accounting for climate change risks in their risk assessment (11 banks); providing venture capital for environmental innovation; participating in or establishing climate change funds; promoting SRI funds based on climate change mitigation criteria (eight banks). It is interesting to highlight that even though around half of the sample deals with indirect aspects of CSR, strong policies, such as avoiding lending to projects with intense GHG emissions and preferring investments in companies with low GHG emissions, are still carried out by only a few banks (five and one, respectively).

How banks are promoting gender equality has been investigated through the exploration of four sub-issues: promoting equal opportunities and equal pay for women and men; promoting work-life balance; ensuring anti-discrimination with respect to sexual harassment; and ensuring gender equality/diversity and equal treatment regarding access to and supply of banking services. The first three sub-issues refer to in-house activities (direct aspects), while the latter is linked to financial products and services (indirect aspects). Internally, banks carry out a variety of activities aiming at the promotion of work-life balance of employees,[5] equal opportunities and equal pay for women and men,[6] and have established preventive measures against sexual harassment and bullying. Indirect aspects are concerned by two activities carried out at a significant level: ensuring equal access to banking services for all women – irrespective of their marital status, race, ethnic or national origins, religious or political affiliation – (14 preferences, even though this activity is required by law in some countries); and programmes of microcredits to support female entrepreneurship (nine preferences). Other activities concerned with indirect aspects mentioned by a smaller number of banks are the following: three banks adopt programmes for loans to founders and/or other forms of credit services in economic sectors dominated by female entrepreneurs, while just one considers the participation in/or the establishment of funds dedicated to women's empowerment.

Voluntary activities related to countering bribery were surveyed according to four main sub-issues: countering the risk of bribery; countering money laundering; countering the risk of bribery in asset management, lending operations and SR funds; transparency in resource-backed lending.[7] The first two sub-issues encompass in-house (or internal) activities, such as the setting of programmes and internal control systems for countering bribery and money laundering, but also external activities, such as the provision of sanctions for business partners' violations of the management systems for countering bribery and the co-operation with other banks and government agencies to strengthen measures to counter money laundering throughout the banking system. All these internal and external activities represent direct aspects of banks' responsibilities. The third and the fourth sub-issues are instead related to the products and services concerned with indirect aspects. This issue area is regarded as very important throughout the sector, even though countering bribery is not required by law while anti-money laundering is a highly regulated area of the banking activity. For what concerns countering the risk of bribery, 16 banks control the exchange of gifts with third parties, while 14 have already in place or are developing guidelines for employees on countering bribery, as well as providing safe issues reporting channels (whistle blowing) and sanctioning violations of the management systems for countering bribery (called the Programmes). Despite these efforts, though, only four banks sanction business partners for violations of the Programmes, three train business partners on the issue, while only two banks report publicly on the Programmes' performance and have channels or hotlines for them. There is a consistent difference between internal and external aspects: if internal countering bribery activities are quite frequently used, their external dimensions are still in an embryonic phase.

Countering money laundering is tackled more systematically by banks, being an issue partly required by law.

The indirect aspects of banks' responsibilities (countering the risk of bribery in asset management, lending operations and SR funds) gave the following results: 15 banks account for risks of bribery associated with management of banks' assets and lending operations; 13 companies take into account criteria for countering bribery in managing assets; and nine banks manage SR funds taking into account criteria for countering bribery.

Conversely, there are negative results collected on the transparency in resource-backed lending issues.

Results concerning CSR activities in the three issue areas differ if we consider the banks' direct and indirect CSR activities. Banks do work on all sorts of aspects of climate change. However, just a few banks are developing strong and effective policies to deal with climate change indirectly, that is, encouraging other actors to engage in climate protection activities.

This however should be the 'hot issue' for sustainable banking. For what concerns the gender equality and bribery-money laundering issues we get positive findings both on the direct and indirect sides.

7.2.4   Measuring Performance: Difficulties of Indirect Impact Measurement

Measuring performance is the key to understanding whether CSR policies and structures are efficient in contributing to societal and environmental prosperity. Therefore, the implementation of a CSR monitoring system delivers partial evidence of its real embedment within corporate strategies and actions. The survey questionnaire investigated whether companies are measuring their performance in the three issue areas.

Climate change and gender equality performances are internally measured by all 17 banks and the frequency of external reporting and external verification of this performance is quite high (15 and 14 banks as regards external reporting and 11 and nine on external verification, respectively).

Countering bribery is the most difficult issue area to measure (11 banks do it internally while only four banks report on their performance externally and use third party verification): bribery being illegal and the issue therefore well hidden, it is difficult to assess whether measures for countering it are effective. One bank provides comments concerning the unavailability of appropriate indicators.

When banks measure their performance to show improvement, there are differences as to whether direct or indirect impacts are considered. The key question of this section is whether banks can appreciate an actual improvement of performance on the basis of their own key performance indicators (KPIs).

Among the direct impact, banks measure 'reducing greenhouse gas emissions' and 'promoting equal opportunities-equal pay for women and men' (covered by 12 banks out of 17), 'switching to renewable energy sources' (ten banks), 'promoting work-life balance' and 'countering money laundering' (seven banks). Sexual harassment along with countering bribery were found to be the most critical sub-issues, probably due to the difficulty in unveiling and assessing surreptitious activities. Still, the measurement of indirect impact is more problematic: only four banks could demonstrate their performance improvement in 'accounting for climate change in lending and investment policies', and only three in 'countering bribery in project financing', plus one in the 'equal treatment in the access/supply of services for women and men'. This shows a gap between the formal commitment of banks in taking up indirect responsibility and the consequent capability to manage and monitor their indirect impact.

As we were interested in identifying the factors that support the social and environmental performance of the banks, we asked companies to specify which of the CSR instruments contributed most to an improvement of their performance. ISO 14 000 with regard to climate change and company-specific codes with regard to bribery are the instruments most often referenced. None of the other instruments we enquired about stand out (frequencies are too low). Three banks cite other factors rather than instruments: dialogue with rating agency and NGOs, non-financial rating and activities to mitigate climate change (buy energy from renewable sources, increase energy efficiency, neutralize CO_2).

Moreover, it was interesting to understand which mechanisms companies use when implementing the chosen instruments. Definition of procedures – regular monitoring of compliance, evaluation and control – and internal verification as well as employee training programmes seem to be the most frequently used mechanisms in relation to the ISO 14 000 (mitigating climate change) and company-specific codes of conduct (countering bribery). 'Regular review and improvement processes' are considered by banks as the most relevant implementation mechanism for enhancing an instruments' impact (eight entries equally distributed both on instruments related to mitigating climate change and countering bribery) followed by 'setting of targets' that is mainly referred to climate change-related instruments. Instruments related to countering bribery (all represented by company-specific codes) score higher than the others with regard to the following mechanisms: regular monitoring of compliance, internal verification, internal and external communication, and disciplinary action in case of breaches.

The fact that banks attribute a greater effectiveness in improving their performance to internal procedures and to the proper implementation of CSR instruments rather than to external mechanisms, such as external-independent verification, external communication and stakeholder engagement, can be read as a sign of CSR embedment into corporate organizational structure.

Finally, we investigated the companies' awareness concerning the impact created by their social and environmental activities. There is a quite high awareness of the impact created outside the banks: ten companies (representing two-thirds of respondents) state that their activities serve as a model for other companies and help to spread knowledge or technologies. More than half of the respondents stress that their activities are building the conceptual basis for new legislation and are contributing to building capacity for society. Seven banks highlight that their CSR activities contribute to raising the standards of integrity and transparency of their business partners.

The results from the section on policy makers' intervention are very interesting. The question addressed to companies was if they wish policy makers to lend specific types of support or action. The majority of banks expect policy makers to 'help in increasing awareness' – mainly among consumers (12 entries), investors (11) and companies (ten) – and to 'build a receptive environment for CSR through the means of multi-stakeholder dialogue' and 'build the demand for SR funds by incentives or transparency requirements' (nine entries). Notably, companies do not wish policy makers to introduce new laws or better regulation. They rather see the role of policy maker in developing or encouraging voluntary standards and instruments in emerging issue areas, therefore confirming a greater trust in their voluntary intervention rather than in the normative one.

7.3 CONCLUSIONS: EMERGING ROLE OF INDIRECT ASPECTS OPENS NEW SCENARIO OF CSR IMPACT

Overall, the survey results confirm that the banking sector is putting a consistent effort on CSR practices and activities, attaining significant results: a large number of instruments are adopted, the surveyed banks state that CSR is not only used as a communication measure but is rather integrated into strategies and policies, even though this is done to a different degree and with different means. The banks questioned also show awareness on the importance of the impact they generate on the level of society and the environment. With the focus of our analysis on the three issue areas, it is worth specifically considering how these issue areas have been tackled in the different phases of the CSR process.[8]

Commenting on Figure 7.2 and reminding about the survey results, the specific issues are considered relevant by the large majority of banks which have declared to formulate policies and strategies to tackle them. At first sight we can observe that the three issue areas perform similarly with no significant differences along the whole CSR implementation process, except for countering bribery, which registers a decrease in the measurement of performance.

In general, the banks in our sample show a certain dynamic in considering the social and environmental consequences of their business even though some problems arise when it comes to the measurement of the CSR-related performance. As Figure 7.2 shows, the frequencies collected in the performance measurement are lowest. A partial explanation can be found with a typical measurement issue: the banks themselves in some cases declare that KPIs are hardly identified and sometimes are not

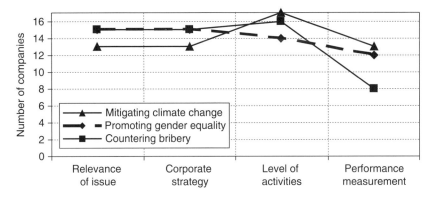

Source: Authors.

Figure 7.2   CSR implementation process

appropriate. A proof can be found in the bribery field where intermediary or proxy measures are often used instead of specific key performance indicators. Moreover, the number of answers given decreases considerably when looking at the perceived improvement of performances related to products and services provided (indirect impact via customers).

Focusing on the social and environmental responsibilities of the banks, the emerging role of indirect aspects of CSR is one of the main findings. Banks recognize the impact of their lending and investment operations. Also, the adoption of certain CSR instruments has a substantial influence on the loan appraisal process and clients' behaviour. For instance, the Equator Principles, a voluntary code regarding sustainability issues in investment and project financing, have been adopted by almost half of the banks.

The lack of adequate KPIs and capacity to tackle new issues in general clearly point to the need for greater co-operation among researchers, companies and policy makers in order to better deal with the multifaceted topic of sustainability.

NOTES

1. We would like to thank Sabina Nicolella (FEEM) and Peter Wilkinson for valuable comments.
2. The ethical and sustainable orientation is increasingly considered by different stakeholders: lenders/savers would like to know how banks channel their money; NGOs ask banks to indicate what the economic sectors financed by banks are; investors are worried that

the value of their shares can decrease if banks are involved in financial scandals or if banks finance companies that damage the environment or violate human rights. An evident sign of the progressive environmental care is the growth of the market for funds that invest exclusively in responsible companies (Jeucken 2004).

3. Germany (Deutsche Bank, Dresdner Bank, KfW Bankengruppe, West LB and HypoVereinsbank); United Kingdom (the Royal Bank of Scotland and the Cooperative Bank); Switzerland (UBS); France (Caisse Nationale des Caisses d'Epargne); The Netherlands (ABN AMRO); Italy (Unicredit Group, Gruppo San Paolo IMI and Gruppo Monte dei Paschi di Siena); Belgium (DEXIA and KBC); Spain (Banco Bilbao Vizcaya Argentaria and Caja Madrid).

4. The desk selection was an important starting point for our survey. It was conducted between May and October 2005 according to five criteria: (1) analysis of market leaders/ multinational enterprises (our elaboration on the basis of Mediobanca's (2003) banking sector research); (2) analysis of CSR reporting tools and websites; (3) SRI indexes composition and SR funds (Sustainable Investment 2005); (4) ranking of CSR performances (Stock at Stake 2004; Clausen et al. 2005; SustainAbility 2005; The Global 100 2005); and (5) interviews with selected CSR sector experts.

5. All of the banks have established flexible working time arrangements; 14 banks (representing 82 per cent of our sample) support employees with care responsibilities; ten banks (59 per cent) have established return regulations after parental leave.

6. 15 companies (representing 88 per cent of our sample) have established a regular statistical review on gender equality and diversity; 13 banks (76 per cent) have a range of means for supporting professional careers and consider gender equality and diversity at different stages of employment; and 11 (65 per cent) ensure gender equality of full-time workers and part-time workers/home workers.

7. These are loans secured against future resource revenues, especially oil revenues. Banks risk being complicit with the misappropriation of state funds unless provisions are in place to check that loans are properly used and to ensure that the fiscal management of the borrowing government is transparent.

8. The results have been organized systematically around different steps. In order to appear in the index, banks should have: (1) attributed a high/rather high strategic importance to the issue areas (relevance of issue); (2) set up a separate policy on the issue concerned or integrated the issue into existing corporate strategies and policies (corporate strategy); (3) ticked more than one-third of the activities given (level of activities); and (4) must have declared to be able to demonstrate an improvement of performance within the three issue areas (performance measurement).

8 Driving on CSR: SMEs in the automotive supply chain

**Tamás Pálvölgyi, János Szlávik,
Noémi Csigéné Nagypál, Miklós Füle and
Mária Csete**

8.1 INTRODUCTION

Small and medium-sized enterprises (SMEs)[1] play an important role in the economy of the European Union: 99 per cent of the companies operating in the enlarged EU are SMEs and they employ about two-thirds of all employees working in the EU. As EU Commissioner Günter Verheugen states, '[t]hey are an essential source of jobs, create entrepreneurial spirit and innovation in the EU and are thus crucial for fostering competitiveness and employment.' (European Commission 2005b, p. 3).

Although Corporate Social Responsibility (CSR) is mostly linked to big multinational enterprises, the role of SMEs is not negligible given their economic role, their social embedding and their primary relation with local communities. Therefore, their voluntary, beyond-compliance responsibility can contribute substantially to sustainable development. While there is some research on the CSR activities of European SMEs,[2] there is scant information available about their resulting performance and impact.[3] This impression was also underlined by the European Multistakeholder Forum on CSR in 2004, which stated that 'we know relatively little about the scale and impact of CSR amongst SMEs' (EU MSF 2004b, 2004c).

In the present chapter we present the results of a survey that was carried out among 20 Austrian and Hungarian SMEs from the automotive sector in 2005 and 2006. Its aim is to contribute to a better understanding of CSR in SMEs by applying the methodology presented in Chapter 4.

The survey focuses on how companies commit themselves to CSR, how they implement CSR instruments and devote resources to it, and how the CSR activities by companies influence the companies' social and environmental performance. Finally, indicative findings as regards the sustainability impact achieved outside of the companies is examined. In terms of CSR issue areas and in line with this book's emphasis, we focus on the environment as well as gender equality and countering bribery. With regard to the environment, we widen the field of issues beyond those of the mitigation of climate change and chemical risk to include a category of other environmental impacts, for example, those on waste, water and air. This is to achieve a more comprehensive picture of SME environmental activities as a known focus of their voluntary activities.

8.2   THE SURVEY

Since CSR is typically linked to multinational enterprises and SMEs are less active in explicitly engaging in this field, our survey concentrates on companies with some experience in CSR-related activities. This includes environmental management, support of NGOs and donating or sponsoring. In order to represent the differences between old and new EU Member States, it was decided that companies from both groups of countries would be incorporated in the survey. Two countries were selected: Austria and Hungary.

In terms of industry, we chose the automotive sector because it is a significant sector in both countries and SMEs are the typical kind of supplier in this sector. Furthermore, the issue areas in which we are interested are relevant in this sector.

Fifteen of the 25 (40 per cent) Hungarian and five of the 28 (17.8 per cent) Austrian companies answered our questionnaire. With a sample of 20 SMEs, our survey results are not representative, especially with regard to Austria, but can provide a good qualitative impression. A comparison of the two countries is possible only to a limited extent because of the small sample in the case of Austria.

When now presenting the survey results, we shall distinguish between the Austrian and Hungarian SMEs only when there are significant deviations between them; in all other cases we shall treat them as one sample.

8.2.1   Commitment of SMEs to CSR

In the first set of survey questions we enquired about the companies' understanding of their voluntary commitment to society and the environment, their motivation and the aims connected to carrying out CSR. Additionally, we questioned them on their view as concerns the benefits they provide to the local community. The main results are presented below.

Sixty per cent of the companies state that compliance with mandatory legislation is 'very relevant' for their social and environmental activities. The remaining companies consider compliance as 'fairly relevant'. While this may indicate that some companies are not absolutely compliant with legislation, it is more likely that some of them are not absolutely aware of the relevant legislation as concluded by the Observatory of European SMEs (Observatory of European SMEs 2002a, 2002b). All respondents state that they meet non-mandatory government recommendations to some extent. However, only 20 per cent of companies regard their social and environmental activities as going clearly beyond compliance; however, more than 50 per cent said that it is very or fairly relevant. This focus of the sampled SMEs on compliance as opposed to beyond compliance is at odds with the European Commission's understanding of CSR as a clear beyond-compliance instrument.

When it comes to the motivation for engaging in CSR, cost saving is the most important factor, being marked by more than half of the companies. It seems that SMEs perceive CSR to be a 'win-win' solution. The cost aspect is followed by the desire to 'meet a fundamental value of the company', 'to contribute to sustainable development' and to 'meet customer or supply chain expectations'. None of the companies through CSR aims to 'improve access to capital', to 'prevent or obviate anticipated legislation', to 'benefit from public programmes and subsidies' or to 'from networking activities'. It is realistic that SMEs cannot influence legislation, especially if networking is not a motivation factor for accepting responsibility. From this survey, cooperation between SMEs, at least in the field of social and environmental responsibility, seems to be negligible. Socially Responsible Investment (SRI) is also an instrument available only to larger companies; therefore improving access to capital is not a significant motivation for SMEs.

When asked about what benefits the SMEs provide for the local communities in which they operate, the most important benefit that our respondents highlight is the provision of good workplaces. This is followed by the reduction of negative environmental impacts. About half the respondents think that their company contributes to local competitiveness while only one-third estimates that it serves as an example for others. Investment in the local community was not seen as 'very relevant' by any of the respondents, but at least as 'fairly relevant' by 20 per cent (three respondents).

8.2.2 CSR in Strategy and Planning Activities

After examining the companies' commitment to CSR, we investigated the integration of CSR into strategy or planning. We first aimed to gain information about which social and environmental issues the companies regarded as the most relevant for their operation. The question was open – issues were not specified.

The areas that the participating companies declared to be the most important include the reduction of energy and resource use as well as cost saving (five companies) – which is not, strictly speaking a CSR issue. Though judging on the basis of a low number of respondents, these answers suggest that issues are attributed strategic relevance that imply cost reduction – although economic benefit is only one of the motives for engaging in CSR that were specified by the SMEs. Furthermore, providing good workplaces was mentioned as being important by two companies, improving workplace safety by one company and raising environmental awareness by an additional two companies. This shows that employees are important for the voluntary commitment of SMEs in general and may even indicate that they are also relevant actors in the conceptualization and implementation of the CSR engagement of SMEs. This is also in accord with the fact that SMEs see their most important role in the local community as providing good workplaces.

Interestingly, we find that companies implementing the ISO 14 001 standard are more active in answering this question and that their answers are more specific than those by the other companies. Management standards seem to be useful in defining strategic issues and targets for the company.

When focusing on the predefined CSR issues, the most important issue is mitigating negative environmental impacts other than climate change and chemical risks, which was ascribed high importance by 68 per cent of the respondents (Figure 8.1). The countering of bribery is considered highly important by 47 per cent and the promotion of gender equality by 34 per cent. Chemical risk management is of uncertain importance – the relevance of the issue is mostly dependent on the technology used by the company. It is interesting that climate change is assessed as less strategically important

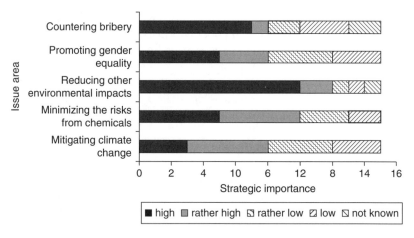

Source: Authors.

Figure 8.1   Strategic importance of selected CSR issue areas

than the other issues. This might indicate that local challenges – ranging from female representation in the company to direct pollution – are given more weight than global ones.

How systematically do our SME respondents tackle the social and environmental issues which they consider to be strategically relevant? Our survey shows that none of the companies state that they use voluntary activities 'as a reaction to pressures'. This is in line with the fact that, contrary to multinational enterprises, societal pressure is not typical for SMEs. Most of the respondents see voluntary activities as 'a useful addition' to their operations (six out of 15). However, it is striking that only four respondents carry out voluntary activities 'as an integral part of their operations'. Four companies consider them as 'nice to have'.

When enquiring in more depth about how the SMEs plan and select voluntary activities, most of the respondents say they 'react to opportunities'. Five out of 15 respondents – mostly those that regard voluntary activities as an integral part of their operation – 'select activities strategically'. 'Employees' suggestions' are named by three companies and the 'needs of external stakeholders' by two. Though on a low empirical basis, this may indicate that bottom-up initiatives can be more relevant for SMEs than stakeholder pressure. We also evaluate how the companies translate their social and environmental responsibility into daily operations (Figure 8.2).

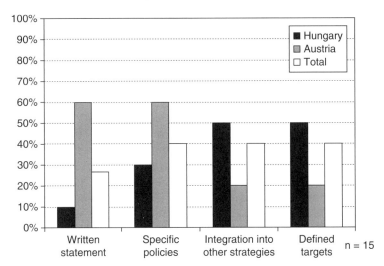

Source: Authors.

Figure 8.2   Ways of translating corporate responsibility into daily operations

The high proportion of written statements and specific policies among Austrian respondents can partly be attributed to their widespread use of ISO 14 001 which requires such statements. Relatively more Hungarian than Austrian companies claim to integrate responsibility into other strategies and define respective targets. Those ways of translating responsibility into daily practices that are more formal (for example, specific policies) and easier to publish (in a written statement instead of defined targets that are not necessarily given in written form) seem more popular among Austrian companies. This might reflect that the application of specific instruments is more 'professional' in Austria than Hungary. However, it should be kept in mind that the rate of medium-sized companies was higher in the Austrian sample which might bias our result.

8.2.3   Implementation of CSR

We assumed that implementation plays a crucial role in achieving a high CSR performance. As a consequence, the survey enquired in some detail about implementation. First, we asked the companies about the formal CSR instruments. The number of companies who (a) know the instrument but do not use it, (b) do use the instrument and (c) are planning to use it in the near future are summarized in Table 8.1. The general CSR instruments enquired after in our survey are relatively unknown to the respondents and are rarely used by them. Two groups of instruments are an exception, however, management systems and ways of connecting to employees and external stakeholders.

Quality management is the most widespread, especially ISO 9001, but also sector standards. While it is not directly related to sustainability, the management system's second one in terms of being widespread is ISO 14 001. It is the only environmental management standard applied by the sample companies, and is used by almost half of the companies (7 out of 15). Split up nationally, these make up 30 per cent of the Hungarian respondents and 80 per cent of the Austrians – a significant difference. Among the tools to connect with internal and external stakeholders, 'monitoring employee satisfaction' is the most common. Our survey reveals that some of the sample SMEs are required to use specific CSR instruments by their customers. For example, ISO 9001 is a requirement for half of the Hungarian respondents (five out of ten) and TS 16 949 is required from 40 per cent of the Austrian companies (two out of five). In Hungary environmental management standards are completely neglected by the customers of our sample companies, while in the Austrian sample quality and environmental management standards are equally important for customers.

Table 8.1 CSR instruments used, known and planned to be implemented by SMEs

Instruments	The respondent SME... (n = 15)		
	knows the instrument	uses the instrument	plans to start using it in next 2–5 years
Codes of conduct			
Global Compact	1	–	–
Partnership agreement with trade unions	4	–	–
Guidelines by your industry association	1	1	–
Company-specific code(s)	–	2	2
Management systems			
ISO 14 001	4	7	–
EMAS	3	–	–
ISO 9001	3	11	1
ISO/TS 16 949	2	5	–
VDA 6.1, 6.4	2	3	–
SA 8000	1	–	–
Company-specific management system(s)	1	–	1
Ways of connecting to employees and external stakeholders			
Monitoring employee satisfaction	1	13	–
Involving employees into decision making	3	8	–
Collecting information about/from external stakeholders (for example, surveys, complaints management, focus groups)	3	8	–
Consultation with external stakeholders and dialogue (for example, in non-financial accounting or auditing, roundtables)	2	6	–
Including external stakeholders in decision making (for example, in working groups, joint initiatives)	2	2	–

Table 8.1 (continued)

Instruments	The respondent SME . . . (n = 15)		
	knows the instrument	uses the instrument	plans to start using it in next 2–5 years
Participation in local partnerships	3	2	–
Non-financial accounting and reporting			
Non-financial reporting	4	3	–
Labels, awards (known, gained)			
National eco-label	4	–	–
EU Eco-label	4	–	–
Gender, diversity or family-friendly workplace awards	2	1	–
National entrepreneurship award	3	2	–

Source: Authors.

As regards other forms of supply chain relations, a third of the 15 companies do not receive any support for engaging in CSR from their customers. The most common form of relating to their SME suppliers is customers' communication of their own company values to them and encouraging customers to reflect them. Few customers collect data about their SME suppliers' environmental and social performance or monitor it. Only one company marked that it received training or assistance from their customers.

When it comes to corporate citizenship activities, SMEs in our sample mostly support sport, culture and youth, as already revealed by earlier surveys (see Observatory of European SMEs 2002a, 2002b). The most frequent types of community activity are donating and sponsoring. Environmental protection is not supported by any of the companies asked; even those companies that are committed to improving their environmental performance remain passive in terms of environmental protection in the community context.

Geographically, corporate citizenship activities are mostly local (10 out of 15 respondents). Some bigger companies marked the regional level, while only one company, operating in Budapest, claims to engage at national level. This means that the smaller the company is, the more likely it is to concentrate its voluntary activity at local level.

8.2.3.1 Activities in selected CSR issue areas

In order to gain an indication as to the companies' performance in selected sustainability issues, we asked the companies what concrete activities they carry out in the field of mitigating climate change, chemical risk management, combating other environmental effects, promoting gender equality and countering bribery.

Most respondents (8 out of 15) admit that they do not contribute 'beyond compliance' to the mitigation of climate change. The most frequent reason they mention is the self-assessment that their 'company's activities do not contribute to climate change significantly'. However, some of these companies that say on a general level they do not go beyond compliance with regard to climate issues, ticked climate-related activities listed in the questionnaire. This might indicate that some companies do not link energy saving or efficiency to the mitigation of climate change, or that they consider their activities only as cost saving efforts. The most frequent activities marked are improving energy efficiency and the monitoring of energy consumption. Working to reduce CO_2 emissions from transport is less frequent. One of the reasons might be that SMEs concentrate on manufacturing – although they will probably produce CO_2 through transporting inputs and final products. Changing to renewable energies and technology change are also less frequent, presumably because these activities require more resources and a more strategic approach.

With regard to chemical risk management, 10 out of 15 (66 per cent) companies claim to work towards reducing the risk from chemicals. Five companies answered negatively to this question; three of them because the use of chemicals was assessed as not significant, and two because they think an engagement in this area is not expected from the company. Still, the majority of the companies polled deal with the issue. The reason for this might be that, in contrast to climate change as a global problem, the risk from chemical use affects not only the immediate environment of the company but also the health of employees, and, as indicated earlier, SMEs are committed to providing good workplaces and improve working conditions. Another reason for the high activity might be that chemical risk management is a strictly regulated area and control is also quite developed.

Four out of five (80 per cent) Austrian and only four out of ten (40 per cent) Hungarian companies state they are engaged in the promotion of gender equality. This might point to the difference between the regulatory and socio-cultural environments in the two countries with regard to this issue. The most frequent reason mentioned for not engaging in gender equality was that the issue is not seen as a problem in the company because of the low representation of female employees. The most frequent CSR activities that the SMEs carry out in this regard are the consideration of gender equality in staff recruitment and flexible working time solutions.

With regard to the countering of bribery, most of the companies (12 out of 15) indicated no activities in this field. Only three companies have relevant guidelines, one also claims to review risk and another to rely on informal processes. None of the companies has a fully-fledged anti-bribery policy. These results point to a gap between the rhetoric and reality of CSR with regard to this issue: in the first section of the survey the SMEs questioned indicated that countering bribery was of high strategic importance to them, but we later found that they had hardly taken any action to implement this strategic assessment.

8.2.3.2   CSR responsibilities and expenditure

Organizational responsibilities represent the frame for implementing CSR. Our survey shows that environmental protection is the issue area for which most of the SMEs have established responsibilities. These are either assigned to the functional (6 of 15) or top management (5 of 15) level. Gender and bribery issues are primarily dealt with by the top management, which reflects that SMEs usually are not so functionally differentiated as to have functional managers for these issues. Only one company indicated that gender equality is handled by the human resource manager, which strengthens the impression that the issue is not very developed in organizational terms. The responsibility for corporate citizenship activities lies with the top management in all responding companies.

In order to deepen our impression of implementation efforts, we asked the SMEs about their expenditure as regards implementation of CSR in the past three years and in the future. None of the companies state that their expenditure on CSR activities has decreased during the last three years. Rather, the majority of SMEs (7 out of 11) that answered state that their costs have increased. Among these, five firms plan further minor increases, and one further major increases in CSR implementation costs. The remaining four companies claim that their CSR expenditure was stable. For the future, these SMEs plan to increase it a little. According to these figures, the SMEs that replied seem to regard CSR as a 'growth' area.

8.2.3.3 Barriers to social and environmental activities of SMEs and desired policy support

We asked the SMEs about what barriers they experienced in carrying out social and environmental activities, and what barriers they suspected existed generally for SMEs (Figure 8.3). The most frequently mentioned barrier both generally and for the company itself was the lack of financial and/or time resources – an answer, however, that jars with the SMEs' frequent indication that they carry out CSR in order to reduce costs. The lack of market demand was considered similarly problematic in general, but

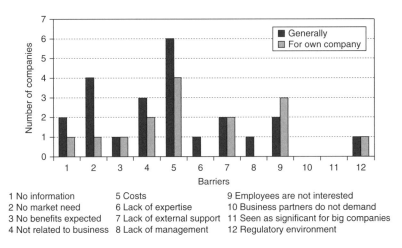

1 No information   5 Costs   9 Employees are not interested
2 No market need   6 Lack of expertise   10 Business partners do not demand
3 No benefits expected   7 Lack of external support   11 Seen as significant for big companies
4 Not related to business 8 Lack of management   12 Regulatory environment

Source: Authors.

Figure 8.3   The barriers to social and environmental activities of SMEs

it was less frequently mentioned as a barrier for the given company. For the company itself, the lack of employees' interest, however, was highly important. This is the only factor that companies marked more frequently as a barrier for themselves than generally. The reason for this might be that companies see internal factors more clearly within the company than in the case of other companies.

Respondents were furthermore asked how industrial associations (open-ended question) and policy makers can foster CSR. With regard to associations, most companies suggest training (seven companies) or assistance and information (four). Some also mentioned enabling communication, financial and legal support. From policy makers, companies mostly expect financial support (8 out of 15). Also, governments should provide an appropriate legal framework for corporate action on social and environmental issues and should encourage respective international agreements (8 out of 15). While they should raise awareness (above all among consumers) and provide training, support though networking, mandatory reporting requirements and the special recognition of sustainable products in public purchasing was not or rarely demanded.

8.2.4   Sustainability Impact through CSR

Since the impact that corporate social behaviour generates with regard to society and the environment is the core interest of our research, the last section of the questionnaire addressed the sustainability performance of the companies and its measurement.

Less than half of the companies (8 out of 15) state that they measure their social and environmental performance, with a further respondent indicating that its measurement system is under development. Only three companies specify indicators by which they measure their sustainability performance in the issue areas we focus on.[4] When asked how they use their performance data, most respondents point to internal control but four of them referred to reporting as well. Data is verified externally only in one case. This picture shows that in the surveyed SMEs, measurement and verification of sustainability performance – which is a crucial precondition for improving this performance – are still underdeveloped. The use of environmental management systems, which typically require performance measurement, is a crucial determinant for collecting data in the first place.[5]

Lastly, we asked companies how they themselves estimated their CSR activities to have affected their sustainability performance and respective impact.[6] In the area of energy saving and climate change 6 of the 15 respondents experience their improvement as low, while one claims a medium and one a high improvement of their performance through CSR. The rest could not specify performance changes. This rather poor result is in accord with the fact that this area is regarded as being of low strategic importance. In the case of chemical risk management the picture is slightly more positive, with five of the SMEs presuming low and five medium improvements, and the rest not providing any estimates. Although this area was of higher strategic importance, none of the companies indicated high improvement. In the area of 'other environmental problems' the sustainability performance of the SMEs is most positively affected by CSR: two companies claim low, six companies medium and three companies a high improvement. Improvement in the realm of gender equality is evaluated by seven companies. Most of them (five respondents) experience low, one company medium and one high improvement. Bribery is the least frequently evaluated area; only two companies state low improvement in this area. One of the reasons for not evaluating countering bribery might be that respondents might have had the impression that by stating improvement in this field, they would have admitted earlier poor performance.

8.3   CONCLUSIONS

This chapter presented the results of a survey on CSR practices of 20 Hungarian and Austrian SMEs in the automotive supply chain. Summing up our main results, we find a majority of the companies (60 per cent) state that compliance with mandatory legislation is 'very relevant' for their social and environmental activities; the remaining companies consider compliance as 'fairly relevant'. It is likely that some companies are in reality not absolutely compliant with legislation, but more likely some of them are not absolutely aware of the relevant legislation. All of the respondents state that they meet non-mandatory government recommendations to some extent, but only three out of 15 companies regard their social and environmental activities as going clearly beyond compliance.

Cost saving is the most frequently mentioned factor for motivating acceptance of responsibility, marked by more than half of the companies. This motive is followed by 'meeting a fundamental value of the company', 'contributing to sustainable development' and meeting 'customer expectations'. This contrasts with earlier research which suggested ethical considerations to predominate.

SMEs, even those that are committed to CSR, know and apply relatively few instruments, and they do not plan to implement more in the near future. Quality management is common, and ISO 14 001 is also applied by almost half of the respondents. However, it should be kept in mind that this was one of the company selection criteria.

Employees seem to be considered as a crucial resource by responding SMEs. They are important actors in the case of CSR too, as bottom-up initiatives (involving employees in decision making, reacting to employees' suggestions to select voluntary activities) are relatively important. Most companies monitor employee satisfaction and many of them mention improving working conditions or awareness raising among employees as the most important social and environmental issues for the company's operation.

The difference between Austrian and Hungarian respondent companies is less significant than we expected. One of the reasons can be that Hungarian companies (after two years of accession to the EU) are very motivated and companies in our sample and in the sector analyzed work for the international market. Practical implementation, however, is more developed in Austria; four out of five respondents operate ISO 14 001, while only three out of ten Hungarian respondents. CSR instruments are more consciously and professionally applied.

Regarding sustainability impact achieved through CSR, it is difficult to track the results of the implementation of specific measures. This is both because measurement of performance is not widespread among SMEs and because the survey did not provide for triangulation of whether improvements were indeed caused by CSR, rather than other factors. The companies' estimation of their own relative improvement, however, can provide an indication. The companies gave different estimates for different fields and seem to have provided cautious answers, not wanting to overestimate the improvement of their performance. Minimizing environmental impacts other than energy use and efficiency, climate change and chemical risk management is the issue area in which the highest improvement is claimed. Countering bribery is a critical area as companies usually cannot measure performance in spite of its high strategic importance. Success factors for sustainability improvements are difficult to identify through a survey. However, ISO 14 001 can be assumed to be a useful instrument to define targets, foster measurement and improve environmental performance. SMEs have less capacity to develop company-specific instruments; therefore standardized instruments are more important than in the case of large enterprises.

The sample companies find that further SME involvement in CSR can be fostered by training and assistance from associations. From policy makers they would welcome not only financial support, but also awareness raising. As the results of our survey indicate, such measures could help in enhancing small businesses' sustainability, especially in the environmental realm.

NOTES

1. On the definition of SMEs, see European Commission (2003).
2. DTI et al. (2002); EU MSF (2004a); Hillary (2000); Observatory of European SMEs (2002a, b), Sarbutts (2003).
3. Among the few studies, the clear focus is on environmental performance. See Ammenberg and Hjelm (2003) or Friedman and Miles (2001).
4. The indicators include 'energy use', 'number of hazardous materials/total number of materials' and 'rate of recycling of waste and waste water' as environmental indicators. Indicators for gender equality are 'rate of women in management' and 'employee satisfaction'.
5. Six out of seven SMEs with a performance measurement system operate ISO 14 001.
6. Since the companies use various indicators, a comparison of improvement based on concrete indicators was impossible.

9 CSR practices across four sectors: a synthesis of the surveys

Katharina Schmitt

9.1 INTRODUCTION

This chapter synthesizes the four sector surveys presented in the preceding chapters. It provides evidence from the empirical research carried out among 49 European companies in four sectors in late 2005. The aim of the synthesis is to present similarities and differences in companies' Corporate Social Responsibility (CSR) perceptions, policies and implementation approaches (and hence CSR output and outcome) across sectors, issue areas and company sizes. The comparison is made in percentages in order to compare the fractions of the samples at hand. Given the sometimes small and also varying sizes of the samples, and given the fact that the samples are not random, this is not meant as a representative characterization. Through the synthesis, we identify three remarkable patterns. Firstly, independent of sector and size, the companies frame the concept of CSR not so much as a beyond-compliance strategy but rather as a means to enhance compliance with law. Secondly, by and large, the companies' CSR approaches are linked to and coherent with their core business, rather than 'bolt-on'. Thirdly, there is a distinct divide between the oil and banking sectors, on the one hand, and the fish processing industry and automotive sector SMEs, on the other, with regard to the development stage (or 'maturity') of their CSR approaches. In general, sector differences seem to better account for variance in CSR output and outcome than differences in issues or company size.

9.2 COMMON INTERPRETATION OF RESPONSIBILITY: FOCUSING ON COMPLIANCE

When asked how they understand their social responsibility, an overwhelming majority of companies, independent of sector and size, emphasizes the relevance of complying with legislation in relation to carrying out activities that go beyond legislation: all respondents in the oil and fish processing sector, 80 per cent in the banking sector and 60 per cent in the SME sample answer that 'compliance' is very relevant to their understanding of their responsibility. In each of the sectors at least twice as many companies answer that 'compliance' is highly relevant compared to 'going beyond compliance'. A large proportion of the companies thus have perceptions which are at odds with the widely used definition of CSR as voluntary, that is, beyond compliance that is upheld, among others, by the European Commission (2001, p. 6). Rather, the surveyed companies' interpretation stands in line with a definition first postulated by Carroll in 1991. He differentiates four kinds of social responsibilities that constitute total CSR: economic, legal, ethical and philanthropic. According to Carroll, legal responsibilities are 'the ground rules under which businesses must operate' (Carroll 1991, p. 41) and, thus, complying with the law is defined as a central part of CSR. For companies, this definition implies that by merely fulfilling legal obligations, they can already claim to be acting 'responsibly'.

9.3   CSR APPROACHES IN LINE WITH CORE BUSINESS OPERATIONS

Another finding across the different sectors is that the companies develop CSR approaches that are largely in line with their core business operations. This starts with the definition of which CSR issues are relevant for the companies. As could be expected, companies in the four sectors give varying prominence to different CSR issues when translating their commitment into strategies (Figure 9.1). Systematically, companies regard such issues as important that are tightly related to their core business: anti-corruption integrity is crucial for the licence to operate for both banks and oil companies, the latter also being concerned about climate change, while fish processors economically depend on sustainable fisheries, and the automotive industry is under pressure from environmental concerns.

When it comes to the implementation of CSR through standardized as well as company-specific CSR instruments and activities, the focus on core business again becomes apparent. In the case of standardized instruments, for example, companies tend to use instruments closely linked to their core business – such as the Responsible Care Initiative in the oil sector; the MSC and HACCP certifications for sustainable seafood and food safety among fish processors; the UNEP Statement by Financial Institutions on the Environment and Sustainable Development in the banks; or ISO 14001

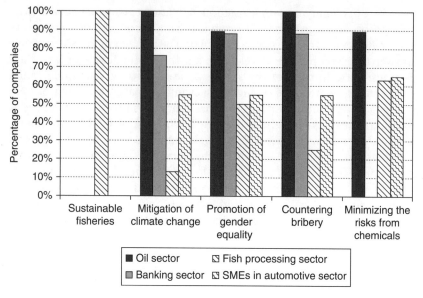

Source: Author.

Figure 9.1   Rating of CSR issues as 'highly relevant', compared across the sectors

and 9001 among automotive SMEs. Especially in the oil and bank samples, however, instruments with a broader coverage – and higher profile – such as the Global Compact and GRI reporting are also popular.

The link of CSR to core business is partially surprising because it could be presumed that changes to core business activities require larger amounts of financial and human resources, while more 'bolt-on' CSR approaches might be a softer and ultimately less costly option for companies. We conclude from this that most of our responding companies seem indeed committed to tackling the sustainability impact of their core operations, though this observation does not yet allow conclusions on the effectiveness of these efforts.

9.4   DIFFERING DEVELOPMENT STAGES IN STRATEGIZING AND IMPLEMENTING CSR

A central theme when comparing the survey results is that the sampled oil companies and banks in many respects seem more advanced in their CSR approaches than the fish processors and automotive sector SMEs. We find evidence for this along the whole implementation path.

This becomes first obvious when the companies formulate their responsibility in corporate statements. The prevalence of such statements and the issues they cover differ significantly across the sectors. Corporate statements are most widespread in the oil and banking sectors where most of the CSR issues targeted are covered. This is followed by the fish processing sector where only a few of the issues are covered and where the statements seem to have been introduced considerably later than in the oil companies and banks.

Secondly, we find sector differences when it comes to developing a strategic approach to CSR. Having described above that companies perceive sustainability issues as relevant that link up with their core business, we also find that companies from the oil and banking sectors more often and more broadly assess a CSR issue as being of high importance to their business as compared to respondents from the SME or fish processing sectors. While this may mean that SMEs and fish processing companies are less affected than the other sectors by the CSR issues we analysed, it can also indicate that the first two sectors are less advanced than oil companies and banks in systematically identifying and evaluating CSR issues and their relevance for the own business.

Thirdly, different development stages of the sectors' CSR approaches can also be discerned when looking at the companies' target setting practices in relation to the issue areas covered in this book. The oil companies again spearhead the trend: almost all of them have introduced targets with regard to issues perceived to be of high relevance, in this case mitigating climate change. The banks in this case lag behind and draw level with the fish processing and SME sectors where about half the companies have introduced targets in important issue areas.

Fourthly, the advancement of the oil companies and banks manifests itself in the use of CSR instruments to implement their social responsibility. If one looks at the total number of instruments implemented within one company, the oil companies and banks use an average of 17 instruments per company. The fish processors lag behind with nine instruments and the SMEs surveyed tend to make use of even less CSR instruments. The high instrument density in the first-mentioned sectors raises questions as regards instrument coordination and the depth to which instruments are indeed translated into changes in corporate behaviour. However, the sheer number of instruments adopted hints at a higher CSR 'maturity' of the oil and banking sectors and possibly to higher public awareness of these industries. Conspicuously, non-financial reporting as an externally-oriented tool is also much more common in the oil and banking samples than in the other

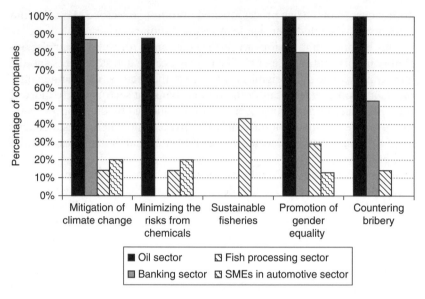

Source: Author.

Figure 9.2   Performance measurement, compared across sectors and issue areas

two samples. Note also that the use of tailor-made instruments, both codes of conduct and management systems, is more common in the oil companies and banks than in the other samples. This points to a greater fine-tuning of CSR approaches to company conditions and the specific business interests, often resulting from prolonged organizational processes.

Finally, the sector divide manifests itself in the systematic measurement of CSR performance. In the oil and banking sector samples performance measurement is rather common (between 70 and 97 per cent on average across the issue areas), while in the fish processing and SME sectors' sample it is rather exceptional (between 13 to 23 per cent on average, Figure 9.2). Looking at issues, we find that the respondents from the oil and banking sectors also tend to measure their performance in more issue areas than the other respondents. Both again point to different development stages in the sector samples' CSR practices. However, an intervening explanation could be the practice of non-financial reporting, based on GRI guidelines and measurement criteria, in most of the oil companies and banks. In contrast, hardly any fish processors and automotive SMEs apply non-financial reporting to their business.

The upshot is that the surveyed companies from the oil and banking sectors operate CSR approaches that are more differentiated, better integrated, implemented and monitored than the sustainability policies in the other two sectors. This may result from the longer-standing involvement of the oil and banking sectors in voluntary initiatives and the respective expertise developed over time. Possibly, it follows from their higher exposure to public scrutiny and pressures – which is, among others, due to the industries' economic power and corporate scandals. Finally, it may also have to do with the fact that oil companies and banks tend to be larger organizations that may be able to devote more resources to elaborating such efforts. However, the observed sector divide does not imply that other industries will lag behind for good: on the contrary, they might be able to learn from pioneer sectors, including which mistakes to avoid.

PART III

Assessing and explaining the sustainability
impact of CSR: case study findings

10 Standardized CSR and climate performance: why is Shell willing, but Hydro reluctant?

Elin Lerum Boasson and Jørgen Wettestad

10.1 INTRODUCTION

As shown in previous chapters, oil companies are, at least in their rhetoric, front-runners when it comes to engaging in Corporate Social Responsibility (CSR). In particular, they apply a large number of standardized CSR instruments. Further, they tend to perceive climate change as the most important of all societal challenges confronting the industry. Thus, one might assume that they would apply the CSR instruments they adhere to as tools in their efforts towards reducing their contribution to global warming.

Whether CSR merely serves to streamline company rhetoric or has an influence on actual efforts has been heatedly debated by stakeholders and scholars alike (for example, Sahlin-Andersson 2006). This chapter explores whether the CSR instruments of the oil industry have merely worked as a rhetorical means or whether they have contributed to alterations in climate-related practices. Two oil companies were selected for study, the comparatively small Norwegian company Hydro and the larger Dutch/British Shell. They were chosen due to their similarity in CSR portfolios and differences as companies, as elaborated below. Hydro's petroleum branch was merged with Statoil in spring 2007, after the period which is the focus of this study (St.prp.nr. 60 2006–2007).

Instruments with standardized approaches for coping with societal issues are central features of the CSR trend. Such instruments involve formal decisions concerning adherence; they are managed and promoted by dedicated secretariats, and they provide global meeting places for their adherents. Against this backdrop, we might expect the rules promoted by the CSR instruments to permeate company practices. On the other hand, the complexity of the societal issues in focus in this chapter, as well as the ambiguity of the instruments, their voluntary character and lack of forceful follow-up mechanisms, all give reason to suspect low effects (Miles et al. 2001; Sahlin-Andersson 2006). These contradictory expectations warrant an in-depth case study of actual effects, although it should also be borne in mind that, due to the recent character of the instruments, they may not yet have displayed their full potential.

The similarity of Hydro and Shell's CSR portfolios as contrasted with their highly differing company-specific characteristics make them interesting objects for comparative case study. This study looks at four instruments adhered to by the companies which include reference to climate change. Both companies participate in the United Nations Global Compact (GC), both apply the reporting framework of the Global Reporting Initiative (GRI), report to the Carbon Disclosure Project (CDP) and participate in the Global Gas Flaring Reduction Public-Private Partnership (GGFR) (Boasson et al., this volume). The first two initiatives target a broad range of societal challenges, including climate change, while the latter two focus explicitly on climate change. Further, GC, GRI and CDP are reporting instruments which indirectly entail changes in corporate behaviour by promoting disclosure practices (such as reporting in terms of targets and timetables) that give rise to specific internal rules and practices. The GGFR directly targets internal rules and practices. All four instruments aim at emission reductions and the development of low-carbon products, such as new renewable energy and the capture and storage of CO_2. This study focuses on the development of company rules and practices related to carbon emissions and low-carbon products. As all four instruments were introduced at the entrance to the millennium, the time span under study is from early 2000 until late 2006.

Despite the similarities in their CSR portfolios for the issues, differences between the two companies seem to have resulted in the CSR instruments affecting the climate practices of the two companies differently. Shell is an international oil giant, with a turnover 11 times higher than that of Hydro. Moreover, it is active in 145 countries. In contrast, Hydro was active in 40, but most of its activities were concentrated in Norway (Hydro 2006; Shell 2007). Both Hydro and Shell have been conglomerate companies encompassing a variety of industrial activities, but Shell concentrated its activities within the petroleum sector at an earlier stage than Hydro.

The core questions in this chapter are: (1) to what extent and how does the oil companies' application of CSR instruments affect their climate performance? and (2) how may any relation between instrument adherence and performance be explained? Answering these questions involves following a three-step causal chain. First, we explore the choice of CSR instruments. Second, we examine the effect of these CSR instruments on internal company rules. Next, we discuss how these CSR-induced rules affect the companies' relevant products and emissions, and then ultimately how the CSR instruments contribute to fighting climate change. Finally, varying explanatory approaches are applied in order to shed light on the relation between the instruments and the companies' practices. The applied approaches are the corporate strategy, the corporate culture and political-institutional settings in the environments in which the companies operate. Following the analytical language of organizational theory, these environments may be categorized in three ways: the companies' countries of origin, the global organizational field of petroleum and the global organizational field of CSR. These three kinds of environment may exert different kinds of pressure on the companies' choice of instruments, rule making and actual performance. A comparison of how the two companies have adapted to the instruments in focus may improve our understanding of how CSR instruments affect company-specific rules and the extent to which such rules actually determine a company's environmental impact.

This report is based on scrutiny of company publications, review of earlier research concerning the two companies and a series of in-depth interviews with company representatives.[1] The next section briefly describes the theoretical basis. The third section examines the relation between the CSR instrument portfolios of Hydro and Shell and their climate-related rules and practices. The fourth section looks at some factors that may have caused this pattern of relations. It discusses both internal organizational factors and the companies' responsiveness to the political-institutional environments in which they operate. Similarities in the companies' application of the CSR instruments may be explained by similarity in the internal or environmental factors, whereas differences may be owing to variations in the explanatory factors. The fifth section sums up the main empirical and theory findings.

10.2   THEORETICAL BASIS

We assume that adherence to an instrument may affect a company's rules relevant to activities that contribute to climate change (henceforth: climate-related rules), and that these rules may in turn govern the company's climate impact. The latter term refers to the company's actual emissions and its balance between high- and low-carbon products. We regard company employees as rule following actors (March and Olsen 1989). By 'rules' we mean the routines, procedures, roles, strategies, policies, organizational forms and methodologies through which the companies' activities are constructed (ibid., p. 22). Rules may be formalized or have a more informal, culturally defined character (Christensen and Røvik 1999).

The CSR instruments explored here involve overarching principles, policies, reporting standards, standardized codes of conduct, procedures and participation in learning forums.

The effects of instruments will be traced through a three-step causal chain – from output, to outcome and then to impact. Adherence to an instrument is regarded as an output of some kind of internal decision process. The nature of the instruments must be taken into account when describing the output. Instruments may vary with regard to scope, specificity and follow-up activities. The more kinds of social activities they encompass, the greater is their scope. Specificity relates to how concrete are the requirements they set. As to follow-up activities, these may vary in form and intensity. Follow-up mechanisms may focus on learning, naming and shaming, more formal sanctions and so on. The intensity will vary according to the capacity and priorities of the secretariats. When we describe the companies' output, this will be regarded as a dichotomy: either they adhere to the instruments or they do not.

Outcome is seen as the introduction of new rules or alteration of the company's original rules. The outcome will be deemed 'strong' when instrument-induced rules replace formerly prevalent rules, 'medium' when a substantial part of the prevalent rules have been replaced, 'weak' in instances of minor alterations and 'non-existent' when no substantial effects can be detected. If the rules of the company were in line with the instrument to begin with, adherence may contribute to raising their status. This we shall regard as a 'weak' effect.

Impact refers to outcome-induced change in company actions which affects the company's carbon emissions or the carbon content of their product portfolio. Thus we apply a more modest definition of impact than found elsewhere in this book. If such instrument-induced rules conflict with other company rules, are unachievable in technical terms or fail to be communicated to the right persons, they may not come to guide action (Brunsson 1993; March and Olsen 1989). The effects will be deemed to be strong when company actions are completely guided by instrument-induced outcomes. Instances of substantial but incomplete changes in actions are termed medium impact, whereas minor alternations are regarded as weak impact. When it is impossible to detect changes, there is no impact. This implies that the level of impact depends heavily on the level of outcome: only a high level of outcome may yield a high level of impact.

Our explanatory approach encompasses five complementary perspectives – two focusing on internal organizational conditions and three on the political-institutional settings of the external environments in which the companies participate. While the internal explanations indicate distinct boundaries between the companies and their environments, the three additional external explanations regard the boundaries between a company and its environment as arbitrarily drawn and quite blurred (Hoffman [1997] 2001, p. 7).

The corporate strategy perspective is the most common approach applied in CSR research (for example, Galbreath 2006; Kakabadse and Kakabadse 2007). The main assumption is that the executive managers will develop business strategies which set out objectives and means that guide actions taken by the company's sub-organizations. Further, that the corporate leaders are in full control of the corporation. The executives will ensure that the corporation as such will act as a unified, rational actor although it consists of bounded rational members (Simon 1947). By its strategic governance the executives will decide which instrument to adhere to, and how to transform these into formal rules and practices (Prakash 2001). Further, the employees will act in line with the strategic choices concerning application of CSR instruments. The leaders may want to use the instruments in order to improve the company's climate performance or to create tangible financial effects; or these aims may also be combined (Galbreath 2006). Formal coordination mechanisms, clear lines of command or internal networks will ensure that the aims of executives are communicated throughout the organization, whereas performance information is transferred back to the top. On this basis, we expect that *the executives will ensure that CSR output, outcome and impact are in line with the corporate strategy.*

Management literature has increasingly recognized that the corporate culture may affect the actions taken by corporations. Internal culture may either hinder or promote the instruments in rendering effects (Bonn and Fisher 2005). This perspective focuses on informal, normative rules and routines, and assumes that members of the organization act in accordance with what is perceived as culturally appropriate (Christensen and Røvik 1999; March and Olsen 1989). It is assumed that the corporations are strongly institutionalized, both vertically and horizontally. Vertical institutionalization implies that the members of the organization follow informal cultural rules rather than formal ones, whereas horizontal institutionalization implies that all of the company's sub-organizations are united by the same cultural traits (Christensen et al. 2004, p. 53; Krasner 1988). The company culture will be marked by events in the early years of its life, but also be malleable to incremental change. The circumstances under which a company was established will crucially affect its internal socialization processes and future development (Pierson 2004; Selznick 1957). Nonetheless, the original trajectory may be adjusted as a result of later events, such as performance crisis or diverse exogenous shocks. Climate-related rules and actions will reflect the general cultural traits and specific organizational experiences relating to environmental concerns occurring prior to adhering to the CSR instruments. On this basis, we expect that *companies will choose CSR instruments that fit the company culture; and the better the fit, the more profound the outcome and impact will be.*

While the corporate cultural perspective focuses predominantly inward, we now turn our focus towards the cultural expectations in the corporations' environments. Several CSR researchers have pointed out that CSR may best be understood as companies responding to pressures within their surroundings (for instance, Kakabadse et al. 2007, p. 30; Sahlin-Andersson 2006). By applying the organizational field concept we aim to specify the different political-institutional settings in which Hydro and Shell operate. An organizational field encompasses those organizations that, in the aggregate, constitute a recognized area of institutional life (Powell and DiMaggio 1991, p. 64). Both private and public organizations are included, and the organizations of a field are socially or functionally interconnected (Hoffmann [1997] 2001; Scott 1995). Organizations may be connected through market arrangements, be linked in legal agreements, work together towards common normative aims or share world views. Relations between the organizations will be maintained through participation in various market constellations, overarching organizations and forums. Each of the three fields may embody legitimatizing concepts (DiMaggio and Powell 1983; Hoffman [1997] 2001, p. 167). These may be at odds with each other. Further, some fields will exert pressure merely towards similarity in instrument adherence, while others may actually shape the companies' specific practices. Complex fields marked by uncertainty are liable to exert pressure towards output similarity, while strongly institutionalized fields may also shape company outputs and impacts (Colyvas and Powell 2006; Powell and DiMaggio 1991).

The corporations will be embedded in the business culture and traditions of their home country (Skjærseth and Skodvin 2003). Accordingly, they can be expected to follow their countries' traditional management approaches and ways of coping with climate change. In addition, the actions of governmental and non-governmental organizations, the national climate policy and the CSR activities of the country will create expectations concerning choice of CSR instruments and how these are to be transformed into rules and practices. On this basis, we expect that *the CSR output, outcome and impact will be in line with expectations in the company's country/ies of origin.*

The global organizational field of petroleum production represents the companies' business sector environment. It encompasses various corporations and countries engaged in petroleum production (Levy and Kolk 2002). Participants may work together on specific projects and joint ventures but will also meet in global petroleum production-related arenas. Expectations may emerge concerning salient CSR instruments and how these are to be transformed into rules and practices. Thus we expect that *the CSR output, outcome and impact will be in line with the expectations in the global field of petroleum.*

Lastly, we presume the existence of a *global organizational field of CSR* consisting of a broad range of organizations including multinational companies, consultants, various NGOs (environmental as well as business-related) and intergovernmental organizations. Although these may not be interlinked with the same stability as the organizations within the former fields, they will be connected through various collaborative arrangements and conferences. Thus common expectations will emerge with regard to the use of CSR instruments. This leads us to expect that *CSR output, outcome and impact will be in line with the expectations in the global field of CSR.*

10.3 EFFECTS OF CSR INSTRUMENTS

10.3.1 Output

Both Shell and Hydro adhere to the Global Compact (GC), the Global Reporting Initiative (GRI), the Carbon Disclosure Project (CDP) and the Global Gas Flaring Reduction Public-Private Partnership (GGFR). In the following we briefly discuss the nature of these instruments to shed light on what the companies accepted in deciding to adhere to these instruments.

The UN Secretary General launched the GC in 1999. It is based on ten principles, of which three are environmental: that business should support a precautionary approach to environmental challenges, undertake initiatives to promote greater environmental responsibility and encourage the development and diffusion of environmentally friendly technologies (Global Compact 2006). Adherence to the GC implies integrating these principles in internal practices (Ruggie 2002, p. 31). Participation requires a letter of commitment from the company's chief executive officer. Participants in the GC may take part in various learning forums at local or global levels (Sahlin-Anderson 2006). Except for soft guidance given through such participation, and a range of handbooks, the secretariat has not established any follow-up mechanisms. Both Hydro and Shell joined the GC in 2000.

The GRI aims to improve the companies' assessments of how they affect society, and ultimately influence their behaviour (GRI 2002, pp. 4, 9). The GRI gives direct guidance on defining report content and ensuring the quality of reported information and provides guidance on specific technical topics. These include reporting on climate issues by recommending measurement and disclosure of direct and indirect emissions and introduction of targets and timetables for emission reductions and development of renewable energy (GRI 2002, 2006b). The GRI guidelines recommend benchmarking against a range of verified indicators. In their reports adhering companies present a table clarifying how they relate to the GRI standard, but they may allow exemptions from the GRI recommendations. Issuing of training material and conferences on how to report are the only follow-up mechanisms. Shell embarked on alignment to the GRI as a pilot test company in 2001, while Hydro started to align to it the following year (Hydro 2002; Shell 2002, p. 48).

The CDP was initiated in 2002 by various environmental stakeholders and major global investors. The aim is to ensure that major multinationals respond to climate change (CDP 2006d). Although the specific focus of the CDP has evolved somewhat over time, its core elements are in line with GRI requirements (CDP 2006c). As a follow-up, the CDP discloses annual rankings of how the various responders perform. The aim is to encourage the companies to compete with each other in climate performance. Shell started to report to the CDP in 2002 and Hydro in 2003.

The GGFR was launched at the UN World Summit for Sustainable Development in 2002. Its aim is to reduce greenhouse gas emissions from flaring and venting at petroleum installations. The World Bank and Norway were initiators (Kaldany 2006). At present, the initiative includes a range of oil states, ten major oil companies and OPEC (World Bank 2004a). The GGFR does not provide any specific rules on how to cope with flaring and venting, but rather promotes learning. In 2004 the GGFR launched a voluntary standard for reducing gas flaring and venting (World Bank 2004b). The GGFR has set forth the goal of 'No continuous flaring and venting of associated gas, unless there are no feasible alternatives.' The standard focuses specifically on how to improve the market for gas – for example, by establishing required infrastructure, and aiming to make it profitable for companies to sell gas. The GGFR provides soft guidance in the form of arranging conferences, publishing reports and assessment tools. Shell engaged in the GGFR in 2002, while Hydro joined in 2003.

Table 10.1 sums up the features of the four instruments.

10.3.2 Outcome

Both Shell and Hydro have participated in GC learning forums, and both refer to the GC in their annual reports (Hydro 2002, 2006; Shell 2005). It was indicated in the interviews that the GC adherence confirmed their companies' good intentions and support to the UN. Neither of the companies

Table 10.1   CSR output: features of the instruments adhered to by Hydro and Shell

	Scope	Specificity	Follow-up
GC	Multi-issue	Unspecific	Learning forums/material
GRI	Multi-issue	Indirectly specific	Learning forums/material
CDP	One issue	Indirectly specific	Ranking
GGFR	Parts of an issue	Unspecific	Learning forums/material

Source: Authors.

seems to have launched internal efforts aiming to transform the principles of the GC into company-specific rules. Our respondents made it clear that those responsible for climate efforts had little knowledge of the GC, whereas the CSR persons considered it irrelevant with regard to climate concerns. Thus, for the GC, the pattern of no significant outcome is the same in the two companies.

Turning to the GRI, Shell was already in line with the requirements of the GRI Sustainability Reporting Framework for reporting targets and timetables for overall greenhouse gas emissions, flaring and energy efficiency prior to its adherence to the instrument (Shell 1998, Shell 2005). More recently, Shell has started to follow the GRI requirements concerning reporting on emissions stemming from use of its products. Our interviewees pointed out that Shell's adherence to the GRI confirmed its strategy chosen in the late 1990s. Nonetheless, this approach is strengthened albeit not induced by the GRI as such. In contrast to this, there are substantial discrepancies between Hydro's internal rules and the GRI Sustainability Reporting Principles. Neither Hydro's business principles nor its climate policy are aligned to the GRI framework for reporting on climate-related targets and timetables (Hydro 2003, 2004). Neither has Hydro followed the recommendation to report on indirect emissions. Hydro does, however, report its direct emissions – a practice started before it began reporting in alignment to the GRI. Hence, we may conclude that adherence to the GRI has hardly produced tangible effects on Hydro's company-specific rules.

Both Hydro's and Shell's first reports to the CDP were brief, but their most recent responses have been far more detailed (CDP 2006a, 2006b). The patterns of company responses are the same as for the GRI: Shell acted much in line with the requirements at the outset and has continued to align itself, while Hydro has refrained from doing so.

Both companies have participated actively in the GGFR collaboration. The initiative was not well known among corporate-level respondents, but

Table 10.2   CSR outcome of instrument adherence in Hydro and Shell

	Hydro	Shell	In line with instruments	Output
Targets and timetables	No	Yes	GRI, CDP	Strengthens Shell's initial approach
Disclose emissions	Yes	Yes	GRI, CDP, GGFR	Strengthens their initial approaches
Disclose indirect emissions	No	Yes	GRI, CDP	Induced by GRI/ CDP in Shell

Source: Authors.

the practitioners interviewed valued it. The practitioners stressed that the initiative spurred learning and increased the focus on flaring and venting within the global field of petroleum production. Further, they underlined that the initiative had improved collaboration between the companies and the national administrations in developing countries, although success here varied from country to country. Moreover, it seems that the initiative has improved the internal focus on flaring and venting in both Hydro and Shell. Further, the GGFR was one of several factors that led Hydro to start publicly reporting on its flaring emissions in 2005, while Shell did so before GGFR was initiated.

Differences and similarities in the companies' climate-related rules relating to the instruments are presented in Table 10.2.

10.3.3   Impact

Let us now turn to the complex issue of impact. In 2005 Shell emitted some 105 million tons of CO_2 equivalents. The company aims to reduce its climate emissions by 5 per cent by the year 2010 in relation to the 1990 levels (Shell 2007). According to our interviewees, this target was not regarded as especially hard to reach at the time it was developed. Nonetheless, they indicated that Shell is now struggling to meet it, mainly because the group has embarked on several new projects that will lead to rising emissions in the future. Several respondents pointed out that these projects were initiated without being assessed in relation to the emissions target. Thus, we may conclude that the target has not hitherto had strong action guiding effects. Our respondents mentioned that new rules had been introduced requiring its national organizations to inform the climate unit of any projects that will lead to increased emissions. Whether these new rules will make the target action guiding is still an open question. Moreover, despite several major energy efficiency programmes, energy efficiency has improved only slightly since 2000 (Shell 2007, pp. 9, 33). Thus, Shell was not able to meet its 2005 target concerning energy efficiency.

Neither is Shell on track for meeting its target of ending flaring by 2008, and the date has been postponed to 2009 (Shell 2007, p. 32). According to our respondents, progress has now been made and Shell may reach the target by this later date. Further, they underlined that the GGFR has contributed positively. Our informants reported that the partnership has facilitated the collaboration with public administrations, in particular in Nigeria, on the infrastructure development required for handling the gas. This has eased infrastructure development. Moreover, the initiative has contributed somewhat to promoting better internal information flows on flaring and venting.

Shell aims to build at least one large-scale business in alternative energy. However, interview data indicate that this overarching and ambitious aim has not been implemented internally. Thus it is hard to assess whether it has been fulfilled. Further, several interviewees stated that the fact that Shell now discloses the emissions caused by its products helps to raise the corporate-level focus on developing low-carbon products. Shell has invested \$1 billion in renewable energy over the past five years (Shell 2007) – but this actually represents only a microscopic portion of the company's annual investments. Nonetheless, Shell has a broad portfolio of new renewable energy activities, encompassing biofuels, hydrogen, wind and solar energy (ibid., p. 13). Moreover, it has recently embarked on several major CO_2 capture and storage projects (Shell 2005).

Hydro emitted around nine million tonnes of CO_2 equivalents in 2005 (Hydro 2006). Emissions from oil and gas activities were slightly reduced in the first years after 2000, but increased from 2003 and onwards (ibid.). Emissions from flaring have been reduced by 2 per cent from 2003 to 2005 (ibid.). It is unclear whether the latter stems from yearly fluxes or reduction efforts. None of our interviewees related this to the GGFR. Moreover, Hydro reports on less successful dialogues with national governments on flaring and venting than does Shell, so the outcomes are also less significant than for Shell. Earlier, Hydro aimed at large-scale carbon capture and storage, but it has not reported major efforts in this respect in recent years. Today, Hydro is active within hydrogen and wind (ibid.), but does not disclose how much it invests in new renewable energy activities.

From our interviews, it does not seem that the minor outcome in Hydro has resulted in action guiding rules. Rather, it appears that emissions are simply adjusted to governmental regulations and that the interest in new renewable energy is spurred by the emerging market opportunities. Thus, we may conclude that impact of climate-related CSR is rare in Hydro.

10.3.4   Similar Output Has Produced Differing Outcomes and Impacts

The companies are marked by output similarity, as they both adhere to the four instruments (see Table 10.3). The GC is the sole example of complete decoupling between instrument adherence and rule making. Adherence to the GC has resulted in neither outcomes nor impacts in either company. As for the GRI and the CDP, these have brought about only minor effects in Hydro in terms of confirming prior choices concerning information disclosure. In general, Hydro has followed the instrument requirements that best fit its initial approach and refrained from all deviating requirements. In Shell more effects may be detected. Adherence to the CDP and GRI has strengthened Shell's original climate approaches. Moreover, as a result of instrument adherence, Shell has aligned its reporting practices to the requirements of the CDP and the GRI. The GGFR has led to minor outcome effects in Hydro and medium ones in Shell.

As the outcome effects are meagre in Hydro, it comes as no surprise that we have not been able to detect impact resulting from these. But also in Shell, despite the (at least comparatively) substantial level of outcome, we have noted few impact effects. Shell's climate targets have not been in evidence in guiding the company's actions concerning energy efficiency, or flaring and other activities which cause emissions. However, they seem to have affected the practices somewhat. It is reasonable to assume that emission volumes would have been greater had it not been for the targets. Concerning the development of new renewable energy, our findings indicate that the fact that Shell has started to report on its indirect emissions has helped to strengthen the company's focus on new renewable energy. It must be noted that the complexity of the causal mechanisms involved here makes the effects less immediately evident. Effects may have occurred, but we have not been able to note them. Moreover, effects may grow stronger in the future.

Table 10.3   CSR output, outcome and impact in Hydro and Shell

Instruments	Hydro			Shell		
	Output	Outcome	Impact	Output	Outcome	Impact
GC	Adherence	None	None	Adherence	None	None
GRI	Adherence	Weak	None	Adherence	Medium	Weak
CDP	Adherence	Weak	None	Adherence	Medium	Weak
GGFR	Adherence	Weak	None	Adherence	Medium	Medium

Source: Authors.

10.4   EXPLANATORY ASSESSMENT

Our examination of the effects of CSR instruments on company practices strongly indicates that, on the whole, the instruments have had only weak effects. Further, the instruments have affected the companies differently. The exception is the GC, which has not produced effects in either Shell or Hydro. In order to detect the importance of the different explanatory factors, the explanatory research question must be specified. In the following we aim to answer three questions: why is the output of the two companies similar? Why have the instruments produced more substantial outcomes in Shell than in Hydro? And why have the CSR-induced rules produced such low impact in Shell?

10.4.1   Counterproductive Strategy in Hydro and Low Level of Strategic Control in Shell

Adopting the lens of the corporate strategy perspective, the decision to opt for the four instruments is expected to be in line with the strategy designed by the corporate executives. Further, we shall expect to find that the leadership of Hydro hindered the instruments from producing effects, while the executives of Shell may have promoted outcomes, but stood in the way of impacts.

Shell claims that it has aligned its climate targets to its main aim of long-term value gain (Mirvis 2000; Shell 2007). It was the Shell Board that decided to join the GC, while the company executives actively engaged in joining the GRI (Veer 1999). According to our informants, the decision to join the CDP and the GGFR was made at lower hierarchical levels at the corporate headquarters. All these decisions seem to be in line with Shell's business strategy and, thus, we may conclude that the corporate strategy perspective may very well explain Shell's instrument adherence.

When it comes to explaining outcome, both the interviews and public statements made by Shell executives indicate that the company's CSR motivation is twofold: to enhance Shell's internal rules and to affect the conduct of other companies (see, for example, ibid.). While both motivations have characterized how Shell executives have approached the GRI, the CDP and the GGFR, the rationale for adhering to the GC seems to have been to improve Shell's outward appearance. Our interviewees indicated that the corporate leaders made no efforts to apply the principles of the GC. On the other hand, Shell executives have aimed to systematically transform the requirements of the other instruments into company-specific rules. Moreover, Shell has engaged in the making of the instruments, and thus helped ensure that many of the instruments' requirements were in line with existing Shell rules when they were adopted. Further, the corporate level has ensured that Shell's business principles and climate policies have been in alignment with the requirements of the instruments.

Shell has developed internal primers with details on how to cope with the various societal issues encompassed by its business principles. Notably, the executives have not initiated such a primer on how to cope with climate issues. The lack of hierarchically imposed routines on dealing with climate issues seems to prevent the impact from being as substantial as the outcome of the instrument adherence. The lack of formal regulations is particularly grave, as the sheer size of Shell hampers the executives' steering possibilities. Since the late 1990s, the main lines of command have gone from the corporate level to the business branch division and subsequently to national organizations (Mirvis 2000, p. 67; Stadler and Hinterhuber 2005). These various organizations are interlinked by a range of complex internal networks. Our respondents pointed out that the business branches have gained in importance in recent years, while the national organizations still have substantial powers. This restricts the executives' possibility to create impacts.

A climate group has been established at a rather low level in the hierarchy, with substantial room for manoeuvring. In addition, there are several loose internal climate networks which ensure information flows. These measures are not strong enough to ensure strong strategic control on how climate concerns are coped with. Recently, routines have been introduced requiring the national organizations to report to the climate group on any new business plans that would involve an increase in carbon emissions. This may indirectly improve the corporate leaders' impact control somewhat, but it is too early to assess the effect. On the one hand, the alignment of the overarching aims and regulations to the instruments is in line with Shell's corporate strategy. On the other hand, the lack of specific translation of the CSR instruments into company-specific rules may also be traced back to Shell's corporate directors' fear of reducing value gain as a result of inducing climate policy-related constraints. The latter also contributes to explaining the low level of impact. The corporate strategy approach cannot explain that the GGFR, which has attracted the least attention among executives, has produced the strongest impact within Shell.

Concerning Hydro's strategy, the company aims for growth and internationalization (Hydro 2002; Hydro 2006, p. 14). This is not matched by any climate sub-goals. On the one hand, some interviewees spoke of CSR instruments as a means towards fulfilling Hydro's main aims. On the other hand, they referred to CSR instrument adherence as a result of ad hoc decision processes. The GC was formally signed by the Hydro Board, but our respondents indicated that the consequences had not been explored prior to adoption. According to the interviews, adherence to the GRI, the CDP and the GGFR were decided at lower hierarchal levels, but were nonetheless related to the aim of improving Hydro's international reputation. Concerning the GGFR, it was assumed that adherence might facilitate development of gas infrastructures in Third World countries. Thus, instrument adherence seems to be at least indirectly related to the realization of Hydro's main strategic aims.

As to outcome explanations, some Hydro interviewees pointed out that instrument adherence as such is sufficient in order to gain a good CSR reputation. Others, however, forcefully argued that a good reputation comes as a result of good performance. They did not see the instruments as appropriate tools in this respect. They tend to deem the environmental performance of Hydro as superior at the outset (due to strict Norwegian governmental regulations) and thus they do not see a need to align Hydro's company-specific rules to the CSR instruments. It does not seem likely that the Hydro leaders have considered transforming the requirements of the CSR instruments into company-specific rules, neither in general nor in relation to climate concerns. The exception is the CDP adherence which gave rise to internal discussions as to whether Hydro should set climate targets and timetables (CDP 2006a). According to our informants, strategic assessments led these plans to be shelved. Hence, it seems clear that the lack of outcome on Hydro's part can be explained by strategic decisions made by the corporate leaders.

It follows from the lack of substantial outcomes that the impact of Hydro has been meagre. Hydro has an internal climate network and a climate unit at a low hierarchical level, but these have not been given any responsibility concerning alignment to the CSR instruments. Although the comparatively smaller size and hierarchical structures of Hydro enable a high degree of corporate strategic control (Lie 2005), these possibilities have not been applied in order to fulfil the requirements of the instruments.

Thus we see that executives in both companies promoted adherence to instruments, while variations in outcome may be traced back to differences in corporate strategy. While the low level of outcome gives little reason to expect impact by Hydro, the low level of impact in Shell may partly be explained by the lack of specificity in the Shell alignment to the instruments. As the complex structure of Shell hampers the executive's ability to directly exert strategic control, this is of high importance.

10.4.2   Low Cultural Unity in Shell and Cultural Path Dependency in Hydro

Adopting the lens of the cultural approach, we may expect Shell to adhere to the CSR instruments because it has a tradition for such adherence, implying that it had adhered to many CSR instruments before it adopted the four instruments in focus here. Further, we expect the cultural features and overarching strategy to be in line with the instruments, but not the company-specific rules and practices. With Hydro, this perspective leads us to assume that it was in line with Hydro's practice to adapt to the instruments, but that the company culture has worked to prevent these instruments from producing outcome and impact effects.

In the final decades of the twentieth century Shell was accused of being inward focused and impermeable (Frynas 2003; Howarth 1997; Ledgerwood 1998). The harsh criticism levelled against Shell during the 1970s and 1980s hardly affected its conduct. In the mid-1990s Shell was attacked for the planned dumping of Brent Spar and had to tackle controversies in Nigeria (Frynas 2003, p. 280; Ledgerwood 1998, p. 272). Parallel to this, it experienced financial problems. This led Shell's headquarters to finally respond to the external criticism and its corporate culture underwent a gradual change. A major campaign aimed at enabling the organization to respond to demands from its environment was initiated (Mirvis 2000; Stadler and Hinterhuber 2005). Moreover, Shell included sustainable development in its Corporate Business Principles, introduced a range of climate targets and increased its renewable energy investments (Frynas 2003, p. 280; Ledgerwood 1998). The instrument adherence decisions seem to follow naturally from this new Shell approach. In addition, interviews and literature indicate that alignment to CSR instruments is regarded as appropriate at the Shell headquarters. Thus the corporate-level culture of Shell seems to have promoted the production of substantial outcomes from the CSR instrument adherence.

The lack of translation into specific rules does, however, contrast with the Shell culture as it was developed in the late 1990s. Further, it is not primarily the culture at the corporate level which is of relevance when we are to understand the low level of impact, but rather the culture of the many sub-organizations. The Shell group has grown organically from the British 'Shell' Transport and Trading Company and the Royal Dutch Petroleum Company since their merger in 1907 (Howarth 1997). Its many national organizations have developed various distinct and strong cultures (Frynas 2003, p. 279, 283; Howarth 1997, p. 370). Interview information confirms that the Shell culture still varies across levels, divisions and countries. To a considerable extent, Shell employees seem to follow locally developed rules and cultures. Thus, overarching climate-related strategies and aims may render some effects on the action taken locally, but will not strongly constrain the sub-organizations' actions. Further, our interviewees indicate that the follow-up activities of the CSR instruments' secretariats have primarily affected the corporate level in Shell, and not people throughout the organization. Thus we may conclude that the lack of horizontal unity of the culture has been an obstacle to creating greater impact.

Turning to Hydro, it developed during the twentieth century an inward looking management style marked by consensus and close dialogue with the government (Johannesen et al. 2005; Lie 2005). Since its creation in 1905, it has become deeply rooted in Norwegian society (Johannesen et al. 2005). The steering principles and decision procedures of Hydro have been largely informal, and thorough socialization processes have ensured cultural unity (Lie 2005). With the new millennium came a major turning point in the company's history. Governmental ownership was reduced to below 50 per cent, and several takeovers and major replacement within the staff occurred (ibid.). Nonetheless, our interviewees indicate that much of Hydro's culture has remained unchanged – at least in the oil and gas divisions.

It did, however, not develop any tradition of voluntarily adopting measures in addition to the regulations during the 1990s. Thus, the cultural approach seems to provide little explanatory value as to why Hydro started to adhere to the instruments after entering the new century. When Hydro in 2004 developed its internal business principles, these mirrored the company's lack of tradition for voluntarily adopting environmental measures (Hydro 2004). Neither did these reflect any of the CSR commitments Hydro had taken on since the year 2000. Hence, we may conclude that Hydro has a strong culture, particularly vertically, which has hindered the instruments from being transformed into operational descriptions and producing impacts. Further, the follow-up mechanisms of the instruments are far from strong enough to intrude on the Hydro culture.

We see that the corporate culture of Shell promoted instrument adherence and outcome, but created obstacles when it came to impacts. Hydro has a somewhat stronger culture, and the cultural features contrast with the CSR instruments. Thus, this perspective does not help to explain why Hydro started to adhere to the instruments in the first place, but it is useful for understanding the low level of outcome and impact.

10.4.3 Hydro: Shielded by its Domestic Field

Turning to the domestic environments of the companies, we posit that the CSR instruments were adhered to by both companies because it was expected within their countries of origin. Furthermore, we assume that both the climate issues and CSR instruments have been stronger in the Netherlands and the UK than in Norway, and thus Shell responded more thoroughly.

By the late 1990s, both the Netherlands and the UK had developed

ambitious climate policies which targeted the carbon emissions of the oil
industry (Jordan et al. 2003; Skjærseth and Skodvin 2003). Corporate
leaders in the UK have traditionally had a fairly autonomous position. In
order to defend this position, they raised a concern at an early date about the
social responsibility of business (Byrkjeflot 2002, p. 123). The Netherlands
has not been as strongly influenced by this Anglo-Saxon approach to corporate management. Nonetheless, the CSR concept attracted attention,
although not as much as in the UK (European Commission 2006c). On this
basis, it seems 'natural' for Shell to adhere to voluntary instruments. The
level of impact indicates, however, that the domestic field has less explanatory value concerning Shell. In fact, the Shell interviewees did not regard
UK and Dutch circumstances as important.

Turning to the domestic scene for Hydro, we find a somewhat different
picture. Hydro interviewees frequently referred to conditions in Norway
as crucial. The Norwegian government targeted the Norwegian oil sector
with climate measures in the early 1990s, but later it gave in to the oil companies and reduced the strength of the measures (Boasson 2005; Lie 2005,
pp. 348–52). Later, oil companies' emissions have hardly been questioned.
The traditional Norwegian corporate management model is based on
close dialogue with groups within the company and the government – not
on contact with external stakeholders. Although this approach has been
challenged by global management trends, it is still prevalent (Byrkjeflot
2002). To date, CSR has scarcely attracted attention in Norway (Graham
2005). Moreover, our interviewees pointed out that there was no pressure in Norway concerning alignment to the CSR instruments. All in all,
the Norwegian field cannot explain Hydro's instrument adherence, but
it seems that domestic conditions have supported Hydro's neglect of the
instruments' requirements. Thus, this perspective helps to explain the low
level of outcome and impact.

Summing up, the domestic fields of Shell seem to have a rather low
explanatory value. Turning to Hydro, this perspective cannot explain why
Hydro adopted the instruments in the first place, but it sheds light on the
low level of effects detected in Hydro.

10.4.4 The Field of Petroleum Hinders CSR Instruments From Producing Effects

If Shell and Hydro are equally embedded in the global field of petroleum,
this approach can hardly contribute to explaining the differences between
them. We may rather expect this field to have promoted instrument adherence but obstructed output and impact.

The companies and the oil producing countries are interlinked by market-based collaboration arrangements. International oil companies of European and US origin are interconnected by common ventures in European and US waters and through the International Association of Oil and Gas Producers (OGP 2006). Both companies may be regarded as deeply rooted in this field, although Hydro also has activities within other industries. Interviewees from both companies indicate that sub-organizations engaged in exploration and processing are heavily exposed to expectations from the field. This goes for both companies. The functioning and structure of the field is based on rather unstable geo-political compromises (Claes 1998). Volatility in oil prices also creates profound uncertainties. The uncertainty has led to the emergence of a range of additional legitimizing strategies in addition to financial results. Throughout the twentieth century, the oil companies mimicked each others' strategic priorities and formal organizational arrangements (Hoffmann [1997] 2001; Levy and Kolk 2002). Further, the companies have aligned their approaches to climate change over time (Levy and Kolk 2002).

The interviewees indicated that climate responsible actions were only seen as relevant to the extent that they might contribute to enhancing financial gains. They had some minor hope of CDP and GGFR adherence yielding future revenues, but their general stand was that adherence to CSR instruments would not be economically beneficial. Thus, it is a paradox that they state that adherence to the four instruments was expected within the field. The traces of hope concerning the economic value of CDP and GGFR may relate to the fact that the follow-up mechanisms of the CDP are in line with the prevailing competitive logics of the field and that GGFR deals with petroleum-specific issues. Moreover, GGFR has a proven ability to alter prevailing perceptions of economic value of gas recovery, and thus it has managed to induce more significant effects within the companies than the other instruments in the field.

The upshot is that the petroleum field, on the one hand, has promoted similarity in output, while, on the other hand, this is perceived and accepted as a window dressing exercise. Thus, outputs and impacts are hampered. The exception is the GGFR, which shows that it is possible for low-profile CSR instruments to create deeper effects. As the companies are affected by the petroleum field at all organizational levels, this perspective seems to provide good explanatory value.

10.4.5 Shell: More Profoundly Affected by the Global Field of CSR

If equally embedded in it, the field of CSR can be expected to affect Shell and Hydro similarly. Further, we may expect this field to exert pressure towards instrument adherence, but not towards deeper effects.

The confusion over what CSR actually means is extensive, and the complexity of the issues surrounding it is tremendous (Kakabadse and Kakabadse 2007; Windell 2005). This infuses profound uncertainty to CSR as a concept. Nonetheless, a global CSR field of business, governmental and non-governmental organizations has emerged. Interconnections are provided by UN-related arenas, specific CSR ventures and global business arenas like the World Business Council for Sustainable Development (cf. Windell 2005).

According to our interviewees, both Shell and Hydro strive to keep apace of changing fashions, aiming to embrace the 'right' instruments prior to their popularity peak. Moreover, some respondents stated that the company must adhere to the salient CSR instruments; this is not a matter of choice. The instruments seem to gain legitimacy from the kind and number of actors that initiate and adhere to them – and not from their ability to induce performance changes. The GC and the GRI gain legitimacy from their UN affiliation, while the CDP is supported by powerful investors (CDP 2006a; Sahlin-Anderson 2006, p. 598). All three are further strengthened by their affiliation to research communities and NGOs. At the beginning of 2007, there were 3000 organizations adhering to the GC, while some 1000 adhered to the GRI and/or the CDP (CDP 2006e; Global Compact 2006; GRI 2006 a, b). Respondents saw adherence to the GC and the GRI as pivotal. The broad scope of the GC and GRI and follow-up mechanisms are in line with the expectations within this field. Although the CDP has a specific focus on one issue, it shares basic features with other important instruments within the field. The specificity and the few participants involved make the GGFR somewhat anomalous, and in contrast to the other instruments the pressure towards GGFR adherence is not particularly strong.

Many of our informants were surprised that we should approach them about CSR instruments and their effect on climate change measures. Some seemed puzzled by the thought that the instruments might render tangible effects on practices. As one remarked, 'You have to realize that climate issues have moved out of what is classified as CSR . . . All companies treat this issue seriously.' It is the declaration of good intent and not actual performance which seems to count for a company to be seen as a shining CSR example. An example of this is how the CDP Secretariat has highlighted Hydro as a climate leader even though it hardly followed the CDP recommendations (CDP 2006a). Shell did seem to be more concerned about being targeted for their possible lack of implementation than Hydro. Due to the many Shell scandals, such as their vast overstating of reserves in 2004, it is particularly eager in its striving towards a better reputation (see, for example, Stadler and Hinterhuber 2005). Further, our interviews indicated that it is mainly the corporate level that is engaged in this field. This contrasts with the petroleum field, which affects all parts of the oil companies' organizations.

Summing up, we see that the global field promotes instrument adherence, but the uncertainty and the 'window dressing' character of the field obstructs stronger effects. Shell's reputation liabilities seem to have influenced its corporate level to focus somewhat more on outcomes. Hydro has limited freedom in the choice of instruments, but in general it feels far less constrained than Shell.

10.5 EXPOSED GIANT AND IMPERMEABLE JUNIOR

Hydro and Shell are marked by output similarity, as they both adhere to the same four instruments. Despite similar output, both outcome and impact differ between the companies. In general, the instruments have affected climate-related rules more strongly within Shell. The exception is the GC, which is decoupled from how the two companies have opted to cope with climate change. Both the GRI and the CDP are decoupled from Hydro's practices, whereas Shell has aligned its reporting practices to these instruments. The GGFR is the instrument that has affected the two companies the most, with effects somewhat greater in Shell than in Hydro. To a large extent, Hydro has picked those elements of the instruments that fit with its own established practices and omitted the elements that would necessitate changes. Shell has adapted to the instruments over time. The main reason why the outcome has not been stronger in Shell is that the company was acting in line with many of the instrument requirements even prior to adherence. It must be noted that the complexity of the causal mechanisms involved here makes the effects less immediately evident. Effects may have occurred, but we have not been able to note them. Moreover, effects may grow stronger in the future.

When we turn to the question of how to explain the output, outcome and impact, Table 10.4 shows that the relationships are complex and draws on all of our theoretical approaches.

The corporate strategy approach has fairly strong explanatory value. The reluctance of the leaders in Hydro and the strong CSR motivation of Shell's executives result in significant differences. Hydro executives are able to constrain the outcome and impact from the instruments, but they did not exert the same level of control concerning instrument adherence in the first place. With Shell we note the opposite pattern: its leaders promoted adherence and to some extent outcome, but without exerting the same level

Table 10.4   Explanations to CSR output, outcome and impact

Explanatory approach	Hydro			Shell		
	Output	Outcome	Impact	Output	Outcome	Impact
Hierarchy	Slightly promotes	Hampers	_	Promotes	Promotes	Slightly promotes
Culture	Hampers	Hampers	_	Promotes	Promotes	Hampers
Domestic	Hampers	Hampers	_	Slightly promotes	Slightly promoting	Slightly promotes
Petroleum	Slightly promotes	Hampers	_	Slightly promotes	Hampers	Hampers
CSR	Promotes	Slightly promotes	_	Promotes	Slightly promotes	Hampers

Source: Authors.

of impact control. If Shell's rules had not been so much in line with the instruments prior to adherence, its outcomes would probably have been greater. However, Shell leaders must take some of the responsibility for the low level of impact, as they decided against developing detailed rules for climate conduct. Moreover, Shell generally lacks hierarchical structures that could ensure strong top-down control. Indeed, it may be questioned whether it is at all possible to control a vast company such as Shell. Moreover, stronger hierarchical control would probably have constrained the company's ability to adapt to local conditions and societal demands. This remains a crucial paradox while the Shell executives strive to make the company more responsible.

The cultural perspective yields interesting insights in the CSR responses of both companies. The Hydro and the Shell cultures differ in terms of both strength and content. While Shell has a tradition of engaging in voluntary initiatives, Hydro has not. Moreover, the strength of the Hydro culture makes the corporation resistant to external pressures. The very diversity of the Shell culture helps to explain why the efforts of its executives have resulted in limited impact. The value of the cultural explanation increases when viewed in conjunction with the domestic field approach. Even though the Hydro culture is quite strong, it clearly bears the marks of a general Norwegian approach to climate measures and to business management. Hydro's boundaries towards its domestic field are permeable. Further, by virtue of its strong position within the Norwegian field, the company is strikingly shielded from instrument claims which warrant changes in practice. While the Norwegian field serves to limit output, outcome and impact, Shell's UK and Dutch fields slightly promote effects at all levels. Although the domestic fields may have had some effects on Shell's reactions, the explanatory value of this field is far lower for Shell than in the case of Hydro.

Shell emerges as more strongly affected by the two global fields than Hydro, and has not been able to protect its original culture in the way Hydro has. When it comes to the global field of petroleum, Hydro is also affected, although not as profoundly as Shell. The global field of petroleum sheds light on why both companies have chosen to adhere to the instruments – and to the GGFR and the CDP in particular. Nonetheless, the uncertainty of the field acts as an obstacle to outcome and impact effects within both companies. The relative success of the GGFR is linked to its ability to reduce this uncertainty. In the case of Hydro, this field amplifies the influence of the domestic field, the company culture and the motivations of its executives. As for Shell, the influence of the petroleum field contradicts the internal factors and expectations in the domestic field. However, as Shell lacks firm boundaries towards this field, it is easily influenced by the prevailing field logics.

Lastly, it seems as if the global field of CSR merely produces superficial, isomorphic effects. Nonetheless, it is of considerable value in helping to explain why the companies decided to adhere to the instruments in the first place. This is especially true of Hydro, whose adherence contrasts with executive motivations and the company's internal culture. Shell is clearly more vulnerable to the expectations within this field than Hydro. Thus, this field has had effects beyond output for Shell, while the effects are rather superficial concerning Hydro. Our study indicates that Shell is far more capable of affecting the development of institutional standards in this field than Hydro. Shell seeks to take advantage of this by trying to make other companies – oil companies in particular – copy its practices. The downside of this strategy is that it leads to high expectations that Shell will follow the approaches it recommends for others. The question of whether Shell succeeds in its efforts to change the conduct of others demands a more far-reaching research strategy than applied in this chapter, and thus it has not been explored here.

This study has explored a highly complex issue. The examination of Shell and Hydro has indicated that oil companies are not affected similarly by the CSR instruments to which they adhere. In the case of Shell, the inability of its executives to govern the conduct of the company's various sub-organizations emerges as the most probable explanation of why 'willing Shell' has not been more effective than 'reluctant Hydro'. However, the causal mechanisms are far from straightforward or easy to grasp. Nor have all possible explanatory factors been dealt with here. Unfortunately, it has been beyond the scope of this study to examine how, in the case of the various Shell organizations, their approaches to CSR and climate issues are influenced by the countries in which they operate.

The fact that some effects are detected indicates that the CSR instruments are not without potential. As the four instruments in scrutiny are quite new, there is reason to believe that they have not yet displayed their full potential.

NOTE

1. Throughout the chapter we refer to the interviews (Hydro Interview 2006a, 2006b, 2006c, 2006d, 2006e; Shell Interview 2006a, 2006b, 2006c, 2006d, 2006e, 2007a, 2007b, 2007c, 2007d) without specifying the actual interviews the information was drawn on. This is done due to the sensitivity of the issues at hand. The interviewees are experts on the topics in focus.

11 In hunt for sustainable seafood: sustainability effects of CSR in three fish processing companies

Franziska Wolff and Katharina Schmitt

11.1 INTRODUCTION

In the past 30 years demand for seafood has doubled and wild fish stocks worldwide are under serious pressure. The United Nations Food and Agriculture Organization (FAO 2007) estimates that in 2005 about half of the stocks were fully exploited while one-quarter of stocks was over-exploited, depleted or recovering from depletion. Impacts of fishing on biodiversity and habitats threaten the function and integrity of marine ecosystems.

The fish processing industry can play a major role in rendering fishing more sustainable: their sourcing and product decisions are levers vis-à-vis the fishing industry at the one end and consumers at the other end. Corporate Social Responsibility (CSR) as a concept to voluntarily integrate social and environmental concerns into business operations is only just taking roots in the sector. CSR here translates above all into sourcing seafood from sustainable stocks, including from fisheries certified by the Marine Stewardship Council (MSC), and requiring suppliers to abandon environmentally harmful fishing practices.

In this chapter we look at the concrete effects and impacts of selected fish processors' CSR claims. We also analyze what factors within the companies and in their environment can explain the achievement of sustainability effects through CSR. In particular, we examine the role of explanatory factors deduced from management and institutionalist literature. They include corporate strategy and organization; corporate culture; the business environment; civil society stakeholders and the political-institutional setting. Discussing their relevance will provide insights not only on success factors and obstacles to the achievement of CSR effects, but will also shed light on the debate between these two complementary approaches.

The focus is on wild capture fisheries[1] and our empirical basis is provided by three company case studies of the Dutch-British multinational Unilever, the British processor Young's and medium-sized German Gottfried Friedrichs KG. The companies were selected from among the respondents of a CSR survey in the processing industry (Schmitt and Wolff, Chapter 6), because they all featured high levels of CSR commitment and strategizing (CSR 'output') and have accordingly adapted their practices (CSR 'outcome'). This suggests real benefits in terms of sustainability (CSR 'impact'). Selecting high-performing companies makes it possible to learn about drivers of impact. The fact that – on a high level – CSR outcomes of these companies differ somewhat provides us with the interesting puzzle why some variance remains despite the companies' similar CSR outputs.

The chapter starts by outlining our analytical framework and by introducing the three case study companies. We then assess the CSR effects (output, outcome and impact) that the processors have achieved by the time of our research. Subsequently, we try to explain these effects, discussing hypotheses presented in the analytical framework. Finally, we draw conclusions from the findings. Empirically, our study is based on interviews with company representatives and civil society stakeholders. The interviews were carried out between autumn 2006 and spring 2007. In addition, we make use of company-specific information from the mentioned CSR survey, of publicly available documents and academic literature.

11.2   ANALYTICAL FRAMEWORK

Our study aims to assess and explain CSR effects created through the CSR efforts of the three case study companies. CSR effects include 'output', 'outcome' and 'impact'.[2] They are the results of responsible behaviour of varying depth and can be issue-spanning ('overarching') or issue-specific.

CSR output describes the extent to which companies change their commitment and strategies with regard to social and environmental performance, including the adoption of specific CSR instruments. With regard to the issue of sustainable fishing, fish processors may, for example commit themselves to sourcing fish from healthy stocks and decide to undergo a MSC certification. CSR outcome denotes concrete changes in the companies' social and environmental practices, resulting from changes in CSR output. There are three relevant mechanisms for fish processors to create outcome with regard to the sustainable fishing issue. All of them relate to sourcing and the composition of product portfolios. The first mechanism is withdrawal or abstention from overexploited or depleted fisheries. The second is the shift to buy fish from more sustainable fisheries. Both aim at substituting unsustainable with (more) sustainable fish. The third mechanism is the implementation of supplier requirements on responsible fishing practices. Finally, CSR impact covers the substantive consequences for society and the environment outside the company, induced by the sustainability changes in corporate practices (outcome). Environmental impact includes relief for both target stocks and marine ecosystems. Note the specific challenge that fish processors have no immediate influence over the creation of environmental impact: it is fishermen whose fishing practices impact the marine ecosystem in the first place; only by influencing their behaviour[3] can processors create environmental impact.

In order to account for the achievement of these effects, we draw on the framework developed by Viganò et al. in Chapter 3, and test the relevance of five explanatory factors. Exploring, firstly, the creation of CSR output, we focus on what factors determined the companies' choice of CSR instruments. This is because instruments provide a systematic mechanism to translate output into outcome. With instruments being more or less conducive to impact, preference of one instrument over another may affect the sustainability impact that a company can achieve. Secondly, with regard to outcome, we ask what factors drove the effective implementation of instruments within companies, leading to the high levels of outcome observed in the three companies. Thirdly, since environmental impact in our case lies outside the processors' immediate sphere of influence and we cannot determine it empirically on the basis of the data available to us, we confine ourselves to analysing the causal links between outcome and impact across all three companies. This includes a discussion of how conducive to creating impact different instruments are (Section 4.3.2).

The explanatory factors we consider were identified on the basis of (environmental and strategic) management literature, on the one hand, and organizational and institutional scholarship, on the other hand (see Chapter 3). They include corporate strategy and organization, corporate culture, civil society demands, companies' business environment as well as the political-institutional setting in which they operate. For each of the factors, we now formulate propositions on their expected effect on (a) instrument choice (output) and (b) effective implementation of seafood policies, leading to outcome.

Corporate strategy and organization encompasses both the rules and roadmaps companies develop to attain their objectives and their formal organizational structures, capacities and resources. Based on management literature (Hitt et al. 2003; Roome 1992), we expect that in their choice of instruments (output), managers will systematically examine whether or not an instrument can contribute to achieving pre-existing strategies and whether the instrument can be easily implemented within the organizational structures. We also expect that the creation of outcomes is supported by tying CSR into routine business operations; by integrating it vertically and horizontally with other strategies; by creating process ownership and by hierarchical control through corporate leaders.

Corporate culture denotes the informal, normative rules and routines within companies discussed by cultural and institutionalist approaches (March and Olsen 1989; Mintzberg et al. 1998). While we do not expect corporate cultures to influence such concrete decisions as choice of specific instruments (output),[4] we expect that in particular a long-standing and well-developed identity of an organization as being socially responsible will create intrinsic pressures to achieve a high level of CSR outcome.

A company's business environment represents prevailing patterns of interpretation and legitimacy as well as (perceived) business opportunities and restrictions within the sector.[5] In institutionalist terms, we assume that instrument choice is influenced by the legitimacy of an instrument within the sector. An instrument may hence be selected because it is used by prestigious peer companies which are 'imitated' (DiMaggio and Powell 1983). We furthermore posit that the extent to which sustainable fishing represents (or is perceived as) a business opportunity in relevant markets (Steger 1993) will determine the rigour with which a processor implements its CSR policies and instruments, and will thus influence outcome levels.

Civil society demand describes the expectations, pressure or support of societal stakeholders on corporate (CSR) processes (McIntosh et al. 2003; Suchman 1995). We expect civil society not to influence the choice of a specific instrument, although it may affect a company's general decision to adopt (any) instrument. However, we do assume that civil society demand accounts for the achievement of CSR outcome. This may happen both through pressure (by creating publicity and affecting market opportunities) and through support (by providing knowledge and gaining influence within NGO-business co-operations).

The political-institutional setting includes governmental expectations, public policies and wider regulations pertaining to the social systems of production (Hollingsworth et al. 2002). We posit that choice of a specific instrument becomes more likely if this instrument is politically promoted. Similarly, we expect the political-institutional setting to foster the effective implementation of CSR. Indirectly, national cultures of corporate voluntarism may drive such outcomes (Midttun et al. 2006). More directly, outcomes may be fostered by governments voicing expectations of 'appropriate' behaviour in the seafood business or influencing supply of and demand for sustainable seafood.

11.3 INTRODUCING THREE FISH PROCESSORS COMMITTED TO CSR

We shall briefly introduce the three companies to be researched: Unilever, Young's and Gottfried Friedrichs.

Operating in 150 countries worldwide, with 206 000 employees and a 2005 turnover of 39.7 billion euros, Unilever is one of the biggest companies in the area of fast moving consumer goods. Formed in 1930 from a Dutch-UK business merger, the company today operates as a single business entity with two separate legal parent companies: Unilever NV (Netherlands) and Unilever PLC (UK), headquartered in Rotterdam and London. Its business operations cover food as well as home and personal care products. One sub-segment is the Unilever Frozen Food business, which accounted for 16 per cent of overall Unilever sales in 2005 and is the focus of our subsequent analysis. It covers wild-capture fish exclusively, that is, no aquaculture fish. Unilever was one of the world's largest whitefish buyers in 2005 (Unilever 2005), sourcing fish from around 100 suppliers worldwide and operating a vertically integrated fishing business in Germany. Unilever fish products were uniquely sold as frozen food and under Unilever's premium brands, largely on the European market. In 2006, Unilever sold the majority of its European Frozen Foods business (Unilever 2006a). This resulted from a steady decrease in sales of (especially premium branded) frozen food, competition by (cheap) fresh fish and price-fighting discounters. The sale reduced Unilever's fish business by more than half.

Young's is a British business with a total turnover of around half a billion pounds a year and some 4500 employees (2005), focusing exclusively on seafood products – frozen and fresh, smoked and natural, from wild-caught and farmed fish. The company's formation dates back to 1805, with the Young's family remaining involved until the late 1980s. After it had been part of a number of other food companies, Young's became independent again in 1999 after merging with the seafood company Bluecrest. It is today privately owned by the UK-based holding company Foodvest. Young's is headquartered in Grimsby (UK) but has a total of 16 sites within the UK. Great Britain forms the sole market to which products are being sold and the company claims to be the UK's leader in both frozen and chilled fish. Almost half of its products are marketed under Young's own brands, the rest is manufactured in the form of packaged products under retail brands as chilled seafood to fish counters or as supply to the food service sector.

Finally, Gottfried Friedrichs KG is a medium-sized German enterprise based in Hamburg with around 400 employees and a turnover of 65 million euros (2006). The over 100 year old company is not stock market listed and the founder family still owns the majority of capital resources. Friedrichs specializes in smoked fish of both wild and farmed origin. The products belong to the high-price premium segment and are sold to retailers. For premium salmon and eel products, Friedrichs claims to be market leader in the German-speaking markets that it supplies.

11.4   TAKING STOCK OF CSR EFFECTS

The three selected fish processors have adopted CSR policies on the issue of sustainable fisheries. In this section we shall describe these CSR 'outputs' and discuss the resulting 'outcome' and 'impact' for Unilever, Young's and Friedrichs. We shall put the companies' sustainable fisheries commitment into a broader context by also describing their 'overarching' CSR policies, that is, initiatives spanning a broader set of sustainability issues. However, the description of overarching CSR will be limited to the output level.

Table 11.1 gives an overview of the different CSR effects in our case study companies, which will be substantiated in the following.

11.4.1   CSR Output

Unilever, Young's and Friedrichs: three companies quite different in terms of size, product portfolio and markets feature similar – and rather high – levels of CSR output, that is, of commitment and strategizing including instrument adoption. In each case output comprises some more overarching CSR commitments and a sustainable seafood policy.

Looking firstly at 'overarching' CSR, global player Unilever has developed the most elaborate commitment, including an explicit CSR vision. Unilever has formulated a Code of Business Principles with values and standards for its employees (Unilever 2006b) as well as a Business Partner Code for suppliers (Unilever 2006c). Furthermore, the company's environmental strategy aims at reducing the impact of corporate operations (eco-efficiency), the impact of products (eco-innovation) and at ensuring a sustainable supply of key resources, through three sustainability initiatives in agriculture, water and fish (Unilever 2005d). Young's, while not using the term 'CSR' as such, has adopted a company code for ethical trading and social accountability in its supply chain (Young's Bluecrest 2006a). It also assumes responsibility for the health and safety of its employees and environmental management of its plants. Lastly, Friedrichs has developed a code of conduct and ethics which covers issues such as responsibility towards the supply chain, employees and the community (Gottfried Friedrichs KG 2005).

Table 11.1 CSR output, outcome and impact in the three company cases

	CSR output (changes in corporate commitment and strategy)	CSR outcome (changes in corporate practice)	CSR impact (changes in society/the environment)
Unilever (until 2006)	• *Overarching CSR policy:* sustainability vision; environmental strategy; code of business principles; business partner code • *Sustainable seafood policy* ('Sustainable Fish Initiative'), includes: – MSC CofC certification – company-specific tool to assess sustainability of fisheries ('Traffic Light System') – quantified sustainable sourcing target (100%)	• *Withdrawal from unsustainable fisheries:* withdrawal from North Sea cod • *Switching to more sustainable fisheries:* sourcing fish from MSC stocks **(KPI: 46 % MSC fish in portfolio of wild-caught fish)** or from fisheries supported by 'Traffic Light System' • *Supplier standards*	• *Environmental impact:* – in MSC fisheries: relatively sustainable target stocks, reduced impacts on ecosystems, effective management systems – in fisheries supported by 'Traffic Light System': impact difficult to specify • *Societal/sector impact:* co-founding of MSC

Table 11.1 (continued)

	CSR output (changes in corporate commitment and strategy)	CSR outcome (changes in corporate practice)	CSR impact (changes in society/the environment)
Young's (2007)	• *Overarching CSR policy*: sustainability statement; ethical trading and social accountability code • *Sustainable seafood policy* ('Fish for Life'), includes: – MSC CofC certification – company-specific tool to assess sustainability of fisheries ('Fishery Health Check')	• *Withdrawal from unsustainable fisheries*: withdrawal from North Sea cod and partly from Eastern Baltic cod (as of 2005) • *Switching to more sustainable fisheries*: sourcing fish from MSC stocks **(KPI: 40 % MSC fish in portfolio of wild-caught fish)** or from fisheries supported by 'Fishery Health Check' • *Supplier standards* including supply chain audit, traceability system	• *Environmental impact* – in MSC fisheries: relatively sustainable target stocks, reduced impacts on ecosystems, effective management systems – in fisheries supported by 'Fishery Health Check': impact difficult to specify
Friedrichs (2007)	• *Overarching CSR policy*: company code of conduct • *Sustainable seafood policy* as part of company code of conduct; includes: – MSC CofC certification (since 2002)	• *Withdrawal from unsustainable fisheries*: abstaining from sturgeon caviar and dogfish • *Switching to more sustainable fisheries*: sourcing fish from MSC stocks **(KPI: 90 % MSC fish in portfolio of wild-caught fish)** • *Supplier standards*	• *Environmental impact* – in MSC fisheries: relatively sustainable target stocks, reduced impacts on ecosystems, effective management systems

Source: Authors.

Notes: KPI = Key Performance Indicator
CofC = Chain of Custody

Let us now turn to the companies' sustainable seafood policies. These contain sourcing guidelines which typically refer to instruments by which the sustainability of a fishery is assessed. Unilever and Young's not only use the MSC but additional company-specific tools for this.

Unilever's Fish Sustainability Initiative (FSI), established already in 1996, committed the company to purchase 100 per cent seafood from sustainable sources by 2005. In order to achieve this goal, the company joined forces in 1997 with the World Wildlife Fund (WWF) to set up the MSC. Transformed into an independent not-for-profit organization in 1999, the MSC is today one of the major CSR initiatives in the fisheries sector. It is used by many other companies including Young's and Friedrichs. We briefly describe its functioning.

The MSC provides an international product label to assure consumers that a seafood product stems from a sustainable fishery. Two distinct types of certification exist within the scheme: certification of the fishery itself and chain of custody (CofC) certification. In the fisheries certification a fish stock is assessed against the 'MSC Principles and Criteria for Sustainable Fishing' (MSC 2002).[6] These require healthy populations of targeted species (MSC Principle 1); the integrity of ecosystems (Principle 2); and an effective (public) management system that respects local, national and international law (Principle 3). In mid-2007 22 fisheries around the globe were certified against these standards, making up 5–6 per cent of all global fisheries (MSC 2007; Seafood Choices Alliance 2007, p. 22). Once a fishery is certified, the MSC label may be used on respective seafood products, provided a chain of custody assessment verifies that the products indeed originate from the certified fishery (MSC 2005). CofC procedures are implemented from the fishing vessel through to the wholesaler, retailer, processor or restaurant.

In its early years certification of fisheries through the MSC progressed very slowly and Unilever feared it would not be able to achieve its 100 per cent target in time. It hence developed an additional, in-company fishery assessment tool to guide its sourcing decisions. Through this 'Traffic Light System', fisheries are assessed against a set of five criteria but with less procedural conditions than set by the MSC. The criteria include existence of fisheries research, a quota system, regulatory tools, control systems and a long-term management plan. The impact of fishing on marine ecosystems is also said to be accounted for. Assessment results are graded into three colours: green, yellow and red. Fisheries that get an all green assessment are deemed 'sustainable'. Those with a mix of green and yellow are deemed managed and progressing, whereas those that get one or more red scores are deemed as poorly managed. Unilever stops sourcing from 'unmanaged' fisheries that score red against all five indicators (Unilever 2003; Unilever Interview 2006a, 2006b).

Looking at Young's, the company's 'Fish for Life' policy (Young's Bluecrest 2006b, 2006c) includes a commitment not to sell endangered species and to base fish procurement decisions on 'responsible' procurement criteria. In addition, the company explicitly states to not ever knowingly purchase illegal[7] fish. Since the late 1990s, Young's is MSC chain of custody-certified. Due to the initially low number and slow process of fishery certifications by the MSC, like Unilever, Young's developed its own in-company tool ('Fishery Health Check') to assess the sustainability of additional stocks from which to source fish. The 'Fishery Health Check' takes into account existing data on a fishery's stock status, legality of catch, management as well as levels of by-catch and environmental impact of fishing operations. The fisheries are subsequently rated to be 'low', 'medium' or 'high risk'. Risk relates both to ecological risk and to business exposure risk for the company in commercially engaging with the species or fishery (Young's Bluecrest 2007). A 'high risk' assessment either requires withdrawal from that fishery or species, or definition of conditions under which an engagement with the fishery or species is upheld. By early 2007, the 'Fishery Health Check' was applied to 36 fisheries or species, 14 of which were rated 'low risk'. Though Young's Fish for Life policy promotes the use of MSC certified sustainable species in new product development, a concrete target for sourcing sustainable fish – MSC certified or 'low risk' – does not exist.

Like Young's sustainable seafood policy, Friedrichs has committed itself in its (non-public) code of ethics[8] to refraining from using fish species that are legally protected or threatened with extinction (Gottfried Friedrichs KG 2005). Based on their decision in 2002 to undergo – as the first German fish processor – a MSC chain of custody certification, Friedrichs also aims to expand the share of MSC labelled products in their portfolio of wild-caught fish products. While the company does not have a formal target for the sourcing of sustainable fish, it informally strives for 100 per cent MSC fish in its portfolio of wild-caught fish.

Summing up, overarching CSR commitments are most elaborate in Unilever while the seafood policies are detailed and quite similar in all three companies. Remaining differences include that Unilever is the only company with a formalized and quantified sustainable sourcing target, and that Young's seafood policies are most specific. Both bigger companies have developed own tools to assess fisheries.

11.4.2   CSR Outcome

Changing their practices as a consequence of implementing the above commitments and strategies (CSR outcome), all companies made use of the three mechanisms identified in Section 2: withdrawal from critical fisheries, sourcing from sustainable fisheries and implementing 'green' supplier requirements. Due to differing product portfolios, the companies' exact activities vary.

As regards the first mechanism, none of the companies sources fish from protected or threatened species. For example, both Unilever and Young's have withdrawn from the overexploited North Sea cod fishery. At the time of this study, Young's had furthermore reduced its purchases from the overexploited Eastern Baltic cod stock by a third (Young's Bluecrest 2006g, 2007b). Friedrichs renounced sturgeon caviar and dogfish.

Making use of the second mechanism, the companies have shifted to buy fish from sustainable fisheries. A reliable and verifiable indicator for this outcome is the share of MSC sourced fish in the companies' volume of wild-capture fish (measured in tons). The MSC shares in our sample rank between 40 and 90 per cent. In mid-2006, before it sold its fish business, Unilever had sourced 46 per cent of its (wild-caught) fish from certified fisheries. The company had striven hard to reach its 100 per cent sustainable sourcing target by increasing its share of MSC certified fish. After including certified New Zealand hoki and South African hake in its portfolio, certification of the Alaskan pollock fishery in early 2005 provided the opportunity to boost the MSC share from 4 to 46 per cent. In addition, Unilever declared 10 per cent of its seafood to be sourced from 'green light' fisheries according to its 'Traffic Light System' (Unilever 2006d, p. 13). At the same time, Unilever fully or partially withdrew from fisheries ranked 'red' in the system. It also encouraged managers and stakeholders of 'yellow' fisheries to improve their performance and those of 'green' ones to undergo a MSC certification (Unilever 2003). In absolute terms, no other company sourced so many tons of fish from sustainable fisheries. However, at the same time Unilever explicitly failed to achieve its aim of purchasing all fish from sustainable sources by 2005 (Unilever 2003). As a consequence, the company did not renew its 100 per cent sustainable sourcing target for its remaining fish business. With a 40 per cent share of MSC fish among its wild-capture purchases in early 2007, Young's achieved a somewhat lower share then Unilever. The fish stems from the MSC certified Alaskan pollock, Alaskan salmon, South African hake, Patagonian scallops and Pacific cod fisheries. An additional share of Young's seafood was sourced from fisheries rated as 'low risk' by the company's 'Fishery Health Check'. Let us finally look at Friedrichs. The company began early to give preference to fish from countries with a good fisheries' management.[9] Since sourcing from MSC fisheries in 2002, the share of certified fish in its portfolio of wild-caught fish was at 90 per cent in 2007. This translated into about 1000 tons of wild salmon. The (Alaskan/Kodiak) salmon was at the same time harvested in a comparatively undamaging way, namely by trolling.

The third mechanism to achieve outcome is the implementation of 'green' supplier requirements. Unilever has a set of sustainable sourcing requirements which are communicated to and discussed with its suppliers. However, no specific control systems are in place. This is different in the case of Young's. The British company applies supply chain audits, traceability systems ('Young's Trace') and inspections to make sure that suppliers conform to their standards. These require fishermen to abstain from destructive fishing practices[10] and from illegal (IUU) fishing. For some stocks, the latter requirement is based on standardized buying guidelines by the EU Fish Processors Association (AIPCE 2006).[11] To complement the supplier standards on IUU fishing, Young's introduced an 'open book' policy for its own records of all seafood sources. The company has stopped business relations with suppliers not willing to share Young's policies. Like the other processors, Friedrichs commits its suppliers to sustainable fishing and trading practices.[12] The purchasing agreement is not tied to control or auditing mechanisms.

11.4.3 CSR Impact

To what extent have the described changes in corporate behaviour (CSR outcomes) resulted in impact on society and the environment?

11.4.3.1 Societal impact

The most prominent CSR impact in the societal realm is the creation of the MSC as today's most important non-governmental mechanism for the sustainable consumption of seafood products, applicable worldwide. The scheme has gained legitimacy throughout the fish harvesting, processing and retailing industries, especially on the European and US markets. Beyond applying for a chain of custody certification, a number of companies get involved in the MSC's governance structures and contribute to funding the costs of pre-assessing and certifying individual fisheries. While consumer familiarity with the label in many countries (including the EU and USA) is still relatively low and some civil society organizations dispute the MSC's ecological benefit, the scheme is increasingly becoming a reference standard among policy makers.

11.4.3.2 Environmental impact: causal paths from outcome to impact

Environmental impact of sustainable fishing activities includes the effects of sustainable fisheries' management and fishing practices on targeted fish stocks and the surrounding marine ecosystems. In the context of this study, we cannot verify or quantify these impacts, especially not for individual companies. We can, however, analyze in a qualitative way causal paths from CSR outcome to impact.

Table 11.2   Assessment of instruments' conduciveness to impact

Criteria	MSC	Young's Fishery Health Check	Unilever Traffic Light System
Level of specificity	High	Unclear	Unclear
● quantifiable targets	+	?	?
● specific/substantive activities	+	?	?
Level of obligation	High	Medium	Medium
● independent verification	+	–	–
● sanctions	+	+	+
Overall conduciveness to impact	High	Medium	Medium

Notes: Scale of assessment: high = positive values in both sub-criteria; medium: a positive value in one sub-criterion; low: no positive value in either sub-criterion.

Source: Authors.

Withdrawal from unsustainable fisheries   Stopping sourcing of fish from critically threatened fisheries may create environmental relief to the extent that the company's purchasing stop is not (over) compensated by other actors' demand for the seafood in question. WWF therefore advises companies to withdraw from unsustainable fisheries only when the fish species is indeed endangered. In other cases, greater environmental relief can be created by actively lobbying for a more sustainable fisheries' management (WWF Interview 2007).

Sourcing from sustainable fisheries   The switch to buy fish from more sustainable fisheries initially requires an assessment of how sustainable a fishery is. Both the MSC certification and company-specific assessment tools as developed by Young's ('Fishery Health Check') and Unilever ('Traffic Light System') provide such an assessment (Table 11.2). Can we expect these three tools to create the same impact? In the following, we shall briefly assess to what extent the instruments are in principle conducive to creating environmental benefits. Our underlying assumption is that CSR instruments by their very design can be more or less conducive to creating impact. We posit that instruments are likely to create greater impact when they have a higher level of (i) specificity and (ii) obligation (see Chapter 3). 'Specificity' means that quantifiable targets exist and that specific and sustainable (not only procedural) activities are required. An instrument's level of obligation is higher when an instrument is subject to independent verification and to sanctions. Assessment of these factors is purely analytical, not empirical.[13]

Assessed against the above criteria, the MSC features a high conduciveness to impact. With regard to specificity, an MSC certification sets quantifiable targets and requires implementation of substantive activities in each certification procedure (MSC 2006, pp. 8–14).[14] During these, both targets and activities are specified in the form of so-called 'conditions' (corrective action) which can be set for each MSC Principle (Agnew et al. 2006, p. 10).[15] The MSC's level of obligation is high too, with independent verification and sanctions in the case of non-compliance. For verification, the MSC assigns accreditations to independent bodies. These need to consult independent experts in their assessment of a fishery against the MSC criteria, and assessment criteria have to be published and opened up for stakeholder comments before used in the certification process.[16] Stakeholders can lodge objections on the assessment procedure (MSC 2006). When MSC procedures and conditions are not met, sanctions can be imposed, including suspension or withdrawal of the fishery certificate. Annual audits and surveillance reports (required after five years) help to detect non-compliance. Due to its specific and progressive requirements and independent verification, we can ideally equal a company's sourcing of MSC fish (CSR outcome) with a sustainability effect (CSR impact) in the respective fishery.

However, some reservations have been voiced as to this equation. Greenpeace (2006a) claims that stocks have been certified which were overfished, featured high rates of by-catch, including of threatened species, and whose ecosystem were impaired. Similarly, Wildhavens (2004) finds that Principle 2 is routinely not met. Other observers (Agnew et al. 2006; Philipps et al. 2003) respectively underscore that certification does not necessarily create environmental gains vis-à-vis the pre-certification state of the fishery.

The latter argument, however, is countered by the appraisal that, ultimately, it might not be so relevant whether the good shape and sustainable management of a fishery is a result of the certification process or merely its precondition. In both cases companies would harm the environment less than if they sourced fish from other, less sustainable fisheries. Among the studies pointing to positive impact from implementing the MSC (for example, Hoel 2004; Knapp et al. 2007), Agnew et al. (2006) most concretely identify a number of environmental gains across ten certified fisheries. The value added of the MSC finally lies in assuring that sustainability is not an incidental occurrence but that it is monitored and fostered within a given time frame. There exist additional institutional aspects of the MSC that may indirectly foster impact.[17]

The company-specific tools – Unilever's 'Traffic Light System' and Young's 'Fishery Health Check' – are more difficult to evaluate, since assessments of concrete fisheries and subsequent courses of action are not public. In terms of specificity, both companies claim that they engage in consultation to encourage positive change in fisheries' management structures. However, since their requirements for corrective action are not public, we cannot assess their specificity. With regard to the instruments' level of obligation, unlike the MSC, neither Young's nor Unilever's tool embraces independent verification. When it comes to sanctions, the tools are employed differently: while Unilever claims to 'no longer source from fisheries that are unmanaged' (Unilever 2006e), Young's does not automatically withdraw from a fishery scoring 'high risk'. Rather, they define conditions under which to continue their involvement. These include, among others, engagement in consultations to drive positive changes in management measures as well as internal and third party verification of supply chain traceability and integrity.

Application of 'green' supplier requirements   Fish processors may stir 'on the water' effects also by requiring fishermen to use sustainable fishing practices which cause less by-catch, less high-grading and discards, less bottom impact, and less mammal or sea bird mortality. Achievement of environmental impact through such standards can be said to depend on the levels of specificity and obligation too. Specificity varies, with concrete conditions in the case of Young's and more general guidelines in the case of Friedrichs. Unilever's supplier requirements are not publicly accessible, so we cannot assess them in terms of specificity.

When it comes to the level of obligation (independent verification, sanctions), Friedrichs and Unilever do not have systems in place to monitor and verify whether their suppliers actually meet the supplier requirements. Although violations would be penalized, their detection is left to chance. Young's is the only company in our sample that verifies compliance with supplier requirements through supply chain audits and inspections.

11.5   EXPLAINING THE CSR EFFECTS

How were the CSR effects described above achieved? What factors internal and external to the companies can explain them?

11.5.1   Explaining Instrument Choice as a Core Aspect of CSR Output

All of our case study companies have sustainable seafood policies. To comply with these, they underwent a MSC chain of custody certification and two of the companies developed additional company-specific instruments to assess the sustainability of fisheries (Young's 'Fishery Health Check' and Unilever's 'Traffic Light System'). In the following we try to explain how these CSR outputs were achieved and, more specifically, why the companies chose (or developed) the instruments now in place. The choice of one instrument over another has implications for the creation of CSR impact, as we assume that different instruments have a different potential to create impact. A general caveat is that for sustainable seafood very few standardized instruments exist as alternatives to the MSC.[18] Since these typically have a different scope, businesses are more likely to develop an own instrument than choosing a different standardized one.

Based on the propositions presented in Section 2, we examine the relevance of the following explanatory factors for instrument choice: strategic and organizational fit; legitimacy of an instrument within the business environment; civil society demand; and instrument endorsement within the political-institutional setting.

11.5.1.1   Strategic and organizational fit

In line with our hypothesis, all three fish processors expected the CSR instruments to promote their strategic goals. We found that these strategic goals relate largely to securing the companies' financial performance and supply base. Only in one case a company actually chose between two alternative instruments. The instruments' expected sustainability impact did play a role in this choice. Contrary to our expectation, the instruments' organizational fit was not relevant for the companies' decisions.

In the 1990s, as the then world largest buyer of white fish, Unilever had a keen strategic interest to protect its supply base from medium- to long-term depletion. This interest, substantiated by market research into potential consumer interest in a label, motivated the global player to engage in the creation of the MSC – more than any pre-existing CSR commitment: Unilever's CSR strategy was developed only later. The development of the 'Traffic Light System', as mentioned earlier, was merely triggered because the MSC could not quickly enough certify fisheries relevant for Unilever, both due to its substantive requirements and time-intense procedures. Since this endangered the achievement of the 100 per cent sustainable sourcing target, an alternative tool to identify sustainable stocks was necessary.

For Young's, sustainable sourcing and MSC labelling provided an opportunity to tackle two core strategic challenges they were facing in the late 1990s: with seafood demand being static and marine fisheries' resources depleting, key opinion formers including banks regarded the seafood industry to have no future. This threatened the company's ability to raise finance. At the same time, consumer awareness of fisheries' overexploitation emerged as a constraint to the market. Sustainability labelling provided a strategic means to counter both predicaments. As regards the choice of the MSC, it was stated in interview that 'the vision that we had for years was very similar to that of the MSC. So it was a means to achieve what we wanted to achieve without the need for us to spend all of our time and efforts on creating this in a very fragmented way' (Young's Interview 2006). The perceived conduciveness of the instrument to sustainability impact did play a role here too: 'The MSC was the only one – and still is – that provided *action*' (ibid. italics added). Like Unilever, Young's developed its own tool, the 'Fishery Health Check', only to compensate for the slow progress of MSC fisheries' certifications.

At Friedrichs, the decision to start sourcing certified fish was seen to foster the pre-existing positioning and marketing strategy. In a time of commercial difficulties, when price competition from Eastern European producers forced the company to give up their non-premium product lines and to lay off 30 per cent of employees, sustainability labelling provided an opportunity to reorient the business: Friedrichs perceived (or constructed) a discursive link between the sustainability of fisheries and the long-standing focus on quality and premium products.[19] A label could help to communicate the combination of tradition and innovation, quality and care for the environment. Resulting from a strategic discussion, certification within the MSC scheme was preferred to one within the Naturland scheme, sponsored by a German organic producers' association. The labels do not compete directly as the MSC refers to wild-caught fish and Naturland to farmed fish. Friedrichs wanted to invest in the certification of either its wild or its aquaculture salmon, to avoid double costs and difficulties in communicating two labels to the consumers. In a cost benefit analysis of the two options the MSC prevailed over the Naturland standard. This was among others, because Friedrichs expected the latter not to deliver much environmental value added ('impact') as compared to its own supplier requirements for aquaculture. Furthermore, Friedrichs expected the MSC label to become more widely accepted by industry than the Naturland label.

11.5.2   Legitimacy of instruments in the business environment

Our expectation that instruments are chosen because they have a high legitimacy within the sector – for example, are used by prestigious peers – is discussed for standardized tools (the MSC) only. The expectation is confirmed in one case, partly confirmed in another and not applicable in the third.

Since Unilever was the initiator of the MSC scheme, the instrument's legitimacy among peer companies could not have influenced instrument development (hypothesis not applicable). There is at best a weak indirect influence from an altogether other sector – forestry – since the MSC was modelled on the successful timber certification scheme of the Forest Stewardship Council (FSC) (Gulbrandsen 2005). However, more generally, by developing the MSC, Unilever wanted among other things to increase its reputation within the sector (Unilever Interview 2006b).

On the UK market, Young's was the first to sell MSC products. This implies that in their immediate competitive environment, there were no peers which they followed. Only in a wider context, one might argue that advocacy by the giant and pioneer Unilever had enhanced the instrument's legitimacy and created incentives for Young's not to fall behind as a sustainability committed leader. More directly, Young's was involved in the MSC's set-up and this created an interest in the scheme. One of the company's CEOs had been appointed to the MSC's Board of Trustees, so it came as a natural step to start sourcing MSC certified fish once it was available. The commitment of the CEO spilled over to a larger group of Young's managers who participated in the MSC's institutional development and built up process ownership.

In the case of Friedrichs, 'instrument legitimacy' plays an ambiguous role for its choice of the MSC: on the one hand, when Friedrichs – as pioneer within Germany – had adopted the MSC, peer companies in its market took a downright negative view and communicated this to the company.[20] On the other hand, one of the reasons why Friedrichs preferred the MSC label to the Naturland label was that it expected the MSC to become more widely accepted by industry.

11.5.1.3   Civil society demand

The assumption that civil society demand does not play a significant role with regard to instrument *choice* is largely confirmed. However, in the *development* of instruments, civil society organizations to varying degrees exerted influence over instrument design.

When Unilever thought about developing a certification scheme, they approached WWF because of the NGO's involvement in the FSC and their know-how on certification schemes. At the time, business-NGO partnerships were still rare and Unilever was inexperienced with them. Initial discussions on how a certification scheme could be applied to fisheries revealed that the two organizations 'had different motives, but a common purpose' (Burgmans 2003, p. 22; cf. Fowler and Heap 1998). Subsequently, WWF and other NGOs significantly influenced the design of the MSC scheme, including with regard to ecosystem-related rules.

In the development of individual policies under the 'Fish for Life' framework, Young's consulted a number of organizations, such as WWF, the Marine Conservation Society and partly Greenpeace. Co-operation however was not as intense and 'on a par' as in the described case of

Unilever and WWF. Young's underscores that the company was not directly pressurized by NGOs to develop or select a specific instrument.

Similarly, civil society stakeholders did not influence Friedrichs' choice of the MSC, neither through pressure nor support.

11.5.1.4 Instrument endorsement within the political-institutional setting

A final hypothesis on why a company chooses a specific instrument is that the instrument is supported within the political-institutional setting. This hypothesis has to be refuted for our three cases: there was no explicit encouragement from state actors to adopt or develop the MSC or any of the company-specific tools.

Rather, the political-institutional setting provided a negative incentive: the failure of fisheries' managers to sustain fish stocks, EU-wide as well as internationally, was a driver for the MSC's development. As this failure threatened their supply base, Unilever felt private action was required.

11.5.1.5 Summary

Table 11.3 summarizes the above findings. The dominant factor influencing instrument choice or development – apart from the non-availability of alternative ready-made instruments with a comparable scope – were expectations that the instruments would foster the achievement of strategic goals. The strategic goals in question related above all to economic viability.

Apart from the instruments' strategic fit, their legitimacy in the sector influenced at least to some extent their choice or development. We could not identify a clear pattern as regards the role of civil society: while NGOs did not directly influence any of the companies' instrument choices, they influenced the design of newly developed own tools. The assumption that instruments were chosen because of governmental endorsement could not be confirmed.

11.5.2 Explaining CSR outcome

What factors were relevant for achieving the relatively high levels of outcome that result from the implementation of the companies' sustainable fisheries' policies? To recapitulate: all processors stopped sourcing from problematic fisheries and shifted to purchasing seafood from more sustainable sources. The shares of MSC certified fish in their portfolio of wild-capture seafood products range from 40 per cent (Young's) to 46 per cent (Unilever) and 90 per cent (Friedrichs). These shares go well beyond the averages in the sector, with the best score representing somewhat of a one-off value, based on one species and a comparatively low tonnage. In

Table 11.3   *Influence of different explanatory factors on instrument choice or development (CSR output)*

Explanatory factor	Expected influence	Actual influence			Hypothesis
		Unilever	Young's	Friedrichs	
Strategic (and organizational) fit	Yes	Yes (strong)	Yes (strong)	Yes (strong)	Confirmed
Business environment: instrument legitimacy in sector	Yes	n.a.	Yes (weak)	Yes (partly)	Partly confirmed
Civil society demands	No	Instrument design: Yes (strong)	Instrument choice: No Instrument design: Yes (weak)	No	No pattern
Political-institutional setting: public instrument endorsement	Yes	No	No	No	Not confirmed

Source: Authors.

addition, the processors implemented 'green' supplier requirements. We first try to explain these generally high levels of outcome. In the summary we shall also account for the remaining differences in outcomes, focusing on the companies' MSC shares.

11.5.2.1   Strategic and organizational integration

Our assumption is that the high levels of output, as just described, may be explained by corporate leaders linking their seafood policies to the companies' core strategies' company and integrating them organizationally. Indeed we can confirm that in all case study companies, strategic and organizational integration was high. This extended to the interface of company and supply chain in the implementation of supplier requirements.

In Unilever's Frozen Fish business, sustainability issues were included in product development and the company's brand strategy (Unilever Interview 2006b). Brand development pull was seen as the crucial success factor for putting the company's Fish Sustainability Initiative into practice:

sustainability was the vehicle by which Unilever strove to perpetuate market leadership of its Iglo brand on the frozen fish market. Once the ambitious 100 per cent sustainable sourcing target had been established, implementation was, of course, also a question of reputation for a highly 'visible' player like Unilever. In terms of organizational integration, a specific challenge for a large corporation is to maintain hierarchical control and implement strategic decisions. It was hence advantageous that the Fish Sustainability Initiative was headed directly by the director of Unilever's Frozen Food business group who pushed forward the initiative against sceptics within the company. Within the initiative a steering group served to enable communication across the relevant corporate functions and different geographical locations. It comprised fish buyers, a product developer and a representative of external relations. Internally, Unilever did not communicate its sustainable fishing policies beyond the borders of the initiative, so as to avoid information excess in the huge organization. Externally, communication with suppliers on 'green' supplier requirements was intense. Their implementation was fostered by the fact that Unilever, unlike many competitors, does not purchase fish on the spot market but through tight supplier relations. The very fact that these relations were durable and reliable was used as a lever to convince suppliers to accept the requirements.

Young's made sustainable fishing a core business principle as it perceived its respective efforts to be a differentiator against competitors. The firm integrated sustainable fishing issues into its sourcing, brand, manufacturing, growth and marketing as well as employee training strategies (Young's Bluecrest 2005). Fish species were added to the portfolio which Young's had not sold historically, such as MSC labelled Thames herring and Cornish mackerel, to actively enlarge the company's share of sustainably sourced fish. Brand rules were adapted to integrate sustainability issues and the MSC. Within the marketing strategy advertising changed from focusing on the product to focusing on the problems behind the product. In organizational terms, the company strove to design robust implementation mechanisms for their 'Fish for Life' policies. Examples are the supplier audits and traceability systems that go beyond what is usual in the sector. Internally, cross-functional communication channels strengthened the policies' implementation: in 2004 the company set up a sustainability group consisting of the purchasing, marketing, operations, and health and safety units, which was chaired by Young's deputy chief executive. The group advises the executive board on sustainability issues. In addition, efforts were taken to roll out sustainability thinking to the business, among others, through training of staff. As Young's policies increasingly limited the company's behaviour on the sourcing market, it became important for their implementation and in-house acceptance 'to communicate with people and to explain to them why it is necessary to stick to our rules while competitors do not do it' (Young's Interview 2006). Like in the case of Unilever, not trading fish on the open market and maintaining close supplier relations were the preconditions for effectively implementing supplier standards. A priority of Young's in the past years was to limit the number of suppliers and focus on those that share its sustainability concerns.

Becoming Germany's first fish processor with MSC certification, allowed Friedrichs to develop a unique selling proposition. The commitment to raise its MSC share was largely marketing-driven and integrated (beyond the sourcing strategy) into marketing and product development. About half of 2006's marketing measures related to sustainability and MSC labelled products. In product development the company states it examines for each new product whether it can be based on MSC labelled fish. A positive decision requires that the MSC product is deemed profitable and compatible with predetermined taste and recipe specifications. In terms of organizational integration, firstly, the relatively high level of control and flexibility of a medium-sized company in setting itself guidelines and changing its practices was conducive to CSR implementation. Secondly, cross-functional communication lines were tight. A management committee consisting of the director and the heads of purchasing, marketing and quality control deals with sustainability issues and reports them regularly to the board. Finally, Friedrichs' sustainable fishing policy was actively and consensually advocated by executives, mid-management and company owners. Measures to communicate the sustainable sourcing practices to employees were rare, and the extent to which the policies were supported by the wider staff is difficult for us to assess.[21] Communicating and asserting sustainability standards vis-à-vis suppliers was eased by the company's long-standing and trustful supplier relations.

11.5.2.2   Corporate culture

Can the high levels of CSR outcome be explained by the corporate cultures of our case study companies? We assume that a change in corporate practices will be fostered in particular if CSR is rooted in a long-standing and well-developed identity of the organization as being socially responsible. We find that only one company has a record and explicit identity with regard to social responsibility – though it is so large that many sub-cultures coexist. The other companies have no comparable history but feature corporate beliefs and storylines that support rather than conflict with greening corporate practices.

Unilever's tradition of social responsibility and community involvement goes back to the very foundation of the company. William Lever had provided employee benefits that preceded the establishment of a comprehensive welfare state (Rowan 2003; Wilson 1954). Its partial foundation in the Netherlands, where one-third of its land has been reclaimed from the sea, is interpreted to have given rise to a long-standing concern of Unilever with environmental sustainability (Werhane 2000, p. 360). While such a history certainly does not directly determine present day CSR performance, it might shape the identity of employees and promote interest in a satisfactory outcome. Also, as a legacy of its dual country origin, corporate culture in Unilever emphasizes consensus and discussion (Jones and Miskell 2005, p. 137). Decisions tend to become better implemented in consensual cultures than in hierarchical ones, as potential veto players are involved in the decision-making processes and are then bound by the decisions. This may support the creation of CSR outcomes. On the other hand, the corporate culture in Unilever – though distinct – coexists with numerous sub-cultures (Jones 2005). Evidence of this fragmentation is that Unilever's vision of CSR is named and understood differently within its two headquarters: while the British branch views CSR as an umbrella with sustainability as its environmental pillar, the Dutch branch understands sustainability as an overarching approach and social responsibility as part of it. Despite such subtleties, we may assume that the identity of Unilever as a responsible company with a tradition in voluntary activities will have supported rather than obstructed implementation of its sustainable fisheries' goals.

Young's predecessor companies did not have a strong tradition in acting as a 'corporate citizen'. However, the merged company strongly believes in the own influence in the supply chain, market and industry, and in getting engaged. This belief was stimulated by the frustrations of the pre-merger time when Young's and Bluecrest were 'some sort of Cinderella companies of large PLCs[22] that were involved in all sorts of things and there was no real empathy with the seafood industry' (Young's Interview 2006). Corporate managers perceive involvement in the industry to be a value, and this is reflected in the company's active participation in the MSC, in industry associations and initiatives at UK and EU level and in its intense supply chain management. This perception may have influenced positively the implementation of Young's commitment to sustainable fisheries.

Like Young's, Friedrichs does not have an explicit identity as socially responsible. However, its corporate culture builds on a strong sense of tradition, valuation of premium quality, careful manufacture and what was described to us as a 'normative approach' to the raw material fish. This culture was synergetic with or could be used as a basis for a sustainability orientation: 'sustainability' is strongly connotated with a long-term time perspective, with a careful and responsible treatment of nature and, more generally, with a commitment to a 'better world'. The described corporate culture supports rather than obstructs effective implementation of sustainable fishing policies.

11.5.2.3 Business environment

We expect that the high levels of CSR outcome can be explained by the fact that companies experience implementation of their sustainable seafood policies as a business benefit. This expectation is confirmed on the demand side as sustainable seafood met with consumer and partly retailer interest in relevant markets for all case study companies. However, at the same time the firms met with business obstacles on the supply side which prevented them from expanding their outcomes. This applies in particular to the shares of sustainable (and especially MSC labelled) fish in their purchasing volumes.

All case study companies expected that their sustainable fishing commitment could tap the increasing consumer interest in sustainability issues, thus creating a business case.[23] Unilever had this substantiated by market research before setting up the MSC.[24] Retailer or investor interest, though, are said not to have promoted the implementation of the Fish Sustainability Initiative (Unilever Interview 2006a). In Britain the 1990s were characterized by an increasing public awareness of seafood issues. Consumer pressure on the retail sector created back-pressures on Young's: major retailers were interested in offering sustainable seafood, so that customer pull complemented consumer pull (Young's interview 2007). When the UK supermarket chain Sainsbury's signalled an interest in sustainable fisheries' issues, Young's even got involved in setting up the retailer's fish policy. In Germany, while retailers at the time neither called for nor supported the marketing of MSC labelled fish, a survey by Friedrichs indicated meaningful consumer support for sustainable fisheries' issues. Indeed the company's sales volumes of its Alaskan salmon products rose steeply once these had become MSC labelled.

While the companies' expectation of business benefits supported their efforts to implement the commitments of their sustainable seafood policies, these policies were at the same time counteracted by additional costs and obstacles. In financial terms, such costs include the charges of an MSC chain of custody certification and its annual reviews, plus royalties for using the label. Significantly higher costs accrue when processors contribute to funding an MSC fisheries (pre-) assessment or when sustainability considerations require substituting one fish species by another (certified) species. Substitution involves a number of challenges for fish processors: price, quality and the reliability of supply vary when a processor sources fish from a new fishery. So do performance levels – for instance, with respect to fish bones or filleting – and taste. As a consequence, for example, replacement of cod by certified Hoki in Unilever's fish fingers was not welcomed by European consumers. Moving into new fisheries furthermore requires the cost- and time-intense establishment of quality control systems. Finally, focusing one's supply base on fewer (certified) stock implies that processors' bargaining power vis-à-vis their suppliers shrinks and prices threaten to go up. In all three case study companies these additional costs could to some extent be 'cushioned' by the premium margins of their brand products.

More severe restraints, however, existed on the supply side. For instance, in the case of Unilever's Fish Sustainability Initiative, the achievement of the 100 per cent sustainable sourcing target was hampered by limits in the availability of sustainable fish. The major problem was the scarcity of fisheries that qualified as sustainable and, if possible, were certified. It had already taken Unilever rigorous efforts to raise its MSC share to 46 per cent. This had only been achieved by engaging with fishing industries and fisheries' administrations, pushing for and actually co-funding the MSC certification of the New Zealand hoki and Alaskan pollock fisheries. Especially, Alaska pollock is a huge resource used in numerous of Unilever's products. For Unilever, going beyond the 46 per cent share depended on additional fisheries being certified. This, however, was hampered by the fact that many of the fish stocks relevant for the company were (and still are) not in a good enough shape to be certified. This fundamental problem was aggravated, especially in the MSC's early life, by the fact that fishermen were hard to convince of the benefits of certification. Finally, certification procedures took longer than expected (3.5 years in the case of Alaska pollock). Similar to the situation in Unilever, crucial wild-capture fish species sold by Young's (cod, haddock, plaice or tuna) and by Friedrichs (herring and eel) were – and partly are – not available with an MSC label, thus limiting the companies' CSR outcome levels.

11.5.2.4 Civil society demand

Confirming our hypothesis, civil society stakeholders contributed to behavioural changes and high levels of CSR outcomes in all companies. This happened both through pressure and co-operation – for instance, in helping to set up an industry-wide CSR instrument (Unilever), providing advice in the implementation of internal instruments (Young's) or in product development (Friedrichs).

In the case of Unilever, implementing its sustainable seafood policy was based heavily on the company's co-operation with WWF in the set-up of the MSC. Certification of fisheries worldwide against the MSC's principles provided the basis for Unilever to source sustainable fish and work towards its 100 per cent target. WWF provided not only expertise on certification schemes, but lent the scheme legitimacy essential for its acceptance by consumers.

In Young's, the provision of knowledge by academic and civil society experts was an important success factor of implementing their sustainable seafood policy. When first applying the 'Fishery Health Check', the firm was faced with problems in accessing and understanding scientific fishery data. As a response, two experts were co-opted to a sub-committee of the firm's sustainability group to cover gaps in the company's expertise on fisheries' economics and science. In addition, Young's developed communication lines to ICES,[25] an intergovernmental organization concerned with marine and fisheries' science. Company representatives say that the involvement of external expertise led to a better understanding of sustainability issues and to learning processes within the company. From outside the company, NGOs in Britain worked from the 1990s to build consumer awareness. Milestones were Greenpeace UK's 2004 campaign 'A Recipe for Disaster' and its follow-up 'Recipe for Change' (Greenpeace 2005). They put pressure on supermarkets and indirectly on fish processors to change their sourcing practices (Seafood Choices Alliance 2007, p. 22).

Civil society stakeholders influenced Friedrichs' sustainable fishing outcome both in an indirect and a more direct way. Indirectly, purchasing guides for sustainable fish by WWF and Greenpeace Germany supported awareness and consumption of certified fish and thus Friedrichs' efforts. More directly, Friedrichs in 2005–06 co-operated with WWF in the development of a new product. In this process the NGO exerted pressure so that the final product contained 100 per cent rather than 50 per cent MSC salmon (WWF Interview 2007).[26] In the end, the company changed its recipe to accommodate for the demands of WWF.

11.5.2.5   Political-institutional setting

Finally, we assume that the high fisheries-related CSR outcomes of our case study processors can be explained by expectations and norms formulated within the political-institutional setting in which the companies operate. This expectation is only partly confirmed. Voluntary corporate commitment is traditionally rooted above all in the British system of socio-economic governance. National policies try to varying degrees (again strongest in the UK) to stimulate supply of and demand for sustainable seafood. However, cross-pressures exist with regard to fisheries' policies in all countries: within the EU, where national fisheries' policies are governed to a large extent by the Common Fisheries Policy, many fisheries are outside safe biological limits (ICES 2007). Accordingly, the possibility for the case study companies to purchase fish from sustainable sources was more often advanced by fisheries' administrations outside the EU.

Though Unilever operates internationally, the political-institutional setting of its home countries, UK and the Netherlands, can be assumed to affect its voluntary activities on sustainable seafood to some extent. There is a longer tradition of voluntary corporate commitment within the liberal market system of the UK (Hall and Soskice 2001) than within the neo-corporatist, co-ordinated market economy of the Netherlands (Visser 1998). Here, the CSR concept was introduced more recently, but with government support (Cramer and Loeber 2004). In addition, governmental initiatives, especially in Britain (see below), strove to support demand for sustainable seafood and to stimulate supply by funding fishery certifications. However, public policies in countries of origin such as Alaskan pollock management that enabled an MSC certification were more vital for Unilever in achieving its 46 per cent MSC share.

In Young's domestic environment, the British government has commissioned and funded the MSC certification of a number of (relatively small) UK fisheries, thus enhancing the supply of sustainable seafood. Triggered by a series of food scandals during the 1990s, the government developed initiatives to foster sustainable (sea)food consumption that addressed both the supply and demand side.[27] The publicly funded Sustainable Consumption Roundtable recommended encouraging procurers to purchase MSC fish (SCR 2006, p. 45). Prominent support is also lent to the MSC by the Prince of Wales. These signals from politics met with the long-standing Anglo-Saxon culture of corporate community commitment.

Friedrichs' CSR activities were affected by the German setting, both in a tempering and supportive way. Industrial relations in Germany are generally characterized by neo-corporatist networks between state and private sector and a regulatory approach (Streeck 1999). Following this logic and against a recommendation of its advisory council for sustainable development (RNE 2006), the German government refrained from developing a public CSR strategy. Neither were there substantial initiatives on sustainable fisheries. Only in 2005, the environmental ministry hosted a symposium on seafood labelling. This workshop motivated Friedrichs in that it promoted legitimacy of sustainable fisheries' activities within the sector and supply chain. A year later, the government at least formally declared sustainable fisheries and especially certification to be a new focus of its sustainability concept. The Alaskan state government, however, played a more decisive role for Friedrichs: it funded the original MSC certification and surveillance processes of its salmon fisheries, thus helping to ensure the supply of certified fish.

11.5.2.6 Summary

Our expectations – that all five of our explanatory factors would contribute to the achievement of the relatively high CSR outcome levels – were largely confirmed by the three cases analyzed (Table 11.4). Outcome includes changes in sourcing practices and product portfolios. It is difficult to state which factor was most conducive to turning CSR outputs into outcomes. In any case, business benefits were countervailed to some degree by extra costs and by supply restrictions. The supportive role of the political-institutional setting was also qualified, since unsustainable EU fisheries' policies at the same time prevented many stocks within common waters from becoming MSC certified.

The relatively high levels of outcome across the three companies were explained by quite similar factors in each of the company cases. But how can we then account for the remaining differences in the companies' outcome levels? For this question, we shall focus on the companies' shares of MSC fish only. These vary between 40 per cent (Young's), 46 per cent (Unilever) and 90 per cent (Friedrichs). Unlike the other factors described above, the availability of MSC labelled fish to substitute less sustainable seafood in existing portfolios varies markedly. Differences in the companies' MSC shares result from the complexity of a processors' product portfolio; the number and relative weight of (non-) certified species within this portfolio; and the processors' clout to actually push or (co-) fund a fishery certification. In the case of Unilever, the quota of MSC-sourced fish can be attributed to the early and large-scale availability of certified species relevant for Unilever's portfolio. Also, Unilever as a huge player pushed actively for certification of fisheries commercially relevant for the firm, thus being able to raise the own outcome level. Young's only gradually achieved its 40 per cent MSC share. This was due to the initially low number of certified fisheries and a mismatch of certified species with those required in its multifaceted portfolio – Young's sources more than 60 species from 30 countries. Compared with this, Friedrichs accomplished its 90 per cent share (which corresponds to a relatively low tonnage of fish as compared to Unilever and Young's) by sourcing just one MSC species – the early available Alaska salmon. The company had sourced from this fishery already before it became MSC certified, and additional costs were negligible.

11.6   CONCLUSIONS

What sustainability effects (output, outcome and impact) were achieved through CSR in the three European fish processing companies we analyzed? And what factors contributed to the achievement of these effects?

Table 11.4 Influence of different explanatory factors on changes in sourcing practices and product portfolios (CSR outcome)

Explanatory factor	Expected influence	Actual influence			Hypothesis
		Unilever	Young's	Friedrichs	
Corporate strategy and organization: strategic and organizational integration	Yes	Yes	Yes	Yes	Confirmed
Corporate culture: long-standing identities as corporate citizen	Yes	Yes	(Yes)	(Yes)	Largely confirmed
Business environment: business benefits of changing sourcing practices and product portfolios	Yes	Yes, with restrictions	Yes, with restrictions	Yes, with restrictions	Confirmed with qualification
Civil society demands: support; pressure	Yes	Yes	Yes	Yes	Confirmed
Political-institutional setting: role of CSR in socio-economic governance; public policies on sustainable seafood	Yes	Yes, partly	Yes, partly	Yes, partly	Partly confirmed

Source: Authors.

Looking at these questions helps us to understand success factors of CSR in the issue area of sustainable fisheries.

With regard to CSR effects, our analysis underscored that fish processors have much leeway in committing themselves to ambitious policies (output) in the issue area of sustainable seafood. However, their ability to change their own sourcing practices and the composition of their product portfolio (thus influencing their own outcome and impact) is to some extent limited by structural factors, above all the availability of the required fish from sustainable sources. Environmental impact can be imputed most reliably when processors source fish from MSC certified fisheries and when implementation of specific and ambitious supplier requirements is audited and sanctioned. Company-specific tools to assess the sustainability of fisheries are an intermediate solution but should be made more transparent with regard to assessment criteria.

A general caveat to fish processors' influence over the sustainability of their business is that environmental benefits to a large extent depend on the behaviour of fishermen – and of course on (public) fishery management. Since fish processors neither own nor manage the fish resource they source from, their capacity to influence actual 'on the water impact' is limited, especially for smaller businesses. As Hoel (2004, p. 50) points out, 'ecolabelling schemes in fisheries rest on an assumption that the producers of fish products will be able to influence governments to modify management practices so as to satisfy the standards set by the label, alternatively that governments will be sensitive to the market concerns of the industry and modify resource management practices accordingly'. This points to the limits of certification schemes especially for fisheries in the global South. Here, low data availability and governance capacities for stock management make MSC certifications virtually impossible. Also, seafood labelling schemes depend on consumer demand, and such demand at least for the time being is largely limited to EU and North American markets. For a more encompassing solution to the degradation of oceans, CSR will hence not suffice.

What were the causes for the sustainability effects described above? To explain these causes, we tackled in a first step factors that affected 'output' and more concretely the choice of the MSC as the most effective instrument available. While the lack of alternatives restricted the choice between instruments in the first place, it was decisive that an instrument fitted into the company's strategic considerations and was expected to create environmental impact. Instrument legitimacy in the sector created at least some interest in the instrument, as did – unpredicted by us – involvement in the instrument development. In accordance with our assumption, demands by civil society stakeholders were less relevant with regard to instrument choice, but against our expectation no incentives existed in the political-institutional setting that suggested the choice of a specific instrument. However, policy failure to sustain fisheries and thus processors' supply bases had triggered development of voluntary instruments in the first place.

In a second step we discussed factors that supported the translation of output into outcomes. Most of our hypotheses on why the companies achieved relatively high outcomes levels were supported by the empirical material. In all cases we found implementation of sustainable seafood policies strengthened by: high degrees of strategic and organizational integration, including into the supply chain; distinct corporate cultures (though only one built on a traditional identity as corporate citizen); the expectation to reap business benefits, in particular through consumer demand; civil society support and pressure; and to some extent by supportive public policies and institutions. Against our expectation, supply restrictions within the business environment at the same time discouraged CSR outcomes. Analysing the differences between the companies' outcome levels, the main insight was that within their existing product portfolios processors have varying opportunities to source MSC fish. This is due to the limited number of certified fisheries worldwide.

With regard to our analytical framework, our findings show that the set of explanatory factors is fruitful. It enabled us to capture major influences on instrument choice and on the creation of CSR outcomes while leaving enough flexibility to cope with one-off effects. Interestingly enough, the two complementary views inherent in the framework – the managerial vs cultural-institutional perspective – did both yield empirical results. For example, strategic concerns and the business case certainly fostered CSR effects, indicating that corporate actors follow a 'logic of expected consequences' that features prominently among the behavioural assumptions of management literature (March and Olsen 1989). At the same time, corporate cultures, sectoral legitimacy of instruments and civil society expectations were relevant too. This suggests that corporate actors to some extent also comply with a 'logic of appropriateness' as suggested by institutionalist literature (ibid.). These cultural-institutionlist factors, however, tend to be more difficult to uncover, as they are often less intentional and explicit.

NOTES

1. That is, we do not look into farmed fish (aquaculture) or into the wider aspects of environmental responsibility or community commitment.

2. For the terms, which originate in policy analysis, see for example Prittwitz (2003) or Oberthür and Gehring (2006).
3. Either directly (through supplier requirements) or indirectly by lobbying for 'greener' fisheries' management systems.
4. Since we did not receive sufficient information in the interviews to determine the effect of corporate culture on instrument selection, this hypothesis cannot be discussed in Section 11.5.1.
5. And hence the preferences of investors, suppliers, customers and consumers.
6. The 'MSC Principles and Criteria' were developed following international stakeholder consultations and are based on the FAO 'Code of Conduct for Responsible Fisheries'. They were made compliant with the FAO 'Guidelines on Marine Eco-Labelling and Certification' when these came out in March 2005.
7. More specifically: fish from illegal, unreported and unregulated (IUU) sources. This is relevant for the sustainability of fisheries as it includes fish harvested by exceeding quota limits, fish outside prescribed areas, fish caught by ignoring size regulations or using banned fishing methods, or non-target species. Compare Young's Bluecrest 2006c, 2006d, 2006e.
8. The four-page document is informally adapted from time to time by the management committee. Its sustainable sourcing chapter evolved out of an earlier and still rather vague statement on sustainable salmon sourcing (Gottfried Friedrichs KG 2003).
9. This implied purchasing salmon from Alaska rather than from Canada.
10. Such as bottom trawling in specific habitats, shark finning, the most destructive fishing methods as well as methods that incur unacceptable and unnecessary by-catch of non-target species such as turtles, dolphins and seabirds (Young's Bluecrest 2006c, 2006f).
11. Both Young's and Unilever had pushed the development of these guidelines within the Association.
12. Suppliers need to confirm that the fish they trade is not threatened by extinction or legally protected; that it originates from catch areas for which Total Allowable Catches (TACs) or similar rules apply; that the company has adhered to all legal requirements during harvesting; that they state catch area and harvesting method for each consignment; and finally that they act to the best of their knowledge to avoid by-catch and negative impacts on the environment. The requirements follow recommendations by the German fish producers' association (Bundesmarktverband der Fischereiwirtschaft). WWFs consider these to be 'very general'.
13. This is because we consider instrument design an intervening variable with regard to CSR impact, and its influence is empirically difficult to disentangle from other influences, for example, the concrete instrument implementation.
14. With regard to step 4 in the certification procedure, the full fisheries' assessment, the MSC guidelines read: 'An evaluation of the fishery against the MSC's Principles and Criteria for Sustainable Fishing, including, if relevant, the drafting of *measurable, outcome-oriented and time-bounded conditions of certification.*' (italics added)
15. Examples of such conditions are: 'elimination of ghost fishing' or 'reduction in the number of discarded hooks' (Agnew 2006, p. 17).
16. In a more encompassing sense, independence of the MSC is fostered by the fact that both in the MSC Board and Stakeholder Council all major stakeholders are equally represented and that the MSC profits from its certification procedures only to a small extent (for example, licence agreements to use the MSC logo).
17. Firstly, the industry-wide 'model nature' of the MSC helps to raise awareness and to contribute to the diffusion of higher fisheries' standards throughout the entire sector as other fisheries take the MSC standards as a basis for own improvements. This may occur among others through the MSC's pressure on political institutions to set more precautionary levels of Total Allowable Catch in order to allow for a certification. Secondly, the MSC as a joint initiative of industry and civil society bundles the interests of the actors involved and increases their influence to promote sustainable fisheries' issues. Stakeholder inclusiveness has fostered learning and coverage of a broader range

of issues, increasing the scope of potential impacts. Thirdly, the MSC chain of custody certification increases transparency throughout the supply chain and thus prevents illegal fishing.

18. For example, the KRAV or Naturland labels, dolphin-safe labels, retailer marks and so on.

19. This link is debatable, as the quality of wild-capture fish is often more strongly influenced by concrete fishing practices than by a fish stock's level of exploitation.

20. Only later, the MSC's legitimacy began to rise in the sector. Along with this development, a working group was established in the German fish processors' association that developed a purchasing agreement to promote 'stock-conserving' fisheries.

21. The company managers claim that employees relate to the company's high quality and sustainability orientation: 'Our staff appreciate that the fish is trolled . . . that we deal with "happy" fishermen and "happy" fish' (Friedrichs' Interview 2006).

22. Public limited companies.

23. For early research on consumer preferences for eco-labelled seafood see, for example, Wessells et al. (1999).

24. Recent consumer research confirms that environmental considerations are important in European consumers' seafood purchases (Seafood Choices Alliance 2005, p. 7).

25. The International Council for the Exploration of the Sea.

26. For taste reasons, Friedrichs' quality assurance unit had advised to complement the certified wild-capture by (fattier) aquaculture salmon. WWF reasoned that in this case they could not keep up the co-operation, which was to involve the WWF logo on the product's package. Also, the MSC rules stipulated that the MSC logo might only be used for a product that exclusively contains MSC fish.

27. These include the Sustainable Farming and Food Strategy, the Food Industry Sustainability Strategy and the Public Sector Food Procurement Initiative. The latter is part of the government's sustainable procurement strategy aiming at the UK to be among the EU leaders in sustainable procurement by 2009. Furthermore, the environmental ministry in 2005 awarded a £405 grant on sustainable seafood consumption of children, co-funded by the MSC.

12 CSR for gender equality: a new approach for dealing with long-standing inequalities? Insights from two banks

Irmgard Schultz

12.1 INTRODUCTION

This contribution presents the findings of a comparative case study on CSR activities for gender equality in two banks in Europe: Caja Madrid of Spain and Dexia Group, which is headquartered in Belgium, France and Luxembourg. The focus of the study is to elaborate the effects of the banks' Corporate Social Responsibility (CSR) activities on gender equality: do the banks' CSR activities indeed contribute to gender equality? What were the drivers and barriers that can explain the effects?

In order to obtain information about the effects of CSR activities of the two banks, an impact assessment is carried out. It shows surprising findings in the comparison of the two banks' gender equality-related CSR activities and societal impact. Furthermore, we identify the factors within the banks and their environment which can explain these results. The empirical bases of our findings are in-depth interviews with representatives of the banks who are in charge of CSR and human resource management and with stakeholders of the banks; the interviews were carried out in late 2006.

12.2 GENDER EQUALITY IN EUROPEAN POLITICS AND BUSINESS

First of all, it should be borne in mind that political activities to promote gender equality in the economic sector have a long-standing history in the European Union (EU). Already the Treaty of Rome that established the European Economic Community (EEC) defined a principle of equal opportunities in 1957, providing that women and men receive equal pay for equal work (Article 119 of the Treaty of Rome, 1957). Since then a comprehensive body of legislation on this subject and different EU strategies to promote gender equality have been implemented. Nevertheless, there are to be found persistent inequalities in the annual gender equality reports of the EU.[1]

Our following analysis focuses on five gender issues that are discussed predominantly in the debate on gender equality in work and employment: equal opportunities of male and female employees; equal pay; reconciliation of work and family life (work-life balance); anti-discrimination with regard to sexual harassment; and – relevant with regard to the role of banks – the creation of equal access to and supply of financial services. The first, second and third gender issues concern first of all the activities of selection of workforce, career promotion, equal numeration and working time regulation. Above all, a lack of opportunities for women to advance in business careers, unequal pay between women and men and unequal conditions as regards the work-life balance are discussed in the relevant literature. The annual European equality reports and other literature paint the following picture:

- Every third European businesswoman in the top firms aspires to obtain a senior leadership position within her organization (Catalyst 2002, 2004). However, there are still only few women in management positions across the continent. In the banking sector the participation rate of women among the whole workforce is relatively high compared to other sectors (Kreetz 2005, p. 29) whereas the proportion of women in top management positions is still only average (8 per cent) (EPWN and Egon Zehnder International 2004, p. 15). Women are even under-represented in training and seminars relevant to career advancement (Ebner 2004, p. 208; Kreetz 2005, p. 2).

- With regard to equal pay there is a substantial gap between the average earnings of men and women in general, which can only partially be explained by the differences in qualifications and jobs. Even if women have positions in higher-level occupations their pay lags behind that of males across all employment categories (Thewlis et al. 2004, p. 91). In 2004 the estimated pay gap between women and men in the EU was 15 per cent, one point below its level in 1999 (European Commission 2006d). A lack of paternity leave, the over-representation of women in short-term employment and unstable contracts contribute amongst other factors to this gender pay gap (Browne 2002; EGGSIE 2005; European Commission 2006a, 2006f).

- Concerning reconciliation of work and private life the remaining gender gap in part-time work indicates unequal gender relations (European Foundation for the Improvement of Living and Working Conditions 2006). In Europe four-fifths of the part-time workforce and other forms of flexible working arrangements are female, while training is often exclusively offered to the full-time staff. In almost all European countries women (aged 20–49) with children have lower employment rates than those without. In 2004 32.6 per cent of women worked part time, while this was the case for only 7.4 per cent of men (European Commission 2006d).

These facts illustrate a lack of equal opportunities in the European labour market. Deficits also exist for the issues of sexual harassment and equal access to and supply of financial services. Though these two gender issues indicate quite different dimensions of anti-discrimination, both are relevant in the context of banks. Companies can enhance gender equality in European societies both by increasing compliance with legislation and by going beyond compliance through CSR.

12.3   BRIEF DESCRIPTION OF THE CASE STUDY BANKS CAJA MADRID AND DEXIA GROUP

For our study on the effects of gender-related CSR in banks, we selected Caja Madrid, headquartered in Spain, and Dexia Group, operating in Belgium, France, Luxembourg and other countries. These businesses were chosen because both of them are well known for their social engagement including gender issues and for their involvement in CSR.

Caja Madrid is a Spanish savings bank with 12 731 employees, 43.4 per cent of them women. It is not stock market listed. The bank operates all over Spain with more than 1900 branches and more than 6.7 million clients. The bank ranks at fourth place in the Spanish financial sector with respect to total assets, loans and customer funds. The net operating income in 2005 was 1408 million euros. The main activities and products of the savings bank are business with clients as well as investment banking. As a supplement to its financial activity, the Group holds a portfolio of investments in firms operating in strategic sectors. A series of companies are owned by Caja Madrid directly or through the Corporación Financiera Caja Madrid.

Caja Madrid is a financial institution with a social remit and tradition. In 2005 Caja Madrid allocated the amount of 1612 million euros for *Obra Social* (social work) and Caja Madrid Foundation (Caja Madrid 2005a).

Dexia Group, our second case study bank, resulted from a 1996 merger of two major European players in local public finance: Crédit Local in France and Crédit Communal in Belgium. Since this first merger, the stock market listed bank is characterized by strong development activities (and more mergers). Dexia serves two principal markets: local authorities and similar institutions on a global scale and the retail market, mostly in Belgium and Luxembourg. It has developed private banking business for affluent customers in Belgium, Luxembourg and France. In 2004 the net banking income amounted to 5392 million euros. Dexia has developed specialized activities in the field of asset management, insurance services and fund administration. Today, Dexia Group ranks amongst the 15 largest banking groups of the Euro zone (Dexia 2005a). In 2004 Dexia had 24 019 employees, 54 per cent of them male and 46 per cent female.

Dexia Group, similar to Caja Madrid, has a social remit and tradition. Some 50 per cent of Dexia's financial activities concern infrastructure, building of schools, the environment and societal issues. These financial activities are accompanied by a strong citizenship commitment which deals with different objectives depending on the features of the respective countries and on the expectations of the local communities. The Group's financial commitment in this area totalled slightly above 7.1 million euros in 2005.

12.4 IMPACT ASSESSMENT: THE EFFECTS OF GENDER EQUALITY-RELATED CSR

What are the concrete CSR policies of Caja Madrid and Dexia Group? To what extent are these effectively implemented and lead to changes in the banks' daily practices – such as staffing, training, promotion or payment practices? Can we trace wider societal impacts of these changed practices? In the following we shall discuss these questions for each of the banks, distinguishing in our impact assessment between 'CSR output', 'CSR outcome' and 'CSR impact'. Output describes corporate commitments and strategies on sustainability, including adoption of CSR instruments. Outcomes are changes in the companies' concrete practices resulting from CSR output. Impact includes the direct effects on society (and – not relevant for this case study – the environment), that is outside the company. The focus is on gender-related CSR, but in the section of 'output' we shall also provide a brief overview of overarching and non-gender-related CSR policies.

12.4.1 Caja Madrid: Substantial Outcome and Impact Despite Lack of an Overall Gender Strategy

Concerning CSR output, Caja Madrid applies some 'overarching' CSR policies and instruments which are not directly gender-related. Above all, the bank has a CSR commitment in which it refers explicitly to sustainability ('sustainable growth of society', Caja Madrid 2005a, p. 2) and which applies to the entire Caja Madrid Group. Voluntary instruments include the quality standard ISO 9001 (since 1998) and EFQM (since 2003). Targeting sustainability, the bank applies the environmental management standard ISO 14 001 (since 2005), discloses non-financial information against the Global Reporting Initiative (GRI) indicators – including some gender-related information – and plans to join the 'Equator Principles' as a benchmark for financial institutions to manage social and environmental issues in project financing.

With regard to gender equality-related CSR, Caja Madrid's CSR commitment does not explicitly mention gender equality and the principle of equal opportunity (Caja Madrid 2005a). Neither does the bank have an overall strategy on this issue. However, equal opportunity is integrated into its human relations' programmes via internal codes and agreements. Respective targets are annually identified. One of these targets, for example, involves achieving a share of 40 per cent women in management positions.

In this context, two self-tailored instruments play a particular role: Caja Madrid's Integrated People Management System (CMIPMS) and the Integrative Personal Guidance System (SGIP). The former is an integrative management tool that defines the topics of human resources. The CMIPMS existed before the establishment of CSR policies, but is now very closely connected to CSR. Thus, CSR serves as an orientation principle to all management systems of Caja Madrid (internal communication systems, human resources' communication systems and management by groups). With respect to leadership rules, the human resources' management in Caja Madrid is conducted by the guiding principles of its Integrative Personal Guidance System (SGIP: *Sistema de Gestión Integral de Personas*). It guides several tools of career selection and career promotion which have a strong impact on gender relations. Gender equality is integrated implicitly into all these tools by the banks' catalogues of 'Norms and Criteria of Behaviour in the Professional Field', which includes a separate chapter on equal opportunities (Caja Madrid 2005b).

Apart from applying its own instruments, Caja Madrid participates in the Spanish gender award system *Empresa Optima* (Optimal Company). Gender award systems are a kind of management system. They have been developed independently of CSR activities – most of them with initial financial help of governments – to promote 'positive action' for women (Instituto de la Mujer Interview 2006; Busch 2004). However, in many companies including our two case study banks these systems have now become part of the companies' gender equality-related CSR portfolio. The award system *Empresa Optima* is governed by a national programme named *Programa Optima* (Optimal Programme) which the Spanish government initiated in 1996 with the help of the EU Structural Fund. *Programa Optima* is managed by the Spanish Institute for Women (Instituto de la Mujer) which is affiliated to the Spanish Ministry of Work and Social Affairs (Oficina Internacional del Trabajo 2006; Mujeres Universia 2006). Together with the company's responsible officer for *Programa Optima*, the Ministry's officials identify objectives for equal opportunities. On this basis, both are jointly able to formulate a tailor-made gender action plan for the company. At company level, the programme of the gender award system distinguishes six areas of action, including communication and sensitization, continuous education and training, and workforce selection. Within a specified time frame performance is measured and new objectives and actions need to be agreed upon (Instituto de la Mujer Interview 2006). Concerning our five selected gender issues, this management system addresses concrete aspects of the issue of equal opportunities and of work-life balance. The issues of equal pay, sexual harassment and equal access to financial resources are not included.

The bank's CSR outcomes concern changes in the concrete practices of companies as stimulated by CSR output. In the following we focus on gender-related practices. Mention should be made first of all of gender-related reporting in Caja Madrid's inaugural CSR report in 2004. For the first time, it showed all CSR activities connected with the CMIPMS and thus – via links in the electronic CSR report – with all activities of the company. This specific electronic form of the report is accessible to every employee and stimulated the discussion about CSR within the company ('The CSR report is more than a report', as stated by company representatives, Caja Madrid Interview 2006a). In the bank's CSR report 2005 gender issues are published in relation to human resources. Indicators and data were adopted from GRI reporting (GRI 2 indicators), which used only a few categories. Concerning the issue of equal pay between women and men, the 2005 CSR report states a relationship of 1:1 (Caja Madrid 2005a, p. 107). Since then the gender-related categories within the CSR report have become more differentiated because the new GRI 3 categories entail more gender reporting. Internally, Caja Madrid's human resources unit uses additional indicators. They are related to the human resources' annual action plan into which the action plan of the gender award system *Empresa*

Optima is integrated. Caja Madrid was certified as *Empresa Optima* in 2002 and has maintained certification since that time. A person was appointed to have responsibility for *Programa Optima* which included the follow-up processes.

The first participation in *Programa Optima* caused little change in the bank's daily practices (Caja Madrid Interview 2006c). However, since 2002, visible changes and improvements are reported. According to responsible officers of the human resources unit, the best performance was reached by actions aimed at making employees, especially people from the human resources' department,[2] aware about equal opportunity (Caja Madrid Interview 2006c, 2006d). The most substantial improvement within the six defined areas concerns communication and sensitization. Furthermore, different programmes promoting the conciliation of work and family life are considered as very successful and their outcome as high. This is based on the implementation of projects such as 'Working Close to Home', 'Help with Childcare', or 'Help for External Training and E-learning'. Furthermore, Caja Madrid provides a specific maternity/paternity service offering information related to parenthood, nursery support for children up to three years of age, a full subsidy for access to the website during maternity leave, as well as subsidized activities for children during out-of-school periods. It supports part-time work, flexible working time arrangements and return regulations after parental leave which go beyond legal entitlements. Furthermore, the programme supports parents' initiatives.

With regard to equal opportunities, the share of women in the bank's total workforce has continually risen in recent years: from 42.3 per cent in 2002 to 43.4 per cent in 2005. This may signal that the bank is an attractive employer for women, possibly – though not necessarily – as a direct result of its voluntary initiatives on equal opportunities. A more reliable indicator of the bank's success in promoting women's careers is the ratio of women in management positions. This share has increased by more than 6 per cent points from 22.8 per cent in 2002 to 29.2 per cent in 2005; the organization's ultimate target is 40 per cent (Caja Madrid Human Resource unit 2007). An improvement of about 6 per cent more women in top positions within three years indicates that CSR activities for gender equality have substantial effects in the area of equal opportunities for women and men.

With respect to the gender issue of sexual harassment, Caja Madrid has established a confidential complaints channel. Cases of non-compliance with respectful behaviour are handled according to the internal codes and agreements on professional behaviour.

Finally, regarding the gender issue of equal access to and supply of banking services, Caja Madrid promotes equal treatment by offering equality training to its customer consultants for developing skills and behaviour for equal treatment in consulting. However, Caja Madrid does not offer microcredits as a financial product with specific relevance for female customers.[3] In summary, the bank's improvements with regard to gender-related CSR outcomes are considerable.

These outcomes also indicate the achievement of CSR (or sustainability) impact at a societal level. First of all, it should be noted that the changes in corporate practice can partly equal the desired societal impact. For example, an increase in female representation at board level as an (in-company) outcome at the same time enhances the societal quota of women in top positions (impact). The identification of outcome and societal impact is not quantifiable to date and quite difficult. In order to gain an impression of the level of societal impact, it helps to relate the identified CSR outcome (performance) data of the analyzed company to the national and/or European average situation. We argue that societal impact could be achieved when a company's level of outcome is considerably above that achieved by the same industry at a national or European level.

A study on the banking sector provides European data on this matter (Kreetz 2005, p. 29). Regarding equal opportunities, it detected that British and Scandinavian banks have the highest proportion of females among employees and managers (61.5 per cent among all employees and 22.2 per cent among the managers), while the numbers of females are lowest in Southern European banks: only every third employee is a woman and only 7.9 per cent of the managers are female (ibid.). Hence, Caja Madrid performs significantly better than its southern competitors, though weaker than Scandinavian and British banks.

Let us also take a look at the ratio of women in the total workforce related to the share of women in top positions – a key performance gender equality indicator used by analysts of the Ethical Investment Research Service (EIRIS, see Grosser and Moon 2006, p. 7). According to this indicator, having 42.7 per cent of women in the total workforce and 28.1 per cent in top positions, Caja Madrid outperforms its Southern European peers. On average, the latter contains only 33 per cent of women in the total workforce, in relation to 7.9 per cent in top positions.

Concerning the issue of equal pay between women and men, the 2005 CSR report states a relationship of 1:1 (Caja Madrid 2005a, p. 107), which means no gender pay gap at all. This is an excellent result considering the persistent average pay gap in Europe: in 2005 the difference between men's and women's income was around 15 per cent on average for all branches. In Caja Madrid the statement refers to salaries within the same remuneration classes. Hence, a hidden pay gap may exist should women be systematically classified into lower remuneration classes despite fulfilling the same tasks. Also, the report is unclear on the subject of bonuses.

Nevertheless, the very fact that there is no difference in the pay of male and female employees within the same remuneration class already indicates a situation that is better than in many other banks.

Relating to the issue of work-life balance, a further indicator for equal opportunities is the percentage of women and men with unlimited contracts. In Caja Madrid 97.7 per cent of female employees have an unlimited contract, whereas the comparative figure from the Spanish National Statistics Institute indicates only 36.9 per cent for the private sector (Caja Madrid 2004, p. 2). The increasing trend of limited contracts especially for female workers and employees is discussed critically in the debate on work flexibility and work security. Against the background of this predominant societal trend, Caja Madrid serves as a role model by giving an example and providing high contract security. Furthermore, the bank's strong commitment and activities to the issue of work-life balance can be seen as a pilot form of public-private partnership. The bank is taking responsibility in this field and unburdens the social system (for example, the local and regional governments of Spain) of this task. One further point concerning the work-life balance should be mentioned: given its leading position in offering flexible working hours, Caja Madrid is a forerunner with regard to some internal agreements.

Finally, Caja Madrid has elaborated a system for identifying societal needs to be used when initiating programmes of Obra Social, that is social work projects implemented outside of the bank. Gender equality concerns and the needs of diversity groups are systematically considered within the *Obra Social* programmes on an annual basis. *Obra Social* includes many activities which are related to gender equality issues, including programmes of welfare activities, education and training as well as cultural activities (Caja Madrid Interview 2006b).

The upshot of this is that we consider Caja Madrid's CSR gender activities to have a traceable societal impact. In the light of the finding that Caja Madrid communicates its responsibility publicly and hence serves as a role model for other banks in Spain (European Savings Banks Group 2006), this impact can even be seen as substantial. However, with respect to the different gender issues, the depth of societal impact differs.

12.4.2 Dexia Group: Explicit Gender Equality Strategy – but Similar Levels of Outcome and Impact

Dexia's CSR output is considerable. With regard to 'overarching' CSR and issues other than gender equality, Dexia applies several codes of conduct. This includes the UN Global Compact (since 2002), the UNEP Statement by Financial Institutions on the Environment and Development (since 1998), the Equator Principles (since 2003) and all four Wolfsberg Anti-Money Laundering Principles (since their publication). In addition, Dexia operates the environmental management systems ISO 14 000 and EMAS, the Social Accountability 8000 standard for improving working conditions, the OHSAS 18 000 management system for occupational health and safety as well as the EFQM quality management model. Standardized management systems are used differently in different entities of Dexia Group. Dexia has a Sustainable Development Action Plan and a Sustainable Development Report (Dexia 2005a; Dexia Interview 2006a) that includes CSR reporting.

With respect to gender equality, the UN Global Compact is the most interesting of the above instruments. It refers to anti-discrimination in its Principle 6 and has established an alliance with the GRI. Thus, gender equality issues defined by the GRI have been reported in the annual sustainability reports. Dexia also has taken part in national gender award systems. Dexia's branch in France (Dexia Sofaxis) participated in the French Diversity Charter in the Company; the Belgium bank participated in the Belgium *Charte de l'Apprentissage* while Dexia bank in Luxembourg (Dexia BIL) received the award *Prix Feminin de l'Entreprise*. The systems are similar to that of the Spanish gender award *Empresa Optima* with regard to promoting equal opportunities, but the main action categories as well as the institutional set-up differ. Actions triggered from the different gender award systems are hence different in the individual national entities of Dexia. This can be seen as an obstacle to the overall unification process of the human resources' management of all national entities (including data unification of human resources' data) because of a lack of human resources' data harmonization. To a certain extent, the case of Dexia thus illustrates the limits of gender award systems in companies that operate in different countries.

In addition to participation in these award systems, Dexia Group has developed a company-specific strategy for promoting the situation of women which is applied equally across the Group's different national branches. In September 2004 the bank initiated a project on the position of women within the bank ('White Paper on the place of women within the Dexia Group', Dexia 2004), which made the bank a prominent example of gender activities within the sector. The 'White Paper' project led to the company's gender equality strategy. It underlined the need for Dexia to create better conditions for equal opportunities. The commitments of the 'White Paper' include ten objectives, among others, innovative ones regarding the career promotion of women and the work-life balance. For example, the following commitments are included: to favour the recruitment of feminine talents (not positive discrimination, but allows for an equal number of male and female candidates to be presented to managers); and to demonstrate more respect for private time; to promote non-linear career development (which means to develop a mechanism for employees to succeed in bringing up their children whilst not being penalized in their professional career should they decide to pick up on a developing career (ibid.). The commitments deriving from the 'White Paper' were introduced into the 2005 Human Resources Quality Charter that defined for the first time principles for a human resources' management strategy common to all national entities of the company (Dexia 2005b). In summary, the gender-related CSR output of Dexia addresses equal opportunities and the work-life balance while equal pay, sexual harassment and equal access to and supply of financial services are not specifically targeted.

Dexia's gender-related CSR outcome – the changes in gender-related practices resulting from the above commitment, strategies and instruments – is to a certain extent structured by the targets set in the 'White Paper'. The action plan derived from the 'White Paper' defines four equal opportunity targets with indicators: percentage of women in top executive positions; percentage of women in the 'nursery' of high potential executives; recruitment percentage of women for executive positions in the main entities; and a proportion of women presented for entry into the Dexia Assessment of Leadership Device (DEAL). They are monitored every year for progress on the basis of these indicators. According to the human resources' manager of Dexia (Dexia Interview 2006b), first monitoring shows different results for the four targets. Yet a specific progress can be generally observed: the proportion of women at the top executive level has risen to almost 10 per cent. The share of women is 9.3 per cent only amongst the 259 top executives of the Group, 24 per cent of the Dexia high-potential executives and 28 per cent of all executives. Thus, an imbalance is particularly evident on the level of high-potential executives. Regarding the second and third indicators – the percentage of women in the nursery of high-potential executives and recruitment percentage of women for executive positions in the main entities – progress was qualified as 'rather high'. However, the proportion of women presented for entry into the DEAL as the fourth indicator features only a 'rather slow' improvement (Dexia 2005c; Dexia Interview 2006b).

With respect to closing the gender pay gap, Dexia's impact compares with that of Caja Madrid. Within the same income categories remuneration is almost equal between women and men. However, similar to the Spanish savings bank, there may be a hidden pay gap as women are less often found within the highest income brackets in Dexia.

Dexia's activities to promote work-life balance cause varied effects. More than 17 per cent of the bank's salaried staff was hired under part-time contracts in 2004 compared to 15.5 per cent in 2003. This fact can contribute to a better work-life balance, but can also be seen critically with respect to a tendency towards involuntary flexibilization. In this context one should note that 5.5 per cent of male staff had part-time contracts in 2004 compared to 4 per cent in 2003.

Concerning the gender issue of sexual harassment, the Belgium entity of Dexia has a commitment on this issue and has established preventive measures, though no targets.

With regard to gender considerations related to the bank's portfolio of financial products, and hence the issue of equal access to and supply of banking services, Dexia Group provides both microcredits and a basic banking service for everybody.

To obtain an impression of the level of the societal impact of Dexia's gender equality activities, we again compare the bank's performance with comparable European or national data in the sector. As regards equal opportunities, Dexia compares favourably with other Western European banks, having 46.4 per cent of women in the total workforce and 35.12 per cent of women in top positions (2004). These feature on average 45.6 per cent of women in the total workforce and 14 per cent of women in top positions (Kreetz 2005, p. 29). Dexia's share of women in executive positions increased by 10 per cent within only three years (from 25 per cent in 2002 to 35.12 per cent in 2004). This indicates a remarkable outcome and compared to average data also societal impact. However, Dexia has a weak gender ratio with respect to women's representation at board level. Since the only woman on the highest hierarchical level of the company had left the board due to retirement in 2006 and was replaced by a man, there was no longer a woman at this level at the time of our research (Dexia Interview 2006b).

The comparison between outcome and average data concerning the sub-issue of men in part-time work that refers to the gender issue of work-life balance provides an interesting insight. Men are increasingly doing part-time work in Dexia, the ratio having risen from 4 to 5.5 per cent between 2003 and 2004. But compared with the average of 6.6 per cent of male part-timers in EU cross-sector data (European Commission 2006d), Dexia still performs substandard.

As regards financial products and providing equal access to and supply of banking services, the bank's engagement in microcredits and in guaranteeing a basic banking service has to be interpreted in the context of statistics on poverty risks and social exclusion in Europe, which appear somewhat greater for women than for men during all stages of life. The risk of poverty, in particular, is higher amongst older women and amongst lone parents with dependent children, a group predominantly composed of women (European Commission 2006d; European Women's Lobby 2005, p. 7).

In short, when defining societal impacts as having a significantly better performance than the average performance of other banks (and alternatively, companies from other sectors) in the same country or in other European regions, Dexia's wider impact can be regarded as substantial, though a few points have been identified where societal impact is unclear. Having received several gender and diversity awards in different national branches, Dexia can however be seen as a role model for issues of equal opportunities and work-life balance. Most importantly, the bank is directly contributing to societal gender relations by offering financial products to poorer people, which is an important point of social inclusion mainly with respect to elderly and migrant women.

12.4.3 Summary

Table 12.1 summarizes the above findings on the effects of gender-related CSR in Caja Madrid and Dexia Group. Please note that the assessment is qualitative and ordinal, based on the comparison of the two case study banks.

Table 12.1 makes clear a paradox concerning the results of the gender impact assessment on the issue of equal opportunities: though there is no explicit commitment on equal opportunities at board level in Caja Madrid in contrast to Dexia Group, we have detected a little stronger outcome in Caja Madrid than in Dexia. This result needs further analysis and explanation. Furthermore, the results concerning the gender pay gap are interesting because in both banks corporate practices have changed visibly (outcome) although there was no explicit CSR output concerning this issue – such as a commitment at board level with respect to the gender pay gap. Additionally, societal impact could not be shown because of unclear categories (for example, concerning bonuses). The clearest contribution of gender-related CSR activities to societal impact was detected in the sphere of the conciliation of work and private life. In contrast, the gender issue of sexual harassment was difficult to assess because of its very internal character in companies, meaning that societal impact is unclear. Our fifth gender issue – equal access to and supply of financial services – clearly shows better results for Dexia from output to outcome to impact. This is caused by its provision for microcredits and a basic banking service. However, it should be noted that the contribution of Caja Madrid to societal impact brought about by the banks' high 'social dividend' for social work (*Obra Social*) is not evaluated in Table 12.1 besides its contribution to the work-life balance. Furthermore, we did not evaluate the societal impact of the fact that all

Table 12.1 Impact assessment of CSR for gender equality in Caja Madrid and Dexia Group

CSR issue	Caja Madrid			Dexia Group		
	Output	Outcome	Impact	Output	Outcome	Impact
Equal opportunities	No explicit commitment, but integration in human resources programmes (CMIPMS, SGIP, gender award system)	++	+	Explicit commitment, 'White Paper', gender award systems	+ (+)	O
Gender pay gap	No commitment	+	O	No commitment	+	O
Work-life balance	Commitment via human resources programmes (CMIPMS, SGIP, gender award system)	++	++	Commitment; 'White Paper', gender award systems	++	++
Sexual harassment	No commitment	+	O	Commitment (Belgium Bank)	+	O
Equal access to and supply of financial services	No commitment	+	O/++[a]	No commitment	++[b]	++

Notes:
O = no improvement through CSR or unclear; + = improvement; ++ = substantial improvement.
a. Due to Caja Madrid's activities in this field as 'double-bottom line institution'.
b. Due to Dexia's 'basic banking service for everybody' and microcredits.

savings banks are so-called double bottom-line institutions, that is, they offer access to banking services to as many household members in society as possible (even in peripheral regions) (Peachy 2006; WSBI 2006).

12.5 EXPLAINING THE EFFECTS OF GENDER-RELATED CSR: PROMOTING AND HAMPERING FACTORS

The findings of the CSR activities of Caja Madrid and Dexia Group show many similarities and some differences. Above all, in both banks CSR policies for gender equality have indeed resulted in visible changes of corporate behaviour and sustainability impact at societal level. Against this background the overall leading question of the following analysis is how to explain this success. How can two banks which are very different in size, type and scope of their activity fields achieve similarly high levels of CSR outcome and impact on gender equality? What are the drivers for the detected effects of the banks' CSR activities?

The impact analysis showed that concerning the three categories of CSR effects (output, outcome and impact) it is mainly the CSR output which differs. Thus, the analysis focuses on this point. This concerns both the use of overarching CSR instruments and the commitments to gender equality. Why does the weak CSR output of Caja Madrid – with no explicit commitment on gender equality – not lead to a low level of gender outcome (that is, changes in corporate practices) and impact? Dexia, in contrast, has a very explicit commitment on gender equality including a company-specific strategy (the 'White Paper') with target setting and an action plan to better the situation of women. Literature greatly emphasizes the relevance of the integration of a CSR commitment into internal business operations to the effectiveness of CSR. This emphasis will be followed in the analysis. In a more general sense, this raises questions regarding the relevance of the implementation model ('the integration model', Grosser 2004) for explaining the effects of CSR.

With this focus the analysis of factors promoting and hampering the achievement of outcome and impact through CSR follows (but adapts) the following operational research questions:

- Why are some CSR instruments more conducive to impact than others? We assume that some instruments will promote outcome and impact more than others on the basis of their very design.
- What factors determine a company's choice of instrument? Considering that instruments may vary in their conduciveness to

impact, the firms' choice of instrument is relevant to the subsequent achievement of impact.

- What factors drive an effective implementation of CSR instruments within companies? We posit that an instrument may lead to more impact when it is effectively implemented.

In accordance with this book's analytical framework as presented in Chapter 3, factors promoting and hampering CSR success include the design of an instrument and, in particular, its levels of specificity and obligation. Further aspects address a set of five factors which we posit will influence whether companies will choose specific (effective) instruments and implement these in an effective way. These factors include the companies' strategic and organizational embedding of their CSR efforts as well as their corporate culture, the business environment, the role of civil society and the political-institutional setting.

12.5.1 The Design of CSR Instruments and Their Conduciveness to Impact

We expect that the very design of CSR instruments can influence the impact they may create. More specifically, we propose that a CSR instrument will be more conducive to producing impact than an alternative instrument when it requires a high level of obligation, for example, when it is independently verified, requires a public commitment and is linked to some form of enforcement – and when it is specific. By specificity we mean that an instrument requires specific and substantive activities rather than procedural improvements, has quantifiable rather than qualitative targets and has more ambitious targets than other instruments. Our question in this section is hence whether the achievement of (substantial) outcomes and impact in Caja Madrid and Dexia Group has been promoted through the use of instruments with high levels of obligation and specificity. The instruments relevant for gender equality performance include reporting according to the GRI indicators and more specifically gender award systems as well as the in-company instruments for human relations' management (CMIPMS and SGIP in Caja Madrid) and for gender equality ('White Paper' and gender strategy in Dexia).

Both banks have reporting according to GRI indicators in their CSR report (Caja Madrid) and sustainability report (Dexia), respectively, and external verification that causes obligation. But for both banks company-specific management instruments have higher levels of obligation and specificity than standardized instruments. Though stock market listed and participating in SRI, in Dexia the annual internal reporting obligation of the 'White Paper' targets is classified as the most important instrument for promoting gender equality, not external reports, verification and index listing (Dexia Interview 2006a). The 'White Paper' action plan implies high obligation by its public commitment and high specificity because its targets are quantifiable and monitored. High obligation characterizes also the internal instrument of Dexia's new Leadership Model because a 'bonus-malus' – system and sanctions for not complying with the anti-discrimination principle was introduced (Dexia Interview 2006b). This can be seen as an enforcement mechanism.

In Caja Madrid the internal management instruments of the CMIPMS in combination with the company's leadership principles (SGIP) are less characterized by obligation, because public commitment is missing. The annual human resources action plans (40 per cent women in management posts) that contain targets derived from the gender award system *Empresa Optima* are more specific and obligatory. This gender award system is characterized by a high degree of obligation. It defines activities (gender action plan) and goal attainment that is externally monitored at the end of the agreed time frame by the civil servants of the Institute for Women and Ministry of Social Affairs and Work. Most importantly, the system implies a follow-up mechanism.

With regard to the gender award systems in the French, Belgium and Luxembourg entities of Dexia, specificity is also given to the identified activity fields. However, they are less obligatory and specific in comparison with the internal 'White Paper' targets. The same instrument – gender award system – seems to cause different levels of obligation and specificity in the two banks. In the case of Caja Madrid it brings about results in combination with the internal management system CMIPMS; in the case of Dexia the internal project and action plan of the 'White Paper' are more relevant.

12.5.2 Choice of CSR Instruments

To what extent did the banks' choice of CSR instruments contribute to their substantial levels of CSR outcome and impact? Why did the banks choose the CSR instruments described above? In the following we shall examine the relevance of the five explanatory factors elaborated above and will discuss the respective propositions elaborated in Chapter 3.

For Caja Madrid as well as for Dexia the choice of instruments can above all be explained by the factor of *strategic and organizational fit*, confirming one of our initial expectations. Strategically, the decision to produce a CSR report 'fits' with the CMIPMS that is already in place and could be used as an additional element of a strong system-led managerial integration model. The commitment to the gender award system *Programa Optima* was already made in 2002 (before adopting an explicit CSR strategy) and then integrated into the company's CSR activities. Gender equality is related to the strong social tradition of the company. Social commitment is stipulated in a certain way by the 'dual column' approach of savings banks. Also for Dexia, the instruments' strategic and organizational fit was decisive for the choice of instruments. The main management instruments had been implemented before the CSR strategy was established. Later on, these instruments became interlinked. Dexia Group decided in 2002 to become a pioneer in sustainable development and thus also to become engaged in CSR. Under the two-fold business strategy of becoming recognized as pioneer in sustainable development and relating all CSR activities to the business case, it made sense for the bank to adopt a large number of publicly well-known codes of conducts. On the other hand, the project of the 'White Paper' is connected to the business case in so far as it mitigates the 'search for talents'.

Furthermore, the banks' choice of instrument was related to their wider corporate organization in both cases. Caja Madrid's corporate organization is very specific because the board is represented by societal stakeholders, including the municipality of Madrid and representatives of the employees. This leads to a strong necessity for the internal integration of different stakeholder demands, including those of the employees. Thus, integrative instruments such as the internal management and leadership systems have been developed. In contrast, the corporate organization of Dexia is highly dependent on the unification process after the merger of different former companies into one company. The main standardized management instruments are used differently in the individual national entities of the Dexia Group. The strong demand of unification leads to the important role of internal management instruments and a strong orientation towards reporting and monitoring cycles. The project on the situation of women in Dexia ('White Paper') and its action plan can also be understood as a contribution to the unification process.

Other explanatory factors, such as the corporate culture, business environment and civil society demand were less relevant. This largely confirms the respective Chapter 3 hypotheses, as does the fact that the political-institutional setting in the various countries where the banks are headquartered did have a quite substantial (though differing) influence on instrument choice: namely by providing gender award systems, which the banks used as templates for own activities.

12.5.3 Effective Implementation of CSR Instruments

As was shown in Section 4, changes in corporate practices (that is, the achievement of CSR outcome through the implementation of – more or less explicit – CSR output) and resulting societal impacts have been substantial in both banks. When focusing on the process of implementing CSR instruments, what factors promoted this success?

As regards the CSR implementation processes of the banks, we can identify two different patterns. In Caja Madrid the factors of corporate culture, civil society demands and the political-institutional setting were the most important for a good implementation of gender-related CSR. By contrast, in Dexia strategic and organization integration, corporate culture and to a certain extent the business environment were more driving.

In accordance with our Chapter 3 proposition that corporate culture fosters change in an organization's social and environmental practices (in particular if CSR is rooted in a long-standing and well-developed identity of the organization as being socially responsible) both banks confirm that their corporate cultures have been very important for CSR implementation. This can be seen as an explanatory factor of the policy field of gender equality: the long-lasting persistency of gender inequalities in employment is caused by deep cultural stereotypes, gendered images, ideals and role definitions that build 'cultural prerequisites for corporate social responsibility' (Hardjono and van Marrewijk 2001). In Caja Madrid norms and values which are related to the social tradition of the savings bank are claimed to be important factors for the implementation of CSR in general as well as of gender equality policies. Culturally, internal commitments are said to have a high relevance, though the paragraph on gender equality within the bank's catalogue of 'Norms and Criteria of Behaviour in the Professional Field' is somehow 'hidden'. In contrast, the corporate culture of Dexia is directly addressed by the 'White Paper' (amongst others by promoting 'female skills' and requiring 'respect for private time'). High level women functionaries were involved in establishing the gender action plan that was communicated internally as good practice. Dexia Group had to build up a new coherent corporate culture after the mergers. The bank made strong efforts to this end by installing a system of internal mobility (of the employees between the different national entities) that received a prize for its social benefits and learning capacities. The activities of the 'White Paper' project and the gender action plan contributed to building up a modern corporate culture with respect to gender relations.

With regard to strategic and organizational integration it was proposed that CSR instruments are likely to render the highest level of effects if corporate leaders link the CSR approach to the core strategies of the company and integrate it organizationally. We find evidence for this in the case of Dexia. As regards strategic integration, Caja Madrid developed what we will call an 'implicit implementation model'. Equality issues are highly integrated into other policies. The implementation of gender equality was led by internal management systems which included normative principles in human resources and *Obra Social* (social work). In Dexia, in contrast, the implementation model is 'explicit'. Gender and diversity management has a high strategic importance at board level, which has been translated into a strategy and a company-specific project to better the situation of women. The project was communicated by the bank's CEO in late 2004. In general, leadership support is acknowledged to have been a significant driver of its implementation. The project is part of a wider diversity approach which tackles a broad range of areas (for example, languages, culture or training) and does not just boil down to the 'non-discrimination' principle or ethnic diversity (Dexia 2005a). Decisive for effective implementation of gender equality was the company's decision to continue the project in the long term and maintain a clear focus on women/gender even when the scope of diversity activities was widened in 2006 to people with disabilities, ethnic minorities and seniors and juniors.

Integration of CSR into organizational processes played a relevant role for both banks. In Caja Madrid regular reviews on gender issues take place at the human resources' management leadership level and within the social work department. The gender equality-related human resources' activities are mostly governed by mid-management representatives, such as the directors of the human resources' unit and of the resources unit. Bottom-up initiatives of employees are given high priority. With regard to gender equality issues, the involvement of internal opinion makers, especially of the six different trade unions within Caja Madrid, play an important role in pursuing effective CSR implementation. They develop initiatives and projects aimed at enhancing gender equality within the company. The employees are seen as the most important stakeholders by medium-level managers, pointing to a participatory corporate culture within the bank. In Dexia hierarchical integration seems to penetrate the organization even more deeply. The board carries out regular reviews of the developments of Dexia's figures concerning gender diversity. Staff representatives at board level, organized within the European Work Council of Dexia, are participating in the CSR strategy building process. The establishment of internal training courses for functional officers on gender equality is one means to reach the four objectives of the 'White Paper' and is thus tightly integrated into the human resources' strategy. One person is in charge of gender diversity for the entire Dexia Group and since 2004 respective positions have been introduced at local level. Furthermore, Dexia created a cross-functional 'business partner function' in its different human resources' departments to improve the transition from commitment to action concerning gender and diversity issues in 2005.

The business environment is a driver for the implementation of CSR for both banks, though more so with regard to 'overarching' CSR than to gender-related activities. Our earlier proposition that CSR instruments are implemented all the more successfully the more the respective changes in social and environmental practices are experienced as a business benefit for the company is hence confirmed only partially. The Spanish union of savings banks (la Confederación Espanola de Cajas de Ahorros, CECA), conducted a public campaign to communicate and promote the 'social dividend' of savings banks, that is, the amount of money that savings banks are giving to the public via financing *Obra Social* and other social and cultural activities. Caja Madrid within its sector environment of the Spanish savings banks in general aims at being a benchmark and showing leadership in social action. However, gender equality was not a topic within the CECA campaign. Within Dexia as a stock market listed company, financial investors influence sustainable development activities. SRI indexes and the debate about them are assessed as comprising a positive influence on CSR implementation. Again, however, this is evaluated as weak with respect to gender equality.

In accordance with our initial hypothesis, the factor of civil society demand was decisive for the implementation of gender equality instruments in Caja Madrid – more so than in the case of Dexia. The influence of civil society was very important because of the specific stakeholder model of this savings bank and the substantial influence of the employees. The women's units of the trade unions (for example, COMFIA) organize actions for women. Furthermore, Caja Madrid's department of social work has installed a 'needs identification channel' that functions as a 'social monitor'. In Dexia the CSR stakeholder approach helps to monitor the positions of civil society organizations. They might influence the company's activities to a certain degree, but this factor has not the same importance as in the case of Caja Madrid.

The political-institutional setting, which we hypothesized to foster the achievement of CSR outcomes within companies, played an important role in CSR instrument implementation in Caja Madrid, if not so much in Dexia. First, it determines the specific form of Caja Madrid's Board which was shown above to have contributed to effective CSR implementation. Second, for both banks the national gender award systems played a role in effectively implementing gender activities, providing a framework for target setting, monitoring and review, though less so in Dexia. In Spain a further factor of the political-institutional setting was the discussion about a new law on gender equality[4] which obliges large companies like Caja Madrid to elaborate an equality action plan. Already the announcement of this law functioned as a 'shadow of hierarchy' in the sense that the bank's human resources' officers had compared the targets expected by this law and their targets concerning gender equality. However, it functioned not as a new driving force as Caja Madrid had joined *Programa Optima* already years before the discussion on the new law came up. Finally, EU gender politics and the spatial proximity to EU bodies in Brussels did not play a crucial role for Dexia according to the human resources' responsible officer of Dexia. This was a more important factor for the gender-related CSR activities of Caja Madrid in the national context of Spain.

12.5.4 Summary

In summary, Caja Madrid and Dexia Group show progress and substantial effects of their CSR activities to promote gender equality. The causes include their selection of CSR instruments with high levels of specificity and obligation and the effective implementation of these instruments. The factors that promoted the effective implementation are summarized in Table 12.2.

The similarly high levels of gender equality outcome and output in the two banks were surprising – not only because the two companies differ in type and size, but also because their CSR output regarding gender equality differed considerably. Possibly, this can be accounted for by the fact that at least implicit gender commitments existed in both cases and that both companies have adopted an effective (more 'explicit' vs more 'implicit') implementation model that fits with their respective strategies, organization and stakeholder relations, and that was in both cases supported by public policies (though with different levels of importance).

12.6   CONCLUSIONS AND RECOMMENDATIONS

Against the backdrop of the findings and arguments in the previous sections, this last section presents some conclusions and recommendations (set in italics) addressed to policy makers, including the European Commission, to business actors and to further research on CSR for gender equality.

CSR approaches need clearer definition with regard to sustainability impact in general and specifically to the CSR dimension of gender equality. Gender-related CSR politics would be clearer if they were defined with regard to societal impact and if they were tied to the normative and strategic tools of EU gender mainstreaming (see also Grosser and Moon 2005). The gender mainstreaming strategy and the gender-related CSR politics are not well interconnected so far.

Gender award systems are successful instruments to introduce CSR gender

Table 12.2   Factors driving the effective implementation of CSR

	Caja Madrid		Dexia Group	
Strategic and organizational integration	Implicit leadership support; weak actor commitment on gender equality, but nevertheless organizational integration	O	Explicit leadership support, strong actor commitment on gender equality, total organizational integration	++
	Regular reviews on human resources' management level; Staff representation at board level; Influence of trade unions (women units); Bottom-up initiatives within human resources' unit for gender activities	+	Regular reviews at board level; Staff representation at board level; Internal communication; Business partner function for gender and diversity; Leadership principle with strong obligation for complying with gender equality	++
Corporate culture	Corporate culture is the norm and value oriented towards social tradition of savings bank, including gender equality	++	Corporate culture is in the making after mergers; Gender diversity is future oriented, 'fits' with the unification process	++
Business environment	CECA, social dividend, benchmark orientation	O	SRI, benchmark orientation	+
Civil society demand	Strong trade union influence and 'needs identification channel' (*Obra Social*)	++	Stakeholder dialogues	+
Political-institutional setting	Law on gender equality; Spanish gender award system	++	National gender award systems (varying in Dexia's entities)	O

Notes: O = no driver for effective CSR implementation or unclear; + = driver for effective CSR implementation; ++ = strong driver for effective CSR implementation.

activities into companies. They need to be standardized in Europe to increase effects in globalized companies. Both companies are participating in gender/diversity award systems but with different effects. The case of Caja Madrid demonstrates exemplarily that this instrument has the potential to bridge a company's performance and societal demands. The case of Dexia demonstrates the limits of this instrument for globalized companies. The award's contribution to outcomes at company level would be higher for globally acting companies if they were standardized and there were a stronger tie with European gender statistics.

CSR stakeholder dialogues should include more representation of women and gender lobby organizations. CSR networks such as the European CSR Multi-Stakeholder Forum lacked in its representation women and gender lobby organizations (see also Committee on Women's Rights and Gender Equality 2006). Criteria and strategic goals for civil society representation including women and gender lobby organizations in CSR stakeholder dialogues would make this important CSR instrument more equitable.

Business associations and local authorities can provide more impulses for CSR activities for gender equality. The Spanish Confederation of Savings Banks (CECA) demonstrates that business associations can constitute an important driver for implementing CSR activities. The issue of gender equality could be more visible within these. Gender equality could be promoted more explicitly.

Instruments that address corporate culture are indispensable to promote gender equality. Sensitization and internal communication are given high importance in both banks. Within companies, middle level managers and functional officers are an important target group for this. Companies should develop more sensitization activities to create intrinsic motivations of the actors involved. So-called 'softwiring instruments' (Wit et al. 2006) are indispensable for integrating CSR gender equality. Leadership principles that imply high levels of obligation to deal with commitments on CSR and gender equality promote genuine changes in corporate practices.

Further research on successful CSR implementation models for gender equality with a focus on sustainability impacts is needed. Both cases demonstrate the relevance of a fitting integration model with strong feedback on societal demands regarding gender equality. In Caja Madrid this is exercised through the social monitor of *Obra Social* and to a certain extent through the Spanish gender award system. In Dexia stakeholder dialogues, continued observation of stakeholder demands as well as the gender award systems provide feedback on societal demands. Research is necessary on how this feedback function could be strengthened by political and instrument innovations.

Interlinkages between CSR reporting of gender issues with national and

EU statistics could make CSR gender impacts more transparent. New concepts and research on this are needed. Caja Madrid as well as Dexia Group show a high amount of gender activities with substantial societal impact. The significance of CSR reporting and public disclosure of gender indicators for the realization of sustainability impacts cannot be evaluated on the basis of only two case studies. Yet one conclusion can be posed against the background of data and indicators used in the two banks: more systematic disclosure of data in comparison with national and European average data could enhance the transparency and effectiveness of data disclosure. For example, conceptual work is required on the interlinkages between GRI data and European data on gender equality and on how reporting can be linked to sustainability indicators and EU gender equality goals.

NOTES

1. The legislative framework for equality policies of the EU was broadened in the last decade. Additional to gender the following 'diversity categories' have been added: age, religion, ethical background, disabilities and sexual orientation.
2. The human resources unit has about 100 employees.
3. The Spanish national report of the 'Entrepreneurial Environment Study', which fosters gender equality in entrepreneurship and microfinance challenge (Casteigts and Women's World Banking in Spain 2007), shows the high relevance and impact of microcredits for work and gender equality in Spain.
4. The law (*La Ley Orgánica para la igualdad efectiva de mujeres y hombres*) was adopted on 22 March 2007 in a modified version.

13 Banking on integrity: CSR helps counter bribery and money laundering in two banks

Peter Wilkinson

13.1 INTRODUCTION

This chapter examines the role of Corporate Social Responsibility (CSR) in countering bribery and anti-money laundering (AML) and hence in creating sustainability impact. Corruption is one of the most serious issues for societies leading to, for example, abuse of human rights, instability in markets, risks to life, environmental damage and keeping societies in poverty. Bribery and money laundering are among the most significant forms of corruption. Bribery is typically viewed as prevalent in large public contracts and extractive industries in developing countries but recent scandals in developed nations have underlined that bribery can be a risk in any country or sector. Money laundering is a counterpart of bribery used to dispose of the proceeds of corruption but receives intense attention for its role in terrorism. The World Bank estimated corrupt transactions at about $1 trillion per annum (Kaufmann 2004) and the FBI estimated money laundering at an annual amount of $2.8 trillion dollars (FBI 2001, p. 1).

Countering corruption is seen by companies as primarily a compliance or risk management issue. It is of particular importance for banks for countering bribery and fraud in lending and investments and preventing illegally acquired funds using the banking system. However, despite legal obligations for countering bribery and AML, the banks can go beyond compliance with regard to the measures they carry out to attain existing legal goals, or they may decide to strive for more ambitious goals than the legally set ones. Thus, countering bribery and anti-money laundering provide opportunity to exercise CSR and at the same time can give opportunities for building reputation and business opportunities.

The case study for this chapter was carried out on two banks, leaders in their markets, Caja Madrid, Spain, and Monte dei Paschi di Siena, Italy, selected from respondents to a survey among 17 European banks committed to CSR (see Chapter 7). They were chosen as they had similar origins and markets and differed in their risk assessments of bribery. They had equivalent approaches to AML.

The case study starts by setting out the analytical framework used to assess CSR effects in the banking sector and then the banks are introduced. Section 4 assesses CSR in the banks with a description of their CSR output, CSR outcome and, to the extent that it can be determined for these complex issues, the CSR impact. Having assessed the CSR effects within the companies, Section 5 tries to explain these effects and why both banks indicate output, outcome and impact for AML but cannot show evidence of CSR effects for countering bribery. Finally, some conclusions are drawn based on the assessment against the analytical framework. The empirical basis for the study was an initial questionnaire survey of the banks, study of materials including academic literature, public documents and internal documentation provided by the banks and interviews with representatives of the banks and stakeholders.[1]

13.2   THE ANALYTICAL FRAMEWORK

The aim of this chapter is to investigate whether the banks' beyond compliance activities for the issues of countering bribery and AML lead to tangible CSR impact and, if so, why. The framework for analysis is summarized below and is presented in full in Chapter 3. 'CSR effects' means an entire sequence of CSR output, outcome and impact. 'CSR output' is the extent to which companies introduce changes in commitment and strategies for sustainability issues and adopt CSR instruments. 'CSR outcome' denotes substantive changes in practices resulting from CSR output. 'CSR impact' covers any substantive beneficial consequences for society outside the banks that follow from the changes in the banks' CSR practices. The guiding question for this study was 'What factors contributed to the banks achieving similar CSR effects for AML but no evident CSR effects for countering bribery?' In making this analysis it will not be possible to quantify the CSR effects owing to the inability to separate out CSR from compliance and risk management practices. Also, countering bribery and AML are preventive activities – the number of bribery attempts or instances of money laundering deterred cannot be assessed.

Three process stages of commitment, strategy formulation and implementation must occur before CSR impact can be achieved. As shall be seen later, the case study varies from this model as the banks' strategies and implementation were made for reasons of compliance and risk management and any CSR effects came from a non-formalized CSR process.

The focus of this case study is to examine what factors are responsible for influencing CSR impact through the use of CSR instruments. The term 'instrument' means a standardized voluntary instrument[2] or a company-specific system defined as an integrated management system comprising policies and implementation processes. To enable analysis, the guiding question is split into three operating research questions.

1. Why are some CSR instruments more conducive to impact than others? The analysis looks at the instruments chosen by the banks assuming that the level of impact the instrument creates is determined by inherent characteristics of specificity and obligation. More mature instruments are proposed to have greater specificity and obligation.
2. What factors determine a company's choice of instruments? If some CSR instruments are more conducive to impact than others, instrument choice will offer potential for creating subsequent CSR impact.
3. What factors drive an effective implementation of CSR instruments? 'Effective implementation' means CSR implementation processes that achieve a comparatively high level of outcome. Apart from effects coming from the inherent characteristics of CSR instruments, it is assumed that company-specific implementation is decisive for impact.

In analyzing these research questions, five sets of internal and external explanatory factors are proposed as influencing the level of CSR effects. These are: corporate strategy and organization, corporate culture, the business environment, civil society and the political-institutional setting. Corporate strategies and organizational structures provide formal rules. Strategies are roadmaps for organizations to attainment of long-, medium- and short-term goals and objectives. Corporate culture denotes the shared values, knowledge, symbols, beliefs and assumptions that characterize a company. It represents the informal rules and norms of an organization that have developed over time. Business environment comprises the prevailing business opportunities and restrictions within a sector and the understanding and legitimacy of CSR among peer companies and competitors. Civil society affects corporate responsibility when companies acquiesce or respond to expectations, pressure or support. The political-institutional setting includes governmental expectations and public policies on social and environmental issues, and CSR and generally may exercise support or pressure with regard to CSR processes.

13.3   INTRODUCING THE BANKS

Caja Madrid, Spain, and Monte dei Paschi di Siena, Italy, are now described briefly.

Caja Madrid is a savings bank, the fourth largest bank in the Spanish financial sector ranked by total assets, loans and customer funds and the second largest Spanish savings bank after La Caixa. It was founded in 1702 to grant interest-free loans to the poor. The savings bank is the dominant entity within the Caja Madrid Group. The Group operates in different areas of the financial sector including a portfolio of investments in firms operating in strategic sectors. It is active in financial asset brokerage and management, private banking, insurance, real estate and development capital. Caja Madrid operates throughout Spain with some 1984 branches and 6.8 million clients. It ended 2006 with assets of 136 952 million euros, 13 047 employees and a net operating profit of 1033 million euros (Caja Madrid 2007, p. 4). Savings banks have a strong social remit and voluntarily allocate funds to social work and their foundations. Caja Madrid has allocated for many years around 25 per cent of its net profit to social contributions and in 2006 contributed 192.6 million euros to community activities.

Monte dei Paschi di Siena is the world's oldest bank, founded in 1472. Like Caja Madrid it was created as a savings bank to aid the poor. In 1993 savings banks were converted into commercial banks and foundations were formed or separated from the main entity. Monte dei Paschi di Siena was split in 1995 into a foundation and a joint-stock company, Banca Monte dei Paschi di Siena SpA. There are about 900 banks operating in Italy but a growing concentration of the larger banks. In May 2004 the then five largest banks had a market share of deposits of 47.5 per cent but now MPS Group is the only one of the five remaining untouched by merger or acquisition. Banca Monte dei Paschi di Siena heads the MPS Group and performs banking, financial and insurance activities. Public listing has allowed the bank to expand, including investments in a number of regional banks and inauguration of new branches. MPS Group is active throughout Italy and in the main international financial centres, with operations ranging from traditional banking to asset management and insurance and an emphasis on the retail sector. The Group at the end of 2006 had some 24 300 employees, 4.5 million customers and over 1903 branches in Italy representing 6 per cent of total national bank branches. In 2006 the Group recorded a net profit of 910.1 million euros, the highest in its history. Its foundation like Caja Madrid's, is influential in the bank's governance, owning 49 per cent of the capital and appointing five of the bank's ten directors. In 2006 MPS Group contributed 305 million euros to the foundation.

13.4 ASSESSING CSR EFFECTS FOR COUNTERING BRIBERY AND AML

This section assesses the CSR output, outcome and impact in the two banks. It focuses on CSR aimed at countering bribery and money-laundering, but also takes account of more 'overarching' CSR. The latter comprises voluntary initiatives relating to a broader set of sustainability issues but including anti-corruption.

13.4.1 CSR Output

'CSR output' incorporates commitment and strategies for social and environmental performance and the adoption of CSR instruments. Both banks are similar in their formalization and commitments to overarching CSR and to countering corruption. They differ in their public commitments to no-bribes policies and adoption of instruments. They both use strategic planning for CSR.

A high level public commitment is the starting point for countering bribery according to voluntary instruments for anti-bribery.[3] Both banks have made overarching commitments for countering corruption and both have committed publicly to AML. MPS Group commits to countering corruption: 'We do not tolerate any form of corruption' (MPS Group 2007, p. 39); and makes a respective commitment in its sustainability principles 'Correctness and transparency; anti-corruption and anti-crime; active opposition to any type of corruption; fight against money laundering and terrorist activities' (MPS Group 2007, p. 24). Caja Madrid has a Code of Ethics that makes a broad commitment to ethics and integrity (Caja Madrid 2005b, p. 5). Both banks accept a special responsibility to tackle AML. MPS Group stated in interview that as a bank it considered it had a responsibility to counter money laundering which it viewed as 'a blight on society' (MPS Group Interview 2007). Caja Madrid also stated that it saw social responsibility as placing a greater responsibility on the bank for AML (ibid.). It has made a public commitment to AML saying strict compliance with money laundering legislation forms part of its key values for corporate citizenship (Caja Madrid 2007, p. 69). However, despite their commitments for countering corruption and AML, neither of the banks made an explicit commitment to countering bribery though this is expressed implicitly within their anti-corruption commitments and that they have carried out risk assessments of the issue.

Three CSR voluntary instruments selected for overarching CSR reasons had some effects for the issues and are now described.

MPS Group is a signatory to the Global Compact (GC) which was founded in 1999. Caja Madrid chose not to become a signatory. The GC is the world's largest corporate citizenship initiative with more than 6200 participants committed to align policies and practices with ten principles including a Tenth Principle against Corruption which states 'Businesses should work against corruption in all its forms, including extortion and bribery.' Participants must submit an annual Communication on Progress (CoP), a description of practical actions taken in the previous year to implement the principles.

The Global Reporting Initiative (GRI) Sustainability Reporting Framework is used by both banks as a framework for their social responsibility reporting. Both banks stated in interview that they saw social reporting as a CSR tool (Caja Madrid Interview 2006e, MPS Group Interview 2007). The GRI framework provides guidance for disclosure of sustainability performance and aims to give stakeholders a framework to understand disclosed information. Companies can select whether or not to report against particular indicators. The GRI provides for reporting on the management system for countering corruption and specifically indicators for anti-corruption risk assessment and training.

The GRI also offers a Financial Services Supplement issued in 2002 and it is being used by Caja Madrid as part of a pilot test led by CECA, the Spanish association for savings banks. The supplement's CSR section provides for reporting on sensitive issues including bribery and AML and companies may add quantitative data to demonstrate how such issues are managed.

These three instruments cover CSR generally and anti-corruption is only one aspect. Though there are standardized voluntary instruments specific to bribery and AML (these are the Wolfsberg AML Principles and three anti-bribery codes), neither of the case study banks use any of these. Bank-specific instruments are the prime CSR tools for countering bribery and AML driven primarily by compliance with law and risk management. Company-specific instruments for anti-bribery and AML are defined as integrated management systems and this accords with the approach of anti-corruption laws, the GRI and also the leading anti-bribery and AML codes. A management system will include policies, board and management oversight, risk assessment, organizational responsibilities, business relationships, communication, training, internal controls, monitoring, reporting and possibly verification. Caja Madrid has developed an AML instrument but not one for countering bribery whereas MPS Group has instruments for both issues.

13.4.2   CSR Outcome

Now the CSR outcome is considered. These constitute changes in the banks' anti-bribery and AML practices coming from the CSR output described in the previous section. The case study banks show that integrated management systems for the issues produced changes in practices related to risk assessment, lending and investment, oversight, training, internal controls and others.

Risk assessment is important as it sets the scope, approach and degree of commitment for anti-corruption systems and it offers opportunities for beyond compliance activity for countering bribery and AML. MPS Group identified bribery as a fairly high strategic risk and both banks assessed money laundering as a high risk. Both banks have defined strategies for risk management, strong cross-functional working and use various technical instruments, such as internal risk models.

Organizational responsibility, and in particular board and senior management oversight and responsibility for implementation, are vital for an effective anti-corruption management system. The banks have structured to provide oversight for compliance with laws and their commitments to ethical behaviour and countering corruption. In MPS Group the parent company's board of directors defines the overall risk approach and the Group's social policy, assures implementation and has established board committees for internal audit, control and CSR. Caja Madrid's compliance and ethical business conduct commitment is overseen by a regulatory compliance team forming part of the General Secretariat unit. Money laundering prevention policy is handled internally by a designated control unit located in the compliance department that reports directly to the general secretary.

As regards lending and investment, due diligence in banks is critical for the issues. Both Caja Madrid and MPS Group account for the risk of bribery in their management of assets and lending and apply anti-bribery criteria in managing assets including project investments. MPS Group furthermore applies anti-bribery criteria in managing Socially Responsible Investment (SRI) funds. MPS Group said in interview that it asked suppliers to comply with provisions on corruption and all contacts included a contractual no-bribes requirement.

Communication and training make anti-corruption commitments come alive for employees and build anti-corruption cultures. Both case study banks use intranets and training to communicate their policies, procedures and guidelines. Both provide substantial AML training, which they consider to be beyond that required by compliance. Caja Madrid provides guidelines for employees on countering bribery and both banks have established whistle-blowing channels. Caja Madrid gives AML courses as part of individual annual training plans. All group employees are given the opportunity to undertake intranet-based training in AML. In quantitative terms, Caja Madrid in 2004 invited all its 10 775 employees to use an intranet-based ten-minute training module and 40.6 per cent took part. In 2005 620 employees were invited to attend AML training from geographical areas of risk in Spain and 81.8 per cent took part (Caja Madrid Interview 2007). MPS Group stated in interview that it saw its training as going beyond Italian AML law which is precise but does not prescribe how communications and training should be carried out. MPS Group provides this online and in the classroom (MPS Group Interview 2007). The bank reported that 1081 employees were given AML training in 2006 totalling 3290 hours and it also reported sanctions for employee negligence in AML, seven in 2005 and two in 2004 (MPS Group 2007, p. 39). Measures for the effects of this training were not provided.

Information technology tools are crucial to AML, required by law and an area where the banks stated in interview that they go beyond compliance by investing heavily in their development. The tools are used to detect and analyse irregular transactions and forward them electronically to the responsible authorities in line with legal reporting requirements. Caja Madrid's AML tools include sophisticated IT monitoring systems. Caja Madrid improved the quality of its reporting consistently over four consecutive years according to assessment by the Spanish AML authority SEPBLAC using the key parameter for evaluating the efficiency of AML practice – the quality of the suspicious transaction notifications (Caja Madrid 2007, p. 64). MPS Group uses various tools to assist in countering crime and money laundering. For example, in 2006 it developed an electronic procedure that compares and links a 'blacklist' supplied by AML authorities with its general customer list and accounting services. But there were no external assessments of effectiveness.

Internal controls are important for both issues. In MPS Group the Internal Controls unit acts as the parent company's internal auditing unit. It reports to the general manager, with precise processes for reporting to the Internal Audit and Control Committee and the Board of Statutory Auditors to the Board of Directors. Caja Madrid sees auditing as an important element of the controls to counter bribery and AML. Caja Madrid has an Internal Audit unit which is overseen by the Control Committee. Its work is written up in a yearly report using an audit risk map as a guide.

Public reporting: transparency is an important weapon in countering corruption and the case study banks provided some reporting in their CSR reports on AML but none on their measures for countering bribery. The only reference to countering bribery was made by MPS Group in a one-line mention in its social responsibility report to implementing rules and procedures for countering bribery (MPS Group 2007, p. 39). Both banks structure their annual reporting to use the GRI Sustainability Reporting Framework.

This section on CSR outcome has indicated that banks have management systems for countering bribery and AML and these are driven primarily by compliance with law and risk management. The examples of the case study banks show that the management systems also fulfil commitments to integrity and AML (CSR outputs). Laws define AML management systems in detail but are less prescriptive for bribery. Thus, Caja Madrid assessed bribery as a low risk and does not have an integrated anti-bribery management system whereas MPS Group assessed bribery as a high risk and has an integrated system.

In conclusion, corporate practices changed for AML for both banks but it is difficult to separate out the CSR outcome from those engendered by compliance and risk management which were the driving forces for changes in practices. For example, Caja Madrid, despite a commitment to integrity (output) and use of a voluntary instrument containing reference to anti-bribery (GRI Sustainability Reporting Framework), does not have a company-specific instrument. This is because of the low risk assessment of bribery.

13.4.3   CSR Impact

Proxy measures must be used to assess the impact outside the banks of any CSR-induced changes in corporate practices. The measures obtained were restricted to AML as proxy measures for impact of countering bribery were not available for either bank. These could have included, for example, enhancement of employees' skills, sharing of practices with banks and peer companies, and practices contributing to enhancement of the reputation of the banking sector and thereby to the economy in general. There was an implicit measure for impact for countering bribery as neither of the banks had been subjected to bribery allegations, investigations or prosecutions. This section looks, therefore, at the banks' impacts for AML in three areas: contribution to national AML efforts and thereby to the national banking reputation; influence on other savings banks; and positive contribution to integrity of the banking sector through high reputations and the absence of scandals or prosecutions.

The national AML system in Italy shows positive performances and because MPS Group is one of the largest banks, some of the national performance can be attributed to the bank as CSR impact. Reporting is a vital area specified tightly by laws and therefore any CSR effects cannot be separated out. The Financial Action Task Force (FATF) reported in 2006 that overall the Italian AML framework was extensive and mature, and achieved a high degree of compliance with most of the FATF requirements (IMF and FATF 2006, p. iv). Suspicious transactions reporting (STRs) and prosecutions are among indicators used to measure national effectiveness of AML. The report said that STRs increased by 32 per cent from 2003 to 2004 and signalled a remarkable commitment of Italian financial intermediaries in the fight against money laundering. It also said that legal enforcement efforts against money laundering had been quite successful, and almost 600 cases of money laundering led to convictions every year, which was one of the highest rates of successful prosecutions in Europe (ibid., 2006, p. 3). A 2005 FATF review of Spain compared unfavourably, expressing concerns about the relatively low numbers of STRs, especially from outside the banking system and that a large number of STRs had been filed by a small number of financial institutions. Also, there were no statistics showing how many investigations had led to prosecution (FATF 2006, pp. 6, 32). However, Caja Madrid has consistently received good annual ratings from the Spanish AML authority for its reporting and this can be taken as an indicator of CSR impact through the bank's contribution to national AML (Caja Madrid 2007, p. 64).

There was evidence that the case study banks' practices influenced other banks for CSR and AML but no evidence relating to countering bribery. MPS Group stated in interview that it wanted to be a leader in CSR and to receive recognition for this taking into account that with MPS Group's history and tradition, it would be a genuine and natural aim to be a responsible bank (MPS Group Interview 2007). Both banks are prominent in the national banking associations which play strong roles in CSR. Caja Madrid, as a leader in AML, has acted as an example for smaller savings banks starting to tackle AML and has also shared experience with other savings banks, AML being an area where banks co-operate rather than compete. Similarly, MPS Group has a strong link with the Italian Banking Association (ABI) where there is a permanent working group on AML.

Banking is built on trust and confidence – loss of trust leads to banking instability and repercussions in the economy. Thus, practices that contribute to enhancing or maintaining confidence in the banking system can be viewed as an impact. The absence of any scandals or prosecutions means there are no negative effects for the banks' reputations or the sector. There is positive evidence that both banks have enhanced the reputation of the banking sector. Caja Madrid was ranked 12th in a survey of Spanish companies with the highest reputations (Analisis e Investigación, Villafañe & Asociados 2007). This is a noteworthy result because very few savings banks were included in the ranking. MPS Group too has fared well being placed among the top 20 corporations with the highest reputation in Italy. These reputational rankings are the product of many factors but ethical behaviour can be considered as a contributor. The Italian survey identified ethical management as one of the factors creating added value for corporations (Cohn and Wolfe Research International 2006).

CSR effects can have dual value. For example, quality of AML reporting is a measure of internal effectiveness but also can be an external impact if it is assumed (it cannot be proven) that it leads to reductions in money laundering in the economy. Similarly, enhancement of a bank's reputation for integrity can be an outcome (positive changes in employees' perception of their employer, thereby building the anti-corruption culture of the bank) and an impact (enhancing society's confidence in the banking sector). Reporting too can create both internal outcomes and external impact. It can demonstrate to employees commitment and performance of the bank and can contribute externally to the overall reputation of the banking sector.

It is impossible to measure directly anti-bribery or AML CSR impact by banks as compliance and risk management are intervening (and dominant) forces for the banks' efforts in dealing with these issues. However, some impact can be attributed to AML by both banks using proxy measures for the quality of reporting of STRs, sharing good practice with other banks and generally through the banks' reputations contributing to an overall positive image of the banking sector. There were no proxy measures for countering bribery and impact could not be discerned. Table 13.1 summarizes the CSR output, outcome and impact for the banks.

13.5   EXPLAINING CSR EFFECTS IN THE BANKS

This section explores factors that explain the level of CSR effects described in the preceding sections. The three research questions are considered in turn and related to the five internal and external explanatory factors: corporate strategy and organization, corporate culture, civil society pressure, the business environment and the political-institutional setting. Independent of these factors, the actual instrument design may play a role in achieving sustainability impact.

13.5.1   The Instruments' Conduciveness to Impact

It is proposed that the design of an instrument can assist in creating high levels of outcome and subsequently impact. This can be through its specificity and obligations placed on the user, as discussed in Chapter 3. An instrument's level of specificity is the extent to which it prescribes specific and substantive activities and uses quantifiable targets rather than setting out procedural improvements. We shall first discuss the design of voluntary

Table 13.1 *CSR output, outcome and impact for the banks*

	CSR Output (changes in corporate commitment and strategy)	CSR Outcome (changes in corporate practice)	CSR Impact (changes in society/the environment)
Caja Madrid	**Anti-corruption** • Commitment to CSR and anti-corruption • Company-specific code of conduct • Use of voluntary CSR instruments: GRI and GRI Financial Services Supplement **AML only** • Use of company-specific AML management system	**AML only** • Risk assessment practices • Employee training; participation in e-learning and classroom courses; skills enhancement • Use of IT tools for AML • Internal controls • Reporting of suspicious transactions to authorities • Employees' perception of bank's integrity • Reporting on AML in CSR report	**Anti-corruption** • Enhanced reputation of the bank and the Spanish banking sector (as an influencer and leader in banking and also no scandals) **AML only** • Numbers and quality of suspicious transactions; sanctions; reports • Training of smaller savings banks • Participation in Spanish Savings Banks Association working groups
MPS Group	**Anti-corruption** • Commitment to CSR • Chart of Values • Use of voluntary CSR instruments: GC, GRI **AML and anti-bribery** • Use of company-specific AML management system	**Anti-corruption** • Risk assessment practices • Reporting on commitment to anti-corruption in social responsibility report **AML and anti-bribery** • Staff training • Sanctions • Due diligence in lending and investments • Employees' perception of bank's integrity **AML only** • Use of IT tools for AML • Internal control • Reporting of suspicious transactions to authorities	**Anti-corruption** • Enhanced reputation of the bank and the Italian banking sector (as an influencer and leader in banking and also no scandals) **AML only** • Numbers and quality of suspicious transactions; reports • Participation in Italian Banking Association working groups • Sharing of expertise in risk management with the building sector • Sanctions applied by authorities

CSR instruments with relevance for anti-corruption (GC, GRI) and then that of the company-specific instruments.

There are obligations attached to the CSR instruments relating to anti-bribery and AML. One of these instruments is the GC, which was signed by MPS Group. Signatories are required to observe ten Principles including a 10th Principle against Corruption and to make an annual CoP. This is a low obligation set firstly by an organization's own assessment of how non-compliance could affect its reputation and, secondly, by assessment by the GC whether the company has made an adequate CoP. The GC has delisted companies that have not submitted CoPs. Whilst such exclusion from the GC might not be a high penalty for some organizations, for a bank this could be damaging to reputation. Thus, commitment to the GC can be viewed as creating an obligation commensurate with the signatory's assessment of its corporate reputation and any vulnerability.

CSR reporting was identified by the banks as an instrument for implementing CSR, including anti-corruption. It provides a logical framework, self-imposed obligations of producing a continuing series of reports, year-on-year commitments to targets and reporting on achievements. Failure to meet expectations of stakeholders, achieve targets or not living up to public commitments can damage reputation. The GRI sustainability reporting framework is an instrument that supports CSR reporting but because it allows flexibility to companies in what they report on and there is a lack of sanctions, it can be assessed as having a low level of obligation. The GRI uses only a limited set of indicators for countering corruption including countering bribery and AML. For instance, Caja Madrid reported against anti-corruption indicators but the information provided was sparse and omitted to provide a required report on the management system used.

A third instrument is the MPS Group's company-specific instrument for countering bribery; Caja Madrid does not have a comparable instrument. Finally, there are the company-specific instruments for AML, developed both by MPS Group and by Caja Madrid. Law defines some specificity for MPS Group's anti-bribery management system but there was no evidence of further specificity due to CSR. Specificity for AML is defined in detail by national laws rather than CSR strategy. The laws, in accordance with highly prescriptive EU directives, specify procedures and targets for the thresholds and quality of reporting of suspicious transactions and checking on customers' identities but there is no specificity for other components of the management systems, such as communication, training, information technology tools and external reporting (this provides an opportunity for beyond compliance by the banks).

The obligations for the company-specific systems apart from legal compliance were meeting the company's values, integrity commitments and the expectations of stakeholders. Performing satisfactorily in internal and external audits also provides a strong obligation.

Table 13.2 describes the conduciveness of the voluntary instruments used by the banks that provide for countering corruption. Both the GC and the GRI have low specificity and low obligation. GRI reporting by both banks can be assessed as providing some small improvement in reporting on the issues but otherwise the instruments are not strongly conducive to producing impact. Therefore, any CSR impact for bribery or AML is more likely to come from the effective implementation of the company-specific instruments (management systems).

13.5.2   Factors that Determined the Banks' Choices of Instruments

The choice of CSR instruments is an important aspect of companies' commitments to CSR, both for the instruments' potential to create CSR impacts and for business benefits, such as enhancing reputation. Choice means selecting from existing external CSR instruments, initiating instruments where none exist or developing company-specific instruments. The action to choose an instrument may derive from a prior commitment to CSR or lead to a CSR commitment such as fulfilling the obligations of the GC. The two banks had made commitments to CSR before they selected their voluntary CSR instruments for countering bribery and corruption. They chose to deal with anti-bribery and AML by developing company-specific instruments, that is, integrated management systems rather than adopting existing voluntary anti-bribery or AML instruments.

Chapter 3 posits five hypotheses why a company will choose a CSR instrument. The assumptions relate to: strategy and organization, corporate culture, the business environment, civil society demand and the political-institutional setting. One expectation is that a company will adopt an instrument over another because it has a better fit with its strategic goals or its organizational structure. The prime influence for the banks for selecting the voluntary CSR instruments was indeed strategic fit. Both banks used evaluation processes to select their instruments. MPS Group became a signatory of the GC as it fitted a strategy to be associated with established instruments offering engagement with external stakeholders and good external visibility. The bank judged that it would promote the bank's CSR commitment (MPS Group Interview 2007). MPS Group stated in interview that it wanted to be a leader in CSR and to get recognition for this.

Caja Madrid has a strategic preference for a small number of tightly focused management systems selected through a rigorous analysis. This originates from successful use since 2003 of the EFQM[4] Excellence Model which is the basis of the bank's integrated management model. Caja

Table 13.2 Assessment of voluntary instruments' conduciveness to impact for countering corruption

Instrument	Specificity		Obligations	Assurance	Sanctions	Overall conduciveness to impact
	Quantifiable targets	Specific/ substantive procedures	Commitment			
Global Compact (MPS Group only)	No	Low	Commitment against corruption	Low: annual communication on progress	Low: inclusion in CoP non-reporting category; reputation damage	Low
GRI sustainability reporting framework (both banks)	Some	Low	None	Low: year-on-year reporting; requirement to publicly disclose plans, targets and performance but to level chosen by the bank	Low: stakeholder criticism; GRI evaluation of completeness of reporting	Low

Madrid has chosen a small number of CSR instruments that integrate into this model and generate a cross-cutting CSR approach. Caja Madrid advised in interview (Caja Madrid Interview 2007) that the GC would have had a strategic fit with its management systems approach but it chose not to sign up as the GC did not go beyond the bank's existing CSR commitments and would not bring any additional CSR effects. Caja Madrid also considered the GC to be aimed more at companies operating in developing countries.

Familiarity with and high legitimacy of an instrument in the business environment afffected only Caja Madrid's decision to use the GRI Financial Supplement. This was part of a field test by the Spanish Savings Banks Association among its members.

The GRI Sustainability Reporting Framework is used by both banks as a framework for their social responsibility and CSR reporting. It can be argued that this is because the instrument has a strategic CSR fit – the instrument has a comprehensive approach to reporting CSR matching the commitments and strategies of the banks. Organizationally, it matched MPS Group's wish to obtain recognition for its CSR by association with leading CSR instruments and it fitted with Caja Madrid's systems approach. Culturally, it suited the stakeholder cultures of both banks.

There was no evidence of civil society stakeholder demand influencing the banks' choice of any voluntary instruments. The banks were not aware of the three voluntary instruments[5] for countering bribery and this can be attributed to low promotion of the instruments by their originators (civil society and business associations).

Both banks developed company-specific instruments for AML and MPS Group developed one for anti-bribery but not Caja Madrid. The prime factors were the political-institutional environment setting laws, the business environment posing risks and internal strategies.

When looking at why the two bank's CSR outputs (commitments, strategies, instruments) differ, we can again draw on the set of above explanatory factors. One relevant factor for the difference between the banks is the political-institutional environment. MPS Group's instrument was developed to comply with Italian law 231 which requires Italian banks to develop anti-bribery instruments and provides severe sanctions for non-compliance. The law does not specify what banks must have exactly in their code and covers only main issues. Thus, there is scope for beyond compliance. There is no equivalent Spanish law.

The business environment is an explanatory factor too for the different approaches. MPS Group in the survey reported bribery as of fairly high strategic importance while Caja Madrid assessed bribery as a fairly low risk and did not have a management system. There are different perceptions in

Italy and Spain about the levels of corruption. According to Transparency International's 2007 Corruption Perceptions Index, Italy was ranked at 41st, amongst the worst of the EU countries. Spain performed better being ranked at 25th (Transparency International 2007) and this suggests that nationally bribery has been regarded as less as a risk than in Italy. However, there is now an environment of exposure of serious issues of corruption with major scandals involving local authorities, land speculation and property development. Corruption is a risk to banks as the building sector has offered potentially lucrative markets. More than half the loan portfolio of Spanish banks is tied up with mortgages and loans to property developers and has led to public criticism. (Caja Madrid advised that it did not have significant investments in land but this was for market reasons and not because of corruption risk.)

Lack of peer activity in the business environment may also explain why Caja Madrid did not implement a company-specific anti-bribery instrument. A 2006 survey of the 35 companies on Empresa Ibex 35, the Spanish stock market index, revealed that only 15 companies had clearly formalized their commitment to anti-corruption (Fundación Carolina y Fundación Ecologia y Desarrollo 2007). This absence of reference to countering bribery might reflect an issue which applies in many countries of a reluctance to publicly address the sensitive topic of bribery for fear that it will be interpreted as an indication of an underlying issue.

Both banks have developed their own AML company-specific instruments. The driving forces were in compliance with existing legislation (that is, the political-institutional setting) and the business environment according to the assessed risk of money laundering.[6] The pressure for compliance is extremely high. Money laundering is the subject of detailed and extensive international and national legislation responding to the threat of terrorism but also countering money laundering from the results of crime. National legislation is prescribed by EU directives and defines precisely what banks should do for AML. A further influence is the FATF, an inter-governmental body, that has issued influential instruments used by banks as a reference though they carry no direct obligation (FATF 2004). Another influence is Basel II, a standard for risk approaches and countering improper business practices including AML (Bank for International Settlements 2006). In both countries sanctions for failure by financial institutions to report money laundering are generally severe. Italy faces risks from money laundering but has taken countermeasures. The review by the FATF in February 2006 reported that the AML framework was extensive and mature and that law enforcement efforts were quite successful (IMF and FATF 2006, p. 2). Spain too has high money laundering issues but according to the 2006 FATF review, the Spanish legal framework for combating money laundering and terrorist financing is generally comprehensive (FATF 2006, p. 6).

The case studies suggest that when dealing with the issues, banks primarily look to internally developed management systems that comply with the requirements of laws (political-institutional) and also their assessment of risks (business environment). Growing pressure from civil society means the banks are looking to voluntary codes, such as the GC and the GRI, and sector developed codes, such as the Equator Principles to build credibility, enhance reputation and express leadership in integrity. However, whilst the Wolfsberg AML Principles have been developed for AML, there is no sector initiative for countering bribery.

13.5.3   Factors that Influenced Effective Implementation

The previous two sections looked at the inherent characteristics of the instruments that could lead to CSR outcomes and at why the banks chose the respective CSR instruments. This section considers the proposition that CSR impact also depends on the effectiveness with which companies implement the instruments. Effective implementation means that the instruments induce significant changes in corporate practices. In other words, that high levels of CSR outcome are generated and these in turn are assumed to induce high levels of CSR impact. The findings in Section 4.2 confirm such high levels of outcome for the issue area of AML, but not for countering of bribery. This section analyzes the external and internal factors responsible for the high AML outcomes and for the weak anti-bribery outcomes.

Both banks showed identical factors contributing to the effective implementation of CSR instruments for overarching CSR and AML (not, though, for countering bribery). These were the internal factors of corporate culture, strategic and organizational integration and the business environment.

The assumption for the first factor is that substantive outcomes will be obtained where CSR matches corporate culture and there was evidence that the banks' cultures were highly conducive to overarching CSR. The banks stated in interview that they considered their strong CSR cultures to be generally supportive in countering corruption generally. Evidence was given specifically for AML but none could be provided for countering bribery. CSR took place through initiating more extensive AML training or greater investment in AML information technology than that prescribed by laws. It can be surmised that the effective implementation of overarching CSR will provide a supporting environment in which countering bribery and AML activities are more likely to flourish. Both banks have long histories of stakeholder ownership and community commitment with few parallels in other European companies. Caja Madrid is governed by stakeholders and MPS Foundation nominates half the MPS Group's ten directors and owns 49 per cent of the bank. The banks make substantial contributions to the community directly and through associated foundations. This has created a culture where employees appear to be committed to the banks' community links and CSR practices. A further factor is that the banks have strong local ties in their cities of origin and through their local branches. This cultural background suggests that employees and stakeholders understand and endorse the banks' CSR practices and this may enable effective implementation of CSR. There was no evidence available of what the banks' employees thought about their banks' CSR activities or specifically about integrity.

A further aspect of corporate culture is that if CSR is rooted in a long-standing and well-developed identity of being socially responsible, intrinsic pressures are created to produce genuine CSR impact. Interviews with the banks' personnel showed the prevalence of the banks' histories and community commitment in the thinking of those interviewed but there was no additional evidence identified to enable this assumption to be explored further. It can be deduced that the weight of the banks' history, the role of stakeholders (notably their foundations), their closeness to authorities and deep root in local communities all create an expectation and imperative for the banks to undertake and be leaders in overarching CSR and develop impact.

The assumption for the second factor is that CSR will be effectively implemented where there is strategic and organizational integration of CSR instruments. This was indicated to be a strong factor for the banks. There was evidence of advocacy by the senior management, for example, both chairmen of the banks made public commitments to CSR in the social responsibility and CSR reports. CSR strategic plans were embedded in both banks' business activities though MPS Group had yet to link it to the MPS Group business plan, but this was being remedied.

Externally, the business environment, above all the national banking sectors was a strong influence for the implementation of both overarching CSR and for AML (but not for countering bribery). Banking associations were the prime influences. The Confederation of Spanish Savings Banks (CECA) stated in interview that it wanted to inspire CSR among savings banks, but not to be prescriptive (CECA Interview 2007). CECA's stated aim for CSR is to provide members with useful tools and training and to express a corporate image for savings banks as leaders in CSR in Spain. CECA has organized working groups for CSR improvement including piloting the GRI Financial Services Supplement, and at the time of our research planned to present the conclusions to the European CSR Alliance. Both banks are among the largest in their countries and each has accepted a leadership role in CSR among the banking sector and specifically in AML practice, taking part in workshops and providing advice to smaller banks in the case of Caja Madrid. Another assumption is that effective CSR implementation depends on whether the social and environmental activities are perceived as a business opportunity or an organizational benefit for the company. CSR can be driven by the desire to compete on reputation for social responsibility. CECA concurred, stating in interview that a highly competitive atmosphere among savings banks managers could directly lead to as high a level of competition in CSR as in competition for market share (ibid.).

The reason for support from the business environment to AML but not for countering bribery in Italy and Spain may be because of the association of money laundering with terrorism and the high profile and specificity of AML legislation. Also, bribery remains a sensitive topic for companies in many countries, not a subject easily discussed publicly, and this could include Italy and Spain. As shown by the survey in Spain of top companies referred to earlier in this chapter, it is an issue that is neglected (Fundación Carolina y Fundación Ecologia y Desarrollo 2007). This contrasts with the survey sample where 15 of the 17 banks surveyed reported countering bribery as of high or rather high strategic priority.

13.6   CONCLUSIONS

Corruption, of which bribery and money laundering are significant parts, is one of the greatest ills facing societies, lying behind major issues, such as poverty, environmental damage, abuse of human rights or processing the proceeds of crime. Yet, corruption was low on the CSR agenda until the United Nations Convention against Corruption was adopted in 2003 paving the way for the addition of the GC 10th Principle against Corruption in 2005. The purpose of this chapter was to examine the CSR impact in countering corruption and AML but there are impediments to reaching conclusions about possible CSR effects in the case study banks. The prime aim of banks in countering bribery and AML is compliance with laws and risk management and as such, CSR effects are masked by these overriding objectives and cannot be separated out. Further, the issues do not provide direct measures of performance – banks' activities are preventive and the ultimate measure of success is that the violations are prevented or minimized. The issues are clandestine so there is no way of knowing how successful a company is in countering issues in relation to undetected violations. What is certain is that the global scale of corruption is considerable and is an area where banks can exercise a particular social responsibility in dealing with issues which damage societies substantially.

This chapter looked at CSR output, outcome and impact in two European banks. It showed that there was high explicit commitment to AML but less so to countering bribery though many of the banks surveyed identified bribery as of high or relatively high strategic importance. Neither of the case study banks had explicit no-bribes policies. The two banks both used company-specific instruments for AML but only MPS Group had one for countering bribery. Changes in practices (outcomes) could be identified for the case study banks for AML, such as organizational structures, risk assessment, communication and training, internal controls, monitoring and reporting including use of IT tools. Evidence was provided for quality of reporting of STRs but it was impossible to attribute which portion of this was due to CSR. There was little or no evidence for countering bribery in both banks either in the implementation of anti-bribery systems or measures of effectiveness.

It is difficult to measure impact of voluntary anti-bribery or AML activities by banks as compliance and risk management are the prime reasons for the banks' efforts in dealing with these issues but some impact can be attributed to AML by both banks. Quality and volume of STRs is an internal CSR outcome but it is also a CSR impact as STRs contribute to the overall national performances for AML through their preventive effect and also may lead to prosecutions. Outcomes, such as training, attitudes of employees to the integrity of their employers or enhancement of corporate reputation also have external impact. The reputations for integrity of the case study banks can also be taken as an impact as they add in this way to the overall reputation of the banking sector and ultimately contribute to the national economy's success. Although there were no concrete measures for countering bribery, the absence of violations has protected the banks' reputations and can be an imprecise indicator of successful prevention (though it can also be argued that lack of evidence of violations may indicate a lack of effective detection).

We also explored factors that explain the achieved levels of CSR effects. It was proposed that the design of an instrument can assist in creating high levels of outcome and subsequently impact. The GRI and GC were assessed as providing low levels of specificity and obligation for countering bribery or AML and any CSR impact for bribery or AML will come from the effective implementation of the bank-specific instruments.

The choice of CSR instruments is an important aspect of companies' commitments to CSR. The prime influence for the case study banks for selecting their voluntary CSR instruments for the issues was strategic fit.

MPS Group had a strategy to be associated with established instruments offering engagement with external stakeholders and good external visibility whilst Caja Madrid had a strategic preference for a small number of tightly focused management systems. Accordingly, MPS Group had become a signatory of the GC and both banks used the GRI Sustainability Reporting Framework. Both developed their own instruments (management systems) for AML and MPS Group developed an instrument for countering bribery. There was no evidence of civil society stakeholder demand influencing the banks' choices of voluntary instruments. The banks chose to develop bank-specific AML instruments as they saw the issue of such strategic importance that they wished to use instruments with high specificity which went beyond compliance and matched or exceeded the voluntary instrument (the Wolfsberg AML Principles). This could be largely due to the need to ensure compliance and risk management but the banks' CSR and stakeholder cultures may also have encouraged a beyond compliance approach. The lack of use of the anti-bribery instruments can be attributed to the banks' experience in developing company-specific instruments for AML and therefore in the first instance adopting a similar consideration for anti-bribery and not seeking out the voluntary codes. Also, low promotion by the originators of the anti-bribery codes may mean that the banks were unaware of the codes.

Differences in the political-institutional and business environments can explain why MPS Group had an anti-bribery company-specific instrument whereas Caja Madrid did not. Italian law requires an anti-bribery system and there is no equivalent in Spain. The perceived levels of corruption in Italy are higher than in Spain according to Transparency International's 2007 Corruption Perceptions Index and this could explain why the banks differed in their risk assessment of countering bribery with MPS Group judging it as of fairly high strategic importance and Caja Madrid as low.

Externally, the business environment, above all the banking associations, were the prime influences on the case study banks for the implementation of both overarching CSR and for AML (but not for countering bribery). Both banks are among the largest in their countries and each has accepted a leadership role in CSR in the associations and in AML practice. It can be surmised that support from the business environment to AML but not for countering bribery in Italy and Spain is to AML because of the threat of terrorism and associated AML legislation, but bribery remains a sensitive topic for companies in the countries.

Although compliance and risk management were the dominant reasons for AML for both banks and for countering bribery for MPS Group, both banks said in interview that CSR made anti-bribery and AML activities more effective by harnessing positive employee attitudes shaped by long traditions of commitment to the community and stake-holder governance of the banks. However, it can be judged that any CSR output or impact for the banks for AML or countering bribery occurred independently of the CSR strategy and was driven by compliance and risk management. There was a 'top and tail' approach. The banks made commitments to integrity or AML and reported on AML and counter-ing bribery in their social responsibility and CSR report but CSR was absent in-between.

The high level of CSR outcomes for AML may be ascribed to two factors shared by both banks. Organizationally, the two banks have similar his-tories of stakeholder governance. Stakeholder ownership may provide an environment in which CSR can flourish as the banks must take account of a wide base of interests other than pure market forces. Culture of the banks is intertwined with the organizational structure and was indicated in inter-views to be a strong influence for CSR. This provides a climate in which CSR can be supported and endorsed by employees and stakeholders.

There may be several explanations why neither bank has incorporated anti-bribery and AML into the banks' CSR strategies. One is that there has been little pressure until recently from civil society for incorporating countering corruption as part of CSR. A second reason could be that bribery and money laundering are assessed so highly as compliance and business risks that CSR is overlooked. Another reason could be that the highly technical issues of countering bribery and especially AML do not lend themselves to easy presentation to stakeholders. As mentioned before, the issue of bribery may be an uncomfortable topic for companies and, finally, the absence of measures for concrete impacts means that the CSR benefits cannot be promoted easily and thereby the lack of visibility is further enforced.

To conclude, whilst there is no concrete evidence from the case studies that CSR impact can be achieved for countering bribery, the evidence from AML suggests that there is a strong case to include the issues in CSR strategies. The causes are important as the issues are highly detrimental to societies. Successful countering of bribery and AML depends on build-ing cultures among employees so they not only comply with policies but carry out activities in a way that leads to prevention and CSR can help in this.

The two ultimate measures for countering bribery and AML are favour-able perceptions by stakeholders of the integrity of a company and the absence of serious violations. On both measures the two banks demon-strated achievement and, though not measurable, CSR can be deduced to have contributed to this.

NOTES

1. References are given for the interviews but are not attributed to individuals.
2. Such as the Business Principles for Countering Bribery or the Wolfsberg AML Principles.
3. The Business Principles for Countering Bribery and the Partnering Against Corruption Initiative (PACI) Principles for Countering Bribery (PACI 2005).
4. European Foundation for Quality Management.
5. The Business Principles for Countering Bribery, Combating Extortion and Bribery: ICC Rules of Conduct and Recommendations (ICC 2005) and the PACI Principles for Countering Bribery (PACI 2005).
6. Note that the scope of the instruments developed is broader than required by law, which is why the instruments classify as CSR instruments.

14 CSR effects across four issue areas: a synthesis of the case studies

Franziska Wolff

14.1 INTRODUCTION

In this chapter we synthesize the previous case studies and highlight major similarities and differences. All case studies had the same goal: to take stock and explain sustainability effects (output, outcome and impact) resulting from Corporate Social Responsibility (CSR) in specific issue areas and sectors. In doing so, the authors discussed propositions developed by Viganò et al. in Chapter 3. The case studies tackled their common goal with slightly different approaches and structures in order to adapt to their specific contexts. For instance, the study by Boasson and Wettestad focuses the research question by analysing the outcomes and impact resulting from adoption of four specific CSR instruments, rather than from CSR output more generally. As a consequence, the term 'CSR outcome' is also used in a narrower sense.[1] Some case studies made slight alterations with regard to the explanatory factors and hypotheses. Nevertheless, there is a good basis for comparison across the issue areas.

In the following we shall show that the outcomes and impact resulting from CSR output were more often low or medium rather than high. The factors that most strongly influenced the adoption of CSR instruments – as crucial elements of output – were strategic considerations, corporate cultures and civil society demand. When it comes to choosing one specific instrument over another, legitimacy of an instrument in the business sector and its political support were decisive. Looking at the changes in corporate practices resulting from voluntary instruments and from CSR output more generally, no clear pattern could be established. Strategic and organizational integration, corporate cultures, business benefits and expectations from within the political-institutional setting all played important roles in most of the cases.

14.2   TAKING STOCK OF CSR EFFECTS

Our synthesis of CSR effects in Europe is based on the four preceding multi-case studies. They cover voluntary efforts on mitigating climate change (in two oil companies); on promoting sustainable fisheries (in three fish processors); on enhancing gender equality (in two banks); on countering bribery and anti-money laundering (AML) (in two banks). We first take a look at the transformation of CSR output (commitment, strategies, instruments) into outcome (resulting changes in corporate practices) and subsequently into impact (consequences for society and the environment).

Within the two oil companies a specific segment of the companies' overall CSR output was focused on: adherence to four specific standardized instruments relevant for mitigating climate change – the Global Compact, the Global Reporting Initiative, the Carbon Disclosure Project and Global Gas Flaring Reduction public-private partnership. In terms of outcome, these instruments contributed little to climate-relevant behavioural changes within the companies, such as the setting of targets and timetables or disclosure of direct and indirect emissions. Outcome effects were somewhat stronger in one of the companies. In line with the generally weak outcome levels, impact that could directly be attributed to these changes was low as well.

In the case study on sustainable fisheries the three fish processors feature a similar (and rather high) CSR output. It includes sustainable seafood policies, partly with quantitative sourcing targets; the use of a standardized instrument (MSC[2] certification); as well as the use of company-specific instruments with a similar purpose in two companies. As a consequence, unsustainable fish were substituted in the processors' product portfolios and supplier standards were implemented. These outcomes were at medium to high levels in the analyzed companies. Environmental impact could not be directly measured, but existing studies suggest that the MSC's ecosystem benefits are relevant, though they may vary for different fisheries. No evidence could be obtained on the impact of company-specific instruments.

Gender equality output in the banks included, above all, participation in gender award systems and integration of selected sub-issues (gender opportunity, work-life balance) into human resources' strategies, supported in one of the two banks by an explicit gender equality commitment. Improvements in corporate practices were high with regard to those sub-issues for which a CSR output existed. Interestingly, outcomes were also achieved with regard to gender-related sub-issues that had not been addressed by outputs. Societal impact, specified in the case study as performance above national/sectoral averages, was high only with regard to improving the work-life balance of employees and either medium or not measurable so far with regard to other sub-issues.

When it comes to fighting corruption, CSR effects were masked by the banks' aims for compliance and risk management. The banks' level of commitment and strategizing (output) were relatively low with regard to countering bribery but high with regard to money laundering. Instruments adopted for broader CSR aims but with anti-corruption components included the GRI Sustainability Reporting Framework (both banks), and the Global Compact plus issue-related company-specific instruments for AML in both banks and for countering bribery in one bank. In accordance with the output, the changes in corporate practices – relating to anti-corruption management systems incorporating risk assessment, communication and training, internal control and external reporting – were low for countering bribery and high for AML. However, the banks indicated that CSR helped further their compliance performance. Societal impacts for countering bribery could not be discerned because positive effects are preventive while proxy indicators for AML showed some improvements, such as increases in the number and quality of reporting of suspicious transactions as assessed by good ratings from governmental bodies. Less tangible impacts include the two banks' high reputations for integrity and their sectoral influence as leaders with regard to anti-bribery and AML practices.

In summary, we can state that no general pattern is discernible with regard to the relation of output-outcome-impact. CSR outputs were generally the starting point for selecting companies for case studies, and for most case studies companies with rather high output were selected in order to learn from best practice. The levels of outcome and impact resulting from these outputs were more often low to medium rather than high. Interestingly, in some cases low output (for example, with regard to some gender equality sub-issues) induced unexpectedly high levels of outcome. The example also shows more generally that levels of CSR effects differed not only between the issue areas analyzed, but also between sub-issues within the same issue area. The case study on mitigating climate change demonstrates that standardized CSR instruments influence corporate behaviour to differing degrees, depending on their implementation.

Finally, while the case studies focused on issue-specific activities, more overarching CSR was looked at as well, mostly at the level of output. The case studies confirmed the finding of Chapter 9 that the targeted sectors differ in terms of the development stage (or 'maturity') of their CSR approaches, with the fish processors lagging behind on more overarching CSR activities. Furthermore, in companies with both overarching and issue-specific CSR, these two strands of CSR were often not well integrated. Respondents from the two oil companies even voiced their surprise at the study treating beyond-compliance action on climate change as a CSR issue; in their perception this was a 'core business' issue. Both banks examined for their voluntary action on countering bribery and AML managed these issues independently of the CSR strategy, though these were 'topped and tailed' with overarching commitments to integrity and to AML ('top') and reporting of both issues in their sustainability reports ('tail'). In contrast to this, the banks investigated under the gender equality perspective over time had integrated gender concerns into their overarching CSR management at least to some extent.

14.3   EXPLAINING CSR EFFECTS

In order to explain the achievement of CSR effects, the case studies made use of a set of explanatory factors internal and external to companies. These include the design of CSR instruments, a company's strategy, organization and culture, as well as its business environment, civil society and the political-institutional setting. Propositions on the role of these factors were elaborated in Viganò et al. Chapter 3. When looking at the four case studies' findings, what can we learn about the plausibility of these propositions? We shall focus on the hypotheses relating to output and outcome. The reason is that propositions on the conduciveness of instruments to CSR impact were only discussed in an a priori analytical way but could not be researched empirically in the case studies.[3]

14.3.1   Factors Explaining CSR Output

Our operating research question with regard to CSR output read: 'What factors determine a company's instrument choice?', and we distinguished between adoption of an instrument in general, and preference of a specific instrument over others. The influence of different factors on these choices may be positive, neutral or negative.

We assumed that companies decide to adopt an instrument because they expect it to promote their strategic goals. Indeed, the influence of the factor 'corporate strategy and organization' on output was positive in almost all cases. Among the fish processors, the instruments were adopted to contribute to the core strategic concern of protecting the supply base. With regard to gender equality, one of the banks studied developed an own instrument to fit with its general systems-led management systems, while the other bank adopted existing high-profile codes to promote its strategy of becoming (perceived as) a CSR pioneer. In the case study on countering bribery and money laundering, voluntary instruments were either developed for reasons of compliance or risk management. An example for a 'negative' form of strategic alignment is the following: one of the banks had a low strategic priority for countering bribery, and in line with this, settled for non-holistic procedures. Only among the oil companies, adoption of the four CSR instruments analyzed was somewhat ad hoc in one of the businesses (while strategically aligned in the other).

We had also assumed that when choosing between alternative instruments, companies would prefer one instrument to another because it had a better fit with their strategic goals or their organizational structure. However, we found that for many issues the number of instruments was limited so that strategic choices were not possible. Also, where there were several instruments to choose from, strategies and organizational structures tended to be sufficiently flexible not to 'prescribe' selection of any one specific instrument.

Corporate cultures did not play a significant role with regard to instrument choice, confirming our proposition. However, we found that in most of the companies selected, specific cultures existed that may have promoted the adoption of voluntary instruments in the first place. For example, in one of the oil companies its traditional approach to climate change policy drove adherence to the four CSR instruments. In the fish processing sector all analyzed companies had particular traditions or identities which indirectly linked up with the sustainable fisheries' issue. The banks that were examined for both gender equality and anti-corruption CSR had cultures characterized by stakeholder governance and histories of societal commitment which were said to be important in imbuing employees with an understanding of and commitment to beyond-compliance approaches.

With regard to companies' business environment, we had hypothesized that companies would choose the instruments they were most familiar with and which had the highest legitimacy within the sector. This can be said to have been true in about a third of our companies. Both oil companies' deep rootedness in the global petroleum field and their involvement in the global CSR 'scene' had positively influenced adherence to the four instruments. Also with regard to gender equality instruments, we find that one bank had opted to adhere to standardized instruments and in this was indeed influenced by the instruments' high diffusion and legitimacy. The other bank, though familiar with these instruments, decided against using them. In the fisheries sector institutional involvement in developing the instrument was more decisive than its (at the time not yet developed) legitimacy. The least influence of the business environment was discernible in the case of countering corruption: while the banks were aware of the relevant AML instrument, they chose not to adopt it, and in the case of anti-bribery they were not even familiar with the existing instruments.

With regard to civil society, our hypothesis was that civil society demand would not play a significant role in instrument choice, but would be more broadly related to the uptake of social and environmental activities and hence to instrument adoption as such. In the two case studies that analyzed the role of civil society with regard to CSR output this role was found to be neutral to positive. While non-governmental organizations (NGOs) had exerted no pressure either on adhering or on selecting specific anti-bribery or AML instruments in the banks (hence partly refuting our assumption), they had had an important part in developing the major sector-wide instrument for sustainable fisheries and were involved in designing company-specific instruments.

As regards the political-institutional setting, our hypothesis that companies may choose a specific CSR instrument because the instrument is favoured within the political-institutional context was confirmed only for three of the eight companies: one of the oil companies was directly pushed by a national government to adopt a particular instrument, and in the issue areas of gender equality relevant CSR instruments were provided directly by governments (national gender award systems). In other cases more indirect influences were at work: for example, domestic patterns of industrial relations and cultural traditions of voluntary company commitment stimulated the second oil company to adhere to the targeted CSR instruments. In the fish processing sector the failure of governments to stop overfishing triggered CSR instrument development in the first place. With regard to countering bribery and AML, strong legislative frameworks exist and governments have not stimulated voluntary action in this field.

14.3.2 Factors Explaining CSR Outcome

With regard to the CSR-induced changes in concrete practices (outcome), we had asked: 'What factors drive an effective implementation of CSR instruments within companies?' To what extent were our propositions on the explanatory factors confirmed or refuted?

As regards strategy and organization, we had proposed that CSR output was likely to render greatest effects if corporate leaders were to link it to the core strategies of the company and integrate it organizationally. This could widely be confirmed. With the exception of one oil company – which made few efforts to translate instrument requirements into practice – the CSR processes in the other businesses featured high degrees of strategic integration, organizational embedding and internal communication. These processes were both horizontal (between functional units) and partly vertical (through in-house training in one fish processor, and inclusion of trade unions and bottom-up initiatives on gender equality within the banks).

We had proposed that corporate culture fosters change in an organization's social and environmental practices in particular if CSR is rooted in a long-standing and well-developed identity of the organization as being socially responsible. While we found that surprisingly many of the companies had such identities, their concrete effect on achieving outcome was not always straightforward. Cultural changes in one of the oil companies in the 1990s had a positive influence on creating outcome, but strong vertical institutionalization combined with weak horizontal integration actually hampered achievement of impact. Among the fish processors and banks, specific traditions of all companies were seen at least partly to support CSR implementation.

Our assumption with regard to the business environment had been that the level of CSR outcomes depended on whether the social and environmental activities were perceived as a business opportunity or an organizational benefit for the company. In the climate change study fundamental market uncertainties functioned as obstacles to producing deeper outcome and impact effects for most instruments analyzed. In the fish processing sector sustainable sourcing was perceived by all companies as a business opportunity, but its strength varied according to differences in customer and consumer pull. Relevant other business factors affecting outcome included tight supplier relations and availability of certified fish. The case study on gender equality showed that the framing of gender equality as a business case helped banks to promote outcome. With regard to anti-corruption, it can be surmised that the assessment of bribery as a lower risk than money laundering in one of the banks was partly responsible for its achieving lower anti-bribery outcomes compared with AML outcomes.

Civil society stakeholders had promoted effective implementation of CSR instruments and high levels of CSR outcome, as suggested, only in the issue areas of sustainable fishing and gender equality.[4] Environmental groups had been involved in implementing sustainable sourcing policies (in one case even in product development) and complementary external NGO pressure had focused the companies' attention. With regard to gender issues, especially internal stakeholders such as women units of trade unions pushed CSR implementation. There was no evidence of civil society influence on banks' policies and systems to counter bribery and money laundering.

Finally, we had proposed that expectations and norms within the political-institutional setting as regards the effective implementation of CSR instruments also fostered the achievement of CSR outcome. To varying degrees, this proposition was confirmed by all case studies. While implementation of climate instruments was supported in one of the oil companies by strong national climate policies, the opposite was the case for the other company whose domestic policy context was less ambitious. In the sustainable fisheries' study a low positive influence could be detected where governments funded or otherwise stimulated the certification of fisheries. In the case study on gender equality the factors' influence was probably most direct as performance of banks within national gender award systems was publicly verified. With regard to AML, strong EU and national legislation provided an impetus for beyond-compliance activities and, similarly, for countering bribery in one of the banks where there was prescriptive legislation.

NOTES

1. In this narrow sense, it denotes only those changes in company practices that result from the use of the selected CSR instruments. Behavioural changes induced by other changes in commitment and strategy are not included.
2. Marine Stewardship Council.
3. See the explanation in Chapter 3.
4. The role of civil society was not looked into in the case study on mitigating climate change.

PART IV

CSR and public policy

15 CSR and public policy: mutually reinforcing for sustainable development?

Franziska Wolff, Maria Bohn, Irmgard Schultz and Peter Wilkinson

15.1 INTRODUCTION

How does Corporate Social Responsibility (CSR) relate to and interact with public policy? How and why do policy makers 'make use' of CSR, and what functions can CSR develop in systems of public governance? And, importantly, can CSR contribute to achieving public policy goals on sustainability? These are the questions to be addressed in the following.

We argue that public policy plays an important role for CSR. Apart from coining societal expectations for companies' responsibility, it can stimulate and procedurally regulate CSR. Motives of policy makers for stimulating CSR differ from those for regulating CSR. A 'retreat' of the state, a reduction in or avoidance of further regulation of companies, is only one of these motives. Placing CSR within a debate on the transformation of the state, we develop a typology of functions that CSR can have in systems of public governance: apart from being a beyond-compliance self-regulation approach, CSR can be a means to improve compliance with command and control governance and to enhance the social and environmental steering effects of incentive-based regulation. In each of these ideal-typical cases CSR contributes to sustainability in a distinct way. Whether or not CSR actually produces sustainability impact, however, is a question to be decided empirically. Approaching this question with evidence spelled out earlier in this book, we discuss to what extent, if any, CSR activities address public policy goals on sustainable development. We find that companies' voluntary action to a remarkable extent tackles EU policy goals, though from what we see at company level this contribution may not always suffice to ultimately fulfil the public policy goal in question.

15.2   THE ROLES OF PUBLIC POLICY FOR CSR

The most obvious and fundamental role of public policy for CSR is that it defines its very baseline: when setting mandatory social and environmental standards, public policy marks off companies' compliance activities from CSR activities. It has been pointed out that these baselines vary nationally since what is a codified responsibility of businesses ('implicit CSR') in one society may be voluntary in another (Matten and Moon 2005). Less tangibly, public policies also influence the expectations of citizens and companies as regards the roles and responsibilities of business. And increasingly, public policies recognize CSR as a means of sustainability governance. As sketched out in Chapter 1 and illustrated now in some greater detail, public policies have been developed to stimulate or procedurally regulate CSR (Aaronson and Reeves 2002; Buckland et al. 2006; European Commission 2004b and 2006b; Fox et al. 2002; Wolff and Barth 2005). Policy makers can opt for such types of 'new governance' in order to provide sustainability governance where so far none existed, to complement more traditional public policies or to substitute them (cf. Moon 2002).

To stimulate CSR and ultimately sustainability, governments encourage companies to adopt and adhere to CSR instruments and policies. They may do so, for example, by (co-) authoring CSR instruments – from codes of conduct to management systems – that can be used by companies on a voluntary basis. For example, industrialized countries' governments drafted the OECD Guidelines for Multinational Enterprises and the British government co-authored the Ethical Trade Initiative (ETI) and the Voluntary Principles on Security and Human Rights for companies in the Extractive and Energy Sectors. In the field of management standards the EU established a public policy framework with the Environmental Management System (EMAS), and governments represented in the International Organization for Standardization (ISO) have contributed to formulating norms for the environmental management system ISO 14 000, the quality management system ISO 9 000 and the future guidance standard ISO 26 000 on social responsibility. With regard to labelling, many countries as well as the European Community developed eco-labelling schemes in the 1980s. Social labels emerged later: in 2000 Denmark launched a Social Index which can be used as a label, and Belgium introduced its social label in 2002. National gender award schemes existed in some countries (for example, Spain) already in the 1990s. Capacity building is another way to foster CSR. This can range from funding CSR research and training to spreading good practice and anchoring CSR in a public administration department. Governments can also tie public procurement to social and ecological criteria and provide financial incentives for Corporate

Citizenship activities, such as tax deductions for social foundations or for company donations to sustainability projects. Finally, the public sector can stimulate CSR by calling into being or participating in CSR stakeholder networks. In addition to initiatives directly geared towards stimulating CSR, there are a number of public-private partnerships relating to social and environmental issues, as well as voluntary agreements that include businesses and governments – the latter as partners and, rarely, as the controlling and sanctioning authority.

Governments can also regulate CSR to a certain extent. Two examples are transparency and accountability norms. Such regulations define procedural obligations only and leave it to the companies whether or not they go beyond substantive social and environmental standards.[1] Legal transparency obligations can require investment (predominantly pension) funds to disclose how social, environmental and ethical criteria are accounted for in the funds' investment policy. Such clauses have been introduced, among others, in Belgium, France, Germany, Italy, Sweden and the UK. Transparency obligations can also require companies to report on their non-financial risks or impacts. In Europe in the 1990s such reporting obligations had an environmental focus. They were legislated, among others, in Belgium (1995), Denmark (1996), the Netherlands (1997) and Norway (1999). A second wave of company reporting laws followed as of 2001 and included social and ethical aspects. Forerunners were France (2001), Denmark (2001), Sweden (2003) and the UK (2005). Since 2005, the EU Accounts Modernization Directive (No. 2003/51/EC) has obliged large and medium-sized companies in all Member States to include non-financial information in their annual reports. Also, Directive 2006/46/EC encourages the provision of non-financial information in annual reports.

15.3 THE ROLES OF CSR FOR PUBLIC POLICY

So far, we have looked at the active role that public policy, conceptually as well as empirically, plays with regard to CSR. In this section we change perspective and look at the functions that CSR has in relation to public policy and, more concretely, to public policies fostering sustainability governance. By 'sustainability governance' we mean institutional arrangements to promote sustainable development, that is, inter- and intragenerational justice. The term 'governance' in general describes 'the different modes of coordinating individual actions, or basic forms of social order' (Mayntz 1998, p. 7). Hierarchies, markets and networks are forms of governance, each based on a different mechanism: authority, price and negotiation.

Note that we use the term 'governance' not as opposite to the hierarchical steering mode of 'government', as some authors do (Peters and Pierre 1998; Rhodes 1996; Rosenau 1992), but as an umbrella concept for both hierarchical and non-hierarchical modes of steering or social order. Governance is exercised not only by state actors but by all kinds of social actors once they coordinate their actions – be it to form a sports club or to devise green standards for business suppliers.

When looking at CSR from the public policy perspective on sustainability governance, we basically classify CSR as a 'policy instrument'. Policy instruments can be understood as 'techniques of governance that, one way or another, involve the utilization of state authority or its conscious limitation' (Howlett 2005, p. 31). This perspective on CSR makes the role and capacity of the state with regard to sustainability governance the focus of attention. These issues have been an object of recent social scientific research on the transformation of the state, and we shall briefly highlight relevant findings.

In the past decades social and environmental governance used to be shouldered primarily by state authorities. Major means were statutory regulation, public ownership and the distribution of funds (Majone 1996). Since then, however, the role of private actors in sustainability governance, both of businesses and not-for-profit organizations, has increased in many OECD countries beyond their traditional influence on policy making (Cutler et al. 1999): companies increasingly provide goods and services so far supplied by the public sector (for example, in utilities, transport, social services) and co-fund public infrastructures and projects. Civil society organizations develop social and ecological standards, such as SA 8000, or the FSC certification and use advocacy networks and markets to enforce their implementation.

The increasing prominence of private actors in (sustainability) governance has been related to economic globalization and the diminishing power of national governments as well as to political self-retrenchment and the liberalization and deregulation paradigm (Graz and Nölke 2007; Kennett 2008). A longer-term cause is the functional differentiation of societies (Schimank 2005).[2] In functionally differentiated societies, the capacities to influence societal change – through knowledge, resources, compliance and so on – are distributed among many different actors: producers and consumers, scientists, interest groups and the media, to name a few.[3] Successful governance needs to involve these actors. This holds all the more in the case of sustainability problems as they have spread during the twentieth century. Evolving from conflicts of long-term social, economic and ecological developments, such problems are characterized by complexity and uncertainty, by the interlinkage of different dilemmas and scales, and often by unexpected consequences of attempts to resolve the very problem (Voß and Kemp 2006).

In parallel to the increasing role of private actors in sustainability governance, the portfolio of public governance has transformed. Although command and control approaches still dominate social and environmental policies, non-hierarchical forms of regulation have spread (Ritter 1979; Voigt 1995; Wolff 2004).[4] This change followed the perception in the early 1990s that traditional command and control approaches were less effective, efficient and innovation stimulating than 'new' (non-hierarchical) policy instruments, such as voluntary agreements, economic and informational instruments. Since the late 1990s and early 2000s, however, it has been recognized that these have limitations as well, such as high transaction costs for monitoring voluntary agreements, legitimacy deficits and (again) limited effectiveness (Jordan et al. 2003b; Golub 1998; Scharpf 1997). More recently, a consensus emerges under the label of 'smart regulation' that policy mixes are advisable which combine command and control regulation, market-based, informational instruments and voluntary approaches, and include 'soft' and 'tougher' measures. These policy mixes need to be adapted to concrete policy fields, problem and actor constellations and should procedurally contain the effective engagement with business and other stakeholders (Gunningham et al. 1998; EPA Network 2005; Jänicke 2007; Zadek 2005).

In the following we develop a matrix on the different functions that CSR can display within systems of public governance.

15.3.1   Three Functions of CSR in Public Sustainability Governance

We argue that CSR can assume three functions in systems of public governance. These functions link up with the three ideal types of public governance, which again relate to the basic governance mechanisms mentioned above: command and control regulation draws on the mechanism of authority; it is exercized, among others, through labour standards, product bans or emission limits. Incentive-based regulation works on the basis of price differentials; specific instruments include taxes, subsidies, tradable permits, environmental liability regimes and the awarding of public contracts subject to social clauses. Finally, procedural regulation and frameworks for societal self-regulation ('regulated self-regulation') is based on a mixture of negotiation, communication, information and other mechanisms, depending on the concrete instrument. Examples are policy networks, participatory approaches such as political mediations or Local Agenda 21 processes, reallocation of property rights, the requirement for companies to install HSE officers, disclosure obligations and consumer

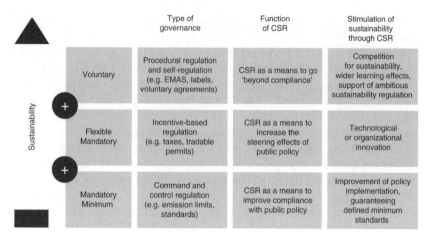

Source: Authors.

Figure 15.1   Functions of CSR in systems of public governance

information rights, product labels, frameworks for environmental management (for example, EMAS) or other CSR activities, voluntary agreements, and the provision of social services, information and advice. Note that the above are ideal types: in reality, command and control governance, for example, is not exclusively based on authority, but includes negotiation and communication as well.

Each type of public governance is based on policy interventions which impose different degrees of constraint on target groups. Command and control regulation is most choice constraining. This is because policy targets, measures and procedures are being defined by law. Incentive-based governance is moderately choice constraining: targets and procedures are being defined by law, but addressees such as companies have options for the measures they take and the degree to which they fulfil the given targets. Frameworks for societal self-regulation pose the least constraints on addressees: targets and measures, and in many cases procedures, are being defined by societal actors themselves.

What does this mean for CSR? We claim that CSR efforts can contribute to different types of public sustainability governance and that they can hence stimulate sustainability in different ways (Figure 15.1). In the context of command and control governance, CSR activities can be a means for companies to enhance and ensure their compliance with laws and regulations. Note that such CSR activities do not produce a sustainability value added in relation to a baseline scenario where companies regularly fulfil their legal obligations. However, they do lead to an improvement of business-as-usual in policy fields where – both intentional and unintended – non-compliance is widespread. Cases in point are the policy fields of countering corruption and fisheries' management. Non-compliance may result, among others, from lacking enforcement structures and it creates an uneven playing field between compliant and non-compliant enterprises.

Incentive-based governance approaches are characterized by giving norm addressees options with regard to their behaviour. For example, an eco-tax with the objective to reduce greenhouse gas emission allows companies (a) to continue emitting greenhouse gases as usual and pay the taxes due (financial effect) or (b) to decrease their tax liability by substituting energy inefficient technology with a more efficient one (environmental steering effect). CSR in such a case means to contribute to the intended social or environmental steering effect of a sustainability policy rather than to its financial effect. Typically, this happens through technological or organizational innovation.

The third governance type of procedural regulation and 'regulated self-regulation' by societal stakeholders is the one typically associated with CSR. Here, the role of CSR is clearly that companies go beyond what is legally required, and respectively become active in fields that are hitherto unregulated. They can do so by defining both targets and measures of their action; as regards procedures, they can and in some cases have to make use of procedures specified by the state. The first is the case, for example, with EMAS, the latter with legal requirements for HSE officers. At a meta-level, businesses can stand up for ambitious framework conditions of sustainability governance (Belz and Pobisch 2004). Companies that accept responsibility would ideally not act as brakemen in social and environmental policy processes nor oppose far-reaching policies through lobbying, threatening, suing or other forms of influence (Töller 2008).

Beyond-compliance CSR may contribute to sustainability in at least three ways. Firstly, the integration of social and environmental concerns into business operations can lead to learning effects within companies. This includes changes of their perception of sustainability problems and acceptance of new norms on how to react to such problems. Secondly, 'beyond-compliance' CSR can change the nature of business competition: a company's competitive edge is not determined solely by its cost leadership or differentiation strategies (Porter 1980) or, indirectly, by its efforts to influence the regulatory environment. Rather, the very sustainability of a company's products, production and organization becomes the source of competitive advantage. This occurs when the costs of social or environmental commitment are offset by process or product innovations that boost energy or resource efficiency; by creation of a unique selling proposition; by improved risk and reputation management; by increased employee satisfaction and labour productivity; or, in the context of countering corruption, by avoiding the costs of sanctions resulting from convictions for violations.[5] Finally, by supporting governments in developing ambitious sustainability regulation, forerunner companies contribute to a collective rise in standards.

We would like to highlight three implications of the above elaboration. Firstly, CSR is not only a beyond-compliance strategy. CSR also has a place in regulated fields, either as a means to ensure compliance with public policy or to enhance its social and environmental steering effects. CSR can have a sustainability impact even when the respective company activities do not go beyond compliance, if only to the extent that the activities actually make a difference to business-as-usual behaviour. Sustainability impact of CSR, however, is not automatic: whether or not a CSR measure makes a difference is subject to empirical study. Secondly, in order to improve sustainability, it is likely that neither a strategy of command and control, of incentives nor regulated self-regulation will suffice on their own. Rather, these approaches are complementary and can be combined in accordance with the 'smart regulation' concept. CSR can play a role in systems of governance both as an independent self-regulation approach and as a means to contribute to the effectiveness of hierarchical and incentive-based governance. Thirdly, however, we do not argue that voluntary business contributions could or should fully substitute for more hierarchical forms of regulation. From a public policy perspective, the linchpin is whether sustainability goals can be achieved effectively through CSR – possibly more effectively than through other approaches. Though in this book we do not make a direct comparison of the effectiveness of CSR and other sustainability instruments, the next section will look how different industries' CSR activities tackle a number of specific policy goals.

15.4   PUTTING CSR TO THE TEST: DOES IT CONTRIBUTE TO ACHIEVING EU SUSTAINABILITY GOALS?

Can CSR contribute to achieving public goals for sustainable development? We acknowledge that companies do not necessarily aim to use CSR activities to fulfil goals set by governments – even if some authors recognize that it can be 'economically rational' for companies to contribute to societal goals (Hahn 2004). At the same time, public sustainability policies do not necessarily directly address companies. We are nevertheless interested in learning to what extent companies' voluntary activities may help in achieving such goals set by the EU. This reflects our view that CSR beyond being a mode of corporate self-regulation is also a means of public sustainability governance.

The following section portrays the most relevant sustainability goals in the fields of EU climate mitigation, sustainable fishery, gender equality and anti-bribery policy. We shall analyze whether and how CSR activities contribute to achieving the sustainability goals defined in these policies. While most of the goals are not immediately directed at companies, some of them are transferable *to* them. That is, businesses can voluntarily contribute to them. Which policy goals are at all addressed by the issue-specific CSR activities? Can we determine the extent to which CSR contributes to the respective sustainability goals, if not in a quantitative then at least in a qualitative way? Are there significant differences between sectors and policy fields as regards these questions? Our assessment makes use of the empirical findings collected in 2006–07 in the European oil, fish processing and banking sectors through the surveys presented in Chapters 5 to 8 and the case studies of Chapters 10 to 13. As these samples are small and include CSR leaders only, the resulting picture is qualitative.

15.4.1 CSR by Oil companies Contributing to EU Goals on Climate Change Mitigation

Climate change mitigation and adaptation has become one of the greatest sustainability challenges ahead of us. EU climate change mitigation policy started in the 1990s and has since developed into a system of both regulatory measures and policy aims. Much of the mitigation policy is directed towards Member States. The following discusses corporate voluntary contributions in eight European oil companies in relation to these goals.

The EU has committed itself to reduce greenhouse gas emissions at the union level by 8 per cent in the period 2008–12, with base year 1992.[6] The European Strategy for Sustainable Development and the Action Plan for the European Climate Change Programme[7] describes measures to achieve greenhouse gas emission reduction targets that go beyond the emissions trading central to the Kyoto Protocol, including the following areas:

- changing energy source (alternative fuels, clean and renewable energy sources, biofuels)
- limiting energy use (demand management, energy efficiency)
- infrastructure use

- limiting other greenhouse gases than carbon dioxide
- and, now being discussed, safe carbon capture and storage.

Examples of corporate voluntary activities in the oil sector that can contribute to fulfilling these objectives include working with energy efficiency, limiting greenhouse gas emissions, developing new renewable sources of energy, and research or pilot initiatives in carbon capture and storage.

In our survey (Chapter 5) we found that all companies were active in the areas of reducing greenhouse gas emissions, development of renewables, and carbon capture and storage – albeit with varying numbers of activities pursued in these areas of work. For instance, six companies work with energy efficiency improvements, but only one company works to switch from fossil fuels to renewable energy sources in operations. Table 15.1 shows the number of sample companies that pursued respective activities. Looking at the companies together, we found, for instance, that eight companies fund research on carbon capture and storage, and that six companies develop bioenergy and wind power.

But although the oil sector companies studied seem to be contributing to the public policy goals related to climate change mitigation, it is not possible from our method to say how great this contribution is, or whether it is progressing rapidly enough to meet the serious climate change challenge. These are two important questions that require further study.

Impacts from a set of selected CSR instruments as examined in the Boasson and Wettestad case study in Chapter 5 were only found to be significant exceptionally. This finding seems consistent with the loose connections between the Global Compact, the Global Reporting Initiative guidelines (and ISO 14000) and corporate activities to mitigate climate change. In our survey oil companies were asked which instrument was most conducive to affect performance – only five companies answered this question, but among these, all answered company-specific instruments for this policy field. There is possibly more to be learnt about climate change mitigation related CSR in the oil sector by studying these company-specific instruments and their relation to climate change mitigation activities.

15.4.2 CSR by Fish Processors Contributing to EU Goals on Sustainable Fisheries

Globally as well as within the EU, wild-capture fisheries are in a sore state: 70–80 per cent of the world's fish stocks are fully exploited, over-exploited, depleted or in a state of fragile recovery (FAO 2007). The EU has formulated goals to tackle this problem, both in fisheries' policy and

Table 15.1   The contribution of CSR to achieving EU policy goals for mitigating climate change

EU policy goal	Do oil companies' CSR activities support EU policy goals?	
	Yes/No	Activities
Reduction of greenhouse gases	Yes	• Offshore activities in North Sea: work with energy efficiency improvements (6 companies); work to reduce flaring (6 companies); work to reduce CH_4 emissions from operations (5 companies); work to switch from use of oil to use of gas in operations (4 companies); work to switch from fossil fuels to renewable energy sources in operations (1 company) • Refining and processing in Europe: apply co-generation technology (4 companies); work with energy efficiency improvements (6 companies); work to reduce flaring (6 companies); work to reduce CH_4 emissions from operations (6 companies); work to switch from use of oil to use of gas in operations (4 companies); work to switch from fossil fuels to renewable energy sources in operations (1 company)
Development of renewables	Yes	• Bioenergy (6 companies) • Wind power (6 companies) • Photovoltaic (4 companies)
Carbon capture and storage	Yes	• Funding research on carbon capture and storage (8 companies) • Pilot projects (6 companies) • Plans for construction of projects of full-scale carbon removal and storage before 2010 (4 companies)

Source: Authors, drawing on Boasson et al. (Chapter 5) (survey sample: n = 8).

in 'neighbouring' fields like biodiversity conservation. Excepting more general objectives such as to '[s]afeguard the earth's capacity to support life in all its diversity' (see the 2006 EU Sustainable Development Strategy) and to halt biodiversity decline by 2010 (6th Environmental Action Programme, EAP), the relevant goals can be clustered as follows:

- To conserve and sustainably use fish stocks and feeding grounds, both within the EU and outside.[8]
- To reduce the impact of fishing on non-target species and the marine ecosystem, including to achieve healthy marine populations, good environmental status and good surface water status.[9]
- To stop illegal, unregulated and unreported fishing.[10]

Table 15.2   The contribution of CSR to achieving EU policy goals for sustainable fisheries

EU policy goal	Do fish processors' CSR activities support EU policy goals?	
	Yes/No	Activities
Conservation and sustainable use of fish stocks and feeding grounds	Yes, business case-driven	• Withdrawal from critically threatened stocks (5 of 8 companies) • Sourcing of MSC fish (5 companies) • Supplier requirements (number of companies varies according to concrete requirement)
Reduction of impact on non-target species and the marine ecosystem	Partly, standard-driven	• Sourcing of MSC fish (5 companies) • Supplier requirements (number of companies varies according to requirement)
Eradicate illegal, unregulated and unreported fishing	Yes, but success not measurable so far	• Supplier requirements, for example based on AIPCE Guidelines (number of companies unknown)

Source: Authors, drawing on Schmitt and Wolff (Chapter 6) as well as on Wolff and Schmitt (Chapter 11) (survey sample: n = 8).

Do the CSR activities of European fish processors tackle the above goals and hence contribute to their achievement? In Table 15.2 we summarize empirical findings gained through a survey of eight CSR leader companies (Chapter 6) and case studies of three of these (Chapter 11).

Conservation and sustainable use of (target) fish stocks is the highest priority for fish processors committed to sustainable fishing. The companies we analyzed use three types of mechanism to address this goal. Firstly, they reduce or refrain from seafood purchases from overfished stocks, such as North Sea or Baltic cod, North Atlantic salmon, dogfish or sturgeon caviar. Secondly, and most importantly, they source fish from sustainable stocks. Presently, the method to determine the sustainability of fish stocks that can be best verified is a certification – both of a fishery and of participating companies – through the non-profit organization Marine Stewardship Council (MSC). The MSC provides an international product label to reward environmentally responsible fishery management and practices. One of its core principles is that healthy populations of targeted fish species are to be maintained or re-established in a fishery – which corresponds to the EU policy goal described above. In April 2007, about 6 per cent of the world's total edible wild-capture fisheries were either certified or underwent certification (over 3.5 million tonnes of seafood), and 608 MSC labelled products were being marketed worldwide (MSC 2007), a majority by European producers. Five out of eight fish processors included in our survey use the MSC label. The best scoring company sourced 90 per cent of its wild-caught seafood from MSC fisheries in 2005, but lower shares are much more common. Two of our sample companies had developed additional, company-specific methods to determine the sustainability of fisheries. These also build on the goal to sustain target stocks. Thirdly, imposing specific standards on fish suppliers is a further means to contribute to the sustainability of target stocks. However, in our survey only three of eight respondents ask fishermen e.g. to prevent high-grading of catch, one calls for technical conservation measures, while five require suppliers to reduce fish waste. Evaluating how effectively such requirements contribute to the EU's policy goal is compounded by the fact that processors only rarely have their suppliers' compliance verified through audits.

The policy goal to reduce impacts on non-target species and on the marine ecosystem is also addressed by CSR activities. Firstly, this goal is institutionalized in MSC certifications. One of the main company measures to tackle the integrity of ecosystems is hence to source fish from MSC stocks. In addition, an – albeit low – number of processors selectively addresses the issue in supplier standards. They require fishermen to minimize by-catch (three of our eight survey respondents); to prevent the mortality caused by loss of fishing nets (two); and to minimize impact on the seabed (one). Three processors reduce coastal pollution of on-land processing activities and two require their suppliers to lessen on-board pollution. Even though supplier requirements have the potential to contribute to reducing ecosystem impacts, the more comprehensive, reliable and verifiable contribution is presently achieved through sourcing of MSC fish.

The EU goal of eradicating illegal, unregulated and unreported fishing has risen on the CSR agenda only recently. A major step was the creation of Barents Sea cod and haddock and Baltic Sea cod buying guidelines by the EU Fish Processors Association (AIPCE 2006, 2007). Being an industry-wide initiative, the AIPCE supplier guidelines may reach a significant scale in future. However, some member organizations were reluctant in developing the guidelines and may in future be unwilling to support them. Due to their recent development, we are unable to assess the guidelines' acceptance and impact so far. Looking at company-specific action, only one of the sample companies requires and audits its suppliers to demonstrate that they operate legally, and itself maintains an 'open book' policy with regard to records of its seafood sources.

Summing up, while we cannot at this time evaluate to what extent CSR committed European fish processors contribute to eradicating illegal fishing, our analysis shows that their voluntary activities tackle the other EU goals of conserving target fish stocks and reducing ecosystem impacts. The contribution is somewhat more robust with regard to conserving target stocks than reducing ecosystem impact. This is unsurprising as securing the industry's supply base (target stocks) is a business case. Contributions to ecosystem conservation in the form of supplier requirements are patchy, and are standard driven when part and parcel of the MSC certification.

15.4.3   CSR by Banks Contributing to EU Goals on Gender Equality

Gender equality has been an issue in European politics since the Treaty of Rome (1957). However, after 50 years of political efforts to realize gender equality in the business and employment realm the annual report on equality between women and men still shows that a gender bias persists (European Commission 2008). The pay gap between women and men, to mention a prominent example, presently amounts to some 15 per cent (ibid, p. 8). In this section we shall present the policy goals that the EU has set with regard to gender equality and shall discuss the extent to which the CSR activities of banks contribute to their achievement.

The Commission's current Roadmap for equality between women and men 2006–10 defines gender equality as 'a fundamental right, a common value in the EU, and a necessary condition for the achievement of the EU objectives of growth, employment and social cohesion'. This strong normative approach is governed by a comprehensive body of EU directives and confirmed by the Renewed EU Sustainable Development Strategy of 2006. The latter understands sustainable development to be based among others on the principles of anti-discrimination and equal opportunities and defines social equity and cohesion as key objectives.

The above mentioned Roadmap, in addition to the Commission's general gender mainstreaming strategy,[11] outlines priority areas of EU action. Though it does not define quantitative goals, it refers to overall EU policy goals and to objectives defined and quantified in the Employment Guidelines of the European Employment Strategy (EES) from 2004. Against this background, we identify five clusters of EU policy goals with relevance for the banking sector:

- Equal opportunities: economic independence for women and men (see Roadmap); an EU-wide female employment rate of 60 per cent by 2010 (see EES and Renewed Lisbon Strategy).
- Equal pay: reducing the gender pay gap by 2010 (Lisbon Strategy, EES, Commission Communication on tackling the pay gap between women and men).
- Work-life balance: improving the conditions for reconciling work and family according to the 'Barcelona targets'. These refer to the provision of childcare facilities for 90 per cent of all children from age three to kindergarten and for 33 per cent of all children under the age of three (see EES, European Pact for Gender Equality 2006).
- Anti-discrimination as regards sexual harassment: elimination of gender-based violence (see Roadmap).
- Equal access to and supply of financial services: this objective can be derived indirectly from the overall EU goal 'social inclusion' (Sustainable Development Strategy) because of its high relevance for the banking sector.

The empirical findings presented in Chapters 7 and 12 demonstrate that banks' CSR activities for gender equality contribute to varying degrees to all five gender-related policy goals mentioned above. Above all, they refer to a better work-life balance and to equal opportunities (see Table 15.3).

To promote equal opportunities, the 17 banks we surveyed use a range of measures, including training activities and promotion of female careers. Almost half of them participate in gender equality or diversity awards. Regarding the effects, the majority of banks that had assessed their own improvement on equal opportunities estimated this to be medium. Furthermore, both our case studies demonstrated that the share of women in management positions rose in relation to the share of women in the total workforce within three years.

To promote equal pay, most surveyed banks make use of performance indicators and tools for monitoring pay data as well as for gender reporting.[12] In contrast, less than half of the banks take specific action to close the gender pay gap.

To improve the work-life balance, all sampled banks have introduced flexible work time arrangements. In addition, 14 of the banks support care responsibilities of their employees beyond minimum statutory requirements, thus contributing to reaching the EU's Barcelona targets for childcare. Our case studies also demonstrate substantial societal impact with regard to this goal. However, less than half of the surveyed banks take specific action to promote parental leave of fathers.

To prevent sexual harassment, more than half of the sampled banks have

*Table 15.3   The contribution of CSR to achieving EU policy goals for
gender equality*

EU policy goal	Do banks' CSR activities support EU policy goals?	
	Yes/No	Activities
Equal opportunities (EO)	Yes	• Company-specific management tools and principles for EO: staff selection, career promotion, gender training, mentoring and so on • Participation in national gender equality or diversity awards • Sensitization measures
Gender pay gap	Partly Lack of response on this question and lack of data (disclosure obligations differ in Europe)	• Internal gender audits • External reporting, mostly based on GRI indicators • Specific action to close the gender pay gap
Work-life balance	Yes, but lack of success with regard to part-time work of fathers	• Flexible working time arrangements • Agreements on parental leave beyond legal requirements • Provision of childcare facilities • E-learning, facilities for home work, and so on
Prevention of sexual harassment	Yes, but success difficult to measure	• Preventive measures against sexual harassment and bullying
Equal access to and supply of financial services	Partly	• Customer training • Financial products: basic banking service for everybody; microcredits

Source: Authors, drawing on Viganò and Nicolai (Chapter 7) (survey sample: n = 17) as
well as Schultz (Chapter 12).

established confidential information channels, take preventive measures
and inform their staff. The success of these measures, though, is difficult
to measure.

To promote equal access to and supply of financial services, a majority of the banks in the survey train their staff on equal treatment. Half of
them offer specific financial products like micro-credits and a basic banking
service for everybody.

In the upshot, the banks we studied indeed addressed EU policy goals for gender equality. However, in our sample this contribution was insufficient with regard to closing the banks' gender pay gap and encouraging part-time work of fathers, as part of improving the work-life balance. Also, the issue of microcredits needs more attention. Contributions to the other goals were more promising.

15.4.4 CSR by Banks Contributing to EU Goals for Countering Bribery and Anti-money Laundering

Corruption, which includes bribery and money laundering, underlies many major social issues. Its ravages include undermining democracy, abusing the rule of law, infringing human rights, damaging the environment, keeping societies in poverty, distorting businesses and markets and funding crime and terrorism. The EU recognizes the scale and risks of the issues but has not yet given attention to the role that CSR can play. Nevertheless, as we shall show on the basis of empirical work presented in detail earlier in this book, CSR can assist in countering these issues, furthering compliance with laws and ultimately contributing to EU goals as far as they are expressed.

The Member States of the European Union have identified the fight against financial crime as a top priority[13] and the EU has introduced disparate instruments and communications covering countering corruption. The EU's policy goals for countering bribery are imprecise and rely largely on other international organizations' conventions to shape Member States' national laws. The EU also uses indirect regulation, such as procurement directives, criteria for the accession of new Member States, trade policy and cooperation agreements, criteria for export credit agencies, debarment, judicial and police cooperation. The EU has issued instruments directed at Member States that include implicit goals for the private sector. A Commission Communication on an EU policy against corruption[14] states that Member States should support the efforts of the private sector to raise integrity and corporate responsibility. A Council Framework Decision[15] requires Member States to enact laws to criminalize private-to-private corruption. In contrast to its anti-bribery efforts, the EU is highly influential for anti-money laundering (AML) with directives binding Member States to enact laws setting goals for the role of financial institutions and companies.

The EU has not identified or acted on the potential role of CSR for countering corruption. Countering corruption is not mentioned in the Commission Green Paper on CSR (European Commission 2001), the CSR Strategy (European Commission 2006b), the EU Sustainable Development Strategy or the European Commission Report on Millennium Development Goals 2000–04.

*Table 15.4　The contribution of CSR to achieving EU policy goals for
　　　　　　countering bribery and money laundering*

EU policy goal	Do banks' CSR activities support EU policy goals?	
	Yes/No	Activities
Fighting financial crime	Yes	● Commitment
Raising integrity and	Yes	● Anti-corruption policies
corporate responsibility*		● Management systems including
Countering bribery*	Yes	communication, training
Anti-money laundering	Yes	● AML: IT tools and reporting
		of suspicious transactions
		● Working with and sharing of
		expertise with other banks

Note: *The goals are expressed for Member States but implicitly are an expectation for the private sector.

Source: Authors, drawing on Viganò and Nicolai (Chapter 7) as well as Wilkinson (Chapter 13) (survey sample: n = 17).

However, the survey presented in Chapter 7 and the case studies of Chapter 13 indicate that CSR by banks can play a strong role in achieving compliance with laws for these issues. This happens mainly through going beyond compliance in communications, training and use of AML information technology tools (Table 15.4). In the survey 9 of the 17 responding banks attributed high relevance to countering bribery and 12 had integrated anti-bribery management systems. The principle activities carried out by the banks including those that did not have management systems covered risk assessment, guidelines for employees, advice and whistle-blowing channels, restricting and controlling facilitation payments and gifts, internal controls and sanctions for violations. Only two banks reported publicly on their anti-bribery policies and procedures. For AML, 14 banks had management systems and all 17 banks trained employees. The other principal activities carried out by nearly every bank are required by law including verifying identities of customers and reporting of suspicious activities.

As the banks see the issues as primarily compliance and risk and reputation management it is difficult to separate out any CSR effects. Standardized voluntary codes were not influential with only two banks using an anti-bribery code and seven banks using the Wolfsberg AML Principles. There was evidence of cooperation and shared working with six banks taking part in multi-stakeholder anti-bribery initiatives and 15 banks working on AML with other banks and government agencies.

Summing up, the activities of the two case study banks and the comparable anti-bribery and AML activities reported by the survey indicate that CSR takes place in AML and may take place for countering bribery. Thus, although bribery and money laundering are governed highly by regulation, these activities appear to further the compliance of the banks and hence contribute to supporting the respective implicit EU policy goals.

15.5   CONCLUSIONS

In this chapter we elaborated a bidirectional relation between public policy and CSR. On the one hand, triggered by different motivations, public policy stimulates and procedurally regulates CSR. On the other hand, CSR can contribute to public sustainability governance through three functions: in relation to command and control regulation it can improve compliance; in relation to incentive-based regulation it can enhance social and environmental steering effects; finally, as a societal self-regulation approach it can induce companies to genuinely go beyond legal requirements. Through each of these functions, CSR can help in increasing sustainability, although this is not automatic.

Empirically, as examined in the previous chapters, we found that enterprises in the European oil, fish processing and banking sectors to a large extent carry out activities that address EU public policy goals on climate change mitigation, sustainable fisheries, gender equality, countering bribery and money laundering. Three points in particular are worth noting. Firstly, considering that public policy goals are not generally perceived in research as major determinants for the design of industry's CSR policies, this fit between private activities and public goals is rather remarkable. Possibly, it is because both public and corporate sustainability goals are responses to the public's perception of and concerns about sustainability problems. Then again, it could well be that corporations lobby the state to have a certain policy that is acceptable to them. Secondly, although we found that the policy goals identified are quite uniformly tackled by corporate action, with no significant variation in terms of sectors or policy fields, the scope and depth by which CSR activities contribute to fulfilling the policy goals differ. Even within our samples of CSR leaders, only a limited number of companies carry out specific sustainability measures (scope). For example, only one of the surveyed oil companies has switched from fossil fuels to renewable energy sources in its operations. Yet, in those companies that carry out the respective measures these may not be fully effective (depth). A case in point is the (hidden) gender pay gap that persists in many companies despite their efforts to close it. Thirdly, our data did not allow us to estimate the extent to which CSR contributes to fulfilling the sustainability goals. This would, for a start, require a much more representative sample of companies both committed and non-committed to CSR (scope), and a better estimate of goal attainment at company level (depth). Here lies a challenge for future research.

NOTES

1. In this the regulations differ from what Matten and Moon (2005) describe as 'implicit CSR', namely the substantive codification of the business sector's social and environmental responsibilities.
2. 'Functional differentiation' is a characteristic of modern societies: social sub-systems, such as politics, science, economy and religion, have evolved which operate fairly independently from each other, while at the same time depending on each other.
3. This is the reason why governments even in societies where the state has a monopoly on the legitimate use of force (Weber 1980) can rarely 'bypass' societal and economic interests for the longer term.
4. Töller (2007) warns not to overestimate these tendencies and announces the 'comeback of the authoritative state'.
5. See the ample literature on the relationship between CSR performance and business competitiveness (cf. Chapter 3.2)
6. Council Decision 2002/358/EC of 25 April 2002 concerning the approval, on behalf of the European Community, of the Kyoto Protocol to the United Nations Framework Convention on Climate Change and the joint fulfilment of commitments thereunder.
7. Communication from the Commission on the implementation of the first phase of the ECCP, COM(2001)580, 23/10/2001.
8. See Art. 2.1, Common Fisheries Policy (CFP) Framework Regulation No. 2371/2002/EC; European Code of Sustainable and Responsible Fisheries Practices; Commission Action Plan to integrate environmental protection into the CFP; EU Council Conclusions on the Community External Fisheries Policy of July 2004; para. 15, Biodiversity Action Plan (BAP) for Fisheries.
9. See Art. 2.1 CFP Framework Regulation; para. 15, BAP Fisheries; Art. 2 and 6.1, 6th EAP; Art. 2, Marine Strategy Directive; Art. 1 and 4(a)(ii), Water Framework Directive.
10. See Community Action Plan for the eradication of illegal, unreported and unregulated fishing, COM (2002) 180, 28/05/2002.
11. Communication from the Commission on Incorporating Equal Opportunities for Women and Men into All Community Policies and Activities, COM (96) 67, 21/02/1996.
12. This needs to be interpreted against the backdrop of various regulations on the disclosure of pay data in EU Member States and the new generation of GRI 3 indicators which demands consequent pay data disclosure.
13. Action Plan of the Council and the Commission on how best to implement the provisions of the Treaty of Amsterdam on an area of freedom, security and justice, OJ C 019, 23/01/1999.
14. Commission Communication on a Coherent and Comprehensive EU policy against Corruption, COM (2003) 317, 28/05/2003.
15. Council Framework Decision 2003/568/JHA of 22 July 2003 on combating corruption in the private sector.

16 Striking oil? CSR and the EU integration processes: the example of Hungary

Tamás Pálvölgyi, Noémi Csigéné Nagypál, János Szlávik, Hajnalka Csáfor and Mária Csete

16.1 INTRODUCTION

The integration of the European Union (EU) is a complex and ongoing socio-economic and political process which has the aim of 'creating an ever closer union among the peoples of Europe' (Art. 1, Treaty of the European Union). This process has been challenged by successive rounds of enlargement, that is, of the accession, tied to specific conditions,[1] of new countries to the EU. The fifth round of enlargement in 2004 was special in the sense that it concerned formerly socialist countries, which meant that their integration into the Community went quasi hand in hand with their transformation to market economies. Along with the adoption of the EU's body of common rights and obligations (*acquis communautaire*), the accession countries were called upon to introduce policies on Corporate Social Responsibility (CSR) – a concept rather unfamiliar to businesses as well as stakeholders in the transformation economies.

In this chapter we shall discuss how EU integration affects and interacts with the practice of CSR in the new EU Member States using the example of Hungary. More concretely, we shall address three research questions: what are the effects of EU accession and integration on the (social, political and economic) framework conditions in which CSR is practised? How does EU integration impact on the concrete CSR practices of companies, and what, in turn, are the effects of companies' CSR activities on EU integration?

Section 2 tackles the first research question. We shall describe the socio-economic framework conditions for CSR in the EU's Central and Eastern European (CEE) Member States, and discuss how the integration into the EU influenced these framework conditions. Our assumption is that accession to and integration into the EU do significantly influence the framework conditions for CSR. This may work through market integration effects, on the one hand, and through political-institutional processes such as policy diffusion, on the other hand. Methodologically, we shall use a 'PESTEL analysis',[2] that is, we briefly discuss political, economic, social, technological, environmental and legal aspects with relevance to CSR. The analysis draws on existing literature and the results of a stakeholder roundtable organized for this purpose.

Section 3 addresses the other two research questions. With regard to the impact of EU integration on the concrete CSR practices of companies we expect that the direct impact of EU integration on the adoption of CSR through companies is substantial too. We assume that businesses have a dual motivation for adopting CSR: the potential benefits on EU and international markets – to succeed on the EU internal market, CSR standards may seem a model to copy, employed by numerous EU competitors – as well as political pressures and incentives to adopt CSR practices. Both factors may be equally important and are likely to gather strength upon EU integration. When it comes to the question of the opposite effect, namely the impact of companies' CSR activities on EU integration, we expect that indirect effects will outweigh direct effects on the economic integration process. Indirect effects can emerge when companies contribute to the societal diffusion of CSR knowledge and norms, and influence policy making. We shall discuss these questions and assumptions on the basis of two empirical interview-based[3] company case studies which were carried out in 2006–07. They assess and compare the CSR practices of two multinational oil companies – MOL Group and Shell Hungary – which have a different background in the context of EU enlargement.

16.2 THE IMPACT OF EU INTEGRATION ON FRAMEWORK CONDITIONS FOR CSR IN NEW EU MEMBER STATES – THE EXAMPLE OF HUNGARY

What are the – social, political and economic – framework conditions for CSR in new EU Member States, and how did integration into the EU influence these framework conditions? In this section we shall use a PESTEL analysis – that is, a scrutiny of political, economic, social, technological, environmental and legal aspects – to answer this question. The PESTEL framework is a common method for analysing the macroenvironment factors under which companies operate. With regard to the individual factors, we shall draw on insights from literature as well as the results of a stakeholder roundtable carried out by the authors in Budapest in early 2007.[4]

16.2.1 Political Framework Conditions

With regard to political framework conditions, we shall focus on three aspects: the historic role of the state and state-owned companies in the CEE countries; the democratic system and public institutions; and the policy-making capacities that have been established in Hungary to promote CSR.

Firstly, all formerly socialist countries represent a special challenge for CSR in the sense that the fulfilment of social goals was regarded for decades as the sole responsibility of the state. In addition, there was a long period in the centrally planned economies in which most companies were owned by the state and hence under strong political influence. They had no individual capacity for economic decision making and their economic responsibilities were limited. With EU integration and the transition to a market economy, previously state-owned companies had to culturally come to grips with the concept of economic responsibility before even considering social and environmental responsibilities beyond compliance.[5] On the other hand, large formerly state-owned companies were the 'manifestation' of the communist state regarding the social benefits provided for employees, such as cheap company restaurants, holidays and so on. Despite the transformation, there is still a certain hidden expectation towards the state as well as companies to provide these benefits (Kerekes and Wetzker 2007). European integration might contribute to reducing belief in the omnipotence of the state.

Secondly, while both the public and the business sector expected the political decision makers to solve ethical problems of the business sector at the beginning of the 1990s (DEMOS 2006), there is currently a low level of trust in politics, politicians and the public sector as a whole. In Hungary anti-corruption programmes have not yet achieved their objectives and the risk of corruption in the public sector is still high (OECD 2005; Freedom House 2006). Partly as a consequence of this situation, policy making and implementation are considered not to be very effective; for example, the level of tax evasion is high. This could be a barrier to a successful CSR policy. The EU accession, however, can be advantageous from this perspective: the public trust in the EU level policy making is generally higher than in the national one.[6]

Finally, let us look at the policy context in which national CSR policy is made. Candidate countries realized that CSR is an important issue in the

EU in the early 2000s. There have been some promising efforts in policy making in Hungary. Sustainable consumption is part of the National Development Plan and its Environmental Operative Programme. The National Environmental Protection Programme for the period of 2003–08 aims, among others, to make 'sustainable lifestyles' more popular. In 2006 a CSR director was appointed within the Ministry of Economy and Transport (MET).[7] This was a significant step as the MET is one of the largest, most influential ministries in Hungary. The main tasks of the directorate include: helping Roma entrepreneurs to a better economic integration; improving taxation morale both at individual and company level; improving the environmental performance of companies; countering workplace discrimination and other issues. One of the potential measures to ensure the achievement of these goals is to enable better cooperation between the government and multinational companies that are experienced in CSR. The directorate is also committed to ensuring that public procurement recognizes the CSR performance of companies (Piac and Profit 2006). The establishment of this directorate has created the capacity for popularizing CSR in the Hungarian business sector.

16.2.2 Economic Framework Conditions

The relevant economic framework conditions for CSR which are addressed include companies' inexperience in terms of market economy practices; the attitudes of citizens towards private business; and consumer demand for sustainable products.

After the dissolution of the Soviet Union, the political systems in Eastern Europe collapsed and market economies were established in most countries in the region. There was a keen demand to reach the welfare level of Western countries by ensuring similar consumption levels. However, the former communist countries had little experience in the practices of a market economy and in company management. Many firms, especially small and medium-sized ones, were set up by newly unemployed so-called 'forced entrepreneurs' who had no management expertise. In many CEE economies the business community is dominated by small companies, many of which employ only two or three members of staff and operate in the 'informal' sector (Fekete 2005; Mazurkiewicz 2003). Markets and the (for example, financial) institutions in which they are embedded are even less mature. Today, an increasing share of companies is interested in the concept of CSR – the vast majority of them private firms. The most important consequence of the European integration is that the (legally embedded) business environment has become more stable. This gives them room and planning security for CSR policies.

As regards public attitudes towards private business, profit still has a dubious meaning in the eyes of many citizens in Hungary. Also, corporate leaders are still viewed with a certain level of distrust. Public opinion is that managers of corporations and owners of small and medium-sized enterprises tend to accept consequences that are damaging to society as a whole and to the environment in seeking maximal profit (DEMOS 2006; Fekete 2005). This scepticism towards the private sector can be assumed to weigh upon the credibility of CSR activities. The historical experience of 'forced voluntariness' fosters distrust of the notion of 'voluntary action', which is inherent in the concept of CSR. This situation makes it difficult to create a business case for socially and environmentally responsible company operations. Some authors argue that experiences from the previous regime led to a low level of trust in 'rhetoric', with the result that consumers today might be suspicious towards companies that actively communicate their CSR commitment (Radácsi 2006). This may be aggravated by the observed practice that newly established CSR advisors, often former communication consultants, popularize the view that CSR is 'simply a new way of corporate communication', which can easily be adopted by success-oriented companies. Apart from triggering distrust, the phenomenon may make businesses less open for 'real' CSR. Note that although CSR is a relatively new term in new EU Member States including Hungary, it is becoming very popular. Different actors, however, interpret it in several ways. The meaning of the concept is generally not clear, neither for companies nor for the public. Hence experts maintain that the term 'CSR' has already 'deteriorated' to some extent and that it is very difficult to stop this tendency.

The other aspect of economic environment is the demand for sustainable products and services and products of companies active in CSR. These market opportunities are still quite limited in Hungary (Kerekes et al. 2003). As a consequence, 'CSR initiatives in Hungary seriously risk being seen as naive – the enemy of the bottom line' (Csonka et al. 2004, p. 17), and economic development is known to affect the social preferences in favour of 'post-materialist' sustainability issues (Inglehart 1995). Also, more and more NGOs which have the mission of raising consumer awareness have been established.

16.2.3   Social Framework Conditions

With regard to social framework conditions, we shall briefly discuss attitudes and practices relating to sustainability issues and the role of civil society in post-socialist countries.

Hungarian society is characterized by a low level of commitment towards global social and environmental problems and a low level of responsibility for common property. This is regarded as a consequence of the national emergence of new – or hitherto hidden – serious social problems, such as unemployment and poverty, after the collapse of the socialist regime and the transition to a market economy. Though citizens are interested in sustainability issues, their concern relates above all to those problems that directly endanger their local community and environment (Eurobarometer 2005). Among the environmental issues, nature conservation dominates vis-à-vis CSR inherent issues, such as industrial pollution, the exhaustion of natural resources or the responsibility of individuals for improving the environment (ibid., p. 5). More problematically, surveys show that despite a high level of awareness about environmental problems among consumers, concrete actions, such as the willingness to pay higher prices for ecological products, are less frequent. Civil society organizations can be important pressure groups for sustainable production and consumption, both vis-à-vis companies and consumers. Let us therefore briefly review the role that civil society organizations play in CEE societies. Although politically marginalized, green organizations had been active in this region since the 1980s.[8] In the beginning, their activity was also a form of indirect expression of political dissent. Following the political changes, these civil society groups often lost their importance. Since the 1990s, however, new organizations have been established which have the mission of environmental protection and consumer protection as well. For example, in Hungary the Association of Conscious Consumers was established in 2002 to 'support . . . and promote . . . conscious consumer behaviour, ethical (environmentally aware and socially responsible) consumption and corporate activity, sustainable consumption and production strategies, the eco-social market sensitiveness and awareness of rights and obligations of consumers' (Gulyás et al. 2006).

16.2.4   Technological Framework Conditions

In the context of CSR, technological framework conditions above all play a role with regard to companies' environmental performance. In the Eastern European economies the intensive industrialization from in the 1950s neglected environmental considerations. Moreover, it was part of the socialist ideology to 'fight against nature', that is, to transform it for the benefit of modern society rather than to heed its limitations.

   The polluting technologies that were widely used, however, proved to be economically ineffective (Illés 2002). Above all for this reason, most of the producing capacities had to be gradually transformed or closed after the transition to a market economy. While this meant an enormous burden on the economy, the advantage was that in some cases the latest

– and often least polluting – technology could be adopted (ibid.). While the scarcity of well-qualified workforce is a significant barrier to applying the latest technologies, it is even more problematic that many sustainability issues cannot be solved through technologies alone – they require deeper transformations of industrial paradigms and consumption patterns. Some of these sustainability issues, such as climate change and biodiversity loss, may even increase through the economic growth that is expected to follow a deeper integration of the new Member States into the European economy.

16.2.5   Environmental Framework Conditions

Although intensive industrialization and the state of technologies (polluting, not energy efficient) negatively affected the environment during the socialist era, nature conservation has always been rather developed in CEE countries. On average, biodiversity levels are higher than in the old EU Member States, partly as a result of the strict protection of some areas, for instance, by courtesy of national parks (ibid.). Following the transition, the decline of heavy industry and intensive agricultural production resulted in significantly lower pollution levels. This improvement was partly compensated by the rapid development of the individual mode of transport and changes in consumption patterns (Kerekes and Kiss 2001). However, due to the significant fall of emission levels, environmental problems appeared less grave and expectations that companies should reduce their negative environmental impacts lost their vigour. For example, since many CEE countries were meeting their Kyoto goals without any special effort to reduce greenhouse gas emissions, the pressure on companies to mandatorily or voluntarily reduce emissions was low.

The deficiency of environment-related technological infrastructure, such as waste management and sewage treatment systems, can also be a barrier to improving the environmental performance of companies. With the legal requirements tied to the EU accession, however, this problem is definitely becoming less serious.

16.2.6   Legal Framework Conditions

One of the greatest challenges following the political transformation of the formerly socialist countries in Europe was the formulation of the new regulatory environment after 1990. In preparation for their accession to the EU in 2004, the countries adapted their legal framework to the European Community's *acquis communautaire*. Among others, environmental policy and policies relating to the EU's internal market are Community policies[9] and are therefore harmonized to a large extent; they provide the baseline for corporate compliance and beyond-compliance activity in old and new EU Member States. Examples include the European directives on (sustainable) public procurement and the EU Accounts Modernization Directive.[10] In line with the former, the Hungarian Public Procurement Act promotes corporate responsibility through criteria for sustainable purchasing. The latter was transposed into the Hungarian Accountancy Act in 2005, with the effect that Hungarian companies can publish sustainability or CSR reports, social accounts or corporate citizenship reports. The realm of social policy, which is governed by the Community's open method of coordination, is less harmonized within the EU and national legislation still defines the rules that corporate actors need to comply to or may voluntarily go beyond. With the Government Resolution No. 1025 'for the reinforcement of the social responsibility of employers and for measures to stimulate it', the Hungarian government sketched out a plan for beyond-compliance activities in social policy and labour relations in 2006. Its main points include: starting a debate on the criteria for socially responsible employer behaviour; studying how stronger CSR can promote more regulated labour relationships; elaborating measures that acknowledge socially responsible behaviour; elaborating the criteria for employers to use a social label; preparing guidelines for supporting companies in establishing 'equal opportunity plans'; creating a 'workplace accessible to the disabled' label and a label for products that are designed for disabled persons.

Experts see a consensus among Hungarian businesses and stakeholders that CSR is a 'beyond-compliance' strategy and should be regulated to some extent by the government. Thus, in a simplified and static view, the potential for CSR is narrowed by strengthening regulation – which is a direct consequence of joining the EU in many cases.

16.2.7 Concluding Remarks

To the extent that CSR may increase the private sector's contribution to sustainable development, it is challenging to examine how CEE countries can successfully adopt the concept of CSR in a context that is quite different from the one in which it was originally developed – in terms of markets and political framework, consumer attitudes, knowledge, human and financial resources and the like (Radácsi 2006).

The PESTEL framework guided our analysis of factors relevant to the success of CSR in new EU Member States. It thus fulfilled a similar purpose as the framework developed in Chapter 3 for explaining CSR effects at company level. Compared to that framework – which set out corporate strategy, organization and culture, the business environment, civil society and the political-institutional setting as relevant factors – the focus here was more on factors external to the companies. We may conclude that civil society demand for CSR is presently lower than in old EU Member States on average, but there is definitely a growing demand. For some companies this can constitute a threat, but for those spearheading CSR it means an opportunity. The business environment shows a similar tendency: we may expect growing market opportunities related to CSR, and the increasing interest in CSR shows that the concept's legitimacy is diffusing already. During the socialist era the political-institutional environment was characterized by the omnipresence of the state and has no tradition for the beyond-compliance responsibilities of corporate actors. Factors internal to companies that influence CSR are also less favourable than on average in the EU. Not only the (privatized) companies themselves, but their market practices and their strategy building and organizational development with regard to CSR are relatively new and therefore less developed. Corporate cultures are presumably influenced by the negative aspects of the social environment, but the extent of this influence may vary amongst companies (for example, as a result of different recruitment criteria, workplace conditions and so on). We set forth how these factors have been or are expected to be influenced by the EU integration process. In accordance with our initial expectation, the influence worked in some cases through market processes. This holds for the convergence of business environments, such as consumer demand and sales opportunities for sustainable products and services. In other cases, EU integration affected the framework conditions of CSR through political-institutional processes rather than through market ones. This was the case when EU policies stimulated the establishment of CSR policy-making capacities in Hungary and capacity building for civil society organizations.

16.3 THE IMPACT OF EU INTEGRATION ON COMPANIES' CSR PRACTICES AND VICE VERSA – EVIDENCE FROM TWO CASE STUDIES

While the assessment discussed above focused on the macro (mostly national) level of the framework conditions for CSR, the present chapter concentrates on the micro (company) level of concrete CSR practices. Our guiding questions are: how does EU integration affect the concrete CSR practices of companies? And how do companies' CSR activities, on the other hand, impact on EU integration? The analysis of the company level dimension of CSR is based on two company case studies in the Hungarian oil sector. The oil sector was selected because of its key relevance for sustainability issues, because it features companies within the new EU Member States that are active in CSR and because it makes a comparison possible with insights gathered from the oil sector studies in Chapters 5 and 10.

In order to account for potentially different strategies to deal with the impact of EU integration, we chose two companies operating in Hungary which have a different geographic and historical background: while MOL is a Hungarian based formerly state-owned company that has recently become a multinational, Shell Hungary has its origins in the old EU Member States (the UK and the Netherlands). Both companies have a long-term presence in the region: MOL was founded as the national oil and gas company in Hungary and Shell was the first multinational oil company that settled in Hungary.

The case studies that address the relation between EU integration and companies' CSR practices were carried out in late 2006 and early 2007. When portraying the concrete CSR practices in the company case studies below, we shall follow the structure laid down in Chapter 4, that is, we shall describe the company's CSR commitment, its strategies, implementation and resulting performance in that order. We shall focus on the issues of environmental protection, gender equality and countering bribery, which are focused on throughout this book.

16.3.1   MOL – A Hungarian Oil Company Developing its Own Sustainability Approach

16.3.1.1   Company background
The Hungarian Oil and Gas Company Plc (MOL Rt.) was founded soon after the political changes in 1991 upon the merger of nine state-owned companies. This step represented a milestone in the history of the Hungarian petroleum industry. The following years were dedicated to the preparation of privatization. The Hungarian government remained an important shareholder of the privatized company and had 8.3 per cent of its shares in 2007.

MOL was the first national oil and gas company in the CEE region to be privatized. Although in the beginning there were 'severe efficiency problems inherited from the company's state-run heritage' (MOL 2007a), further fundamental changes took place after its introduction to the stock exchange. The most significant one concerned the new form of responsibility assumed by company management. The need to protect both the interests of the state and of new private investors led to the 'concept of creating and building shareholder value', which became a fundamental aspect of corporate culture.

In 1995 MOL made its first step towards expansion with the opening of its first filling station abroad, in Romania. 1999 was the year in which basic strategic decisions were made: the management decided to replace the company's various areas of operation with only a few highly focused core activities, and to initiate a major expansion programme.[11] Today MOL is not only a company that embraces the entire Hungarian petroleum industry, but also one of the largest multinational corporations in Central Europe. The core activities of MOL Group are: exploration and production of crude oil, natural gas and gas products; refining, transportation, storage and distribution of crude oil products at both the retail and wholesale level; transmission of natural gas and the production and sales of olefins and polyolefins. MOL has around 15 000 employees today. The company strategy includes further extension.

16.3.1.2 CSR at MOL

MOL is a pioneering company in the field of CSR in Hungary and the CEE region. One of the six core values of the company is: 'Health, safety, environmental and social commitment: we want to fulfil our responsibilities towards our employees, hosting communities and societies therefore we aspire to go beyond legally required standards.' The management prefers the term 'sustainable development' (SD), interpreted as the balancing of economic, environmental and social aspects. As the chief advisor of sustainable development highlighted, within the company they usually try to avoid using the term CSR, because of the confusion and misunderstanding about this recently adopted term in Hungary. While CSR is said to be often interpreted as a responsibility to society only, corporate sustainability includes both societal and environmental responsibility.

The commitment of the company to SD is outlined on its home page (MOL 2007b). According to our interviewees, the personal commitment of the CEO was and is an important driver of SD and CSR in the company. In the strategy for 2006–10 the management states its intention to 'remain a pace setter in Corporate Governance and Sustainable Development in "New Europe"' (MOL 2005a, b).

The CSR commitment is implemented, among others, through several CSR instruments. Above all, a company-specific Sustainable Development Management System (SDMS) has been developed.[12] The system encompasses both short- and long-term objectives, such as developing sustainable operations within the company. The purpose of this specific tool was to bridge the gap between standards and everyday operation. The principles of the SDMS are a multi-stakeholder approach and interdisciplinary. The SDMS is more comprehensive than, for example, ISO 14 001;[13] it is tailored to the company and tackles a number of CSR areas (environmental protection, promoting gender equity, human rights and so on).

Target setting and measurement are claimed to be very important to ensure the impact of the companies' CSR practices (MOL 2005). Environmental targets for 2005 included limitation of the amount of hazardous waste, soil contamination and environmental liabilities. A target relating to the mitigation of climate change, however, is only listed among the future challenges: 'Identify project-based CO_2 emission-reduction opportunities to decrease allocation quota deficit by 20 per cent.'

An integrated MOL Group-level SD report is published annually, which reviews the sustainable development performance of the company and includes the most significant company projects and key data (MOL 2005b). Since 2003, MOL Group has taken note of the Global Reporting Initiative Guideline recommendations when preparing SD reports. In 2005 the company joined the UNDP Global Compact network.

Organizationally, MOL's CSR commitment is implemented by a recently established SD Committee, headed by the CEO. The aim of the SD Committee is 'to ensure the highest commitment to and representation of SD issues both in the internal and the external relations of the MOL Group, to enhance long-term sustainable development performance and to foster the positioning of the MOL Group in the market-place in this new strategic area' (MOL 2006). The responsibility of the Committee is to ensure the integrated management of sustainable development issues at the levels of the MOL Group and functional units. The Committee is also mandated to follow up and verify, together with the SD Chief Advisor and SD working team, the operation and the appropriateness of the company-specific SDMS compared to regulations and the best international practices. Another of its tasks is to regularly review, evaluate and comment on all proposals for SD audit and evaluation, the objectives defined, and the results and reports of the SDMS for the Board of Directors.

The SD working team originally had 17 members, one from each department of the company, but as a result of the high interest and openness within the company, it is continuously growing. Beside the SD working Group, another organizational unit of the company is also responsible for some CSR-related issues. The Health, Safety and Environment Protection unit ensures MOL Group's compliance with legal requirements, providing management of health, safety and environment (HSE) tasks. It works similarly to the SD working team: there is a special team focusing on HSE issues and there is one representative from each department.

The resulting CSR performance of MOL is difficult to assess. Major organizational changes were carried out in the past few years, including the expansion and integration of the company as well as the establishment of the SD Committee and introduction of the SDMS. Targets of previous years, such as the reduction of hazardous wastes, of soil contamination and environmental liabilities are claimed to have been met.

16.3.1.3 Interrelations with EU integration
Hungary's EU accession influenced MOL's CSR practices primarily through the implementation of the *acquis communautaire*. It sets new (partly higher) sustainability standards that the company needs to take into account in its compliance and beyond-compliance activities. In addition, the EU accession contributed to a more transparent and stable legal environment. It is also a direct consequence of Hungary's EU membership that at MOL the definition of the European Commission's 2002 Communication on CSR as a 'business contribution to sustainable development' is considered as the relevant definition of CSR. Direct political incentives or pressures to adopt CSR policies, however, did not play a role for MOL.

EU policies for MOL serve as a 'compass' for predicting changes of national level legislation. However, according to a company representative, EU level legislation is often interpreted differently in different Member States. For example, the implementation of EU directives differs between Hungary and Slovakia; therefore the level playing field is only partly realized. In the field of environmental protection two EU policies are regarded as being of crucial importance and as influencing the potential of MOL's beyond-compliance activities. These are Directive 96/61/EC concerning integrated pollution prevention and control (the IPPC Directive) and Regulation (EC) No 1907/2006 on the Registration, Evaluation, Authorization and Restriction of Chemicals (REACH). As in the field of environmental protection, the traditional approach in Hungary was to treat environmental media separately; implementation of the IPPC Directive contributes to the diffusion of a more integrated approach.

Other, indirect effects of the EU integration, such as better performance or compliance of suppliers because of changing economic and legal conditions, were not experienced by the company.

When it comes to the impact of MOL's CSR practices on EU integration, we found that the company actively participated in the economic integration process. For example, in 2002, MOL joined the Hungarian EU Business Council which was initiated by the European Roundtable of Industrialists in 1998. MOL is the only company in the Roundtable from the CEE region and has also become a member of the Business Council. In this sense, MOL contributes to a better economic integration of the region. It is, however, difficult to exclusively trace this commitment back to CSR practices, since such sector commitment is also part of common business practice without sustainability relevance.

16.3.2   Shell Hungary – A Giant Applying Global Policies

16.3.2.1   Company background

Shell was the first foreign company present on the Hungarian petroleum market in 1925.[14] The company had its own refinery on Csepel Island (near Budapest), which started operating in 1930, and by the early 1940s the petrol station chain of Shell spanned the whole country.

Following the transition to a socialist system, the company's assets – similarly to those of other private companies – were taken over by the state. Shell was temporarily not present in the country, but resettled there as early as the 1960s. The first Shell petrol station after World War II opened in a franchise system in Budapest in 1966.

From 1989 onwards, Shell and the Hungarian company Interag cooperated as a joint venture. In 1992 Shell became the major owner, which resulted in the rapid extension of the petrol station network. From 1993 onwards, Shell was the single owner of the Hungarian company, which has operated since this time as Shell Hungary Plc. Today Shell Hungary is among the 30 largest companies in Hungary in respect of turnover.[15] The number of employees in 2004 was 272.

16.3.2.2   CSR at Shell Hungary

In general, Shell's global CSR commitment and policies are valid and implemented by Shell Hungary as well. The principles of CSR are in harmony with the company's business principles, laid down in the Shell General Business Principles. As part of these Business Principles, Shell 'commit[s] to contribute to sustainable development. This requires balancing short and long term interests, integrating economic, environmental and social considerations into business decision-making' (Shell 2005). In Hungary the commitment of Shell's top management is underscored by the fact that the present CEO is the chairman of the national chapter of the Business Council for Sustainable Development. In terms of translating this CSR commitment into strategy, Shell Hungary follows the guidance given by its international headquarters.

When it comes to the implementation of Shell's CSR commitment in Hungary, only a limited group of CSR activities can be identified as specific to the country. This is due to the fact that the company's activities in Hungary are limited to the trading of oil products and, more importantly, that they are a result of the multinational's centralized decision making, which severely restricts the leeway that the Hungarian operating company has to develop its own strategic concepts. An indicator of this is that the sustainability report is only published in English and – although there is demand – has not been translated into national languages. As a consequence of their limited strategic leeway, those social and environmental activities in which Shell Hungary wishes to take part are restricted to corporate citizenship activities. For example, Shell Hungary supports several foundations, such as the so-called Shell ÉletPÁLYA Foundation, which has the aim of providing professional training and practical advice to young entrepreneurs. Within the scope of this scheme, Shell maintains close contact with universities and other educational institutions. The company also participates in the Global Road Safety Partnership (GRSP). GRSP is a cooperation of governments and governmental agencies, the private sector and civil society organizations to address road safety issues in low and middle income countries. Another advanced area of the company's sponsorship concept is public health.

The remainder of the company's CSR practices is not country-specific but rather part of the general practice of the global company. We shall focus our subsequent description of these practices on the issue areas of environmental protection, gender equality and countering bribery, which are key focal points in this book. In the field of environmental protection the renewable energy business of the company, the development of second generation biofuel and the development of CO_2 capture technologies can be considered as the most important; however, neither of these is relevant at Shell Hungary.[16] While the general importance of climate policy for Shell was highlighted by company representatives, there is no concrete, strategically planned action to, for example, promote energy efficiency or the use of renewable energy in Hungary. Suppliers have to comply with the Shell General Business Principles and formulate their own HSE policy. The compliance is regularly monitored by Shell.[17] The HSE system of petrol stations is also of a high standard in order to ensure the safety of employees, customers and the environment. The gender equality strategy is included in the so-called 'Diversity and Inclusiveness' policy. There are two major elements of this global strategy: increasing the proportion of women in top management and improving their career opportunities. The parenting support policy supports parents with small children. They are offered part-time jobs (six hours a day) if they return to their position after six months. Countering bribery, according to one of our interviewees, 'is a direct consequence of the Shell General Business Principles: Honesty, Integrity, Respect for People' (Shell Interview 2006d). Shell has introduced a global whistle-blowing helpline and support, allowing staff to report anonymously concerns about possible bribery, facilitation or other incidents of fraud. However, no case has been reported in Hungary so far. In 2006 the code of conduct was still under implementation at Shell Hungary.

Unfortunately, it was impossible to gain national level data on Shell's CSR performance, that is, on the impact of the activities described above.

16.3.2.3   Interrelations with EU integration

For multinational companies operating globally the relevance of the EU enlargement and its consequences for CSR can be assumed to be less significant than for companies with most of their business activities limited to Europe. This assumption was confirmed in the case of Shell Hungary. While the 'change of legal, economic and environmental conditions resulting from the EU accession is generally beneficial for the business environment, enabling a more professional and transparent business activity', a company representative maintained that 'the CSR activity of Shell in Hungary was not significantly influenced by the country's EU accession' (ibid.).

On the other hand, the CSR activities of multinational companies can still contribute to successful economic and social integration of new Member States into the EU, not only by their very economic operations but also indirectly by diffusing knowledge and norms with relevance to SD. Shell, for example, decided to make those EU policies accepted and recognized at national level that are not sufficiently adopted in certain new Member States. In Hungary, according to our interviewees, the principle of sustainability is not as well known as it should be according to its importance in the EU Sustainable Development Strategy. Therefore, Shell Hungary has committed itself to promoting the concept. In Bulgaria one of the most crucial problems as experienced by Shell is the high corruption level. Therefore, the local subsidiary of Shell is committed to drawing attention to this problem and to diffusing anti-corruption measures.

16.3.3   Comparison of the Company Cases

In the following the two company case studies are compared both with regard to the companies' CSR activities and the consequences of EU integration that they experienced.

With regard to CSR commitment, both companies recognize their responsibility towards society and the environment. Both also participate actively in the discussion on CSR and SD in Hungary. At MOL this commitment seems to be motivated intrinsically (personal commitment, competitive advantage) while the Shell representatives primarily highlighted the importance of Shell General Business Principles and corporate traditions.

When it comes to the integration of CSR into strategies, MOL is still in the phase of strategy formulation and planning. However, it promises that the strategy will be based on screening the company's SD practice. Shell Hungary – as part of a global company – cannot formulate its own strategies. The global strategy is reflected at national level; however, it is

Table 16.1   Comparison of the two companies' CSR processes

	Commitment	Strategy	Implementation	Performance
MOL	Intrinsically motivated	Early stage screening of the company	Involvement of different company units	? (Major recent organizational changes; New SDMS)
Shell	Especially at top management level and headquarters	Automatic, not tailored to local circumstances	Automatic, not tailored to local circumstances	? (Corporate Citizenship activities)

not tailored to local conditions and some elements of the global strategy are not represented. For example, while the general importance of climate policy to Shell was highlighted by company representatives, there is no concrete action to, for example, promote energy efficiency or the use of renewable energy in Hungary.

The situation is similar with regard to the CSR implementation phase. MOL is still in the phase of implementing its own CSR instruments (screening of the company's SD performance, company-specific SDMS). In the case of Shell, globally applied CSR instruments and CSR-related actions are typical. They are not tailored to local circumstances but rather adopted automatically.

Finally, assessment of the CSR performance of the two companies is problematic for different reasons. In the case of MOL the reason is that major organizational changes have been made recently and that the SD Management System was introduced only in 2006. Shell Hungary's business activity is limited to trading oil products and there are no performance data available at national level.

The difference between the two companies' CSR processes is summarized in Table 16.1 and is also reflected in their evaluation by the Accountability Rating Hungary 2006[18] (Braun and Partners 2006). The criteria of the assessment in this latter study included stakeholder engagement, strategy, governance, performance management, public disclosure and assurance. While MOL was the second on the list (the first company from the oil sector), Shell was the ninth (the second from the sector) among the 30 biggest companies in Hungary.

The most interesting conclusion that can be drawn from the two case studies is that EU accession played a relatively minor role for the multinationals in both cases, both with regard to their general business operations and their CSR activities. Some other common observations were made by the representatives of MOL and Shell: CSR and SD are issues of growing importance not only at EU but also at national level in Hungary. Although the circumstances are less favourable[19] than in most old EU Member States, companies (especially those that operate in a multinational environment) still recognized the importance of CSR. Both companies' representatives highlighted that a national SD strategy was indispensable in Hungary. Their communication of the issues of CSR and SD confirmed our conjecture that multinational companies play an important role in the formulation and discussion about these issues.

When it comes to the impact of multinational companies' CSR activities on EU integration, there are both direct effects (participation in the economic integration process) and indirect effects (influence on national policy formulation, diffusion of knowledge and norms, motivation of competitors). In the case of Shell Hungary the latter was dominant. We can conclude that the most important effect of CSR of multinational companies which have a Western European origin is the participation in national level discussion on CSR and the motivation of competitors of CEE origin to adopt a CSR and SD strategy in order to ensure their competitiveness on the European as well as on the global market.

16.4   SUMMARY AND CONCLUSIONS

Our focus in this chapter was to approach the following research questions: what are the effects of EU accession and integration on the framework conditions for CSR? How does the EU integration impact on the concrete CSR practices of companies and what are the impacts of companies' CSR activities on EU integration? On the basis of a PESTEL analysis, a stakeholder roundtable discussion and two company case studies, we have reached the following conclusions: accession to the EU has influenced the business environment and socio-economic framework for CSR gradually and mostly in an indirect way. The impacts of EU accession cannot always be clearly differentiated from those of changing to a market economy since the two processes are interlinked. The most important direct effect of the EU accession is the implementation of the *acquis communautaire*, resulting in a more stable and predictable regulatory environment.[20] Also, the national level formulation of CSR policy, which started in the 2000s, was partly stimulated by the EU accession.

Companies may have dual motivation for CSR: the potential benefits on EU and international markets as well as political pressures and incentives. In the case of MOL and Shell, CSR tends to be experienced as an important factor of business success rather than being triggered by political pressure. We can conclude that companies' CSR activities are primarily motivated by competitive advantage and not so much by political pressures and incentives, although the companies recognize EU CSR strategy and make reference to its definition of CSR. The latter is important for formulating the business environment for CSR. The CSR practice of multinational companies is still not significantly influenced by EU integration.

The impact of companies' CSR practices on EU integration is more difficult to assess. In general, their CSR (and general business) practices might have some positive impact on the region's social and economic integration into the EU to the extent that company strategies support EU policy goals, such as those endorsed by the European Sustainable Development Strategy. Most of this impact is indirect. The companies examined consider EU integration as an external and – mostly for those operating on the global market – as a relatively insignificant factor. Multinational companies that are forerunners in CSR are important in stimulating national level discussion and policy making on CSR, as they are often considered to be example setters. Their role in motivating competitors and suppliers to catch up with their business and CSR practices is at least as important as the direct impact of their CSR practices.

NOTES

1. To accede to the EU, the candidate countries had to be recognized as European States (Art. 49, EU Treaty) and to comply with the principles of freedom, democracy, respect for human rights and fundamental freedoms, and the rule of law (Art. 6, EU Treaty). In addition, the Copenhagen criteria required candidate countries to be stable democracies, respect human rights and the rule of law and protect minorities; to have a working market economy; and to adopt the common rules, standards and policies which make up the body of EU law (see Presidency Conclusions of Copenhagen European Council of December 2002).
2. The PESTEL analysis is described in, for example, Campbell and Craig (2005, p. 501).
3. See MOL interview 2006a and 2006b; Shell interview 2006a and 2006b.
4. The roundtable tackled the impact of EU integration on the CSR environment and on national CSR policies in Hungary and other CEE countries. Participants included representatives of multinational companies, trade unions, NGOs with an environmental management and law profile, the government and academia.
5. Newly established companies, on the other hand, are typically struggling to find their feet in the market and therefore have less capacity for CSR.
6. For instance, while there is similar trust on average in national governments and the EU regarding environmental issues, in Hungary the difference is significant: 38 per cent trust the EU and only 21 per cent the national government the most (multiple answers question, maximum three answers) (European Commission 2005a).
7. The budget of the CSR directorate for the first year of its operation was 300 million forints (approximately 1.2 million euros).
8. The first attempt to establish a green civil society organization in Hungary was in 1984, when the so-called Duna Kör (Danube Circle) tried to disseminate secret information on a plan for damming the Danube in Czechoslovakia and in Hungary (Gabcikovo-Nagymaros). It organized several protests from 1986 onwards.

9. That is, these policies are governed by the Community procedure of the first pillar of the EU as opposed to the intergovernmental procedure of the EU's second and third pillar.
10. Directive 2003/51/EC of the European Parliament and of the Council of 18 June 2003 amending Directives 78/660/EEC, 83/349/EEC, 86/635/EEC and 91/674/EEC on the annual and consolidated accounts of certain types of companies, banks and other financial institutions and insurance undertakings.
11. The first significant steps in order to implement this strategy were made in 2000, when MOL became the first Central European oil company to establish a cross-border partnership through acquiring 32 per cent of the Slovakian national oil company, Slovnaft. In the same year the company extended its activities by entering the chemical industry business, purchasing nearly 30 per cent of one of the most significant Hungarian chemical companies, Tiszai Vegyi Kombinát (Tisza Chemicals Company).
12. According to MOL's SD chief advisor, oil companies usually have their own system as they are complex organizations and have big capacities in the area of environmental protection.
13. ISO 14 001 is also implemented and verified at the company.
14. It was a corporation owned by Shell (75 per cent) and by a Hungarian company, Mayer and Co. (25 per cent).
15. In 2004 the turnover totalled at 171 214 000 000 forints (approximately 680 million euros).
16. The introduction of a new diesel fuel was mentioned by the CEO as the most significant step towards environmental benefits in Hungary.
17. For instance, there are regular audits by Shell auditors in the case of lubricant suppliers.
18. The Accountability Rating Hungary ranks companies on how they develop a corporate strategy that responds to stakeholders' expectations, while ensuring long-term profitability. The national list has been prepared by Braun and Partners (2006).
19. For example, the lack of national SD strategy and the lack of sufficient attention on the part of the government were mentioned as important barriers by several interviewees.
20. This is important for the companies' CSR activities as well, as it enables them to see more clearly what is 'beyond compliance'. Furthermore, they have more capacity for CSR if they do not have to adapt continuously to the changing and unpredictable regulatory environment.

17 Rhetoric and realities in CSR: main findings and implications for public policy and research

Franziska Wolff, Regine Barth, Christian Hochfeld and Katharina Schmitt[1]

17.1 INTRODUCTION

In the previous chapters we presented conceptual considerations and empirical findings on the question to what extent and how Corporate Social Responsibility (CSR) leads to sustainability impact, and what the relevance of this is for public policy. Our focus was on four sectors and a selection of sustainability issues. Empirically, some 50 companies were surveyed, and ten of them studied in-depth. This final chapter serves to sum up some of the main insights of and conclusions from this research, albeit with a specific focus: our interest here is with the implications for public policy and research. We hence present a selective synthesis, which complements the synthesizing work of Chapters 9 and 14.

We first take a critical look at the framework which we used to assess the sustainability impact of CSR. Summing up core results on the sustainability effects of CSR (output, outcome and impact) we identified, we then venture upon an answer to our guiding question: is CSR – in the cases we examined – more than mere rhetoric? With a cautious 'yes, if . . .' we go on to set out patterns where CSR is more likely to lead to sustainability impact, and where there are systematic limits for CSR impact. The patterns we describe result from such factors as visibility and measurability of a CSR issue, whether the issue affects a company's core business, institutional density in an issue area and others. This knowledge is relevant for public policy making when choosing the most promising instrument mix. Fostering CSR can be considered as an option to complement social and environmental regulation. We shall wrap up the chapter by giving respective policy recommendations. These recommendations especially aim at sharpening public policies to focus on CSR 'reality' by addressing directly or indirectly those framework conditions and factors which lead to improved sustainability impact. Similarly, research should address the impact question and look into the interface of public and private sustainability policies.

17.2   ASSESSING THE ASSESSMENT TOOL

What lessons can we learn from applying the framework for assessing sustainability impact of CSR, as elaborated in Chapter 2? This framework by Skjærseth and Wettestad draws on two strategies: a strategy for identifying how CSR activities contribute to a relative improvement in the social or environmental performance (relative improvement strategy) of companies, and a strategy for evaluating how they contribute to the achievement of absolute goals – in our case EU policy goals for sustainable development (goal attainment strategy). In both strategies it is necessary to draw a hypothetical baseline of corporate performance without voluntary action; to establish causal relationships between CSR and observed improvements; and to extrapolate from changes in corporate behaviour to impact on society and the environment, outside the company.

Having applied the framework across our four surveys and case studies, it helped to develop a systematic research design, to structure interview guidelines and to avoid methodological pitfalls. However, there were still significant challenges and these are described below.

The challenge of causally identifying CSR effects: firstly, as CSR is defined as a 'beyond compliance' strategy, voluntary company activities need to be distinguished from mandatory ones – yet companies themselves rarely make this distinction when developing and assessing sustainability measures. Corporate decision makers as well as the in-company measurement of social and environmental performance rarely distinguish between CSR-induced improvement and other improvements. Secondly, factors other than CSR (for example, developments on resource markets) can contribute to sustainability impact, yet such factors are sometimes presented retrospectively as CSR.

The challenge of delimitating CSR effects: the distinction between changes in commitment and strategy (output), in corporate practice (outcome) and in resulting effects outside companies (impact) was not always as obvious as expected. It should be noted that in the social issue areas analyzed a CSR outcome often at the same time represented a CSR impact. For example, increasing female representation at board level would be a change in corporate practices, but at the same time would contribute to enhancing the quota of women in top positions in the entire society. In environmental fields the delimitation between outcome and impact tends to be clearer. For instance, substituting an old technology by a new, more energy-efficient one translates into a reduction of CO_2 emissions in the outside world.

The difficulty of quantifying CSR effects: sometimes there are issues which cannot be directly measured, for instance, because the intended effect is primarily preventive (for example, countering bribery). But even when issues can be measured, problems of data availability emerged: it was difficult to obtain quantitative data on the CSR-induced changes of companies in practice, and even more difficult to get hold of data to conclude from changes in corporate behaviour to social and environmental effects. This was due to confidentiality concerns as well as deficiencies of companies in measuring their own sustainability performance and external impact, often resulting from the difficulties mentioned above.

The difficulty of determining goal attainment: interlinked with the difficulty to quantify the sustainability impact of CSR, we had difficulties working out the extent to which CSR contributes to achieving absolute goals (in our case EU sustainability goals). Among others, this had to do with the small samples underlying our (qualitative) research design; the lack of pre-existing data to determine a baseline of what those companies contribute to the goals that do not actually engage in CSR; and the fact that the goals were themselves often qualitative, impeding a quantitative assessment. More methodological research is needed to operationalize the goal attainment strategy in CSR impact assessment.

Summing up, assessing the sustainability impact of CSR is a challenging endeavour, even with a systematic framework as developed in this book. While some of the described difficulties are inherent to the task, others might be overcome by further methodological investigation when elaborating the framework in future research.

17.3   RHETORIC OR REALITY? CORE RESULTS ON THE SUSTAINABILITY IMPACT OF CSR

This book is dedicated to empirically exploring the effectiveness of the CSR practices of a number of European companies, targeting a small selection of issues. What can we conclude on the overriding question of the balance between the rhetoric and reality of CSR? Very briefly, we may state that the rhetoric of CSR is still stronger than its reality; that the reality of CSR is strong enough to allow for some rhetoric; and that there still is a potential to improve reality. We shall support these claims by summarizing evidence on the levels and substance of CSR output, outcome and impact identified in previous chapters.[2] The assessment is based on a rough ordinal differentiation between low, medium and high CSR effects. The relative strength of CSR outcome results from its 'distance' to CSR output, and the level of impact to that of outcome found within a sector.

CSR output becomes manifest in the sustainability commitment of companies, their respective strategies and adoption of instruments. With some variation across the sectors and issues targeted, we found rather high levels of CSR output. In our sector surveys large shares of companies express their commitment to society and environment in a written statement. Concretely, 100 per cent of the oil companies, 94 per cent of the banks and 63 per cent of the fish processors have such a corporate statement. The bulk of companies then 'translate' this commitment into strategies. Depending on the issue, 70 per cent to 90 per cent of the respondents integrate commitment into strategies either by creating self-standing policies on sustainability issues, by integrating responsibility for issues into other, cross-cutting (growth, sourcing, R&D and other) strategies, and/or by setting concrete performance targets for the issues. The frequency with which these forms of strategic 'translation' are employed decreases slightly in the order of translation mechanisms listed above. With regard to target setting, it is more common in all sectors to have targets for the companies' own operations than for suppliers and other partners. Both formal commitments and strategies reflect the different strategic prominence that the different industries give to the CSR issues targeted.[3] In terms of instrument use, the surveyed companies in the banking and oil sectors have adopted a wide selection of an average of 17 instruments per company. Among these instruments, a significant number is standardized and pertains to a wider variety of sustainability issues (that is the Global Compact, the OECD Guidelines, or the Global Reporting Initiative), rather than being issue-, sector- or company-specific. Fewer instruments are used by the fish processors (nine CSR instruments on average) and the small and medium-sized enterprises (SMEs) surveyed in the automotive sector (five instruments). These instruments, however, tend to be more issue-specific and, in the case of SMEs, more informal. As was shown in Chapter 15, CSR output reflects to a high degree sustainability goals codified by EU policies.

These high levels of CSR output in general correspond to somewhat lower levels of CSR outcome, that is, changes in corporate practices. Looking at activities that companies carry out to implement their CSR output in the issue areas of climate change, chemicals, sustainable fisheries, gender equality and countering bribery, our surveys show that the level of CSR activities is at least medium for all issue areas analyzed in the oil and the banking sectors. The companies surveyed in the fisheries' sector and in the SMEs sector, however, feature a greater heterogeneity as to whether or not they carry out activities to tackle certain issues. Generally, it can be summarized that when a company makes a commitment to a certain issue, there will be a minimum of activities to manage the issues in its business operations. In the case of promoting gender equality in the oil sector and mitigating climate change in the fisheries' sector we even find far more activities implemented than commitment at output level would suggest. The same applies, for example, to one of the banks analysed in-depth in Chapter 12: while its gender-related CSR output itself is low, changes in corporate practice (outcome) to improve gender equality are assessed to be medium to high. Contrary to these scenarios, the CSR output on countering bribery among the automotive SMEs surveyed is higher than their implementation efforts would actually suggest. The case studies of Chapters 10 to 13 allow us to draw some causal inferences on outcome creation. One conclusion is that ambitious levels of CSR output in many cases produced at least medium levels of outcome. In a few cases less ambitious outputs nevertheless induced substantial outcomes. We also found that similar levels and content of output may induce different levels of outcome, as was suggested by the case study on sustainable fisheries. Finally, the case study on climate change mitigation showed that implementation of standardized CSR instruments varies widely and does not necessarily induce the intended behavioural change in companies. This holds true all the more when instruments are not issue-specific.

Determining the levels of CSR impact created in society and the environment is methodologically most difficult. Also, our empirical basis for it is narrower than for assessing outputs and outcome. Here, we rely to a large extent on in-depth case studies of eight companies, since surveys can yield only limited and self-reported data on the sustainability impact of CSR. The surveys among 49 companies did reveal two things, however, which provide a good starting point for further analysis: firstly, even CSR forerunner companies often do not systematically assess their CSR performance and impact.[4] As a consequence, the basis is weak for improvement processes within the companies to substantiate their CSR impact as well as for gaining credibility vis-à-vis the public. Secondly, and this might be a consequence of the above, the survey respondents (with the exception of banks) are rather reluctant to assess their own social and environmental improvements caused by CSR. Where they do so, their self-evaluation is cautiously optimistic, at least with regard to issues the companies perceive as strategically important. Respondents from the banking sector more confidently assert that their impact ranges from rather high in the area of countering bribery to medium in mitigating climate change and promoting gender equality.

With our case studies, we intended to complement the approximate self-assessment by companies of their impact with more in-depth and triangulated data, focused on one issue area each. The studies discern sustainability impact in some sectors and issues (and indeed sub-issues), but less so in others. For example, environmental relief caused by fish processors sourcing MSC labelled fish can be assumed to be rather high. Also, the two screened banks' societal impact on improving the work-life balance of employees was substantial. On the other hand, impact of the same banks with regard to closing the gender pay gap, as another business dimension of gender equality, was not identifiable. In the field of countering corruption there is some medium impact of the case companies with regard to anti-money laundering, but not with regard to countering bribery. Similarly, the impact of four CSR instruments used by the analysed oil companies on their carbon emissions or the carbon content of their product portfolio ranged from medium to weak and zero. So, while there are indeed a few examples for high impact, more often the studies suggest a low to medium impact. These findings are a bit more pessimistic than the self-assessment by the companies in our surveys. This may partly be a result of our specific definition of impact as the effects emerging outside companies. It can be assumed that companies will not have made the analytical distinction that we draw between improvements within companies (outcome) and sustainability effects outside companies (impact).

17.4   THE POTENTIAL FOR AND LIMITS OF CSR IN ACHIEVING SUSTAINABILITY IMPACT: AMONG OTHERS, A QUESTION OF ISSUES

As shown above, the rhetoric of CSR is still stronger than its reality. However, in many individual instances CSR does make a valuable sustainability contribution. In this section we discuss patterns where we could discern that CSR is either more or less likely to increase sustainability. In what cases can we realistically expect CSR to create sustainability impact and where are there systematic limits to the achievement of such impact? The patterns we identify relate to the nature of CSR issues. Hence, they are to some extent independent of the companies' individual behaviour as analyzed in Parts II and III of the book. As Table 17.1 shows, they nevertheless link up with the set of explanatory factors for CSR effects which we used for this analysis.

When considering patterns according to which the likelihood of CSR to produce sustainability impact is systematically higher or lower, we take into account the depth and scope of such impact:

- Scope: CSR may create impact in a different number of issues.
- Depth: CSR may create different levels of impact with regard to an issue.

Table 17.1   Factors influencing the potential for and limits of CSR impact

Strategy and organization	Visibility and measurability of a CSR issue
	Strategic relevance of an issue
	Implications of an issue for core business and the business case
Corporate culture	Companies' control over an issue: the role of cultural norms
Business environment	Companies' control over an issue: the role of business stakeholders
Civil society	Organization of societal and environmental interests in an issue area
Political-institutional setting	Institutional density in an issue area

Source: Authors.

Our findings show that, against the backdrop of specific sectors, sustainability impact is systematically more difficult to achieve for some CSR issues than for others (see also Vogel 2005).

17.4.1   Visibility and Measurability of a CSR Issue

The visibility and measurability of an issue may affect both the scope and depth of sustainability impact. Some issues are hidden and impact of CSR activities cannot be directly measured. This is the case when the intended effect is primarily preventive, such as with countering bribery, and non-occurrence of predefined circumstances is the declared aim. Other issues are more definable and measurable. Examples from our case studies include the share of women in top positions, the volume of sustainably sourced inputs and reduction of greenhouse gas emissions. When issues are hidden and difficult to measure, it is more demanding for companies to assess their impact – proxy indicators are required – and to review their progress. However, to assess impact and review progress are important preconditions for improving sustainability performance. It hence tends to be more difficult to achieve a high sustainability impact in such issue areas.

17.4.2   Strategic Relevance of an Issue

The strategic relevance of an issue affects the scope and depth of CSR impact. At a most general level, sustainability is impaired when companies do not regard the tackling of a CSR issue as strategically important in the first place. In terms of scope, for example, the fish processors surveyed by Schmitt and Wolff in Chapter 6 did not implement CSR activities in the fields of gender equality and countering bribery. In terms of depth, and on a more positive note, one bank in the case study of Schultz in Chapter 12 which framed gender equality as an issue strategically relevant for the recruitment of highly trained and motivated staff had achieved a higher share of women in management positions than the other analyzed bank. Interestingly enough, however, the assessment of an issue as strategically important does not necessarily imply a high level of CSR implementation activities and impact. This was indicated with regard to the issue of countering bribery by our CSR survey among SMEs in the automotive supply chain (Pálvölgyi et al. in Chapter 8).

17.4.3   Implications of an Issue for Core Business and the Business Case

It is a special challenge when CSR requires changes in the core business, that is, in a company's portfolio of products and services. Less sustainable products or services need to be replaced by more sustainable alternatives. The ecological or social value added of the alternative can be created at different (ideally all) stages of a product's life cycle, ranging from sourcing to production, distribution, use and disposal. The extent to which CSR activities cover a product's life cycle influences how deep sustainability impact will be.

In the fields we researched the core business was affected for the issues 'climate change' in the oil sector and 'sustainable fishing' in the fish processing sector. In the first case the challenge ultimately lies in replacing fossil fuel products by lower carbon products; in the second case in replacing seafood from unsustainably managed fisheries by sustainably managed and harvested fish. To a lesser extent, 'gender equality' can also affect the core business of the banking sector, since endorsement of this issue can be reflected in the lending practices of banks. For an enterprise, taking up responsibility with regard to its products and services implies major investment: in adjusting R&D and innovation strategies, production processes, markets and supply chains, marketing and brands. These adjustments may translate into financial losses with regard to a company's market positioning, customers and supply base so far. Also, technical as well as social and organizational learning are required and the changes may need to be legitimized and 'made sense' of vis-à-vis employees.

When they are not seen to provide a business case at least in the long run – for example, because the company does not perceive sufficient demand, policy incentives or other business grounds – the firm is unlikely to carry out such changes: 'turkeys don't vote for Christmas'. Hence, sustainability impact is displaced. In accordance with this logic, the previous case studies showed that banks only reluctantly offered microcredits as a financial product with specific relevance for female customers. More CSR impact was found to result from the portfolio change of fish processors towards sustainable seafood and to some extent from the switch of oil companies to low-carbon products, where business cases had been identified. However, while oil companies added sustainable products to their portfolio, they did – unsurprisingly – not withdraw unsustainable ones (fossil fuel) from it.

Note that the CSR impact of changing to more sustainable products and services is not only likely to be deep, but also long term: the high costs of changing product portfolios will stabilize the commitment to sustainable products, once taken.

17.4.4 Companies' Control Over an Issue: Cultural Norms, Business Stakeholders

The depth of sustainability impact through CSR is affected by the degree of control that a company has over a CSR issue. Impact is more difficult to achieve when the issue lies outside the company's immediate sphere of influence. This may be the case when in tackling a CSR issue (a) it requires changes in wider cultural norms, habits or identities within the organization or (b) it intervenes in the behaviour of suppliers, business partners or other stakeholders outside the organization.

With regard to the first case, sustainability transformations in corporate behaviour require company-wide changes to different degrees in the behaviour of staff. For example, promoting gender equality and countering bribery affect the action, awareness and acceptance not only of executives or specific functional units but of all employees. Achieving sustainability impact through CSR hence presupposes not only a high diffusion of commitment through the organization, but ultimately changes of wider norms, attitudes and practices at societal level. These are long term and difficult to tackle by a company's management alone.

With regard to the second case, some CSR issues require changes not only in the company's own behaviour and performance, but in the behaviour of suppliers, business partners or other stakeholders as well. To exemplify: from the perspective of banks, and respectively of fish processors, achieving impact with regard to countering bribery or sustainable fisheries requires intense communication and co-operation with business partners and suppliers. To achieve behavioural change in the supply chain, incentives are crucial. If the suppliers or business partners are SMEs whose capacities for CSR tend to be more limited, support for organizational change by customer companies to these suppliers is all the more required to achieve impact (see Pálvölgyi et al., Chapter 8).

Sometimes, in order to improve the conditions for achieving sustainability impact through CSR companies need to exercise pressure for public policy changes. This is the case if structural and institutional limitations in the wider business environment of companies ('systems of production'[5] or 'systems of provision'[6]) prevent the achievement of greater impact. Such limitations may refer to the availability of material resources such as sustainable production inputs (in our case eco-labelled fish) but also of immaterial assets. An example of the latter is expertise and leadership competences of women in order to promote their take-up of top positions.

17.4.5   Organization of Social and Environmental Interests

The organization of sustainability interests through societal pressure groups – as an important actor driving corporate sustainability – varies in different issue areas, affecting both the scope and depth of potential CSR impact. In some issue areas civil society organizations are less involved, less widespread, have a lower organizational capacity and a lower potential to 'threaten' companies than in other issue areas.

We found that in the field of countering bribery, civil society did not play any role in driving adoption or implementation of anti-bribery policies in the two banks analyzed (see Wilkinson, Chapter 13). In this field, which attracts low public awareness, only one notable global organization exists (Transparency International). Bribery being a 'hidden' issue, the naming and shaming strategy that non-governmental organizations (NGOs) are often confined to reaches its limits and also this is not Transparency International's policy.

In the environmental field numerous NGOs are active and tackle numerous (sub-) issues. Although their organizational capacity is often limited as well, environmental NGOs can draw not only on moral arguments but on the fact that environmental destruction often harms people's health or livelihood. Civil society groups have developed complementary strategies of putting public pressure on companies and of supporting their sustainability efforts through co-operation. An example is the 'division of labour' between Greenpeace and WWF in the issue area of sustainable fishing (see Wolff and Schmitt, Chapter 11).

The organization of gender interests differs in several respects: firstly, gender equality interests are not 'third party' interests but directly affect a large part of company employees and society, thus giving 'a voice' to the issue. Secondly, gender issues are often organized through trade unions which tend to be directly involved in the implementation of (human resources-related) CSR processes and have direct access to corporate decision makers. Furthermore, they have a relatively high pressure potential in conflicts: unlike environmental NGOs, they are not limited to creating publicity but can also mobilize labour action such as strikes.[7]

17.4.6 Institutional Density in an Issue Area

A high institutional density in an issue area affects depth of impact. It is obvious that issues which are more densely regulated by social and environmental policies leave less room for CSR activities. Hence, in such cases the sustainability impact that can be achieved through CSR is more limited – and at the same time it is less needed.

Our findings confirmed this insight. For example, the issue areas of anti-money laundering and mitigating climate change are highly regulated in Europe – more regulated than companies' behaviour with regard to gender equality or fishing. Here, the value added of the respective CSR activities was either limited to improving compliance with law[8] or, at the other pole, it extended to changes in companies' product portfolios. The 'greening' of climate-relevant production processes, however, is largely required by law in Europe. From this argumentation we may deduce that CSR can make a bigger sustainability contribution earlier on in the policy cycle when a policy field is still less developed, or when enforcement structures are weak. The contribution will also be greater regarding issues which cannot or can only partly be addressed by legally binding instruments.

17.4.7 Summary

The above factors help to determine patterns when CSR is more likely to realize its sustainability potential, and when CSR reaches its limit. Independent of the action of individual companies, they can explain some of the variance in sustainability impact achieved by businesses in the different issue areas we have analyzed.

Table 17.2 sums up the challenges that exist in different issue areas for achieving sustainability impact through CSR. These challenges may overlap and accumulate. Table 17.2 shows that the most structural obstacles exist in the field of countering bribery and money laundering.

It should be noted that the limits of CSR to create sustainability impact relate not only to the 'depth' and 'scope' of impact. A further dimension is the reliability and durability of impact: due to the voluntary nature of CSR, its implementation and resulting impact depend on the discretion of corporate decision makers. As argued above, sustainability impact is most likely to be long term when CSR leads to changes in product portfolios. This is due to the high investment of adapting core business and the resulting 'path dependency'.

*Table 17.2   Issue-related challenges for creating sustainability impact
through CSR*

Issue area	Challenges for creating CSR impact
Mitigating climate change	• Core business: business case only for adding more sustainable products to portfolio, but not for withdrawing less sustainable ones • Institutional density
Promoting sustainable fisheries	• Core business: business case for substituting unsustainable by sustainable products in portfolio • Limited control over issue: relevance of supply chain
Promoting gender equality	• Limited control over issue: relevance of cultural norms
Countering bribery and money laundering	• Hidden and immeasurable issue • Limited control of issue: relevance of cultural norms, relevance of business partners • Low public awareness of issues, low civil society capacities • Institutional density

Source: Authors.

17.5   RECOMMENDATIONS FOR PUBLIC POLICY AND RESEARCH

The following policy recommendations are based on the findings presented in this book. They take into consideration how public policies can stimulate company-internal drivers of CSR impact as well as company-external factors. The latter include the role of civil society, the business and sector environments and, in a cross-cutting fashion, the political-institutional setting itself. We shall focus our recommendations on those selected points of departure that lay within our (EU-oriented) scope of research. Hence, the recommendations will not address the whole range of public measures conceivable to support CSR, for example, in the context of bilateral trade agreements and reporting obligations.

17.5.1   CSR and Sustainability Impact: No General Rule

An important insight for policy makers resulting from our findings is that the sustainability impact of CSR differs according to sectors and issue areas: in some instances relatively high impact could be achieved, in others impact was low. There is hence no general rule as to the value of CSR for fostering sustainable development.

If the political promotion of CSR is to form part of effective policy mixes, then it will be necessary to evaluate in advance whether an issue lends itself to being tackled by voluntary measures or not. Some indications are contained in Section 4 of this chapter. Generally, this requires an issue- and sector-specific impact assessment of CSR in companies committed to CSR.

17.5.2   Put Sustainability Impact High on CSR Agenda

It has so far been largely taken for granted that CSR produces beneficial impact on society and the environment. Major policy and academic discussions accordingly concern the company-internal management of CSR processes and their impact on financial performance, rather than sustainability impact emerging outside the companies.

We hence suggest that policy debates on CSR should be geared more towards the social and environmental impact of CSR. Political actors can give a decisive push for this. A first step could be to assess and then broaden the extent to which existing policy strategies on CSR and policy bodies tackle the question of sustainability impact. Multistakeholder fora on CSR (like the EU Multistakeholder Forum on CSR which is expected to be reconvened) will also be important arenas to discuss this challenge.

Policy makers should communicate explicitly to the business sector and its representative bodies the benefit for companies to measure the sustainability value added of CSR. Governmental agencies could produce a 'State of CSR sustainability impact' report in collaboration with companies. Such a report would stimulate the respective business debate and exchange of best practice. The report would present the state-of-the-art methods for measuring and assessing the sustainability impact of CSR in different sectors, and would also present issue-specific indicators for measuring such impact. The indicators could be linked to public policy goals in the field of sustainable development.

Awareness of the impact question can be increased among stakeholders that play a crucial role for the social and environmental effectiveness of CSR. Consumers and investors should be educated so they can better distinguish between 'rhetoric' and 'realities' when companies report on their CSR impact. A dialogue could be facilitated with the Socially Responsible Investment (SRI) community on how sustainability impact can be better accounted for in SRI screenings.

17.5.3   Communicate Public Policy Goals on Sustainability

Sustainable development is an enormous challenge and a continuing process that requires contributions from all societal actors and governments as well as the business sector and civil society. While our findings indicate that there is a certain overlap of public and business goals, it emerged from the interviews that companies only rarely align their CSR activities consciously with sustainability goals set by the EU or by Member States' governments. Sometimes businesses are not even familiar with these goals. Partly as a consequence of this situation, some EU sustainability goals are targeted by companies while others remain disregarded.

If policy makers wish the private sector to contribute more substantially to the sustainability goals they have set, they need to communicate to companies where exactly they expect companies to become active. An active communication policy would link the promotion of CSR to that of public sustainability goals.

17.5.4 Use a Broad Range of Governance Options to Stimulate Effective CSR

To date, public policies to stimulate CSR are largely restricted to communicative instruments (labels) and disclosure or reporting obligations. If we accept that there is a potential to promote sustainable development through voluntary corporate action, even though CSR can and should not 'substitute . . . appropriate regulation in the relevant fields',[9] policy makers can exploit additional governance options and policy mixes to promote effective CSR.

17.5.4.1 Analyze gaps and mainstream policies

Policy makers have been active in providing frameworks and incentives for CSR in Europe and elsewhere. A gap analysis could help to assess the areas where integration of CSR into public polices is still patchy but could contribute to sustainability.

CSR policies can also be better integrated into other public policies, such as the Marrakesh process on sustainable consumption, economic and social policies. Within the EU the obligatory development of CSR strategies at Member State level might be considered. These strategies can again be integrated with national sustainability, innovation and economic policies. Considering the high sustainability potential of CSR linked to the 'greening' of products and services, public CSR policies should be aligned with programmes promoting sustainability research and innovation. Within Europe capacity building for the development of effective CSR policies (public as well as private) is necessary at national level.

17.5.4.2 Set incentives

The adoption of incentive measures for CSR could generate proactive behaviour in companies to build competitive advantages through organizational and technological innovation. Such inventive measures would include, above all, public procurement policies. Public procurement amounts to 14–16 per cent of EU GDP. In the EU social and environmental aspects can be taken into consideration to some extent,[10] when they relate directly to the product or service at issue. These existing possibilities to make public procurement more sustainable should be fully exploited in EU institutions and Member States while further possibilities to integrate CSR aspects – which are more broadly organization- and process-related – into public procurement need to be explored.

Other incentive measures to promote CSR could include exemption of specific regulatory obligations, for example when companies use EMAS, or provisions for mitigation in sentencing. That is, in the event that a company is convicted for a bribery offence, the authorities may mitigate the sentence if the company can show that it had in place a no-bribes policy and an effective anti-bribery management or compliance system. An area where some work has already started is that of Export Credit Agencies which are setting qualifying social and ecological standards or anti-bribery criteria. A review of such options should be produced and possible trade-offs between creating CSR incentives and relaxing regulatory standards discussed.

17.5.4.3 Influence framework conditions of self-governance: CSR instrument development and civil society

Policy makers can also contribute to strengthening the sustainability potential of CSR by influencing favourably the framework conditions of societal self-regulation. This may, among others, include challenging the development of CSR instruments and initiatives, and strengthening civil society organizations representing sustainability interests vis-à-vis companies.

The role of governments in developing CSR instruments varies: some instruments are purely company-driven, others are developed in joint initiatives with governments and/or civil society stakeholders. Using their influence as (co-) sponsors or as endorsers of CSR instruments, policy makers could take up some of the following lessons learned from our research. Among other things, they can contribute to raising the sustainability impact of CSR initiatives by challenging these initiatives to strengthen the claims they set out for their adherence. Further, there is great potential for strengthening the follow-up mechanisms of CSR instruments, in particular codes of conduct. UN bodies have a particular responsibility when it comes to strengthening CSR initiatives to which they presently lend legitimacy. Concretely, policy makers may:

- initiate public-private partnerships with issue-specific focus targeting particular business communities;
- challenge existing initiatives to strengthen their claims over time;
- challenge existing initiatives to produce sector-specific sub-projects rather than following a 'one size fits all' approach;
- contribute to producing rankings of companies in relation to central CSR claims;
- contribute to strengthening the secretariats of major CSR instruments;
- encourage diversification of CSR approaches.

Our findings indicate that civil society organizations play a crucial role for effective CSR. Policy makers should support civil society organizations in their efforts to challenge companies (capacity building). Stakeholder support is even more important for countries where civil society is weak, including outside the EU. Support may be in financial terms, for example, through a 'Corporate Responsibility Observation Programme'. It could also be in procedural terms, through integrating civil society organizations such as the different 'major groups' of sustainable development as defined by the UN into relevant CSR policy processes and stakeholder bodies.[11] Presently, women lobby organizations are rarely represented in CSR stakeholder bodies.

17.5.5   Set Ambitious Social and Environmental Policies

According to our empirical findings, companies proved to be more active with regard to voluntary sustainability activities in domestic settings where ambitious policies provided clear points of orientation.[12] This is to some extent caused by market and risk expectations which companies form on the basis of assessing their policy environment. In this sense, there seems to be reciprocal reinforcement of public and private sustainability policies.

The political promotion of CSR should hence be supported by ambitious social and environmental policies. These can stimulate the early reorientation of corporate strategies towards respective policy goals. In addition, such policies remain indispensable where CSR fails. This is the case, among others, where companies do not perceive a business case or where corporate responsibility implies a more radical transformation of product portfolios and markets. Other cases in point are issues for which consumer awareness is low (such as gender equality or countering bribery) or where the steering potential of consumers' buying decisions is limited (for instance, with business-to-business goods). In such cases, public policies can facilitate a level playing field that benefits business actors. Ambitious social and environmental policies are also required for the international realm where governments need to promote the vigorous application of internationally recognized CSR standards, on the one hand, while improving global governance structures through multinational agreements, on the other hand.

Regulatory, incentive-based or procedural public policies do not make CSR superfluous. As argued by Wolff et al. in Chapter 15, CSR can still play an at least threefold role in stimulating sustainability.

17.5.6 Consider Particular Conditions in New EU Member States

The socio-cultural and market conditions for achieving sustainability impact through CSR differ in different countries or regions. This was shown by Pálvölgyi et al. in Chapter 16 for the Central and Eastern European (CEE) countries as opposed to old EU Member States. These discrepancies need to be reflected in public CSR policies.

For example, to foster the uptake and effective implementation of CSR, EU and CEE policy makers need to account for the differences in their communication of CSR in the new EU Member States. For instance, they should highlight that CSR is a modern approach in the enlarged EU and not simply the distrusted traditional 'social activity' of companies. It should be examined what additional measures are necessary for the promotion of CSR in these countries, such as strengthening consumer awareness and NGO capacities. Here, too, an emphasis should be on the achievement of concrete social and environmental benefits.

Socially responsible multinationals can take up an important role in setting an example and in promoting CSR in the region. Policy makers can further the dialogue and exchange between such multinationals and national companies in the field of CSR.

17.5.7 Adapt CSR Research Policy

From the perspective of sustainability governance, the acid test of CSR is whether it leads to sustainability impact, and is more than a mere 'management fad'. However, CSR research has not yet sufficiently taken into account the impact of CSR on society and the environment, and the respective knowledge is still limited. One reason is the methodological difficulty of measuring sustainability impact. Hence, respective research efforts need to be intensified. We propose tackling the following questions (in italics):

How can the framework for assessing CSR impact presented in this book be refined to better measure how much CSR contributes to achieving public policy goals (goal attainment)?

The framework by Skjærseth and Wettestad (Chapter 2) draws on a 'relative improvement' and a 'goal attainment' strategy for assessing the sustainability impact of CSR. The latter aims at identifying how CSR activities contribute to the achievement of absolute goals – in our case, EU policy goals on sustainable development. This strategy turned out to be difficult to apply. The approach hence needs to be refined. This applies in particular to its ability to quantify the impact of CSR and to relate it to absolute benchmarks such as public policy goals. This would allow for assertions concerning goal attainment in ordinal scales (such as a high/medium/low contribution of CSR to goal attainment) and, depending on the case, possibly even in numerical scales (calculation of percentages of goal attainment).

How can public sustainability policies (which set standards) and public CSR policies (which may drive forward such standards) effectively interact and complement each other?

Sustainability regulation aims to set concrete social and environmental standards for norm addressees, including companies. Public CSR policies aim to stimulate companies in voluntarily going beyond the standards set by such regulation. How do these two types of public policies interact in practice? Do policy makers consciously employ incentives for CSR to tackle gaps in regulatory approaches? Or to trigger companies' experiments with instruments that they feel they cannot (yet) prescribe? And conversely, do policy makers systematically evaluate corporate beyond compliance practices in order to explore the basis for future sustainability regulation? What are the institutional frameworks for successfully aligning sustainability regulation and public CSR policies?

How do companies influence existing regulation and the development of new regulation – and thus complement or thwart the sustainability impact achieved through CSR?

Certain CSR initiatives, such as the voluntary emission trading scheme initiated by BP and Shell, aim to influence governmental regulatory processes. They do however interact with a range of other factors when it comes to affecting the development of regulation. An important question in this context is how companies' CSR and/or lobbying activities affect existing regulation and policy development processes in different geographical areas, such as in the EU and the USA. Are they strengthening or are they thwarting sustainability governance? Do the effects differ across issue areas?

Which factors explain why CSR instruments are created? Who influences or shapes the characteristics of CSR instruments that lead to low, medium or high sustainability impact?

Standardized CSR instruments, such as the GRI Sustainability Reporting Framework and Carbon Disclosure Project, tend to refer back to the management practices of powerful global players. It can be presumed that the major global corporations try to shape the CSR initiatives in order to have influence on the conduct of other companies within their own sector. However, the development and characteristics of instruments are also influenced by professional associations and NGOs (as in the case of the Marine Stewardship Council). By influencing the characteristics of instruments, these actors also take potential influence on the sustainability impact achieved by the instrument. It is, hence, of interest to investigate which factors may explain why certain CSR instruments are initiated and why they have certain characteristics, which are to varying degrees conducive to sustainability impact. How does adherence to CSR instruments affect the companies that initiated them in the first place and to what extent does it affect others?

How do standardized and company-specific CSR instruments relate to each other? Do standardized instruments create greater sustainability impact than company-specific instruments?

At the outset of our research, we expected standardized instruments to be more effective than the company-specific instruments. However, this proved not to be generally the case. As company-specific instruments for responsible business practice are often derived from (and hence not independent of) standardized instruments, we can presume that there exists an interesting relationship between the effects of the two types of instruments. Are the tailor-made or the standardized instruments more effective? Arguments for the former assumption might be that companies' own instruments are closely adjusted to the companies' processes and routines, and that their standards are not the product of a lowest common denominator between (corporate) sponsors of a standardized instrument. However, by the same token, standardized instruments might be more conducive to impact, for instance, when their standards result from multistakeholder processes driven by ambitious interest groups. Also, independently verified follow-up procedures might guarantee a more stringent implementation than in the case of company instruments. Finally, which type of instrument is more effective under which circumstances?

How does reporting, including mandatory reporting and disclosure obligations, affect the achievement of sustainability impact?

Non-financial reporting is a CSR instrument popular among companies and policy makers alike. In many countries the latter have introduced mandatory reporting obligations for certain categories of companies and mandatory disclosure obligations for specific funds. However, the efficacy of reporting and disclosure to achieve greater sustainability impact through CSR is yet to be tested. Does the information collected and contained in reports shed light on sustainability impact rather than on processes? Does it foster comparability and credibility of CSR and its effects, thus allowing for stakeholders to respond to the information and to pressure companies to increase their performance? Can assurance (third party independent verification) overcome potential limits in credibility and comparability of companies' sustainability impacts? Above all, does disclosure of information induce social and environmental changes in the organizational and production processes of companies? By what mechanisms? Do these mechanisms also work in the case of mandatory CSR reporting?

To what extent do SRI indexes and performance ratings account for the companies' achievement of sustainability impact through CSR?

The SRI market is steadily growing and an increasing number of multinational companies are interested in scoring well in SRI ratings. However, the relation between companies' sustainability impact and their rating within SRI indexes has still to be tested. Do companies that are well positioned in SRI indexes indeed perform better in relation to the environment and society than their lower-ranked competitors? In order to answer such a question, the way SRI indexes are composed has to be investigated: the extent to which stakeholders and/or companies affect their contents and the way that data on CSR performance are collected by the indexes need to be explored. Furthermore, the genuine sustainability performance and impact of companies have to be defined in order to be tested against the score achieved in the SRI index.

How do 'local' cultures in subsidiaries (for example, in new EU Member States) affect the sustainability impact of multinational companies' CSR?

Many multinational companies are among the CSR front-runners. Even though these companies carry out a range of CSR efforts, their main business activities may continue to cause environmental damage and hinder social development. To understand the relation between the CSR initiatives taken at corporate level and the actual social and environmental impact of the companies we need further insights into the internal governance of the companies in order to detect barriers to achieving sustainability impacts. In this context, it is of particular interest to analyze whether CSR initiatives of multinationals are hindered by the 'local' cultures in the sub-organizations of companies. The question could be addressed by carrying out in-depth studies of selected corporations and by comparing their achievements in different locations and across different CSR issues.

What sustainability impact can CSR achieve outside the EU, and in particular in developing countries?

Assuming that CSR can be considered mostly a Western phenomenon, we can expect to have different scenarios when CSR is transferred to an extra-European context and especially to developing countries. Where the demand for and the standardization of responsible business practice are lower, the implementation of CSR as well as the response of the companies' environment will differ. This will ultimately lead to differences in the sustainability impact created by CSR. Hence, there is a need to investigate the different roles that CSR can play in governance contexts outside Europe.

17.6 CONCLUSIONS

In this book our interest has been directed at questions such as: how can the sustainability impact of CSR be assessed? To what extent does CSR produce sustainability impact? What factors drive or hamper the achievement of sustainability impact through CSR? What is the function of CSR in wider frameworks of sustainability governance? To what extent does CSR contribute to the attainment of EU sustainability goals? What is the interrelation between CSR and EU integration within the new EU Member States? These questions underscore three elements that have particularly characterized our research: a European focus; a governance perspective; and a preoccupation with impact. Concluding this book, we shall briefly outline each of these elements and discuss its implications.

Firstly, we focused on CSR in Europe. Prominence was thus given to a region where many social and environmental issues are densely regulated, leaving less leeway for corporate voluntarism than exists elsewhere.

Though in many of the analyzed cases the CSR effects of European companies accrued outside Europe, not all of our findings may be directly transferrable to other geographical contexts, such as developing countries. However, within Europe we covered a number of different institutional contexts. Our case studies, for example, investigated CSR in liberal market systems, in co-ordinated market economies with various degrees of (neo-) corporatism, and in formerly planned economies – settings that feature very different traditions of voluntary corporate commitment. Looking at CSR in Europe hence brings to light a diversity and richness of embeddings which may contain lessons for CSR in comparable institutional contexts outside Europe (cf. Habisch et al. 2004; Perrini et al. 2006).

Secondly, we discussed CSR against the wider backdrop of sustainability governance. By defining CSR as a mode of sustainability governance, for corporate, societal and public policy actors alike, we went beyond the predominant business focus of the CSR debate. On the one hand, we took account of the contribution of societal and state actors to CSR. On the other hand, we systematically looked into the contribution of CSR to societal and in particular to public policy goals. Our findings can hence contribute to the ongoing debate on the role, the potential and limits of CSR in policy mixes.

Thirdly, and most importantly, we focused on the sustainability impact of CSR. Following from our governance perspective, our interest lies in the effectiveness of CSR as a steering mechanism. At this stage, however, it is often impossible to achieve a good measurement of sustainability impact solely attributable to CSR. This will remain so for the near future due to the nature of many CSR activities and the limits of available information. Once CSR has developed a longer tradition of systematic implementation and more is done to integrate regular monitoring and follow-up, measurement will be easier. For the time being, our book can provide first important insights into the societal and environmental benefits of CSR. Judging from this point, the potential as well as the systematic limits of CSR impact justify – and also call for – more research.

NOTES

1. We would like to thank all members of the RARE project team for valuable comments on this chapter. Federica Viganò and Elin Lerum Boasson particularly supported us with regard to Section 5.
2. On the relation between the categories 'rhetoric vs reality' and CSR output, outcome and impact see Chapter 1.
3. While the countering of bribery is the strategically most important issue in the oil and banking sectors 5, followed by the mitigation of climate change in the oil sector and the

     promotion of gender equality in the banking sector, the fish processing sector attributes no strategic relevance to these issues and focuses on sustainable fisheries' issues and on chemicals' issues instead. The SMEs surveyed consider as most important environmental impact reduction – however, not including climate change – and the countering of bribery.

4.   Whether and how intensely they measure performance varies between sectors and for different issues. Often, companies do not differentiate sufficiently between sustainability effects achieved through voluntary measures (that is, CSR) and effects caused by implementing legally required measures. A lack of awareness, but also methodological difficulties might be at the root of these measurement deficits.

5.   Hollingsworth et al. (2002).

6.   Spaargaren and van Vliet (2000).

7.   However, this ultimate threat is rarely employed in the context of gender issues.

8.   Rather than going beyond compliance (in the case of countering bribery and money-laundering in banks).

9.   Para. 4, European Parliament resolution of 13 March 2007 on corporate social responsibility: a new partnership (2006/2133(INI)).

10. In defining the subject matter of the contract, in the selection of bidders, the tender specification and award criteria.

11. This should also apply to the 'CSR Alliance' as a major element of the EU Strategy on CSR.

12. See, for example, Boasson and Wettestad, or Wolff and Schmitt in Chapters 10 and 11, respectively.

References

Aaronson, S. A. and J. Reeves (2002), *The European Response to Public Demands for Global Corporate Responsibility,* Washington, DC: National Policy Association.

Abrahamson, E. (1991), 'Managerial fads and fashion: the diffusion and rejection of innovation', *Academy of Management Review*, **16**, 586–612.

AccountAbility (2003), 'Mapping instruments for corporate social responsibility. Report prepared for the European Commission, Directorate-General for Employment and Social Affairs', www.ec.europa.eu/employment_social/soc-dial/csr/mapping_final.pdf, 30 March 2008.

Ackermann R. W. and R. A. Bauer, (1976), *Corporate Social Responsiveness: The Modern Dilemma*, Reston: Reston Publishing Co.

Adger, W. N., K. Brown, J. Fairbrass, A. Jordan, J. Paavola, S. Rosendo and G. Seyfang (2003), 'Governance for sustainability: towards a 'thick' analysis of environmental decision making', *Environment and Planning*, **A35** (6), 1095–110.

Agnew, D., C. Grieve, P. Orr, G. Parkes and N. Barker (2006), *Environmental Benefits Resulting from Certification Against MSC's Principles and Criteria for Sustainable Fishing*, London: MRAG UK Ltd and Marine Stewardship Council.

AIPCE (2006), 'Purchase control document on IUU fishing', as agreed at the EU Fish Processor's Association (AIPCE) meeting on 29 September 2006.

AIPCE (2007), *White Fish Study 2007*, Brussels.

Albareda, L., J. M. Lozano and T. Ysa (2007), 'Public policies on corporate social responsibility: the role of governments', *Journal of Business Ethics*, **74** (4), 391–407.

Aldrich, H. (1979), *Organizations and Environments*, Englewood Cliffs, NJ: Prentice Hall.

Ammenberg, J. and O. Hjelm (2003), 'Tracing business and environmental effects of environmental management systems – a study of networking small and medium sized enterprises using a joint environmental management system', *Business Strategy and the Environment*, **12** (3), 163–74.

Analisis e Investigación and Villafañe and Asociados (2007), 'Monitor Español de reputación corporativa 2007', www.merco.info/ver/mercoempresas/rankings-merco-empresas/empresas2–2007, 4 December 2007.

Andriof, J. and M. McIntosh (eds) (2001), *Perspectives on Corporate Citizenship*, Sheffield: Greenleaf Publishing.

Annandale, D., A. Morrison-Saunders and G. Bouma (2004), 'The impact of voluntary environmental protection instruments on company environmental performance', *Business Strategy and the Environment*, **13**, 1–12.

Arts, B. (2002), 'Green alliances of business and NGOs. New styles of self-regulation or dead-end roads?', *Corporate Social Responsibility and Environmental Management*, **9** (1), 26–36.

Atkinson G. (2000), 'Measuring corporate sustainability', *Journal of Environmental Planning and Management*, **43** (2), 235–52.

Bank for International Settlements, Basel Committee on Banking Supervision (2006), *International Convergence of Capital Measurement and Capital Standards: A Revised Framework Comprehensive Version*, Basel.

Bansal, P. and K. Roth (2000), 'Why companies go green: a model of ecological responsiveness', *Academy of Management Journal*, **43** (4), 717–36.

Barney, J. (1991), 'Firm resources and sustained competitive advantage', *Journal of Management*, **17** (1), 99–120.

Baron, D. (2001), 'Private politics, corporate social responsibility and integrated strategy', *Journal of Economics and Management Strategy*, **10** (1), 7–45.

Behrman, J. N. (1988), *Essays on Ethics in Business and the Professions*, Englewood Cliffs, NJ: Prentice Hall.

Belz, F.-M. and J. Pobisch (2004), 'Shared responsibility for sustainable consumption? The case of the German food industry', paper presented at the 12th International Conference of Greening of Industry Network, Hong Kong, 7–10 November 2004.

Belz, F.-M. and M. Bilharz (2005), *Nachhaltigkeits-Marketing: Theorie und Praxis im Dialog*, Wiesbaden: Deutscher Universitäts-Verlag.

Bemelmans-Videc, M. L. (1998), 'Introduction: policy instrument choice and evaluation', in M.-L. Bemelmans-Videc, R. Rist and E. Vedung (eds), *Carrots, Sticks and Sermons: Policy Instruments and their Evaluation*, New Brunswick, NJ: Transaction Publishers, pp. 1–18.

Berry, G. (2004), 'Environmental management. The selling of corporate culture', *Journal of Corporate Citizenship*, Winter 2004, 71–84.

Boasson, E. L. (2005), 'Klimaskapte beslutningsendringer?', Masters thesis, Department of Political Science, University of Oslo, Norway.

Bonn, I. and J. Fisher (2005), 'Corporate governance and business ethics', *Corporate Governance: An International Review*, **13** (6), 730–8.

Bouma, J. J., M. H. A. Jeucken and L. Klinkers (2001), *Sustainable Banking. The Greening of Finance*, Sheffield, UK: Greenleaf Publishing.

Bowen, Howard R. (1953), *Social Responsibility of the Businessman*, New York: Harper and Row.

Braun and Partners (2006), 'Accountability rating Hungary 2006', www.arhu.hu/, 30 April 2008.

Brooks, S. (2005), 'Corporate social responsibility and strategic management: the prospects for converging discourses', *Strategic Change*, **14** (7), 401–11.

Browne, J. (2002), 'Gender pay inequity: a question for corporate social responsibility?' University of Cambridge: ESCR Centre for Business Research, Working Paper No. 251.

Bruijn, T. de, O. Fisscher, A. Nijhof and M. Shoemaker (2004), 'Learning to be responsible: developing competencies for organisation-wide CSR', Report, University of Twente, http://doc.utwente.nl/49040/1/Learning_to_be_responsible_v3_jan_2005_giles.pdf, 30 April 2008.

Brundtland Commission (1987), *Our Common Future*, Oxford: Oxford University Press.

Brunsson, N. (1993), 'Ideas and actions: justification and hypocrisy as alternatives to control', *Accounting Organizations and Society*, **18** (6), 489–506.

Buckland, H., L. Albareda, J. M. Lozano, A. Tencati, F. Perrini and A. Midttun (2006), 'The changing role of government in corporate responsibility. A report for practitioners', European Academy of Business in Society (EABIS), www.eabis.org/research-projects/role-of-government-deliverables-4.html, 30 April 2008.

Burgmans, A. (2003), 'Cooperation is catching', www.ourplanet.com/imgversn/134/burgman.html, 30 April 2008.

Burke, L. and J. M. Logsdon (1996), 'How corporate social responsibility pays off', *Long Range Planning*, **29** (4), 495–502.

Busch, C. (2004), 'Total e-quality award: total e-quality – a change paradigm on personnel management', contribution to RARE Workshop Rhetoric and Realities of Gender Activities in CSR, 13 October 2004, Institute for Social-Ecological Research (ISOE), Frankfurt am Main.

Byrkjeflot, H. (2002), 'The Americanisation of Swedish and Norwegian management', in M. Kipping and N. Tiratsoo (eds), *Americanisation in 20th Century Europe: Business, Culture, Politics*, vol. 2, Bergen: Rokkansenteret offprint.

Caja Madrid (2004a), 'Igualdad de Opportunidades Profesionales', Internal document, Madrid.

Caja Madrid (2005a), 'Corporate social responsibility report Caja Madrid 2005', www.cajamadrid.com/Portal_Corporativo/html/RSC05/default.htm, 13 September 2006.

Caja Madrid (2005b), 'Normas y criterios de actuación en materia profesional', Internal document, Madrid.

Caja Madrid (2007), *2006 CSR Report*, Madrid: Caja Madrid.

Caja Madrid Human Resource unit (2007), 'Indicadores de igualdad de genero 2002–2005: datos on gender equality 2002–2005, Internal document, Madrid.

Caja Madrid Interview (2006a), 'Interview with managers of Caja Madrid's Quality and Corporate Social Responsibility unit (Calidad y RSC), Madrid', 27 September 2006.

Caja Madrid Interview (2006b), 'Interview with director of Caja Madrid's department for Social Work (Obra Social), Madrid', 27 September 2006.

Caja Madrid Interview (2006c), 'Interview with manager of Caja Madrid's Human Resource unit (Recursos Humanos), Madrid', 27 September 2006.

Caja Madrid Interview (2006d), 'Interview with managers of Caja Madrid's Quality and Corporate Social Responsibility unit (Calidad y RSC) and with managers of Human Resources (Recursos Humanos), Madrid', 19 December 2006.

Caja Madrid Interview (2006e), Interview with managers of Caja Madrid's Quality unit (Calidad y RSC), Madrid, 29 September 2006.

Caja Madrid Interview (2007), Interview with members of Caja Madrid's Quality unit (Calidad y RSC), Madrid, 23 March 2007.

Campbell, D. J. and T. Craig (2005), *Organisations and the Business Environment*, 2nd edn, Oxford: Butterworth-Heinemann Ltd.

Carroll, A. B. (1979), 'A three dimensional model of corporate performance', *Academy of Management Review*, **4** (4), 497–506.

Carroll, A. B. (1991), 'The pyramid of corporate social responsibility: toward the moral management of organizational stakeholder', *Business Horizons*, **34** (4), 39–48.

Casteigts, C. and Women's World Banking in Spain (2007), 'Entrepreneurial environment study: Spain national report. A study in eight European countries with support from the European Community-Programme and European Microfinance network', www.european-microfinance.org/data/File/Gender_Equality_Project_National_Report_Spain.pdf, 21 December, 2007.

Catalyst, The (2002), 'Women in leadership: a European business imperative', www.catalystwomen.org/publications/executive_summaries/wicl-europesumm. pdf, 15 May 2007.

Catalyst, The (2004), 'Women and men in U.S. corporate leadership: same workplace, different realities?', www.catalystwomen.org/publications/executive_sum maries/wicl4-executivesummary.pdf, 15 May 2007.

CDP (2006a), 'Search CDP responses: Norsk Hydro', www.cdproject.net/results. asp, 30 April 2008.

CDP (2006b), 'Search CDP responses: Royal Dutch Shell', www.cdproject.net/ results.asp, 30 April 2008.

CDP (2006c), 'Download questionnaire and letter', www.cdproject.net/question naire.asp, 30 April 2008.

CDP (2006d), 'Carbon disclosure project report 2006, global FT 500', www. cdproject.net/cdp4reports.asp, 30 April 2008.

CDP (2006e), 'About us', www.cdproject.net/aboutus.asp, 30 April 2008.

CECA Interview (2007), Interview with Secretaría General Relaciones Internacionales, Confederación Española de Cajas de Ahorros, Madrid, 22 March 2007.

Chandler, A. D. (1962), *Strategy and Structure*; Cambridge, MA: MIT Press.

Christensen, T. and K. A. Røvik (1999), 'The ambiguity of appropriateness', in M. Egeberg and P. Lægreid (eds), *Organizing Political Institutions*, Oslo: Scandinavian University Press, pp. 159–80.

Christensen, T., P. Lægreid, P. G. Roness and K. A. Røvik (2004), *Organisasjonsteori*, Oslo: Universitetsforlaget.

Claes, D. H. (1998), 'The politics of oil-producer cooperation', PhD thesis, Department of Political Science, University of Oslo.

Clausen, J., Th. Loew and U. Westermann (2005), 'Sustainability reporting in Germany: summary of the results and trends of the 2005 ranking', www.ethibel. org, 29 April, 2007.

Cohn & Wolfe Research International (2006), *Corporate Reputation Assessment*, Milan.

Collier, J. and R. Esteban (2007), 'Corporate social responsibility and employee commitment', *Business Ethics – A European Review*, **16** (1), 19–33.

Collins, D. (2001), 'The fad motif in management scholarship', *Employee Relations*, **23** (1), 26–37.

Colyvas, J. and W. W. Powell (2006), 'Roads to institutionalisation,' in B. M. Staw (ed.), *Research in Organizational Behaviour*, vol. 27, Greenwich CT: JAI Press, pp. 305–53.

Committee on Women's Rights and Gender Equality (2006), *Communication on Opinion on Corporate Social Responsibility: A New Partnership*, 27 November 2006 (2006/2133(INI)) Brussels: European Commission.

Constance, D. and A. Bonanno (2000), 'Regulating the global fisheries: the World Wildlife Fund, Unilever and the Marine Stewardship Council', *Agriculture and Human Values*, **17**, 125–39.

Costanza, R. (1991), *Ecological Economics: The Science and Management of Sustainability*, New York: Columbia University Press.

Cramer, J. and A. Loeber (2004), 'Governance through learning: making corporate social responsibility in Dutch industry effective from a sustainable development perspective', *Journal of Environmental Policy and Planning*, **6** (3/4), 1–17.

Crane, A. (1995), 'Rhetoric and reality in the greening of organizational culture', *Greener Management International*, **12**, 49–62.

Crane, A. and D. Matten (2004), *Business Ethics – A European Perspective*. Oxford: Oxford University Press.

Csonka, V., A. Kenyeres, S. V. Larsen and C. Szabó (2004), *Corporate Social Responsibility: State of the Art in Hungary 2004*, Budapest: United Nations Development Programme.

Cummins, A. (2004), 'The Marine Stewardship Council: a multi-stakeholder approach to sustainable fishing', *Corporate Social Responsibility and Environmental Management*, **11**, 85–94.

Cutler, C.A., V. Haufler and T. Porter (eds) (1999), *Private Authority and International Affairs*, Albany, NY SUNY Press.

Cyert, R. M. and J. G. March (1963), *The Behavioural Theory of the Firm*, Englewood Cliffs, NJ: Prentice Hall.

DEMOS Magyarország Alapítvány (2006), 'Több, mint üzlet: vállalati társadalmi felelősségvállalás (More than business: corporate social responsibility)', www.demos.hu, 10 April, 2007.

Dexia (2004), 'The Place of Women within the Dexia Group', Summary of the White Paper and action proposals, Internal document, Brussels.

Dexia (2005a), 'No achievement without lasting commitment. Sustainable development report 2005', www.corporateregister.com/a10723/Dexia05-sus-bel.pdf, 14 November 2006.

Dexia (2005b), 'HR Quality Charter', Internal document. Brussels.

Dexia (2005c), 'La place des femmes chez Dexia. Rèunion de suivi – 14 September 2005', Internal document, Brussels.

Dexia Interview (2006a), 'Interview with manager for Sustainable Development', Telephone interview, 12 September 2006.

Dexia Interview (2006b), 'Interview with director of Social Relations', 1 December 2006.

DiMaggio, P. and W. Powell (1983), 'The iron cage revisited: institutional isomorphism and collective rationality in organizational fields', *American Sociological Review*, **48**, 147–60.

DiMaggio, P. and W. Powell (1991), 'Introduction', in W. Powell and P. DiMaggio (eds), *The New Institutionalism in Organisational Analysis,* Chicago, IL and London: University of Chicago Press, pp.1–38.

Donaldson, T. (1999), 'Making stakeholder theory whole', *Academy of Management Review*, **24** (2), 237–41.

Donaldson T. and T. W. Dunfee (1999), *Ties That Bind: A Social Contracts Approach to Business Ethics*, Cambridge, MA: Harvard Business School Press.

Donaldson, T. and L. E. Preston (1995), 'The stakeholder theory of the corporation: concepts, evidence and implications', *Academy of Management Review,* **20** (1), 65–91.

Doppelt, B. (2003), *Leading Change Toward Sustainability. A Change-Management Guide for Business, Government and Civil Society*, Sheffield, UK: Greenleaf.

Dowell, G., S. L. Hart and B. Yeung (2000), 'Do corporate global environmental standards create or destroy market value?', *Management Science*, **8**, 1059–74.

DTI, BITC, IOD, BCC and Accountability (2002), 'Engaging SMEs in community and society issues', http://ec.europa.eu/enterprise/csr/roundtable2/engaging_smes.pdf, 8 December, 2006.

Dummett, K. (2006), 'Drivers for corporate environmental responsibility (CER)', *Environment, Development and Sustainability*, **8**, 375–89.

Dunn, W. N. (1994), 'Monitoring policy outcomes', in N. D. William (ed.), *Public Policy Analysis, An Introduction*, Upper Saddle River, NJ: Prentice Hall, pp. 334–402.

Ebner, H. G. (2004), 'Weiterbildung von mitarbeiterinnen', in G. Krell (ed.), *Chancengleichheit durch Personalpolitik. Gleichstellung von Frauen und Männern in Unternehmen und Verwaltungen. Rechtliche Regelungen – Problemanalysen – Lösungen*, Wiesbaden: Gabler, pp. 205–20.

EGGSIE (Expert Group on Gender, Social Inclusion and Employment) (2005), 'Reconciliation of work and private life: a comparative review of thirty European countries. Synthesis report', www.europa.eu.int/comm./employment_social/ gender_equality/gendermainstreaming/gender/exp_ group_en.html, 14 May 2006.

Egri, C. P. and L. T. Pinfield (1996), 'Organizations and the biosphere: ecologies and environments', in S. R. Clegg, C. Hardy and W. R. Nord (eds), *Handbook of Organization Studies*, Thousand Oaks, CA: Sage, pp. 459–83.

Elkington, J. (1997), *Cannibals with Forks: The Triple Bottom Line of Twenty-First Century Business*, Oxford: Clapstone Publishing.

Elster, J. (1989), *Nuts and Bolts for the Social Sciences*, Cambridge: Cambridge University Press.

EPA Network (Network of Heads of European Environment Protection Agencies) (2005), 'The contribution of good environmental regulation to competitiveness', www.eea.europa.eu/documents/prague_statement/prague_statement-en.pdf, 30 April 2008.

EPWN (European Professional Women's Network) and Egon Zehnder International (2004), 'The first "EPWN European Board women monitor" – looking up: women on boards', www.pnw.link.be/PWN_international/ppt_ pdf/14_06g_boeardwomenpressrelease_eng.pdf, 15 January 2005.

European Commission (2001), *Promoting a European Framework for Corporate Social Responsibility*, Green Paper, COM (2001) 366, Brussels: European Commission.

European Commission (2002), *Communication from the Commission Concerning Corporate Social Responsibility: A Business Contribution to Sustainable Development*, COM (2002) 347, Brussels: European Commission.

European Commission (2003), *Commission Recommendation (2003/361/EC) of 6 May 2003, Concerning the Definition of Micro, Small and Medium-sized Enterprises*, Brussels: European Commission.

European Commission (2004a), *ABC of the Main Instruments of Corporate Social Responsibility*, Brussels: European Commission.

European Commission (2004b), *Corporate Social Responsibility – National Public Policies in the European Union*, Brussels: European Commission.

European Commission (2005a), 'The attitudes of European citizens towards environment', *Special Eurobarometer 217*.

European Commission (2005b), *The New SME definition. User Guide and Model Declaration*, Brussels: European Commission.

European Commission (2006a), 'Report on equal pay', www.bmfsfj.de/bmfsfj/ generator/ RedaktionBMFSFJ/Abteilung4/Pdf-Anlagen/nl-dezember-06-kom-equal-pay,property=pdf,bereich=,sprache=de,rwb=true.pdf, 21 December 2006.

European Commission (2006b), *Implementing the Partnership for Growth and*

Jobs: Making Europe a Pole of Excellence on Corporate Social Responsibility, Communication from the Commission COM (2006)136, Brussels: European Commission.

European Commission (2006c), *Corporate Social Responsibility*, Brussels: DG for Employment, Social Affairs and Equal Opportunities.

European Commission (2006d), *Report on Equality Between Women and Men 2006*, COM (2006)71 final, Brussels: European Commission.

European Commission (2006e), *The Gender Pay Gap – Origins and Policy Responses. A Comparative Review of 30 European Countries*, Luxembourg: Office for Official Publications of the European Communities.

European Commission (2008), *Report on Equality Between Women and Men*, Document drawn up on the basis of COM (2008) 10 final, Luxembourg.

European Foundation for the Improvement of Living and Working Conditions (2006), *Working Time and Work-life Balance in European Companies. Establishment Survey on Working Time 2004–2005*, Luxembourg: Office for Official Publications of the European Communities.

European Multistakeholder Forum on CSR (EU MSF) (2004a), *Final Report. Round Table on the Diversity, Convergence and Transparency of CSR Practices and Tools*, Brussels.

European Multistakeholder Forum on CSR (EU MSF) (2004b), 'Final results and recommendations', http://europa.eu.int/comm/enterprise/csr/documents/29062004/EMSF_final_report.pdf, 21 April, 2008.

European Multistakeholder Forum on CSR (EU MSF) (2004c), 'Report on the Round Table on 'Fostering CSR among SMEs', http://ec.europa.eu/enterprise/csr/documents/29062004/EMSF_final_report.pdf, 21 April, 2008.

European Savings Banks Group (2006), 'Savings banks' socially responsible activities, a wealth of experience', www.savingsbanks.org/DocShare/docs/1/JANHCAGAKDEIHIIEEBDPCMLPPDB19DPNCDTE4Q/ESBG/Docs/DLS/2005–02680.pdf, 21 December 2006.

European Women's Lobby (2005), 'Gender Equality *Road Map* for the European Community 2006–2010', www.womenlobby.org, 16 January 2006.

FAO (1995), *Code of Conduct for Responsible Fisheries*, Rome: Food and Agriculture Organization.

FAO (2007), *The State of World Fisheries and Aquaculture 2006*, Rome: Food and Agriculture Organization.

FBI (Federal Bureau of Investigation) (2001), 'Money laundering', *FBI Law Enforcement Bulletin*, **70** (14), 1.

Fekete, L. (2005), 'Social welfare lagging behind economic growth', in A. Habisch, J. Jonker, M. Wegner and R. Schmidtpeter (eds), *Corporate Social Responsibility Across Europe*, Berlin: Springer, pp. 141–9.

Fieldhouse, D. K. (1978), *Unilever Overseas. The Anatomy of a Multinational*, London: Croom-Helm.

Figge, F. and T. Hahn (2004), 'Sustainable value added – measuring corporate contributions to sustainability beyond eco-efficiency', *Ecological Economics*, **48** (2), 173–87.

Figge, F., T. Hahn, S. Schaltegger and M. Wagner (2002), 'The sustainability balanced scorecard. Linking sustainability management to business strategy', *Business Strategy and the Environment*, **11**, 269–84.

Financial Action Task Force on Money Laundering (FATF) (2004), *40 Recommendations plus Special Recommendations on Terrorist Financing*, Paris.

Financial Action Task Force on Money Laundering (FATF) (2006), *Third Mutual Evaluation Report on Anti-money Laundering and Combating the Financing of Terrorism: Spain*, Paris, p. 6.

Fineman, S. (2001), 'Fashioning the environment', *Organization*, **8** (1), 17–31.

Fineman, S. and K. Clarke (1996), 'Green stakeholders: industry interpretations and response' *Journal of Management Studies*, **33** (6), 715–30.

Fligstein, N. (1991), 'The structural transformation of American industry: an institutional account of the causes of diversification in the largest firms, 1919–1979', in W. W. Powell and P. J. DiMaggio (eds), *The New Institutionalism in Organizational Analysis*, Chicago, IL and London: University of Chicago Press, pp. 232–63.

Fowler, P. and S. Heap (1998), 'Learning from the Marine Stewardship Council: a business-NGO partnership for sustainable marine fisheries', *Greener Management International*, **24**, 77–90.

Fowler, P. and S. Simon (2000), 'Bridging troubled waters. The Marine Stewardship Council', in J. Bendell (ed.), *Terms for Endearment. Business, NGOs and Sustainable Development*, Sheffield: Greenleaf Publishing.

Fox, T., H. Ward and B. Howard (2002), 'Public sector roles in strengthening corporate social responsibility: a baseline study', The World Bank, www.iied.org/docs/cred/csr_wbreport.pdf, 23 July 2004.

Frederick, W.C. (1978), 'From CSR1 to CSR2: the maturing of business-and-society thought', Working paper No. 279, University of Pittsburgh, Graduate School of Business.

Freedom House (2006), 'Nations in transit, democratization from Central Europe to Eurasia', www.freedomhouse.hu/nitransit/2006/hungary2006.pdf, 21 April, 2008.

Freeman, R. E. and D. L. Reed (1983), 'Stockholders and stakeholders: a new perspective on Corporate Governance', *California Management Review*, **25** (3), 88–106.

Friedman, A. L. and S. Miles (2001), 'SMEs and the environment: two case studies', *Eco Management and Auditing*, **8** (4), 200–09.

Friedman, M. (1970), 'The social responsibility of business is to increase its profit', *New York Times Magazine*, 13 September 1970, reprinted in T. Donaldson, and P. H. Werhane (eds) (1988), *Ethical Issues in Business: A Philosophical Approach*, Englewood Cliffs, NJ: Prentice Hall, pp. 217–23.

Friedrichs' Interview (2006), Interview with director and managers of Gottfried Friedrichs KC, Hamburg, 8 September.

Frynas, G. (2003), 'Global monitor: Royal Dutch/Shell', *New Political Economy*, **8** (2), 275–85.

Fuchs, D. (2004), 'The role of business in global governance', in S. Schirm (ed.), *Public and Private Governance in the World Economy. New Rules for Global Markets,* New York: Palgrave Macmillan, pp. 133–154.

Fundación Carolina y Fundación Ecologia y Desarrollo (2007), 'Negocios limpios, Desarrollo Global – La role de las empresas en la lucha internacional contra corrupción', Informe 2006, Spain.

Galbreath, J. (2006), 'Corporate social responsibility strategy: strategic options, global considerations', *Corporate Governance: The International Journal of Business in Society*, **6** (2), 175–87.

Gardiner, P. and K. Viswanathan (2004), *Ecolabelling and Fisheries Management*, Penang, Malaysia: World Fish Centre.

Geels, F. W. (2007), 'Reflections on the multi-level perspective: ontological founda-tions, causality and explanation', Unpublished paper.

George, A. L. and T. J. McKeown (1985), 'Case Studies and theories of organi-zational decision making', *Advances in Information Processing in Organizations*, **2**, 21–58.

Gereffi, G., R. Garcia-Johnson and E. Sasser (2001), 'The NGO-industrial complex', *Foreign Policy*, **125**, 56–65.

Giddens, A. (1984), *The Constitution of Society: Outline of the Theory of Structuration*, Berkeley, CA: University of California Press.

Global Compact (2006) 'The Global Compact network', www.unglobalcompact. org, 21 April, 2008.

Global Reporting Initiative (GRI) (2002), 'Sustainability. Reporting Guidelines', Global Reporting Initiative', www.globalreporting.org/NR/rdonlyres/ ED9E9B36-AB54–4DE1-BFF2–5F735235CA44/0/G3_GuidelinesENU.pdf, 30 April 2008.

Global Reporting Initiative (GRI) (2006a) 'What we do', www.globalreporting. org/AboutGRI/WhatWeDo/, 15 February, 2008.

Global Reporting Initiative (GRI) (2006b), 'Sustainability Reporting Guidelines. Version 3.0. Amsterdam', www.globalreporting.org/, 15 February, 2008.

Golub, J. (ed.) (1998), *New Instruments for Environmental Policy in the EU*, London: Routledge.

Gottfried Friedrichs KG (2003), *Vision in Lachs*, Internal document. Hamburg.

Gottfried Friedrichs KG (2005), *Verhaltens- und Ethikgrundsätze*, Internal docu-ment, Hamburg.

Graham, S. (2005), 'Bedriftenes samfunnsansvar – et politikkområde i støpeske-jeen', tale ved statssekretæren til stasjonssjefsmøte, a speech in Oslo, August.

Gray, R. (1992), 'Accounting and environmentalism: an exploration of the chal-lenge of gently accounting for accountability, transparency and sustainability', *Accounting, Organizations and Society*, **17** (5), 399–426.

Gray, R. H., D. L. Owen and C. Adams (1996), *Accounting and Accountability: Social and Environmental Accounting in a Changing World*, Hemel Hempstead: Prentice Hall.

Graz, J.-C. and A. Nölke (eds.) (2007), *Transnational Private Governance and its Limits*, London and New York: Routledge.

Greenpeace (2006a), 'Greenpeace position zum "Marine Stewardship Council" (MSC)', www.greenpeace.de/themen/meere/fischerei/artikel/ das_marine_stewardship_council_msc/.

Greenpeace (2006b), 'A recipe for disaster: supermarkets' insatiable appetite for seafood', www.greenpeace.org.uk/media/reports/recipe_for_disaster.cfm, 20 March, 2008.

Griffin, J. and J. Mahon (1997), 'The corporate social performance and corporate financial performance debate: twenty-five years of incomparable research', *Business and Society*, **36** (1), 5–31.

Grosser, K. (2004), 'Gender mainstreaming and CSR – how can CSR contribute to advancing gender equality?', Contribution to the RARE Workshop Rhetoric and Realities of CSR Gender Activities, 13 October 2004, Frankfurt and Main: Institute for Social-Ecological Research (ISOE).

Grosser, K. and J. Moon (2005), 'The role of corporate social responsibility in gender mainstreaming', *International Feminist Journal of Politics*, **7** (4), 532–54.

Grosser, K. and J. Moon (2006), 'Best practice reporting on gender equality in the

UK: data, drivers and reporting choices', Research Paper Series, International Centre for Corporate Social Responsibility, No. 35–2006.

Gulbrandsen, L. H. (2005), 'Mark of Sustainability? Challenges for fishery and forestry eco-labeling', *Environment*, **47** (5), 8–23.

Gulyás, E., K. Ujhelyi, A. Farsang and Zs Boda (2006), *Opportunities and Challenges of Sustainable Consumption in Central and Eastern Europe: Attitudes, Behavior and Infrastructure. The case of Hungary*, in, Conference proceedings of Launch Conference of the Sustainable Consumption Research Exchange (SCORE!) Network, November 2006, Wuppertal, Germany, www.score-network.org.

Gunningham, N., P. Grabowsky and D. Sinclair (1998), *Smart Regulation. Designing Environmental Policy*, Oxford: Clarendon Press:

Guthey, E., R. Langer and M. Morsing (2006), 'Corporate social responsibility is a management fashion. So what?', in M. Morsing and S. C. Beckmann (eds), *Strategic CSR Communications*, Copenhagen: DJOF Publishing, pp. 39–60.

Habisch, A. (2003), *Corporate Citizenship – Gesellschaftliches Engagement von Unternehmen in Deutschland*, Berlin and Heidelberg: Springer.

Habisch, A., J. Jonker, M. Wegner and R. Schmidpeter (eds) (2004), *CSR Across Europe,* Berlin: Springer.

Hahn, T. (2004), 'Why and when companies contribute to societal goals. The effect of reciprocal stakeholder behavior', in (eds), *Best Paper Proceedings of the Annual Conference of the Academy of Management 'Creating Actionable Knowledge'*, 6–11 August 2004, New Orleans, USA.

Hall, P. and D. Soskice (2001), *Varieties of Capitalism*, Oxford: Oxford University Press.

Hansen, U. and U. Schrader (2005), 'Corporate social responsibility als aktuelles Thema in der Betriebswirtschaft', *Die Betriebswirtschaft (DBW)*, **65** (4), 373–95.

Hardjono, T. W. and M. van Marrewijk (2001), 'The social dimensions of business', *Corporate Environmental Strategy*, **8** (3), 223–33.

Hart, H. L. A. (1968), *Punishment and Responsibility: Essays in the Philosophy of Law*, Oxford: Clarendon Press.

Hart, S. (1995), 'A natural resource-based view of the firm', *Academy of Management Review*, **20** (4), 986–1014.

Hass, J. L. (1996), 'Environmental ("green") management typologies: an evaluation, operationalization and empirical development', *Business Strategy and the Environment*, **5** (2), 59–68.

Hemingway, A. and W. Maclagan (2004), 'Managers' personal values as drivers of corporate social responsibility', *Journal of Business Ethics*, **50**, 33–44.

Hillary, R. (ed.) (2000), *Small and Medium-Sized Enterprises and the Environment*, Sheffield: Greenleaf Publishing.

Hitt, M. A., R. D. Ireland and R. E. Hoskisson (2003), *Strategic Management: Competitiveness and Globalization*, Mason, OH: Thomson South-Western.

Hoel, A. H. (2004), 'Ecolabelling in fisheries: an effective conservation tool?', Norut Report, No. 13/2004, Tromsø Norway.

Hoffman, A. J. (2001), *From Heresy to Dogma. An Institutional History of Corporate Environmentalism*, Stanford, CA: Stanford Business Books (expanded edn).

Hollingsworth, J. R., K. H. Müller and E. J. Hollingsworth (eds) (2002), *Advancing Socio-Economics: An Institutionalist Perspective*, Lanham, MD: Rowman and Littlefield.

Howarth, St (1997), *A Century in Oil: The 'Shell' Transport and Trading Company 1897–1997*, London: Weidenfeld and Nicolson.

Howlett, M. (2005), 'What is a policy instrument? Policy tools, policy mixes, and policy implementation styles', in E. Pearl, M. M. Hill and M. Howlett (eds), *Designing Government. From Instruments to Governance*, Montreal and Ithaca, NY: McGill-Queen's University Press, pp. 31–50.

Husted, B. and J. de Jesus Salazar (2006), 'Taking Friedman seriously: maximizing profits and social performance', *Journal of Management Studies*, **43** (1), 75–91.

Hydro (2002), *Annual Report 2001*, Oslo: Hydro.

Hydro (2003), 'Hydro climate policy', 10 November 2003, Hydro, Oslo.

Hydro (2004), *The Hydro Way*, Oslo: Hydro.

Hydro (2006), *Annual Report and Form 20-F 2005*, Oslo: Hydro.

Hydro Interview (2006a), 'Interview with member of the New Energy team', Vækerø, Norway, 4 July 2006.

Hydro Interview (2006b), 'Interview with principal engineer', Sandvika, Norway, 7 September 2006.

Hydro Interview (2006c), 'Interview with member of the Reporting and Information team', Vækerø, Norway, 22 August 2006.

Hydro Interview (2006d), 'Interview with member of the Climate and Environment team', Vækerø, Norway, 22 August and 20 October 2006.

Hydro Interview (2006e), 'Interview with member of the Environment team', Telephone interview, 25 October 2006.

ICC (2005), *Combating Extortion and Bribery: ICC Rules of Conduct and Recommendations 2005 edition*, Paris: International Chamber of Commerce, Commission on Anti-Corruption.

ICES (2007), *Report of the ICES Advisory Committee on Fishery Management, Advisory Committee on the Marine Environment and Advisory Committee on Ecosystems, 2007*, ICES Advice, Books 1–10.

Illés, I. (2002), *Közép- és Délkelet-Európa az ezred fordulón: Átalakulás, integráció, régiók. (Central and South-Eastern Europe at the Millennium: Transformation, integration, regions)*, Dialóg Campus, Pécs: University of Pécs.

Inglehart, R. (1995), *Value Change on Six Continents*, Ann Arbor, MI: University of Michigan Press.

Instituto de la Mujer Interview (2006), 'Interview with a manager of the Institute of the Woman', Madrid, Spain, 18 December 2006.

Instituto de la Mujer/Ministerio de Trabajo y Asuntos Sociales (2006a), 'Cuestionaro de diagnóstico', Internal document.

Instituto de la Mujer/Ministerio de Trabajo y Asuntos Sociales (2006b), 'Plan de acción positiva', Internal document.

International Monetary Fund and Financial Action Task Force on Money Laundering (IMF and FATF) (2006), *Third Mutual Evaluation Report on Anti-money Laundering and Combating the financing of terrorism: Italy*, pp. 2, 28, 46 Washington, DC: IMF.

Jänicke, M. (2007), 'Ecological modernisation – new perspectives', in M. Jänicke and K. Jacob (eds), *Environmental Governance in Global Perspective. New Approaches to Ecological Modernisation*, Berlin: Freie Universität Berlin, pp. 9–29.

Jeucken, M. (2001), *Sustainable Finance and Banking. The Financial Sector and the Future of the Planet*, London: Earthscan Publishing.

Jeucken, M. (2002), 'What has been achieved by the lending sector?', *UNEP Report on the Financial and Insurance Industry Sector.* Compiled for the World Summit on Sustainable Development 2002, Paris: UNEP.

Jeucken, M. (2004), *Sustainability in Finance. Banking on the Planet*, Delft, the Netherlands: Eburon.

Johannesen, F. E., A. Rønning and P.T. Sandvik (2005), *Nasjonal Kontroll og Industriell Fornyelse*, Oslo: Pax.

Jones, G. (2005), *Renewing Unilever: Transformation and Tradition*, Oxford: Oxford University Press.

Jones, G. and P. Miskell (2005), 'European integration and corporate restructuring: the strategy of Unilever, c.1957–c.1990', *Economic History Review*, **58** (1), 113–39.

Jones, T. M. (1995), 'Instrumental stakeholder theory: a synthesis of ethics and economics', *Academy of Management Review*, **20** (2), 404–37.

Jonker, J. and M. de Witte (2006), *The Challenge of Organising and Implementing Corporate Social Responsibility*, Houndmills, Basingstoke, Hampshire: Palgrave.

Jordan, A., R. Wurzel, A. R. Zito and L. Brückner (2003a), 'Policy innovation of "muddling through"?', *Environmental Politics*, **12** (1), 179–98.

Jordan, A., R. Wurzel and A. Zito (eds) (2003b): *New Instruments of Environmental Governance*, London: Frank Cass.

Joyner, B. and D. Payne (2002), 'Evolution and Implementation: a study of values, business ethics and corporate social responsibility', *Journal of Business Ethics*, **41** (4), 297–311.

Kakabadse, A. and N. Kakabadse (eds) (2007), *CSR in Practice,* Houndmills, Basingstoke, Hampshire: Palgrave Macmillian.

Kakabadse, A., N. Kakabadse and C. Rozuel (2007), 'Corporate social responsibility', in A. Kakabadse and N. Kakabadse (eds), *CSR in Practice*, Houndmills, Basingstoke, Hampshire: Palgrave Macmillian, pp. 9–45.

Kaldany, R. (2006), 'Global gas flaring reduction: a time for action!', Speech at the Global Forum on Flaring and Gas Utilization, Paris, 13 December.

Karliner, J. (1997), *The Corporate Planet. Ecology and Politics in the Age of Globalization,* San Francisco, CA: Sierra Club Books.

Kaufmann, D. (2004), 'Anti corruption is signed into Treaty', http://info.world-bank.org/etools/docs/library/95071/merida/index.html, 7 January 2004.

Kennett, P. (2008), *Governance, Globalization and Public Policy*, Cheltenham, UK and Northampton, MA, USA: Edward Elgar.

Kerekes, S. and K. Kiss (2001), 'Környezetpolitikánk az EU-elvárások hálójában' (Our environmental policy in the network of EU expectations), AGROINFORM Kiadóház, Budapest.

Kerekes, S. and K. Wetzker (2007), 'Keletre tart a "társadalmilag felelős vállalat" koncepció' (The concept of 'socially responsible company' is going East), *Harvard Business Manager, Hungarian Edition*, **7** (3), 37–47.

Kerekes, S., G. Harangozó, P. Németh and Z. Nemcsicsné (2003), *Environmental Policy Tools and Firm-level Management Practices in Hungary*, OECD National Report Hungary, Budapest.

Kieser A. (1997), 'Rhetoric and myth in management fashion', *Organization*, **4** (1), 49–74.

King, G., O. R. O. Keohane and S. Verba (1994), *Designing Social Inquiry: Scientific Inference in Qualitative Research,* Princeton, NJ: Princeton University Press.

Knapp, G., C. Roheim and J. L. Anderson (2007), 'Analysis of Marine Stewardship Council certification of Alaska salmon', in G. Knapp, C. Roheim and J. L. Anderson (eds), *The Great Salmon Run: Competition between Wild and Farmed Salmon*, Washington DC: TRAFFIC North America/WWF, pp. 247–59.

Knill, C. and D. Lehmkuhl (2002), 'Private actors and the state: internationalization and changing patterns of governance', *Governance*, **15** (1), 41–63.

Kolk, A. and A. Mauser (2002), 'The evolution of environmental management: from stage models to performance evaluation', *Business Strategy and the Environment*, **11**, 14–31.

Kooiman, J. (ed.) (1993), *Modern Governance: New Government-Society Interactions*, London and Newbury Park, CA: Sage Publications.

Krasner, S. D. (1988), 'Sovereignty: an institutional perspective', *Comparative Political Studies*, **21** (1), 66–94.

Kreetz, T. (2005), 'Equal opportunity measures in the private sector in Europe. With a special focus on the banking sector' Literature report for the RARE project, ISOE, Frankfurt and Main www.isoe.de, December 2007.

Lascoumes, P. and P. Le Gales (2007), 'Introduction: understanding public policy through its instruments – from the nature of instruments to the sociology of public policy instrumentation', *Governance*, **20** (1), 1–21.

Ledgerwood, G. (1998) 'New corporate governance paradigms for transnational enterprises', *Corporate Governance: An International Review*, **6** (4), 269–77.

Levy, D. L. (1997), 'Environmental management as political sustainability', *Organization and Environment*, **10** (2), 126–47.

Levy, D. L. and A. Kolk (2002), 'Strategic responses to global climate change', *Business and Politics*, **4** (3), 275–300.

Lewis, M. W. and A. J. Grimes (1999), 'Metatriangulation: building theory from multiple paradigms', *Academy of Management Review*, **24** (4), 672–90.

Lie, E. (2005), *Oljerikdommer og Internasjonal Ekspansjon*, Oslo: Pax.

Lijphart, A. (1984), *Democracies: Patterns of Majoritarian and Consensus Government in Twenty-one Countries*, New Haven, NJ: Yale University Press.

Loew, T., K. Ankele, S. Braun and J. Clausen (2004), *Significance of the CSR Debate for Sustainability and the Requirements for Companies*, Münster and Berlin: Eigenverlag.

Lozano, J. M. (2000), 'Companies and society, ethical responsibilities', in J. Verstraeten (ed.), *Business Ethics – Broadening the Perspectives*, Leuven: Peeters, pp. 11–40.

Maaß, F. and R. Clemens (2002), *Corporate Citizenship - Das Unternehmen als 'guter Bürger'*, Wiesbaden: Deutscher Universitäts Verlag.

Majone, G. (1976), 'Choice among policy instruments for pollution control', *Policy Analysis*, **2**, 589.

Majone, G. (1996), *Regulating Europe,* London: Routledge.

March, J. and J. P. Olsen (1989), *Rediscovering Institutions: The Organizational Basis of Politics*, New York: The Free Press.

Marsden, C. and J. Andriof (1998), 'Towards an Understanding of corporate citizenship and how to influence it', *Citizenship Studies*, **2** (2), 329–52.

Matten, D. and J. Moon (2005), 'A conceptual framework for understanding CSR', in A. Habisch, J. Jonker, M. Wegner and R. Schmidpeter (eds), *Corporate Social Responsibility Across Europe*, Berlin and Heidelberg: Springer, pp. 335–56.

Matten D., A. Crane and W. Chapple (2003), 'Behind the mask: revealing the true face of corporate citizenship', *Journal of Business Ethics*, **45** (1), 109–18.

Mayntz, R. (1998), 'New Challenges to governance theory', Jean Monnet Chair Paper RSC No. 98/50, Florence.

Mazurkiewicz, P. (2003), 'Conclusions. Regional corporate social responsibility conference "Responsible business – a new strategy for development"', 6–7 October, Warsaw, Poland, DevComm-SDO, World Bank.

McIntosh, M., R. Thomas, D. Leipziger and G. Coleman (2003), *Living Corporate Citizenship. Strategic Routes to Socially Responsible Business*, Financial Times London: Prentice Hall.

McWilliams, A. and D. Siegel (2000), 'Corporate social responsibility and financial performance: a correlation or misspecification?', *Strategic Management Journal*, **21** (5), 603–09.

McWilliams, A. and D. Siegel (2001), 'Corporate social responsibility: a theory of the firm perspective', *Academy of Management Review*, **26** (1), 117–27.

McWilliams, A., D. Siegel and P. M. Wright (2006), 'Corporate social responsibility: strategic implications', *Journal of Management Studies*, **43** (1), 1–18.

McWilliams, A., D. van Fleet and K. Cory (2002), 'Raising rivals costs through political strategy: an extension of resource-based theory', *Journal of Management Studies*, **39** (5), 707–23.

Mediobanca (2003), 'Major international banks: financial aggregates', www.nbres. it, 13 April 2005.

Midttun, A. (2005), 'Realigning business, government and civil society: emerging embedded relational governance beyond the (neo) liberal and welfare state models', *Journal of Corporate Governance*, **5** (3), 159–74.

Midttun, A., K. Gautesen and M. Gjølberg (2006), The political economy of CSR in Western Europe', *Corporate Governance*, **5**, 369–85.

Miles, E. L., A. Underdal, S. Andresen, J. Wettestad, J. B. Skjærseth and E. Carlin (2002), *Environmental Regime Effectiveness*, London: MIT Press.

Mintzberg, H. (1979), *The Structuring of Organizations*, Englewood Cliffs, NJ: Prentice Hall.

Mintzberg, H., B. Ahlstrand and J. Lampel (1998), *Strategy Safari: A Guided Tour Through the Wilds of Strategic Management*, New York: Free Press.

Mirvis, P. H. (2000), 'Transformation of Shell', *Business and Society Review*, **105** (1), 63–84.

MOL (2005a), 'Setting the pace from "New Europe". Strategy 2006–2010', www. molgroup.hu/en/mol_group/our_strategy/, 12 March, 2007.

MOL (2005b), 'Sustainable development report', www.mol.hu/repository/245144. pdf, 10 March, 2007.

MOL (2006), 'Charter of the Committees' operated by the Board of Directors of MOL Plc.

MOL (2007a), 'About us', www.molgroup.hu/en/mol_group/about_us/2.

MOL (2007b), 'Corporate sustainability – overview', www.molgroup.hu/en/sd/overview/, 10 March, 2007.

MOL Interview (2006a), 'Interview with sustainable development Chief Advisor', MOL, 13 December 2006.

MOL Interview (2006b), 'Interview with Head of HSE Assurance', MOL, 21 December 2006.

Mol, A. P. J. and G. Spaargaren (2006), 'Sociological perspectives for industrial transformation', in X. Olsthoorn and A. J. Wieczorek (eds), *Understanding Industrial Transformation: Views from Different Disciplines*, Dordrecht: Springer, pp. 33–52.

Moon, J. (2002), 'The social responsibility of business and new governance', *Government and Opposition*, **37** (3), 385–408.

MPS Group (2007), *Social Responsibility in MPS Banking Group 2006*, Siena, Italy.

MPS Group Interview (2007), 'Interview with members of MPS Group's Quality unit', Siena, 28 February 2007.

MSC (2002), *The MSC's Principles and Criteria for Sustainable Fishing*.

MSC (2005), *MSC Chain of Custody Standard*, Version 2, August.

MSC (2006). *Marine Stewardship Council Fishery Certification Methodology*, Version 5, September.

MSC (2007), '2006–2007 – a snapshot of the MSC's recent progress', www.msc.org/assets/docs/fishery_certification/MSC_fisheries_06–07.pdf, 15 March, 2007.

Mujeres Universia (2006), 'Programa Optima. Que es el programa OPTIMA?', www:mujeres.universia.es/empleo/emprendedoras/programas/programa_optima.htm, 24 September, 2007.

Murphy, D. F. and J. Bendell (2002), 'New partnerships for sustainable development: the changing nature of business-NGO relations', in P. Utting (ed.), *The Greening of Business in Developing Countries – Rhetoric, Reality and Prospects*, London: Zed Books, pp. 216–44.

Murray, K. B. and J. R. Montanary (1986), 'Strategic management of the socially responsible firm: integrating management and marketing theory', *Academy of Management Review*, **11** (4), 815–27.

Mutz, G., S. Korfmacher and K. Arnold (2001), *Corporate Citizenship in Deutschland,* Frankfurt am Main: Hg. von der Geschäftsstelle Internationales Jahr der Freiwilligen.

Neef, D. (2003), *Managing Corporate Reputation and Risk: A Strategic Approach Using Knowledge Management*, Amsterdam: Elsevier.

Oberthür, S. and T. Gehring (2006), 'Conceptual foundations of institutional interaction', in S. Oberthür and T. Gehring (eds), *Institutional Interaction in Global Environmental Governance: Synergy and Conflict among International and EU Policies*, Cambridge, MA: MIT Press, pp. 19–53.

Observatory of European SMEs (2002a), 'European SMEs and social and environmental responsibility', No. 4.

Observatory of European SMEs (2002b), 'SMEs in Europe, including a first glance at EU candidate countries', No. 2.

OECD (2005), 'Hungary: Phase 2. Report on the application of the Convention on Combating Bribery of Foreign Public Officials', in *International Business Transactions and the 1997 Recommendation on Combating Bribery in International Business Transactions*. Report approved and adopted by the Working Group on Bribery in International Business Transactions on 6 May 2005, Paris: OECD.

Oficina Internacional del Trabajo (2006), 'Programa Optima "Las acciónes positivas en las empresas" – España', www.logos-net/ilo/195_base/es/init/spa 9.htm, 20 November, 2007.

OGP (2006) 'Vision, mission and objectives', www.ogp.org.uk/About us/Vision & mission, 20 March, 2008.

Oliver, C. (1991), 'Strategic responses to institutional processes', *Academy of Management Review*, **16** (1), 145–79.

Orlitzky, M., F. Schmidt and S. Rynes (2003), 'Corporate social and financial performance: a meta-analysis', *Organization Studies*, **24** (3), 403–41.

PACI (2005), *Principles for Countering Bribery*, Geneva: Partnering Against Corruption Initiative.

Pater, A. and K. van Lierop (2006), 'Sense and sensitivity: the roles of organisation and stakeholders in managing corporate social responsibility', *Business Ethics*, **15** (4), 339–51.

Paul, C. J. and D. Siegel (2006), 'Corporate social responsibility and economic performance', *Journal of Productivity Analysis*, **26** (3), 207–11.

Peachy, S. (2006), 'Saving banks and the double bottom-line – A profitable and accessible model of finance', A study sponsored by World Saving Banks Institute, Oxford.

Perrini, F., S. Pogutz and A. Tencato (2006), *Developing Corporate Social Responsibility. A European Perspective*, Cheltenham, UK and Northampton, MA, USA: Edward Elgar.

Peters, B. G. and J. Pierre (1998), 'Governance without government? Rethinking public administration', *Journal of Public Administration Research and Theory*, **8** (2), 223–43.

Pfeffer, J. and G. Salancik (1978), *The External Control of Organizations. A Resource Dependence Perspective*, New York: Harper and Row.

Philips, R. (1997), 'Stakeholder theory and a principle of fairness', *Business Ethics Quarterly*, **7** (1), 51–66.

Phillips, B., T. Ward and C. Chaffee (2003), *Eco-labelling in Fisheries: What Is It All About?* Oxford: Blackwell Publishing.

Piac and Profit (2006), 'CSR in Great Britain', www.piacesprofit.hu/?r=11663, 25 April, 2008.

Pierson, P. (2004), *Politics in Time: History, Institutions and Social Analysis*, Princeton, NJ: Princeton University Press.

Poole, M. S., A. H. van de Ven, K. Dooley and M. E. Holmes (2000), *Organizational Change and Innovation Processes: Theory and Methods for Research*, New York: Oxford University Press.

Porter, M. (1980), *Competitive Strategy. Techniques for Analyzing Industries and Competitors,* New York: Free Press.

Porter, M. (1990), *The Competitive Advantage of Nations*, London: Macmillan.

Porter, M. and M. Kramer (2006), 'Strategy and society: the link between competitive advantage and corporate social responsibility', *Harvard Business Review*, December, 78–92.

Post, J. E. and J. F. Mahon (1980), 'Articulated turbulence: the effect of regulatory agencies on corporate responses to social change', *Academy of Management Review*, **5** (3), 399–407.

Powell, W. and P. DiMaggio (eds) (1991), *The New Institutionalism in Organizational Analysis*, Chicago, IL: University of Chicago Press.

Prakash, A. (2001), 'Why do firms adapt "beyond-compliance" environmental policies?', *Business Strategy and the Environment*, **10**, 286–99.

Preston, L. (1978), *Research in Corporate Social Performance and Policy*, Greenwich, CT: JAI Press.

Prittwitz, V. von (2003), *Politikanalyse*, 2nd edn, Stuttgart: UTB.

Przeworski, A. and H. Teune (1970), *The Logic of Comparative Social Inquiry*, New York, London, Toronto and Sidney: Wiley-Interscience.

Radácsi, L. (2006), 'CSR and the EU integration: the perspective of the new Member States', presentation RARE Workshop, Budapest, 27 April 2006.

Reinhard, F.(1998), 'Environmental product differentiation', *California Management Review*, **40** (4), 43–73.

Rhee, S.-K. and S.-Y. Lee (2003), 'Dynamic change of corporate environmental strategy', *Business Strategy and the Environment*, **12**, 175–90.

Rhodes, R. A. W. (1996), 'The new governance: governing without government', *Political Studies*, **44** (4), 652–67.

Richards, K. (2000), 'Framing environmental policy instrument choice', *Duke Environmental Law and Policy Forum*, **10** (2), 221–83.

Risse-Kappen, T. (1995), 'Bringing transnational relations back', in T. Risse-Kappen (ed.), *Non-State Actors, Domestic Structures and International Institutions*, Cambridge: Cambridge University Press, pp. 3–33.

Ritter, E. H. (1979), 'Der kooperative staat. Bemerkungen zum verhältnis von staat und wirtschaft', *Archiv des Öffentlichen Rechts*, **3**, 389–413.

RNE (Rat für Nachhaltige Entwicklung) (2006), *Corporate Responsibility in a Globalised World – A German Profile of Corporate Social Responsibility. Recommendations of the German Council for Sustainable Development*, Berlin.

Roberts, J. (2003), 'The manufacture of corporate social responsibility: constructing corporate sensibility', *Organization*, **10** (2), 249–65.

Roome, N. (1992), 'Developing environmental management strategies', *Business Strategy and the Environment*, **1** (1), 11–23.

Roome, N. (ed.) (1998), *Sustainability Strategies for Industry. The Future of Corporate Practice*, Washington, DC: Island Press.

Rosenau, J. (1992), 'Governance, order, and change in world politics', in J. Rosenau, N. James and E. O. Czempiel (eds), *Governance without Government: Order and Change in World Politics*, Cambridge: Cambridge University Press, pp. 1–29.

Rowan, J. D. (2003), 'Imagining corporate culture: the industrial paternalism of William Hesketh Lever at Port Sunlight, 1888–1925', Dissertation.

Ruggie, J. G. (2002), 'The theory and practice of learning networks', *Journal of Corporate Citizenship*, **5**, 27–36.

Russo, M. and P. Fouts (1997), 'A resource-based perspective on corporate environmental performance and profitability', *Academy of Management Journal*, **40** (3), 534–59.

Sahlin-Andersson, K. (2006), 'Corporate social responsibility', *Corporate Governance: The International Journal of Business in Society*, **6**, 595–608.

Sahlin-Andersson, K. and L. Engwall (eds.) (2002), *The Expansion of Management Knowledge*, Stanford, CA: Stanford University Press.

Salamon, L. (ed.) (2002), *The Tools of Government. A Guide to the New Governance*, New York and Oxford: Oxford University Press.

Salzmann, O., A. Ionesco-Somers and U. Steger (2005), 'The business case for corporate sustainability: literature review and research options', *European Management Journal*, **23** (1), 27–36.

Sarbutts, N. (2003), 'Can SMEs "do" CSR? A practitioner's view of the ways small and medium-sized enterprises are able to manage reputation through corporate social responsibility', *Journal of Communication Management*, **7** (4), 340–7.

Schaltegger S., C. Herzig, O. Kleiber and J. Müller (2002), *Sustainability Management in Business Enterprises. Concepts and Instruments for Sustainable Organisation Development*, Berlin: Bundesumweltministerium (BMU) und Bundesverband der Deutschen Industrie (BDI).

Scharpf, F. W. (1997), *Games Real Actors Play: Actor-Centered Institutionalism in Policy Research*, Boulder, CO: Westview Press.

Schimank, U. (2005), *Differenzierung und Integration der modernen Gesellschaft. Beiträge zur akteurzentrierten Differenzierungstheorie 1*, Wiesbaden: VS, Verlag für Sozialwissenschaften.

Schmitt, K. (2004), 'Corporate social responsibility in der strategischen unternehmensführung – eine fallstudienanalyse deutscher und britischer unternehmen der ernährungsindustrie', www.oeko.de/oekodoc/259/2005–011-de.pdf, 30 April 2008.

Scott, R. W. (1995), *Institutions and Organizations*, Thousand Oaks, CA: Sage Publications.

SCR (Sustainable Consumption Roundtable) (2006), 'I will if you will. Towards sustainable consumption', May.

Seafood Choices Alliance (2005), 'Constant cravings: the European consumer and sustainable seafood choices', 20 March, 2008. www.seafoodchoices.com/resources/documents/EUConsumer2005.pdf.

Seafood Choices Alliance (2007a), 'The European marketplace for sustainable seafood. April 2007', www.seafoodchoices.com/resources/documents/SeafoodMarketplaceEurope_FULLApr07.pdf, 15 February, 2008.

Seafood Choices Alliance (2007b), 'The UK marketplace for sustainable seafood', www.seafoodchoices.com/resources/documents/SCAUKMPReport.pdf, 30 January, 2008.

Selznick, P. (1957), *Leadership in Administration,* New York: Harper and Row.

Sethi, S. P. (1975), 'Dimensions of corporate social performance: an analytic framework', *California Management Review*, **17** (3), 58–64.

Sharma, S. and M. Starik (eds) (2002), *Research in Corporate Sustainability: The Evolving Theory and Practice of Organizations in the Natural Environment*, Cheltenham, UK and Northampton, MA, USA: Edward Elgar.

Shell (1998), *The Shell Report 1998,* The Hague and London: Shell.

Shell (2002), *Annual Report and Accounts 2001*, The Hague and London: Shell.

Shell (2005), *Annual Report 2004,* The Hague and London: Shell.

Shell (2006), *The Shell Sustainability Report 2005,* The Hague and London: Shell.

Shell (2007), *Annual Report 2006,* The Hague and London: Shell.

Shell Interview (2006a), 'Interview with member of the Policy and External Relation team at Shell International', Stockholm, Sweden, 23 August 2006.

Shell Interview (2006b), 'Interview with member of the Corporate Climate team', London, UK, 11 July 2006.

Shell Interview (2006c), 'Interview with CEO of Shell Hungary', 31 October 2006.

Shell Interview (2006d), 'Interview with Head of Communications', Shell Hungary, 18 December 2006.

Shell Interview (2007a), 'Interview with member of the Halten CO2 Project team', Telephone interview, 1 February 2007.

Shell Interview (2007b), 'Interview with Advisor in the Europe Environmental Discipline team', Skøyen, Norway, 1 February 2007.

Shell Interview (2007c), 'Interview with member of the Cleaner Production Shell Technology team', Skøyen, Norway, 1 February 2007.

Shell Interview (2007d), 'Interview with Shell Business Development Manager – Gas', Telephone interview, 1 February 2007.

Simon, H. A. (1947), *Administrative Behaviour,* New York, The Free Press.

Skjærseth, J. B. and J. Wettestad (2008), *EU Emissions Trading: Initiation, Decision-making and Implementation*, Aldershot: Ashgate

Skjærseth, J.B. and T. Skodvin (2003), *Climate Change and the Oil Industry*, New York: Manchester University Press.

Smith, G. and D. Feldman (2003), *Company Codes of Conduct and International Standards: An Analytical Comparison*, Washington, DC: World Bank Group.

Smith, N. C. (2003), 'Corporate social responsibility: whether or how?', *California Management Review*, **45** (4), 52–76.

Solomon, R. C. and K. R. Hanson (1983), *Above the Bottom Line*, New York: Harcourt Brace Jovanovich Inc.

Spaargaren, G. and B. van Vliet (2000), 'Lifestyles, consumption and the environment: the ecological modernisation of the domestic consumption', *Journal Offprint on Environmental Politics*, **9** (1), 50–77.

St.prp.nr. 60 (2006–2007), *Sammenslåing av Statoil og Hydros petroleumsvirksomhet*, Norwegian Ministry of Petroleum and Energy, Oslo.

Stadler, C. and H. H. Hinterhuber (2005), 'Shell, Siemens and DaimlerChrysler', *Long Range Planning*, **38**, 467–84.

Steger, U. (1990), 'Unternehmensführung und ökologische Herausforderung', in G. R. Wagner (ed.), *Unternehmen und ökologische Umwelt*, München: Verlag Franz Vahlen, pp. 48–58.

Steger, U. (1993), 'The greening of the boardroom. How European companies are dealing with environmental issues', in K. Fischer and J. Schot (eds), *Environmental Strategies for Industry*, Washington, DC: Island Press pp. 147–167.

Steinberg, P. E. (1999), 'Fish or foul: investigating the politics of the Marine Stewardship Council', Paper presented at the Conference on Marine Environmental Politics in the 21st Century.

Stock at Stake (2004), 'Industry survey: banks-Europe', www.ethibel.org, 5 May 2005.

Streeck, W. (1999), *Korporatismus in Deutschland. Zwischen Nationalstaat und Europäischer Union*. Frankfurt and New York: Campus Verlag.

Suchman, M. C. (1995), 'Managing legitimacy: strategic and institutional approaches', *Academy of Management Review*, **20** (3), 571–610.

SustainAbility (2005), 'The global reporters', www.sustainability.com, 5 May, 2008.

Sustainable Investment (2005), 'Companies', www.sustainable-investment.org, 5 May, 2008.

Swanson, D. (1999), 'Toward an integrative theory of business and society: a research strategy for corporate social performance', *Academy of Management Review*, **24** (3), 506–21.

Swanson, D. L. (1995), 'Addressing a theoretical problem by reorienting the corporate social performance model', *Academy of Management Review*, **20**, 43–64.

The Global 100 (2005), 'The most sustainable corporation in the world. The 2005 list', www.global100.org, 5 May, 2008.

Thelen, K. (2000), 'Timing and temporality in the analysis of institutional evolutions and change', *Studies of American Political Development*, **14**, 101–8.

Thewlis, M., L. Miller and F. Neathe (2004), 'Advancing women in the workplace – statistical analysis', Working Paper Series No. 12 of the Women and Equality Unit of the Equal Opportunities EO Commission, Manchester, www.eoc.org.uk/cseng/research/statanalysis.pdf, 13 June 2006

Töller, A. (2007), 'Die Rückkehr des befehlenden Staates? Muster und Ursachen der Veränderung staatlicher Handlungsformen in der deutschen Abfallpolitik', *Politische Vierteljahresschrift*, **48** (1), 66–9.

Töller, A. (2008), 'Wirtschaftsverbände und Umweltpolitik', in W. Schröder and B. Weßels (eds), *Arbeitgeber- und Wirtschaftsverbände*, Wiesbaden, forthcoming.

Transparency International (2007), *Corruption Perceptions Index 2007*, Berlin, Germany: Transparency International.

Underdal, A. (2002), 'One question, two answers', in E. L. Miles, A. Underdal and S. Andresen (eds), *Environmental Regime Effectiveness. Confronting Theory with Evidence*, Cambridge, MA: MIT Press.

Underdal, A. (2004), 'Methodological challenges in the study of regime effectiveness', in A. Underdal and O. R. Young (eds), *Regime Consequences: Methodological Challenges and Research Strategies*, Dordrecht: Kluwer Academic Publishers, pp. 27–48.

Unilever (2002), *Fishing for the Future*, Unilever's Sustainable Fisheries Initiative.

Unilever (2003), Fishing for the Future II Unilever's Fish Sustainability Initiative (FSI).

Unilever (2005), *Environmental Report 2004*, Rotterdam and London.

Unilever (2006a), 'Press release – Unilever signs agreement to sell European frozen foods business', 28 August 2006.

Unilever (2006b), 'Code of business principles', www.unilever.com/ourvalues/ purposeandprinciples/ourprinciples/, November 2006.

Unilever (2006c), 'Business partner code', www.unilever.com/ourvalues/purpose andprinciples/business_partner_code/, November 2006.

Unilever (2006d), Environmental and Social Report 2005.

Unilever (2006e), *Annual Report and Accounts 2005*, pp. 10–14.

Unilever Interview (2006a), 'Interview with Unilever's Director of Sustainable Agriculture', Rotterdam, 8 December 2006.

Unilever Interview (2006b), 'Interview with Unilever's Director of Sustainable Fisheries', Hamburg, 19 December 2006.

Veer, J. (1999), 'Profits and principles, the experiences of an industry leader', Speech by the Managing Director of Royal Dutch Shell at the Greeport conference, April 1999.

Visser, J. (1998), 'The Netherlands: the return of responsive corporatism', in A. Ferner and R. Hyman (eds), *Changing Industrial Relations in Europe*, Oxford: Blackwell, pp. 283–315.

Vogel, D. (2005), *The Market for Virtue: The Potential and Limits of Corporate Social Responsibility*, Washington, DC: Brookings Institution Press.

Voigt, R. (1995), 'Der kooperative Staat. Auf der Suche nach einem neuen Steuerungsmodus', in R. Voigt (ed.), *Der Kooperative Staat. Krisenbewältigung durch Verhandlung?*, Baden-Baden: Nomos, pp. 33–77.

Voß, J.-P. and R. Kemp (2006), 'Sustainability and reflexive governance: introduction', in J.-P. Voß, D. Bauknecht and R. Kemp (eds), *Reflexive Governance for Sustainable Development*, Cheltenham, UK and Northampton, MA, USA: Edward Elgar, pp. 3–30.

Waddock A. and S. B. Graves (1997), 'The corporate social performance-financial performance link', *Strategic Management Journal*, **18** (4), 303–319.

Waldman, D., D. Siegel and M. Javidan (2006), 'Components of CEO transformational leadership and corporate social responsibility', *Journal of Management Studies,* **43** (8), 1703–25.

Wagner, M. and S. Schaltegger (2003), 'How does sustainability performance relate to business competitiveness?', Greener Management International, **44**, 5–16.

Warhurst, A. (2000), 'Corporate citizenship and corporate social investment: drivers of tri-sectoral partnerships', *Journal of Corporate Citizenship*, **1** (1), 57–73.

Weber, M. (1980), *Wirtschaft und Gesellschaft. Grundriss der verstehenden Soziologie*, 5th rev. edn, Tübingen: Mohr.

Weick, K. E. (1995), *Sensemaking in Organizations*, Thousand Oaks, CA: Sage Publications.

Welford, R. (1998), *Corporate Environmental Management 1: Systems and Strategies*, London: Earthscan.

Werhane, P. H. (2000), 'Exporting mental models: global capitalism in the 21st century', *Business Ethics Quarterly*, **10** (1), 353–62.

Werther, W. and D. Chandler (2005), *Strategic Corporate Social Responsibility: Stakeholders in a Global Environment*, Thousand Oaks CA: Sage Publications.

Wessells, C. R., R. J. Johnston and H. Donath (1999), 'Assessing consumer preferences for ecolabeled seafood: the influence of species, certifier, and household attributes', *American Journal of Agricultural Economics*, **81** (5), 1084–9.

Wheelen, T. L. and D. J. Hunger (2004), *Concepts in Strategic Management and Business Policy,* Upper Saddle River, NJ: Pearson Prentice Hall.

Wildhavens (2004), 'An independent assessment of the Marine Stewardship Council', Report, http://zibycom.com.ru/aboutus/documents/WildhavensMSC.pdf, 25 April, 2008.

Willard, B. (2002), *The Sustainability Advantage: Seven Business Case Benefits of a Triple Bottom Line*, Island, BC: New Society Publishers.

Willmott, H. (2000), 'Culture and symbolism', http://dspace.dial.pipex.com/town/close/hr22/wiswebsite/culture.htm, 5 May, 2008.

Wilson, C. (1954). *The History of Unilever*. 2 vols, London: Cassell.

Wilson, C. (1968), *Unilever 1945–1965: Challenge and Response in the Post-War Industrial Revolution*, London: Cassell.

Windell, K. (2005), 'Professionalization in emerging fields: the contestation of CSR', Paper presented at the 21st European Group of Organizational Studies (EGOS) Colloquium on 'Unlocking Organizations', Berlin, 30 June to 2 July 2005.

Windsor, D. (2001), 'The future of corporate social responsibility', *International Journal of Organizational Analysis*, **9** (3), 225–56.

Winn, M. and L. Angell (2000), 'Towards a process of corporate greening', *Organization Studies*, **21** (6), 1119–47.

Wit, M. de, M. Wade and E. Schouten (2006), 'Corporate governance. Hardwiring and softwiring corporate responsibility: a vital combination', *Corporate Governance*, **6** (4), 491–505.

Wolff, F. (2004), *Staatlichkeit im Wandel – Aspekte kooperativer Umweltpolitik*, München: Oekom verlag.

Wolff, F. and R. Barth (2005), 'Corporate social responsibility: integrating a business and societal governance perspective. The RARE project's approach', www.rare-eu.net/fileadmin/user_upload/documents/RARE_Background_Paper.pdf.

Wood, D. J. (1991), 'Corporate social performance revisited', *Academy of Management Review*, **16** (4), 691–718.

World Bank (2004a), 'Public policy for the private sector: gas flaring and venting', Note No. 279, World Bank, Washington.

World Bank (2004b), 'Global gas flaring reduction. A public-private partnership', World Bank, Washington.

World Saving Banks Institute (WSBI) (2006), 'Looking back – the achievements of 2005. Looking forward – the challenges of 2006', www.wsbi.org/uploadedFiles/WSBI/Introducing_WSBI/075%20link%20WSBI%20annual%20report%20WSBI%20screen%20view.pdf, 15 May 2007

Wulfson, M. (2001), 'The ethics of corporate responsibility and philanthropic ventures', *Journal of Business Ethics*, **29** (1–2), 135–45.

WWF Interview (2007), 'Telephone interview with fisheries expert at WWF Germany', 15 February 2007.

Young's Bluecrest (2005), *Sustainability Statement: A Vision of Seafood Sustainability*.

Young's Bluecrest (2006a), *Information from Young's: Ethical Trading and Social Accountability*.

Young's Bluecrest (2006b), *Information from Young's: Fish for Life – Sustainable Fisheries*.

Young's Bluecrest (2006c), *Information from Young's: Ten Principles for Responsible Fish Procurement*.

Young's Bluecrest (2006d), *Information from Young's: Our position on Illegal Fishing*.

Young's Bluecrest (2006e), *Information from Young's: Barents Sea Cod*.

Young's Bluecrest (2006f), *Information from Young's: Bottom (Benthic) Trawling*.

Young's Bluecrest (2007a), *The Young's/Findus Fish for Life (FFL) Fishery Health Check – Wild Captured Fish*.

Young's Interview (2006), 'Interview with members from Young's sustainability group', Grimsby, 13 December 2006.

Young's Interview (2007), 'Telephone interview with members from Young's sustainability group', 24 October 2007.

Zadek, S. (2001), *The Civil Corporation. The New Economy of Corporate Citizenship*, London and Sterling: Earthscan.

Zadek, S. (2004) 'The path to corporate responsibility', *Harvard Business Review*, December, 125–33.

Zadek, S. (2005), 'Responsible competitiveness', Paper presented at the EU Commission Conference 'Corporate Social Responsibility – Driving European Competitiveness in a Global Economy', Brussels, 19 April.

Zadek, S., P. Pruznan and R. Evans (eds) (1997), *Building Corporate Accountability: Emerging Practices in Social and Ethical Accounting, Auditing and Reporting*, London: Earthscan.

Index